ATLA Monograph Series
edited by Dr. Kenneth E. Rowe

1. Ronald L. Grimes. *The Divine Imagination: William Blake's Major Prophetic Visions*. 1972.
2. George D. Kelsey. *Social Ethics Among Southern Baptists,* 1917–1969. 1973.
3. Hilda Adam Kring. *The Harmonists: A Folk-Cultural Approach*. 1973.
4. J. Steven O'Malley. *Pilgrimage of Faith: The Legacy of the Otterbeins*. 1973.
5. Charles Edwin Jones. *Perfectionist Persuasion: The Holiness Movement and American Methodism. 1867–1936*. 1974.
6. Donald E. Byrne, Jr. *No Foot of Land: Folklore of American Methodist Itinerants*. 1975.
7. Milton C. Sernett. *Black Religion and American Evangelicalism: White Protestants, Plantation Missions, and the Flowering of Negro Christianity, 1787–1865*. 1975.
8. Eva Fleischner. *Judaism in German Christian Theology Since 1945: Christianity and Israel Considered in Terms of Mission*. 1975.
9. Walter James Lowe. *Mystery & The Unconscious: A Study in the Thought of Paul Ricoeur*. 1977.
10. Norris Magnuson. *Salvation in the Slums: Evangelical Social Work, 1865–1920*. 1977.
11. William Sherman Minor. *Creativity in Henry Nelson Wieman*. 1977.
12. Thomas Virgil Peterson. *Ham and Japheth: The Mythic World of Whites in the Antebellum South*. 1978.
13. Randall K. Burkett. *Garveyism as a Religious Movement: The Institutionalization of a Black Civil Religion*. 1978.
14. Roger G. Betsworth. *The Radical Movement of the 1960's*. 1980.
15. Alice Cowan Cochran. *Miners, Merchants, and Missionaries: The Roles of Missionaries and Pioneer Churches in the Colorado Gold Rush and Its Aftermath, 1858–1870*. 1980.
16. Irene Lawrence. *Linguistics and Theology: The Significance of Noam Chomsky for Theological Construction*. 1980.
17. Richard E. Williams. *Called and Chosen: The Story of Mother Rebecca Jackson and the Philadelphia Shakers*. 1981.
18. Arthur C. Repp, Sr. *Luther's Catechism Comes to America: Theological Effects on the Issues of the Small Catechism Prepared In or For America Prior to 1850*. 1982.
19. Lewis V. Baldwin. *"Invisible" Strands in African Methodism*. 1983.

20. David W. Gill. *The Word of God in the Ethics of Jacques Ellul.* 1984.
21. Robert Booth Fowler. *Religion and Politics in America.* 1985.
22. Page Putnam Miller. *A Claim to New Roles.* 1985.
23. C. Howard Smith. *Scandinavian Hymnody from the Reformation to the Present.* 1987.
24. Bernard T. Adeney. *Just War, Political Realism, and Faith.* 1988.
25. Paul Wesley Chilcote. *John Wesley and the Women Preachers of Early Methodism.* 1991.
26. Samuel J. Rogal. *A General Introduction of Hymnody and Congregational Song.* 1991.
27. Howard A. Barnes. *Horace Bushnell and the Virtuous Republic.* 1991.
28. Sondra A. O'Neale. *Jupiter Hammon and the Biblical Beginnings of African-American Literature.* 1993.
29. Kathleen P. Deignan. *Christ Spirit: The Eschatology of Shaker Christianity.* 1992.
30. D. Elwood Dunn. *A History of the Episcopal Church in Liberia, 1821–1980.* 1992.
31. Terrance L. Tiessen. *Irenaeus on the Salvation of the Unevangelized.* 1993.
32. James E. McGoldrick. *Baptist Successionism: A Crucial Question in Baptist History.* 1994.
33. Murray A. Rubinstein. *The Origins of the Anglo-American Missionary Enterprise in China, 1807–1840.* 1995.
34. Thomas M. Tanner. *What Ministers Know: A Qualitative Study of Pastors as Information Professionals.* 1994.
35. Jack A. Johnson-Hill. *I-Sight: The World of Rastafari: An Interpretive Sociological Account of Rastafarian Ethics.* 1995.
36. Richard James Severson. *Time, Death, and Eternity: Reflecting on Augustine's "Confessions" in Light of Heidegger's "Being and Time."* 1995.
37. Robert F. Scholz. *Press toward the Mark: History of the United Lutheran Synod of New York and New England, 1830–1930.* 1995.
38. Sam Hamstra, Jr. and Arie J. Griffioen. *Reformed Confessionalism in Nineteenth-Century America: Essays on the Thought of John Williamson Nevin.* 1995.
39. Robert A. Hecht. *An Unordinary Man: A Life of Father John LaFarge, S.J.* 1996.
40. Moses N. Moore. *Orishatukeh Faduma: Liberal Theology and Evangelical Pan-Africanism, 1857–1946.* 1996.
41. William Lawrence. *Sundays in New York: Pulpit Theology at the Crest of the Protestant Mainstream.* 1996.

Orishatukeh Faduma

Liberal Theology and Evangelical Pan-Africanism 1857–1946

by
Moses N. Moore

ATLA Monograph Series, No. 40

The American Theological Library Association
and
The Scarecrow Press, Inc.
Lanham, Md., and London

Based on the author's Ph.D. dissertation presented to Union Theological Seminary in 1987.

SCARECROW PRESS, INC.

Published in the United States of America
by Scarecrow Press, Inc.
4720 Boston Way
Lanham, Maryland 20706

4 Pleydell Gardens, Folkestone
Kent CT20 2DN, England

British Cataloguing-in-Publication Information Available

Library of Congress Cataloging-in-Publication Data

Moore, Moses Nathaniel, 1952–
Orishatukeh Faduma : liberal theology and evangelical pan-Africanism, 1857–1946 / by Moses Moore.
p. cm. — (ATLA monograph series ; no. 40)
Includes bibliographical references.
1. Faduma, Orishatukeh, 1857–1946—Contributions in theology.
2. Liberalism (Religion) 3. Pan-Africanism. I. Title. II. Series.
BR1360.M66 1996 230′.046—dc20 95-39630 CIP

ISBN 0-8108-3091-4 (cloth : alk. paper)

⊗ ™The paper used in this publication meets the minimum requirements of the American National Standard for Information Sciences—Permanence of Paper for Printed Library Materials, ANSI Z39.48-1984.

Manufactured in the United States of America.

Dedicated to the memory of my father,
Moses N. Moore, Sr.

Contents

Editor's Foreword

Since 1972 the American Theological Library Association has undertaken responsibility for a modest monograph series in the field of religious studies. Our aim in this series is to publish two studies of quality each year. Titles are selected from studies in a wide range of religious and theological disciplines. We are pleased to publish Moses N. Moore's *Orishatukeh Faduma: Liberal Theology and Evangelical Pan-Africanism, 1857–1946.*

After completing undergraduate studies at Eckerd College, the author studied theology, missiology, and church history at Yale Divinity School where he received the Master of Divinity degree. After additional studies in American and African American religious history, he received the doctorate in church history from Union Theological Seminary in 1987.

Moses Moore has published articles in *Church History, American Presbyterians,* and *Union Seminary Quarterly Review*. He is a member of the American Society of Church History and the American Academy of Religion. He has taught at the College of William and Mary and the University of Missouri–Columbia, and currently serves as associate professor of American and African American religious history at Arizona State University.

Preface

This work had its inception in 1976 while I was a student at Yale Divinity School. The young instructor of a course on black religion, James M. Washington, suggested that I examine an early twentieth-century critique of the black church. The critique was "The Defects of the Negro Church." It was written by a West African, serving as a missionary to his "kith and kin" in the American South, who had the intriguing name Orishatukeh Faduma. This unsettling initial encounter with Faduma inspired years of strenuous research as I struggled to understand this complex figure and his equally complex era.

The early stages of this project were facilitated immensely by the assistance of Dean Harry Adams of Yale Divinity School who enthusiastically participated with me in a dusty search of the school's long-neglected alumni files. This search led to my discovery that Faduma had been a prolific commentator on numerous issues affecting the well-being of Africans and diaspora Africans. Equally important was the discovery that most of Faduma's numerous writings were available from a variety of sources in the United States and West Africa.

As I analyzed Faduma's writings, it became apparent that he did not fit into any of the traditional theological or missiological classifications generally reserved for Christians of African descent. Rather than being a defender of evangelical orthodoxy, Faduma was comfortable with the "New Theology" of an emerging Protestant liberalism. Indeed an adapted version of liberal theological, missiological, and pedagogical themes were apparent in most of his writings, forming a dynamic and creative synthesis with his inherent Pan-African ideology and sensibilities.

Yet the discovery of Faduma's liberal inclinations disconcerted me because the established historiography insists that Protestant liberalism had a negligible impact within and upon African and diaspora African Christian communities. Faduma's explicit incorporation of liberal tenets in his numerous writings required that I reconsider the prevailing historical and theological assessment. As I researched and read articles and autobiographies by many of his black contemporaries in West Africa and the United States, I discovered that Faduma was not alone in his selective efforts to appropriate the tenets of Protestant liberalism in order to further the well-being of people of African descent. He was one of a number of influential African and African-American clergy and laity who, like their white counterparts, struggled to reconcile their Christian faith and ideological commitments with modernity. In expanding my historiographical focus I found that Carter G. Woodson, in an apparently long-neglected chapter of his classic study *The History of the Negro Church,* had already noted the general impact that various currents of modernity were having upon progressives and conservatives within the late nineteenth- and early twentieth-century Black Church. It was helpful to discover that a contemporary scholar, David Wills, had also begun to challenge the traditional dogma regarding the impact of theological liberalism upon the African-American religious community.

Finally, Faduma's ready though critical appropriation of the theology, missiology, and pedagogy of Protestant liberalism for the Pan-African cause suggested some connections between these two movements, which emerged as contemporaries and self-conscious products of the modern era. Consequently, efforts to analyze and understand Faduma have been cast in the broader context of the apparent dialectic existing between Protestant liberalism and the maturation of the Pan-African movement up to the Manchester conference of 1945. Ironically, this conference, which formalized a new agenda and leadership of mainstream Pan-Africanism, was held on the eve of Faduma's death in 1946 at High Point, North Carolina. Even in his eighth decade he was still committed to the theological and ideological themes that had shaped his life on both sides of the Atlantic. Faduma was indeed a faithful servant of a liberal Protestant and Pan-African missionary tradition.

Acknowledgments

I am deeply indebted to numerous persons, agencies, and institutions for assistance in completing this work. The Fund for Theological Education provided fellowships that aided completion of my course requirements and preliminary research of this project. Research support was also provided by the University of Missouri at Columbia and Arizona State University. The staffs of Burke Library of Union Theological Seminary and the Schomburg Center also require grateful acknowledgment.

I am especially appreciative of Dean Harry Adams and his sense of historical adventure. To Professor Charles Forman, also of Yale Divinity School, I owe my ever-increasing awareness of the importance of the history of the missionary enterprise. Professor Robert T. Handy of Union Theological Seminary provided the kind and wise encouragement of a consummate scholar and teacher. Hollis Lynch and David Wills provided insight and inspiration as I attempted to navigate the historical waters that they previously had charted.

I am also appreciative of Dr. Kenneth Rowe at the American Theological Library Association and of the staff of Scarecrow Press for their interest in this work and assistance in its publication.

Words alone cannot express my gratitude to my advisor and friend, James M. Washington. His vision, patience, and timely counsel made completion of this work both possible and meaningful.

Finally, I am deeply and forever indebted to my wife Doris, my children, and my parents, Katharine and Moses Moore, Sr., for the encouragement they provided and the sacrifices they endured as I completed this work.

Introduction

Although numerous scholars acknowledge that the roots of Pan-Africanism are to be found in the intensive evangelical zeal and outreach of the Protestant missionary enterprise, few have attempted to analyze fully the complex relationship between these two movements.[1] As a result, little more than superficial attention has been paid to the impact of evolving theological and missiological tenets on the development and maturation of Pan-Africanism.[2]

Most analyses of the relationship between Protestantism and Pan-Africanism assume that nineteenth-century evangelical theology and missiology provided an exclusive and apparently uncomplicated foundation and rationale for the development and evolution of Pan-Africanism. The historiographical liabilities of this simplistic perspective are illustrated by an assertion of Immanuel Geiss. Geiss, a noted student of Pan-Africanism, wrote, "in retrospect one can see an almost smooth line of development from Christian missionary activity through early African nationalism to Pan-Africanism."[3] There is, however, evidence that suggests that for many African and diaspora Africans this "line of development" was neither as "smooth" nor as simple as Geiss and others have assumed.

The writings and activities of numerous Pan-African visionaries and activists such as Martin Delany, Alexander Walters, W. E. B. Du Bois, Edward W. Blyden, James Johnson, Majola Agbebi, Alexander Crummell, Henry M. Turner, Marcus Garvey, and Kwame Nkrumah, as well as the institutional history of the Pan-African movement, illustrate the inherent problem of trying to reconcile an emerging Pan-African consciousness and movement with the traditional tenets of evangelical theology and missiology.[4] While this paradox and its attendant inconsistencies have been noted in studies of many of these figures, their particular theological orientations and responses to the theological and missiological developments of late nineteenth-century Protestantism have not been adequately explored.[5]

Of particular concern in this work is the emergence in the late nineteenth century of the controversial theological and missiological movement generally known as Protestant liberalism and the effect it had upon the maturation of Pan-African thought and activities.[6]

Like the emerging Pan-African movement, Protestant liberalism was self-consciously part of the process of modernization.[7] Rooted in the forces and changes fostered by modernity, it came to fruition during the last half of the nineteenth century as an international movement that sought to interpret the Christian faith in a manner consistent with modern "scientific" thought. It has been described as "the movement in modern Protestantism which during the nineteenth century tried to bring Christian thought into organic unity with the evolutionary world view, the movements for social reconstruction, and the expectations of 'a better world' which dominated the general mind."[8]

A brief profile of Protestant liberalism reveals seven distinctive characteristics: (1) a world view "shaped by the theory of evolution"; (2) a tendency "to modify explicit supernaturalism with a doctrine of the immanence of God"; (3) a tendency to "express the doctrine of man primarily in terms of divine sonship and free moral agency"; (4) an insistence "on the legitimacy of applying the test of rational intelligibility to Biblical and doctrinal matters, as to every other phase of knowledge and experience"; (5) an essentially progressivistic and optimistic eschatology; (6) less emphasis on creeds and denominational ties; and (7) application of the "tools of scientific, literary, and historical scholarship to the study of the Bible."[9] Moreover, Protestant liberalism's interest in freedom from ecclesiastical and creedal bondage, accompanied by scholarly advances in the natural sciences, resulted in "a number of significant scholarly contributions . . . in the fields of religious history, social and psychological analysis, comparative religion, educational theory, and systematic theology."[10]

While much of the controversy related to the rise and spread of Protestant liberalism revolved around theological and scriptural issues—particularly scriptural authority as challenged by the Darwinian thesis and the rise of higher criticism—the rationale, goals, methods, and motivations of the missionary enterprise also came to be a major arena and source of tension and conflict. Drawing on the findings and methods of developing disciplines such as philosophy of religion and comparative religion, liberal mission theorists pronounced that many of the traditional tenets of evangelical missiology were misguided, incorrect, and outmoded.

Surprisingly, few historical studies review in detail the profound impact that Protestant liberalism had on the theory and practice of the Protestant mission enterprise.[11] Fewer still have given even cursory attention to Protestant liberalism's impact on the missiological, theological, and ideological perspectives of the westernized African and diaspora African communities.

Traditional western historiography suggests that the impact of Protestant liberalism and the intellectual and scientific currents that gave rise to it were negligible within the African and diaspora African communities. Christians of African descent have been almost stereotypically identified with the conservative and fundamentalist reactions to the intellectual, scientific, and theological currents that gave rise to Protestant liberalism.[12] There is, however, accumulating evidence that proves that intellectual and theological developments within westernized African and diaspora African communities were neither static nor exclusively encompassed within the context and confines of doctrinal conservatism. It also suggests that during the last quarter of the nineteenth century these communities were far from immune to the intellectual and scientific currents that provoked a major crisis within the western Christian community and the subsequent rise of Protestant liberalism.

David Wills has offered a preliminary assessment of the impact that the intellectual, scientific, and theological currents of the era had on the postbellum African-American Christian community—a community simultaneously confronted with the challenges and responsibilities posed by postemancipation realities:

> Difficult enough in themselves, these tasks were complicated by the challenges which beset the Protestant world as a whole in the post-reconstruction era. The history of theological liberalism and the social gospel has generally been written as if these movements—and the current of thought which prompted them—left no mark on the black churches. Such was not the case. Even as they puzzled over how to apply the traditional beliefs and social norms of evangelical Protestantism to their changing situation, black religious leaders were forced to acknowledge and address the assaults being made on those standards themselves. They were forced to fight on two fronts—to cope simultaneously with both a racial and a religious crisis.[13]

It is increasingly apparent that westernized African and diaspora African Christians, like their white counterparts (and indeed perhaps with more urgency than many of them) were forced to confront in various ways the challenges that these developments presented to their theological, missiological, and ideological beliefs and commitments. And although the vast majority of African and diaspora African clergy and laity were unwilling and unprepared to adopt the biblical, theological, and missiological implications of Protestant liberalism, even in its most moderate form, a relatively well-educated—often seminary-trained—minority of "progressive" church leaders on both sides of the Atlantic found that the emerging movement provided an important and acceptable alternative to the theology, missiology, and ideology of traditional evangelical Protestantism. Consequently, they attempted to adapt its controversial tenets to aid in the amelioration of the dire conditions of black existence in the late nineteenth and early twentieth centuries.[14]

Various schemes for the redemption and revitalization of Africa became a major focus for much of the theological and missiological ferment within the West African and diaspora African communities during the last quarter of the nineteenth century. Progressives and conservatives in both communities were increasingly critical of the practices and assumptions of traditional Protestant missiology and insistent upon greater participation in both the theoretical formulation and the actualization of the missionary enterprise.[15]

The relationship between the era's heightened evangelical interest and Pan-Africanism has been the focus of a number of recent studies.[16] Of particular interest are the inferences made by Walter L. Williams and P. Olisanwuche Esedebe. Williams maintains that the era witnessed a subtle but important shift in the attitudes of a number of African and African-American missionaries and their supporters toward African religions and culture. This revision is discernible in the writings of figures with such diverse ecclesiastical backgrounds as Henry M. Turner, John R. Frederick, Majola Agbebi, James Johnson, and Edward W. Blyden.[17] While critiquing traditional evangelical missiological tenets and stereotypes, which devalued African life and customs, they slowly and inconsistently began to advance views and strategies that fostered more positive attitudes toward African culture. Their ambivalent quest was for a missiology (mission theory and practice) that would provide Africans with the spiritual, technological, and intellectual benefits of modern Euro-American Christian culture without the wholesale denial and denigration of their own racial and cultural identity.[18] A few would find that the most cogent and consistent theological orientation for such an altered missiological and ideological perspective toward both European and African culture was not that of traditional nineteenth-century evangelical theology, but rather the emerging "New Theology" of Protestant liberalism.

The activities and writings of Edward Wilmot Blyden (1832–1912) readily illustrate some measure of the impact that sundry currents of Protestant liberalism had upon this missiological development. Born in the West Indies, Blyden received his secondary education and early vocational motivation from a white Presbyterian clergyman. Upon refusal of admission to Rutgers Theological College because of his race, Blyden migrated to Liberia under the auspices of the American Colonization Society. There he completed his education and served as a missionary of the Old School Presbyterian Church. Exposure to progressive secular and religious thought in both the United States and Britain, coupled with a growing appreciation of Islamic and indigenous African culture and religion, resulted in his increasingly strident rejection of traditional Protestant theology and missiology. While Blyden's primary critique centered on the deleterious impact of missionary Christianity on African cultures and peoples, the central missiological issue was the problem of race, religion, and culture. His reflections on this problem reached a wide audience with publication in 1887 of his major work, *Christianity, Islam, and the Negro Race*.[19]

Although it is impossible to place the theologically eclectic Blyden definitively within a particular theological camp, it is obvious that his theological thought moved away from orthodox evangelical Protestantism and toward liberalism.[20] Gayraud Wilmore notes that "Blyden . . . did not consider himself an orthodox Christian in the tradition of American evangelicalism. Theologically, he felt a greater congeniality with the most nonconforming luminaries of New England Protestantism—the Channings, Theodore Parkers and Emersons . . . ."[21] In 1886 his growing liberalism and preference of a "universalistic deism to a narrow religious creed" resulted in his resigning from the Presbyterian ministry to become a "minister of truth."[22]

The well-read and widely traveled Blyden admired and was conversant with such luminaries of the Liberal Era as Mary Kingsley and Herbert Spencer.[23] Abreast of the most progressive theological and scientific currents of the era, he became one of the first serious advocates and pioneers of the sociological, anthropological, and historical study of Africa.[24] His use of such studies and theories in defense and vindication of the African race induced both West Africans and diaspora Africans to become more appreciative of traditional African religion and culture, and more critical of the professed benefits of Western culture and Christianity.[25] His influence was magnified by the efforts of a growing number of West African and diaspora African churchmen.[26]

An explanation of the importance of this missiological development for the maturation of Pan-Africanism is provided by Walter Williams, who observed that "of the necessary conditions for the growth of Pan-African sentiment, the one that remained the longest unfulfilled and was most necessary was black Americans' willing acceptance of, and identification with, Africa and indigenous African cultures . . . . Once they had accepted the validity of African cultures, some mission supporters developed a full-fledged Pan-African feeling."[27]

Of related significance is P. Olisanwuche Esedebe's explicit linkage of Pan-Africanism to a series of missionary congresses on Africa held in the 1890s. These congresses provided important forums for the presentation of an evolving Pan-African missiology.[28] The first, held in Chicago in conjunction with the 1893 World's Parliament of Religion, reflected in part the new liberal-influenced perspective toward other religions and creeds, particularly as fostered by the comparative study of religion.[29] Included among African-American and African participants at this Congress were a number of figures who would later play prominent roles in the activities of the London Conference of 1900, which is traditionally proclaimed as marking the institutional beginnings of the Pan-African movement.[30] The overlap of sentiments and personnel has prompted at least one scholar to suggest that the 1893 Chicago Congress on Africa "be taken as the beginning of Pan-Africanism as a movement."[31] An explicit call for the Chicago Congress to further the development of a culturally and historically informed missiology that would support and further the indigenization of Christianity in Africa was made by Reverend Abayomi, "pastor of a native church in Sierra Leone." In a letter to the Congress's secretary, Frederick Perry Noble, Reverend Abayomi articulated what would become a central tenet of an evolving Pan-African missiology: "What the negro needs is Christianity, not Anglocanism or Americanism. Give him the Bible. . . then allow him to develop on his own line guided by the Divine Rule. But let not Europe or America stand between us and God."[32] A more explicit linkage of progressive and liberal theological and missiological tenets with an evolving Pan-African missiology was reflected two years later at the 1895 Congress on Africa sponsored by the Stewart Missionary Foundation for Africa.[33]

Despite major deficiencies and liabilities, which became increasingly clear to both its black and white adherents, an adapted version of Protestant liberalism "led the Protestant churches into the world of modern science, scholarship and global knowledge" and performed a similar service for an evolving and maturing Pan-Africanism.[34] Its central tenets, coupled with the findings of disciplines such as comparative religion and the philosophy of religion, provided its adherents of African descent with "modern" theological and "scientific" support for what would become central precepts of twentieth-century Pan-African ideology.[35] By selectively appropriating certain tenets of Protestant liberalism and applying them to the cause of spiritual and material redemption of Africa and her offspring, a small but influential group of African and diaspora African figures helped Pan-Africanism make its initial break from what was increasingly viewed as outmoded theological, missiological, and ideological moorings.[36]

The widening gulf between the goals and ideals of an evangelically rooted Pan-Africanism and an increasingly secularized and politicized Pan-African movement can be noted at least from the 1900 Pan-African Conference and its preparatory sessions. At this conference the evangelical Pan-African tradition was well represented and articulated by Majola Agbebi, Bishop Alexander Walters, and Bishop James Johnson.[37] Yet more prophetic of the developing relationship between the Christian mission tradition and Pan-Africanism was the warning issued in the Conference's "Address to the Nations of the World," drafted by W. E. B. Du Bois: "Let not the cloak of Christian missionary enterprise be allowed in the future, as so often in the past, to hide the ruthless economic exploitation and political downfall of less developed nations whose chief fault has been reliance on the plighted faith of the Christian Church."[38]

Evangelical ideals and concerns continued to inform both the leadership and supporters of Pan-Africanism in the decades to follow. By the mid-1930s, however, it had become evident that the more progressive and radical wing of Pan-Africanism would no longer rely upon evangelical Christianity's "plighted faith" for realization of its increasingly secular vision.[39] A new generation of leaders, decidedly heterodox in their theological as well as ideological orientations, had come to the fore of a revitalized Pan-African movement.[40]

The demise of the old evangelical Pan-African tradition and the shift to a more secular orientation was confirmed in 1945 at the fifth—and in many ways the most important—Pan-African Congress. At this Congress the changed status of the explicitly Christian-rooted Pan-African vision, which generations of evangelical activists had nurtured, was illustrated by its lacking even symbolic representation among the leadership of the Congress.[41]

An accurate assessment of the influence of Protestant liberalism within African and diaspora African communities and its impact on the maturation of Pan-Africanism awaits intensive study of the theological backgrounds and orientations of a host of major and minor figures within the broad expanse of Pan-Africanism as well as the Anglo-African and African-American ecclesiastical traditions. This work seeks to make a contribution toward this end by examining the life and writings of Orishatukeh Faduma, who explicitly attempted to adapt and adopt theological liberalism as well as its missiological and educational theory to the Pan-African cause. Faduma's life (1857–1946), spent primarily in Sierra Leone and the Southern United States (with brief but formative periods in London and Guyana), bridges both a geographical and a chronological expanse of major importance for Pan-Africanism. His activities and writings reflect much of the theological, missiological, pedagogical, and ideological ferment present within the African and diaspora African communities between 1857 and 1946. Indeed, Faduma served as an important mediator of much of this ferment on both sides of the Atlantic.

Born in British Guiana (Guyana) of Yoruba parentage and christened William J. Davis, Faduma, upon repatriation to the west coast of Africa, was exposed to the nationalist and incipient Pan-African thought being nurtured in the West African community by churchmen such as James Johnson, Joseph Claudius May, and Edward W. Blyden. Their teachings induced him to participate in a movement critical of the policies of Western mission societies in Sierra Leone. In response to the cultural arrogance implied in the missionaries' practice of encouraging Africans to accept European names upon baptism, he rejected his baptismal name in favor of the more indigenously significant appellation, Orishatukeh Faduma.[42] Similarly, Faduma's constant plea was for indigenization of Christianity in Africa: "Let us have a Christian life and thought expressed in Africa, not after the manner of a Frenchman, an American, or Englishman, but assimilated into African. Let Christianity planted in Africa become native to the soil growing from within."[43]

Unlike Blyden, whose theological education had been eclectic, Faduma was systematically exposed to the progressive theological, pedagogical, and missiological tenets of the age while studying at the University of London, Yale University and Divinity School, and Chicago Theological Seminary. All provided significant institutional nurture for the development of liberalism.[44]

As early as 1890, Faduma confessed his allegiance to the "New Theology." It was, he optimistically affirmed, "the new science of religion . . . destined to uproot American prejudice against the Negro, elevate and purify the state, the Church, conquer Anglo-Saxon haughtiness, and make all nations confess that 'God is no respecter of persons.' "[45] Thereafter Faduma attempted to use the New Theology to provide theological grounding for his evolving evangelical Pan-Africanism. The result of this conscious effort to ally Pan-Africanism and Protestant liberalism was a Pan-African missiology and pedagogy that Faduma preached incessantly on both sides of the Atlantic and attempted to actualize by participating in Chief Alfred Sam's Back-to-Africa Movement.[46] This Pan-African–oriented missionary-emigrationist venture proved to be an important precursor of the more widely known effort headed by Marcus Garvey. It also served as a major stimulus of nationalist and Pan-African sentiments within the West African community. These sentiments were eventually given institutional focus with the formation of the National Congress of British West Africa in 1920.[47]

A number of contemporary scholars have made mention of Faduma and called for a major study of his life and work.[48] Unfortunately, the brief assessments available focus almost exclusively on the secular dimensions of Faduma's thought and activities. As is the case with most Pan-African activists, little if any attention has been given to the theological undergirdings of his Pan-African ideology.[49] This oversight has often obscured the full breadth of the life and thought of most Pan-African visionaries and made incomprehensible many of the apparent inconsistencies and ambiguities in their writings and activities. It has also contributed to the historiographical failure to appreciate the depth and complexity of the ongoing theological and ideological construction and reconstruction within African and diaspora African communities.

In the case of Faduma, such treatments appear to be especially negligent, given the central and acknowledged importance of theological liberalism in his personal life and the key role that he played as mediator of this crucial shift in Protestant theology and missiology to the African and diaspora African communities and to the Pan-African cause. Of related significance is the importance of a careful analysis of Faduma's similarly neglected liberalism-influenced missiology. In the course of his formulation and advocacy of a Pan-African missiology he was forced to address a number of issues that are still of major concern for contemporary missiology. Most notable among these are the relationship between

Christianity and African culture and the limits of theological and ecclesiastical indigenization or Africanization.[50]

It is hoped that this work will make a significant contribution to the interrelated fields of church history, African history, African-American history, and the history and theology of Protestant missions. In addition to providing factual material on a long-neglected but important figure in both African and African-American history, it illustrates the necessity of examining the religious and theological thought that often shaped and gave impetus to the ideologies and activities of many Africans and diaspora Africans. And while providing insight into the complex and crucial role that the theology and praxis of the evangelical mission enterprise played in the evolution of Pan-Africanism, it also challenges traditional interpretations that have tended to project Africans and African-Americans as passive recipients of western theology and missiology.

Notes

1. Efforts to define, date, and analyze the Pan-African phenomenon have given rise to an extensive, complex, and often conflicting body of literature. For a brief contemporary review of major efforts see P. Olisanwuche Esedebe, *Pan-Africanism: The Idea and Movement, 1776–1963* (Washington, D.C.: Howard University Press, 1982), pp. 3–6. See also Immanuel Geiss, *The Pan-African Movement: A History of Pan-Africanism in America, Europe, and Africa,* trans. Ann Keep (New York: Africana Publishing Co., 1974); Tony Martin, "Some Reflections on Evangelical Pan-Africanism, or Black Missionaries, White Missionaries and the Struggle for African Souls 1890–1930," *Ufahamu* 1 (Winter 1971): 77–92; J. Ayodele Langley, *Pan-Africanism and Nationalism in West Africa, 1900–1945* (Oxford: Clarendon Press, 1973).
2. Ibid.
3. Geiss, *Pan-African Movement,* p. 58.
4. See Alexander Walters, *My Life and Work* (New York: Fleming H. Revell Co., 1917); E. A. Ayandele, *Holy Johnson: Pioneer of African Nationalism, 1836–1917* (London: Frank Cass and Co., 1970); W. E. B. Du Bois, *Dusk of Dawn* (New York: Harcourt Brace, 1940); W. E. B. Du Bois, *The Word and Africa* (New York: Viking Press, 1947); Marcus Garvey, *Philosophy and Opinions of Marcus Garvey,* ed. Amy Jacques-Garvey (New York: Atheneum, 1974, originally published 1923, 1925); Edward Blyden, *Christianity, Islam, and the Negro Race* (Edinburgh: Edinburgh University Press, 1967, originally published 1887); Edward Blyden, *African*

Life and Customs (London: Phillips, 1908); E. A. Ayandele, *A Visionary of the African Church, Majola Agbebi (1860–1917)* (Nairobi: East African Publishing House, 1971); Wilson J. Moses, *Alexander Crummell: A Study of Civilization and Discontent* (New York, Oxford: Oxford University Press, 1989); and Kwame Nkrumah, *Ghana: The Autobiography of Kwame Nkrumah* (London: International Publishers Co., 1957).

5. See Hollis R. Lynch, *Edward Blyden: Pan-Negro Patriot, 1832–1912* (London: Oxford University Press, 1967); *Tony Martin, Race First: The Ideological and Organizational Struggles of Marcus Garvey and the Universal Negro Improvement Association* (Westport, Conn., and London: Greenwood Press, 1976); Clarence Contee, "The Emergence of Du Bois as an African Nationalist," *Journal of Negro History* 54 (Jan. 1969): 48–53; Francis Broderick, *W. E. B. Du Bois: Negro Leader in a Time of Crisis* (Stanford: Stanford University Press, 1959); Harold Isaacs, "Du Bois and Africa," *Race* 1 (Nov. 1960): 3–23; Basil Davidson, *Black Star: A View of the Life and Times of Kwame Nkrumah* (New York, Washington, D. C.: Praeger Publishers, 1974). See also Robert July, *The Origins of Modern African Thought* (London: Faber and Faber, 1968); E. A. Ayandele, *The Missionary Impact on Modern Nigeria, 1842–1914* (New York: Humanities Press, 1967); J. Ayodele Langley, *Pan-Africanism and Nationalism;* Walter L. Williams, *Black Americans and the Evangelization of Africa, 1877–1900* (Madison: University of Wisconsin Press, 1982); Cyril E. Griffith, *The African Dream: Martin R. Delany and the Emergence of Pan-African Thought* (University Park and London: Pennsylvania State University Press, 1975).
6. On the general ferment within the American religious community during this era, see Francis P. Weisenburger, *Ordeal of Faith: The Crisis of Church-Going America, 1865–1900* (New York: Philosophical Library, 1959). See also H. Shelton Smith, Robert T. Handy, and Lefferts A. Loetscher, *American Christianity: An Historical Interpretation with Representative Documents,* vol. 2 (New York: Charles Scribner's Sons, 1963), pp. 213–416; Ferenc Morton Szasz, *The Divided Mind of Protestant America, 1880–1930* (University Ala.: University of Alabama Press, 1982). The existence of this ferment within the West African and African-American communities is noted in Gayraud Wilmore, *Black Religion and Black Radicalism: An Interpretation of the Religious History of Afro-American People* 2nd ed. (Maryknoll, N.Y.: Orbis, 1983); Carter G. Woodson, *History of the Negro Church* (Washington, D. C.: Associated Publishers, 1921, 1945, 1972), pp. 224–303; Ayandele, *The Missionary Impact;* J. F. Ade Ajayi, *Christian Missions in Nigeria,*

1841–1891: The Making of a New Elite (London: Longmans, 1965); and Wilson J. Moses, *The Golden Age of Black Nationalism, 1850–1925* (Hamden, Conn.: Archon, 1978).

7. Geiss notes that Pan-Africanism was "predominantly a modern movement . . . the reaction of the most advanced, most intensively Europeanized Africans and Afro-Americans to contact with the modern world." Geiss, *Pan-African Movement,* pp. 5–6.
8. Daniel Day Williams, *God's Grace and Man's Hope* (Harper & Brothers, 1961), p. 22.
9. Lloyd J. Averill, *American Theology in the Liberal Tradition* (Philadelphia: Westminster Press, 1967), pp. 69–94.
10. Sydney E. Ahlstrom, *A Religious History of the American People* (New Haven and London: Yale University Press, 1972), pp. 783–784.
11. William Hutchison has provided the most focused analysis of the changes fostered in American missiology by Protestant liberalism. See his studies entitled, *The Modernist Impulse in American Protestantism* (Cambridge and London: Harvard University Press, 1976); *American Protestant Thought: The Liberal Era* (New York: Harper & Row, 1968); and especially "Modernism and Missions: The Liberal Search for an Exportable Christianity, 1875–1935," in *The Missionary Enterprise in China and America,* ed. John K. Fairbank (Cambridge and London: Harvard University Press, 1974), pp. 110–131.
12. Martin E. Marty, *Righteous Empire: The Protestant Experience in America* (New York: Dial Press, 1970), p. 193; Leo Spitzer, *The Creoles of Sierra Leone: Responses to Colonialism, 1870–1945* (Madison: University of Wisconsin Press, 1974), pp. 127–131; Vincent L. Wimbush, "Rescue the Perishing: The Importance of Biblical Scholarship in Black Christianity," *Reflection* (Jan. 1983): 9–11.
13. David W. Wills and Richard Newman, *Black Apostles at Home and Abroad: Afro-Americans and the Christian Mission* (Boston: G. K. Hall & Co., 1982), pp. xxiii–xxiv. Also see David W. Wills, "Aspects of Social Thought in the African Methodist Episcopal Church, 1884–1910" (Ph.D. diss., Harvard University, 1975) and Carter G. Woodson, *History of the Negro Church,* pp. 224–241.
14. The significant number of Africans and diaspora Africans receiving postsecondary and seminary training during this era has been noted by Walter Williams, *Black Americans and the Evangelization of Africa, 1877–1900* (Madison: University of Wisconsin Press, 1982) and Milfred C. Fierce, "African-American Interest in Africa and Interaction with West Africa: The Origins of the Pan-African Idea in the United States, 1900–1919" (Ph.D. diss., Columbia University, 1976). Among the list of "progressive and liberal African-American"

church leaders were figures such as Alexander Walters, Sutton E. Griggs, Reverdy C. Ransom, J. Milton Waldron, Adam Clayton Powell, Sr., Hugh Henry Proctor, Gordon Blaine Hancock, George Edmund Haynes, and William H. Ferris. Within the West African context, note Edward W. Blyden, John R. Frederick, and Majola Agbebi.

15. Williams, *Black Americans,* and Ayandele, *The Missionary Impact.*
16. See Williams, *Black Americans,* and Sylvia M. Jacobs, ed., *Black Americans and the Missionary Movement in Africa* (Westport, Conn., and London: Greenwood Press, 1982). See also Edwin S. Redkey, "The Meaning of Africa to Afro-Americans, 1890–1914," *Black Academy Review* 3 (Spring/Summer 1972): 5–37.
17. See Edwin S. Redkey, ed., *Respect Black: The Writings and Speeches of Henry McNeal Turner* (New York: Arno Press, 1971); Edward Blyden, *Christianity, Islam, and the Negro Race;* Ayandele, *Holy Johnson;* and Ayandele, *Majola Agbebi.*
18. Williams, *Black Americans,* pp. 161–171, and Ayandele, *Missionary Impact,* pp. 241–265.
19. On Blyden, see Hollis Lynch, *Edward Wilmot Blyden: Pan-Negro Patriot, 1832–1912* (London and New York: Oxford University Press, 1967), and Edith Holden, *Blyden of Liberia* (New York: Vantage Press, 1966). In addition to Blyden's *Christianity, Islam, and the Negro Race,* see also his *African Life and Customs* (London: Phillips, 1908).
20. Unfortunately, Blyden's major theological work, *Comparative Theology,* has not been located. Lynch, Blyden, pp. 78–79.
21. Wilmore, *Black Religion and Black Radicalism,* p. 117.
22. Williams, *Black Americans,* pp. 13, 167. Hollis Lynch also notes that Blyden was interested in the mysticism of the Swedish scientist, philosopher, and theologian, Emanuel Swedenborg (1688–1772). In 1892 one of Swedenborg's disciples dedicated a book entitled *The African and the True Christian Religion* to Blyden. This work expanded upon Swedenborg's view that Africans were "the people potentially most capable of religious perfection." Lynch, *Blyden,* p. 82. For Swedenborg's interest in Africa and the religious capabilities of Africans, see Philip D. Curtin, *The Image of Africa: British Ideas and Action, 1780–1850* (London: Macmillan, 1965), pp. 26–27.
23. Lynch, *Blyden,* pp. 181; 205–207.
24. Lynch, *Blyden,* pp. 54–83.
25. Lynch, *Blyden,* p.151.
26. Williams, *Black Americans,* pp. 167–169. In 1899 West African Anglican clergyman James Johnson produced a sympathetic theological and philosophical analysis of Yoruba religion entitled *Yoruba Heathenism.* Ayandele notes that James Johnson "was

dumbfounded at the moral code of Yoruba religion, 'which only waits for the superior enlightenment of Christianity to raise it to a higher plane.'" In an address entitled *Africa and the Gospel,* Majola Agbebi noted the importance of such studies for the success of the missionary enterprise in Africa: "To be successful (as missionaries) we have to study the names, designs, and influences of the stone and wooden gods of our fathers . . . . The lives and doings of our heathen sages, the origin of the several gods of whom our brethren worship will be useful instruments in the hands of the aggressive missionary." Ayandele, *Holy Johnson,* p. 301, and *Missionary Impact,* pp. 264–265.

27. Williams, *Black Americans,* pp. 164–169, 173.
28. Esedebe, *Pan-Africanism: The Idea and the Movement,* pp. 45–46.
29. Ahlstrom, *The American Protestant Encounter with World Religions* (Beloit, Wisc.: Beloit College, 1962).
30. Prominent among the participants were Alexander Crummell, Bishop Henry M. Turner, and Bishop Alexander Walters, who would actually chair the 1900 London Conference. Participating by proxy were Edward Blyden and the Reverend James Johnson. Esedebe, *Pan-Africanism: The Idea and Movement,* pp. 45–46 and Frederick P. Noble, *The Chicago Congress on Africa, 1894*. Also see Owen Charles Mathurin, *Henry Sylvester Williams and the Origins of the Pan-African Movement, 1869–1911* (Westport, Conn., and London: Greenwood Press, 1976).
31. Esedebe, *Pan-Africanism,* p. 45.
32. Perry Noble, *Africa at the Columbian Exposition* (Chicago: Newberry Library, 1893), pp. 12–13. On liberal theological and missiological support for such a program, see William Newton Clarke, *A Study of Christian Missions* (New York: Charles Scribner's Sons, 1900), and George A. Gordon, *The Gospel For Humanity: Annual Sermon Before the American Board of Commissioners for Foreign Missions,* delivered at Brooklyn, New York, 15 October 1896 (Boston: ABCFM, 1895). Also see Hutchison, "Modernism and Missions," pp. 116–121.
33. See especially the papers presented by Orishatukeh Faduma entitled "Success and Drawbacks to Missionary Work in Africa by an Eye-Witness," and "Religious Beliefs of the Yoruba People of West Africa," in *Africa and the American Negro: Addresses and Proceedings of the Congress on Africa,* ed. J. W. E. Bowen (1896; reprint, Miami: Mnemosyne Press, 1969), pp. 125–136, 31–36.
34. A less benign legacy is also to be noted. Despite its relatively enlightened view of nonwestern religions and cultures, its ethical commitments, and the active efforts of some of its adherents to usher in the "kingdom of God" on earth, Protestant liberalism suffered from

glaring deficiencies. Most notable was the inability of many of its adherents to confront the resurgent racism and imperialism that paralleled liberalism's rise to influence in the late nineteenth century. Indeed, both found not only acceptance but also advocates among the adherents and nominal adherents of Protestant liberalism. See Marty, *Righteous Empire,* pp.197–198, and Robert T. Handy, *A Christian America: Protestant Hopes and Historical Realities* (New York and London: Oxford University Press, 1971), pp. 117–198. For a broader discussion see Thomas F. Gossett, *Race: The History of an Idea in America* (New York: Schocken Books, 1965), pp. 144–147.

35. Ahlstrom, *A Religious History,* p. 783.
36. Especially appealing was liberalism's nonsectarian emphasis, advocacy of modernization, progressive educational theory, awareness of the historical nature and relativeness of Christianity and other religions, and its theoretical support for the indigenization of Christianity.
37. Mathurin, *The Origins of the Pan African Movement,* pp. 41–85.
38. Quoted in Langley, *Pan-Africanism and Nationalism in West Africa,* pp. 28–29. See also Geiss, *Pan-African Movement,* pp. 180–185, and Walters, *My Life and Work,* p. 253.
39. See Geiss, *Pan-African Movement,* pp. 199–228.
40. Langley, *Pan-Africanism and Nationalism in West Africa,* pp. 326–346.
41. Geiss, *Pan-African Movement,* pp. 402–403.
42. "An Important Notice," *Sierra Leone Weekly News,* 5 Aug. 1887.
43. Orishatukeh Faduma, "Success and Drawbacks in Africa by an Eye-Witness," in Bowen, *Africa and the American Negro,* pp. 125–131.
44. Sydney Ahlstrom, *A Religious History,* p. 776; Roland Bainton, *Yale and the Ministry: A History of Education for the Christian Ministry at Yale from the Founding in 1701* (New York: Harper & Brothers, 1957). On the impact of Protestant liberalism in Britain during this period, see Owen Chadwick, *The Victorian Church,* vol. 2 (New York: Oxford University Press, 1970), and L. E. Elliott-Binns, *English Thought 1860–1900: The Theological Aspect* (London: Longmans, Green and Co., 1956). On the pedagogical significance of the University of London, see Orishatukeh Faduma, "African Negro Education," *Sierra Leone Weekly News,* 3 Aug. 1984.
45. Orishatukeh Faduma, "Thoughts For The Times: Or The New Theology," *A. M. E. Church Review* 7 (Oct. 1890): 139–143.
46. Orishatukeh Faduma, "Success and Drawbacks to Missionary Work in Africa by an Eye-Witness," and "Religious Beliefs of the Yoruba People of West Africa," in Bowen, *Africa and the American Negro,*

pp. 125–136; 31–36. Also by Faduma, "The Problem of Christian Missions among Less Developed Races," *The American Missionary* 61 (Mar. 1907): 69–74; "Africa's Claims and Needs," *Southern Workman* 54 (May 1925): 221–225, and "The African Movement: Its Idea and Methods," *Sierra Leone Weekly News,* 2 Oct. 1915.

47. William E. Bittle and Gilbert Geis, *The Longest Way Home: Chief Alfred C. Sam's Back-to-Africa Movement* (Detroit: Wayne State University Press, 1964); J. Ayodele Langley, "Chief Sam's Movement and Race Consciousness in West Africa," *Phylon* 32 (Summer 1971): 210–247; and J. Ayodele Langley, *Pan-Africanism and Nationalism in West Africa, 1900–1945: A Study in Ideology and Social Classes* (Oxford: Clarendon Press, 1973).
48. Most notable in this group, which includes Hollis Lynch, Kenneth King, and J. Ayodele Langley, is George Shepperson, who calls for a study of Faduma as part of a major shift in the historiography of Pan-Africanism. See Shepperson, "External Factors in the Development of African Nationalism, with Particular Reference to British Central Africa," *Phylon* 22 (Fall 1961): 207–225. See also Rina Okonkwo, "Orishatukeh Faduma: A Man of Two Worlds," *Journal of Negro History* 68 (Winter 1983): 24–36.
49. Note, for example, Walter L. Williams' superficial treatment of Faduma's thought and activities in his *Black Americans and the Evangelization of Africa, 1877–1900,* pp. 146, 156–159.
50. On contemporary efforts to address these issues as they apply to the African context, see E. B. Idowu, *Towards an Indigenous Church* (London: Oxford University Press, 1964); C. G. Baeta, *Christianity in Tropical Africa* (London: Oxford University Press, 1968); Harry Sawyerr, *Creative Evangelism: Towards a New Christian Encounter in Africa* (London: Lutterworth, 1968); Edmund Ilogu, "The Biblical Idea of Partnership and the Modern Missionary Task," in *The History of Christianity in West Africa,* ed. O. U. Kalu, (New York and London: Longman, 1980), pp. 335–339; John V. Taylor, *The Primal Vision: Christian Presence Amid African Religion* (London: SCM Press, 1963); Kwesi Dickson and Paul Ellingworth, eds., *Biblical Revelation and African Beliefs* (Maryknoll, N.Y.: Orbis, 1969); O. U. Kalu, "Peter Pan Syndrome: Church Aid and Selfhood in Africa," *Missiology: An International Review* 3(1975): 15–29; O. U. Kalu, "Traditionalization and Modern Evangelical Strategy in Nigeria," *West African Religion* 16 (1975): 31; Gwinyai H. Muzorewa, *The Origins and Development of African Theology* (Maryknoll, N.Y.: Orbis, 1985), Mercy Amba Oduyoye, *Hearing and Knowing Theological Reflections on Christianity in Africa* (Maryknoll, N. Y.: Orbis, 1986). On attempts to address these issues within the larger missiological arena, see J. Verkuyl,

Contemporary Missiology: An Introduction, translated and edited by Dale Cooper (Grand Rapids: William B. Eerdmans, 1978); Owen C. Thomas, *Attitudes Toward Other Religions: Some Christian Interpretations* (London: SCM Press, 1969); and Peter Beyerhaus and Henry Lefever, *The Responsible Church and the Foreign Mission* (London: World Dominion Press, 1964).

1

The Missiological Roots Of Evangelical Pan-Africanism

Modern missionary efforts aimed at redeeming and regenerating Africa had their source in the transatlantic revivals of the late eighteenth century. Evangelical stalwarts on both sides of the Atlantic directed the energy and commitment evoked by this powerful new appropriation of the gospel into a network of missionary and benevolent societies designed to spread the gospel, redeem humanity, and transform society both at home and abroad.[1] Their efforts gave rise to one of the most dynamic, successful, and controversial epochs in the history of Christian missions. Here was laid the foundation for what would be described as the "great century" of Protestant missionary activity.[2]

Though varying in details, the theories that shaped the evangelical missionary enterprise were rooted in the peculiar theological, ecclesiastical, and ideological tenets and commitments of evangelical Protestantism.[3] Moreover, a profound sense of eschatological responsibility and soteriological concern for the souls of "perishing heathens" was inextricably intertwined with the cultural, racial, and economic presuppositions of the post-Enlightenment West.[4] Exalted opinions of the culture and institutions of the Protestant West were rooted in the seemingly self-evident equation of Euro-American Protestant culture with "progress," civilization, and the Anglo-Saxon race. This equation engendered the racial, spiritual, and cultural chauvinism that became a dominant characteristic of evangelical mission theory and practice throughout much of the "great century."[5]

According to both prevailing assumptions and evangelical scholarship, a symbiotic relationship existed between Protestant Christianity and Western culture: Protestant Christianity provided the generative and shaping influence of Western civilization, while Western civilization provided in turn the nurture necessary for the full flowering of Protestant Christianity. Consequently, many Protestants believed that Christianity and "civilization," spread to nonwestern cultures via the mission enterprise, ensured the eventual regeneration of these cultures along Euro-American lines of development.[6] Thus the dogma that Christianization and civilization meant westernization enjoyed a privileged status in mainstream evangelical missiology. Throughout much of the nineteenth century Christianization, civilization, and westernization would be understood and used as almost synonymous terms.[7]

Although a few mission theorists and members of "liberal" traditions such as the Unitarians and Transcendentalists occasionally expressed an increased sensitivity and respect for nonwestern cultures and religions, adherents of mainstream evangelical Protestantism remained impervious to such reappraisals.[8] Lacking a critical historical understanding of the relationship between Protestantism and their own cultural heritage, most evangelical mission theorists, activists, and enthusiasts drew upon Scripture, evangelical dogma, and a flood of missionary literature to support their equation of nonwestern cultures and religions with degradation, backwardness, barbarism, ignorance, and darkness.[9]

The depiction and treatment of these cultures and religions as evil and illusory also found support in the purportedly scholarly works of evangelical theorists such as William Sprague. His *Lectures Illustrating the Contact Between True Christianity and Various Other Systems* reaffirmed the prevailing theological and missiological truism that "the relations between Christianity and paganism were the relations between light and darkness and that with the spread of missions the kingdom of darkness was being routed and its ruler was in panic."[10]

Such assumptions were amplified when focused on Africa. Spiritual and cultural chauvinism merged with racism caused Protestant missionaries to have an even less savory impression of African life and customs. They saw Africa as a benighted continent, ruled by Satan and ravished by both ignorance and the slave trade. The evangelical mission enterprise therefore projected itself as the primary vehicle for Africa's spiritual and material regeneration.[11] They declared that only through the benefits of Protestant Christianity and Euro-American civilization would Africa's progeny attain the redemption prophesied in Psalm 68:31: "Princes shall come out of Egypt and Ethiopia shall soon stretch forth her hands unto God." Evangelical missiological tenets and this prophecy would take on additional import when linked with the religious and secular aspirations of African-American and Anglo-African converts to evangelical Protestantism.[12]

Having emerged during this era of evangelical zeal and outreach, both African-American and Anglo-African Protestantism were indelibly, though not exclusively, stamped with evangelical Protestantism's theological, ideological, and missiological orientations. Throughout most of the nineteenth century and well into the twentieth century, traditional evangelical Protestantism provided the religious and ideological framework from which most African-American and Anglo-African evangelicals responded to their precarious encounter with modernity and Euro-American civilization.[13]

Like their Euro-American counterparts, African-American and Anglo-African converts to evangelical Protestantism felt compelled to engage in evangelical outreach. Although universal in their evangelical concerns and commitments, these were nevertheless given a special focus. They believed that Africa had a special claim to their evangelical zeal and responsibility.[14] Having been "providentially" exposed to Western Christianity and civilization, they viewed themselves as the primary agents of Africa's redemption.[15]

While soteriological concerns were predominant, Anglo-African and African-American evangelicals were generally concerned with more than spiritual redemption. Their efforts embraced a broader and more temporal soteriological framework. The Ethiopian prophecy, as interpreted and preached by generations of evangelicals of African descent, often implied and promised much more than the salvation of African souls otherwise doomed to perdition.[16] Drawing upon their own existential concerns and emphases, some supplemented the traditional evangelical vision of Africa's redemption with the dream of establishing via the mission enterprise the foundation of a strong modern black Christian nation. Modeled along the lines of Euro-American Protestant civilization, this nation and nationality would be proof of the African and diaspora African capacity for Christian civilization and self-government. As such, it would increase the global status and respect of Africans. The success of the evangelical enterprise so envisioned—as a conduit for providing Africa and her descendants with the cultural and technological as well as the spiritual and political fruits of modern Euro-American civilization—would consequently make Africa "a perpetual and courted power in the life of the world."[17] The Pan-African implications of this evangelical strategy were made explicit by Bishop Henry M. Turner of the African Methodist Episcopal Church, who argued that "Africa will be the thermometer that will determine the status of the Negro the world over. . . . The elevation of the Negro in this and all other countries is indissolubly connected with the enlightenment of Africa."[18]

Thus an incipient evangelical Pan-Africanism with its own missiological agenda and priorities developed within and parallel to the mainstream evangelical mission enterprise throughout the course of the nineteenth century. Though rooted in the basic theological and ideological orientations of the broader movement, it was definitively contoured by existential concerns and dilemmas engendered by the African encounter with Western Christian culture.[19]

This development took on a new urgency as the African and diaspora African encounter with modern Western Christian culture became less benevolent and more ominous in the last quarter of the nineteenth century. In the wake of resurgent racism and emerging imperialism, African and diaspora African evangelicals painfully reexamined perceptions of themselves, relative to both Euro-American Christian culture and the traditional culture and religions of Africa. The mission enterprise as the foremost bearer of modern Western Christian culture became the primary focus of this critical reappraisal.

A small but influential group of evangelical enthusiasts on both sides of the Atlantic began to formulate a distinctive and self-conscious Pan-African–oriented missiology and ideology less ambivalent and less compromised as to their past, present, and future status relative to the modern West and their African heritage. Their often inconsistent quest was for a missiology that offered Africa and her progeny the desired religious, technological, and intellectual fruits of modern Euro-American Christian culture, without the wholesale denial and denigration of their own racial and cultural identity and spiritual gifts. Their efforts would draw upon the new theological, missiological, scientific, and intellectual currents that emerged in the late nineteenth century.[20]

Ironically, Sierra Leone, founded in 1787 as a showcase of the British civilizing mission in Africa, provided an important geographical and historical matrix for this critical reappraisal of traditional evangelical missiology and its attendant ideology. British and American evangelicals had long dreamed of establishing an outpost of Christianity and civilization on the west coast of Africa.[21] The decisive impetus for realization of this dream came in 1772. In that year British evangelical and humanitarian forces led by Granville Sharp scored a major victory over proslavery forces with the ruling of Lord Mansfield in favor of the slave James Somerset.[22] As a result of this judgment, approximately 15,000 slaves in England became free. Their ranks were further swelled after the Revolutionary War when thousands of former American slaves who had fought as British loyalists settled in Britain.[23]

The dilemma posed by the growing number of ex-slaves and "Black poor" in England provided the immediate impetus for the collusion of evangelical, humanitarian, and commercial interests in an ambitious scheme that would not only rid England of a public nuisance, but also establish an outpost of Christianity, civilization, and commerce on the west coast of Africa.[24]

The decision to concentrate their ambitious scheme on the small mountainous West African peninsula that fifteenth-century Portuguese sailors had christened "Sierra Leone" was inspired by the exploratory efforts of an amateur botanist, Henry Smeathman.[25] His vision of the peninsula as the locus of a primarily commercial venture fused with Granville Sharp's antislavery interests and the concerns of a small but influential group of left wing evangelicals within the Church of England called the "Clapham sect."[26] This alliance of commercial, humanitarian, and evangelical concerns projected Sierra Leone as "the fertile ground from which the growth of European civilization and Christianity would soon encompass the entire African continent."[27]

In May 1787 these interests took definitive shape with the establishment of the "Province of Freedom" with emigrants from England, Nova Scotia, and Jamaica. However, the project's ambitious commercial, humanitarian, and evangelical goals were frustrated by "climate, disease, poor soil, and the political vicissitudes of life constantly threatened on one hand by European ship captains and on the other by the local population."[28] It was apparent by 1802 that the venture could not succeed without British governmental intervention and on January 1, 1808, Sierra Leone became a crown colony.[29] When the British Parliament also passed a bill in 1808 that legislated the abolition of the British slave trade, Sierra Leone provided the West African naval base necessary for its enforcement.[30]

These events proved fortuitous for the subsequent development of Sierra Leone. It eventually served as a point of liberation for 40,000 enslaved Africans, "recaptured" by the British antislavery squadron. By 1863 the colony's original population of westernized emigrants from England, Nova Scotia, and Jamaica was outnumbered by recaptives.[31]

The majority of Sierra Leone's founding emigrants were already converts to evangelical Protestantism and brought with them well-organized ecclesiastical structures and firm evangelical convictions.[32] However, as the recaptives came to be the largest population group in Sierra Leone, their spiritual needs became the special focus of British evangelical activists and rekindled efforts to make Sierra Leone the showcase of British Christian culture in Africa.[33]

The powerful mission arm of the Church of England, the Church Missionary Society, became the dominant missionizing and modernizing agency in Sierra Leone.[34] Founded in response to the concerns and efforts of the Clapham evangelicals, the Church Missionary Society initially entered the peninsula in 1804 through the proxy of missionaries from central Europe. It gradually assumed primary responsibility for Christianizing and "civilizing" both the descendants of the earlier settlers and the liberated Africans. Mission agency, church, and school became complementary instruments and cooperative tools in their intensive efforts to recreate Victorian Christianity and culture in Sierra Leone.[35]

This intensive evangelical and acculturative enterprise took root among a population torn from its indigenous cultural heritage and eager to gain access to the perceived benefits of Western culture and technology. This produced a society that retained some aspects of traditional African culture, but was predominantly Eurocentric in its psychological, cultural, and intellectual orientation. A "Creole" elite evolved that avidly imbibed the values, goals, aspirations, and even the names associated with Victorian culture.[36] Having thoroughly embraced the tenets and ideology of the missionaries and educators and having been taught to prize and measure all by European standards, Creoles also tended to despise indigenous African religion and culture.[37]

Despite its obvious impact, the success of the Victorian civilizing mission in Sierra Leone was mitigated by a number of developments that took place in the last quarter of the nineteenth century. Most decisive was "the changing image of Africa" and Africans—even those who mirrored Victorian values—among their European mentors. This change, manifest in the "scramble for Africa," found support in a resurgent racism, bolstered by pseudoscientific tenets such as social Darwinism, that ridiculed and rejected evangelical efforts to uplift Africans to the cultural and moral level of Europeans.[38]

These developments provoked a profound cultural shock and identity crisis among a younger generation of Creoles forced to reappraise their own cultural identity and status vis-à-vis both European Christian culture and the African cultural heritage they had been taught to despise and reject.[39] Their efforts at critical reassessment of both their European and African cultural heritage sparked the emergence of a form of cultural nationalism with decided racial and religious emphasis. The initial focus of this reaction was the two agencies through which Western culture was most potently disseminated—church missions and schools.

Key theoretical and theological support for such a critical reappraisal of traditional mission theory and its educational and cultural corollaries was provided by wider developments within the Protestant theological and missiological arena. Especially significant was the growing impact of theological liberalism and disciplines such as comparative religion and the psychology of religion. These provided an intellectual and theoretical framework for a more positive appreciation of nonwestern cultures and religions and helped to forge a more progressive Protestant missiology.

One of the earliest and most significant indicators of the emergence of a more progressive missiology in British mission circles was the mission theory of Henry Venn, who served as secretary of the Church Missionary Society from 1841 to 1874.[40] Upon becoming secretary of the CMS, Venn brought "to bear on the preconceived ideas of his age a fresh and vigorous mind, which reacted to the events and personalities of not only West Africa but also India, Ceylon and other missionary fields of the CMS."[41] To replace traditional mission tenets and practices that he believed to be ill conceived and counterproductive, Venn formulated and attempted to actualize a progressive missiology. While rooted in traditional evangelical, missiological, and theological concerns, his mission theory evinced a cultural sensitivity and historical awareness that in many respects anticipated the development of the liberal missiology that fully emerged at the end of the century.[42] Central to his missiology was the assumption that there were "irrepressible race distinctions" that eventually took on a national cast. European missionaries, he warned, would have to contend with this development. Rather than "charging the natives with presumption and ingratitude," Venn advised missionaries to prepare for and help facilitate this development. In preparation for this task they were to cease being "reckless iconoclasts," study the culture and "national character of the people," and "show the utmost respect for national peculiarities."

Venn argued that continued paternalism and insistence that African churches be modeled after European patterns of ecclesiastical and theological developments would "be apt to create a feeble and dependent native Christian community."[43] Thus he advocated the establishment of "self-governing, self-supporting and self-propagating" national churches under the leadership of an indigenous clergy.[44] Consistent with his goal of fostering an indigenous church and leadership, Venn also called for the development of an educational curriculum that would broaden the narrow religious focus of most mission schools.[45]

Although they were never shared wholeheartedly or enthusiastically by his missionary colleagues or by Lambeth Palace and therefore never fully implemented, Venn's missiological theories and efforts nevertheless had significant impact within British West Africa—particularly within Sierra Leone. Indeed, one of the most ambitious efforts to actualize Venn's progressive missiology was the establishment of the Native Church Pastorate in Sierra Leone in 1861.[46]

A reformist and progressive missiology, formulated by the foremost mission theorist of the era and appropriated by West African ecclesiastics and intellectuals, helped to provide a new generation of West Africans less sanguine about the "blessings" of Western Christianity and culture with a basis from which both to formulate and to legitimate their own critique of traditional Western missiology and culture. Venn's progressive missiology thus adapted served as a catalyst of incipient cultural, ecclesiastical, and nationalist ferment in Sierra Leone throughout the remainder of the nineteenth century.[47] Orishatukeh Faduma was among the Sierra Leoneans who grew to maturity amid the resulting racial, cultural, and religious strife.

Notes

1. Charles I. Foster, *An Errand of Mercy: The Evangelical United Front, 1790–1837* (Chapel Hill: University of North Carolina Press, 1960); Charles L. Chaney, *The Birth of Missions in America* (South Pasadena, Calif.: William Carey Library, 1976); Oliver Elsbree, *The Rise of the Missionary Spirit in America, 1790–1815* (Williamsport, Penn: Williamsport Printing Co., 1928). Max Warren, *The Missionary Movement from Britain in Modern History* (London: SCM Press, 1965).
2. Kenneth S. Latourette, *A History of the Expansion of Christianity, Vol. 5, The Great Century in the Americas, Australia, Asia, and*

Africa, A.D. 1800–A.D. 1914 (New York: Harper & Brothers, 1943).

3. On the theological roots of Protestant mission theory see Charles Forman, "A History of Foreign Mission Theory," in *American Missions in Bicentennial Perspective,* ed. R. Pierce Beaver (South Pasadena, Calif.: William Carey Library, 1977), pp. 71–72, and R. Pierce Beaver, "Missionary Motivation Through Three Centuries," in *Reinterpretation in American Church History,* ed. Jerald C. Brauer (Chicago and London: University of Chicago Press, 1968), pp. 113–151.
4. R. Pierce Beaver, "Missionary Motivation Through Three Centuries"; Kenneth S. Latourette, *A History of the Expansion of Christianity,* Vol. 4, *The Great Century: Europe and the United States* (New York: Harper & Brothers, 1943), pp. 1–21.
5. Henry Warner Bowden, "An Overview of Cultural Factors" in Beaver, *American Missions,* pp. 50–51, and Williams, *Black Americans,* p. 5.
6. Sylvia Jacobs, *The African Nexus: Black American Perspectives on the European Partitioning of Africa, 1880–1920* (Westport, Conn., and London: Greenwood Press, 1981), p. 19. For an example of African-American appropriation of this belief see Wilson J. Moses, "Civilizing Missionary: A Study of Alexander Crummell," *Journal of Negro History* 60 (Apr.1975): 229–51.
7. Sylvia Jacobs, "The Historical Role of Afro–Americans in American Missionary Efforts in Africa," in *Black Americans and the Missionary Movement in Africa,* ed. Sylvia Jacobs (Westport, Conn., and London: Greenwood Press, 1982), pp. 6–7. For a more critical perception of the association of Christianity with Western culture, see the writings of two of the foremost mission theorists of the nineteenth century, Rufus Anderson and Henry Venn. Rufus Anderson, *To Advance the Gospel: Selections from the Writings of Rufus Anderson,* ed. R. Pierce Beaver (Grand Rapids: Eerdmans, 1967), and Max Warren, ed., *To Apply the Gospel: Selections From the Writings of Henry Venn* (Grand Rapids: Eerdmans, 1971).
8. Sidney Ahlstrom, *The American Protestant Encounter with World Religions* (Beloit, Wisc.: Beloit College, 1962). For one of the earliest liberal arguments "that non-Christians who are faithful to their religions might be saved," see Beaver, "Missionary Motivation," in Brauer, *Reinterpretation,* p. 129. See also Cornelius R. Duffie, *The Salvability of the Heathen No Excuse for Neglect of Revealed Duty by the Christian* (New York: Daniel Dana, Jr., 1860), and Forman, "History of Foreign Mission Theory," pp. 73–74.
9. Forman, "History of Foreign Mission Theory," p. 73.
10. William B. Sprague, *Lectures Illustrating the Contact between True*

Christianity and Various Other Systems (New York: Daniel Appleton, 1837); cited in Forman, "History of Foreign Mission Theory," p. 73.

11. Jacobs, "Historical Role of Afro-Americans," p. 16.
12. See Albert J. Raboteau, "Ethiopia Shall Soon Stretch Forth Her Hands: Black Destiny in Nineteenth-Century America," The University Lecture in Religion at Arizona State University, 27 Jan. 1983, Department of Religious Studies, Arizona State University, Tempe, Arizona. See also St. Claire Drake, *The Redemption of Africa and Black Religion* (Chicago: Third World Press, 1970).
13. Williams, *Black Americans,* p. 3.
14. Williams, *Black Americans,* p. 96, and Jacobs, "Historical Role of Afro-Americans," pp. 16–17.
15. Most African-American and Anglo-African evangelicals, having accepted the basic tenets of orthodox evangelical theology, missiology, and ideology concerning the uniqueness of Protestant Christianity and the unquestioned superiority of Western Protestant culture, also shared the prevailing view of Africa's complete degradation and bondage to heathenism and ignorance. Williams, *Black Americans,* pp. 37, 97, 104–105, 107.
16. Raboteau, "Ethiopia."
17. Williams, *Black Americans,* p. 100.
18. Bishop Henry M. Turner, letter to the *A.M.E. Christian Recorder,* 4 June 1891.
19. Tony Martin, "Some Reflections on Evangelical Pan-Africanism, or Black Missionaries, White Missionaries, and the Struggle for African Souls, 1890–1930," *Ufahama* 1 (Winter 1971): 77–92.
20. The major catalyst and most prominent proponent of this effort was the West Africa-based scholar Edward Wilmot Blyden. As early as 1866 he began setting the agenda for the development of a distinctively Pan-African missiology. Subsequent works such as "Mohammedanism in West Africa" (1871), "Mohammedanism and the Negro Race" (1875), "Christian Missions in West Africa" (1876), *Christianity, Islam, and the Negro Race* (1887), and *African Life and Customs* (1908), reflect the continued evolution of his Pan-African missiology. Lynch, *Blyden,* pp. 66–78. See also the missiological writings of Orishatukeh Faduma, John R. Frederick, Mojola Agbebi, James Johnson, and Henry M. Turner.
21. Joseph A. Conforti, *Samuel Hopkins and the New Divinity Movement: Calvinism, the Congregational Ministry, and Reform in New England between the Great Awakenings* (Grand Rapids: Christian University Press, 1981); Phillip J. Staudenraus, *The African Colonization Movement, 1816–1865* (New York: Columbia University Press, 1961); Floyd J. Miller, *The Search for a Black Nationality:*

Black Colonization and Emigration, 1787–1863 (Urbana: University of Illinois Press, 1975).

22. John Peterson, *Province of Freedom: A History of Sierra Leone, 1787–1870* (Evanston: Northwestern University Press, 1969), pp. 19–20; Christopher Fyfe, *A History of Sierra Leone* (London: Oxford University Press, 1962), 13. See also Lamin Sanneh, *West African Christianity; The Religious Impact* (London: C. Hurst & Co., 1983), pp. 53–89.
23. Peterson, *Province of Freedom,* p. 20. See also Ellen Gibson White, *The Royal Blacks* (New York: G. P. Putnam's Sons, 1976).
24. Peterson, *Province of Freedom,* pp. 18–23.
25. Ibid., pp. 17–18; Fyfe, *History of Sierra Leone,* pp. 14–16.
26. Peterson, *Province of Freedom,* p. 22.
27. Philip D. Curtin, *The Image of Africa: British Ideas and Action, 1780–1850* (London: Macmillan, 1965), p. 39. Peterson, *Province of Freedom,* p. 22.
28. Peterson, *Province of Freedom,* pp. 26–27.
29. Ibid., p. 36.
30. Ibid., p. 45.
31. Robert July, *The Origins of Modern African Thought* (London: Faber & Faber, 1968), p. 66.
32. Peterson, *Province of Freedom,* pp. 37–44; Fyfe, *History of Sierra Leone,* pp. 55–56.
33. Their concerted efforts made Sierra Leone the earliest and most important laboratory of missionization and western modernization in Africa. See Geiss, *Pan-African Movement,* p. 50. For a focused interpretation of the modernization process in Sierra Leone, see Martin N. Kilson, *Political Change in a West African State: A Study of the Modernization Process in Sierra Leone* (Cambridge: Harvard University Press, 1966). For a more contemporary discussion of this relationship, see Stephen C. Knapp, "Mission and Modernization: A Preliminary Critical Analysis of Contemporary Understandings of Mission from a Radical Evangelical Perspective," in Beaver, *American Missions,* pp. 146–209.
34. J. D. Fage, *A History of West Africa: An Introductory Survey* (Cambridge: Cambridge University Press, 1969), pp. 128–129. On the activities of African-Americans such as Paul Cuffe, Colin Teague, Lott Cary, Daniel Coker, and others, see Fyfe, *History of Sierra Leone,* pp. 112–113, 132, 133, 181; Williams, *Black Americans,* pp. 16–17, 34–35. See also Sheldon H. Harris, *Paul Cuffe: Black America and the African Return* (New York: Simon & Schuster, 1972), pp. 38–42; Miles Fisher, "Lott Cary, the Colonizing Missionary," *Journal of Negro History* (Oct. 1922): 380–418; Leroy Fitts, *Lott Carey, First Black Missionary to Africa* (Valley Forge: Judson

Press, 1978); and Matei Markwei, "The Rev. Daniel Coker of Sierra Leone," in *Black Apostles at Home and Abroad: Afro-Americans and the Christian Mission,* ed. David W. Wills and Richard B. Newman (Boston: G. K. Hall & Co., 1982), pp. 203–210.

35. Peterson notes that "schools and churches went together from the outset in Sierra Leone . . . . [T]he importance of the school was indiscernible from that of church or chapel." Peterson, *Province of Freedom,* pp. 63–80. The dominant educational institutions were in fact church-related schools such as the Church Mission Society Grammar School, Wesleyan Boys High School, and Fourah Bay College. The first secular student was admitted to Fourah Bay College in 1864. Lynch, *Blyden,* p. 27. See also Eric Ashby, *Universities: British, Indian, African: A Study in the Ecology of Higher Education* (London: Weidenfeld and Nicholson, 1966), pp. 162–178.
36. The term "Creole" described the Europeanized descendants of all black African groups that settled in Sierra Leone after 1787 and those members of the indigenous population who successfully emulated the Victorian values and manners of Creole society. See Spitzer, *Creoles,* pp. 12–13, 39, 41, Abner Cohen, *The Politics of Elite Culture* (Berkeley: University of California Press, 1981), and Akintola J. G. Wyse, *H. C. Bankole-Bright and Politics in Colonial Sierra Leone, 1919–1958* (Cambridge: Cambridge University Press, 1990).
37. Spitzer, *Creoles,* pp. 40, 75–76, 128–129, 230, 236.
38. Curtin, *Image of Africa,* pp. 238–240, 414–415, 425–426. Spitzer, *Creoles,* pp. 45, 46.
39. Spitzer, *Creoles,* pp. 110–111.
40. As the grandson of one of the leaders of the evangelical revival within the Anglican Church and son of John Venn, founding member of the Clapham sect, Henry Venn had deep roots in the British evangelical and humanitarian movement. Unfortunately, an indepth assessment of Venn's theological orientation and its impact upon his missiology is unavailable. Among the studies that are available, see T. E. Yates, *Venn and Victorian Bishops Abroad: The Missionary Policies of Henry Venn and Their Repercussions Upon the Anglican Episcopate of the Colonial Period, 1841–1872* (Uppsala: Swedish Institute of Missionary Research, 1978); J. F. A. Ajayi, "Henry Venn and the Policy of Development," in *The History of Christianity in West Africa,* ed. O. U. Kalu (London and New York: Longman, 1980), 63–75; and Warren, *To Apply the Gospel.* See also Hollis R. Lynch, "The Native Pastorate Controversy and Cultural Ethnocentrism in Sierra Leone, 1871–1874," in Kalu, *History of Christianity in Africa,* pp. 270–292. Eugene Stock, *The History of the Church Missionary Society,* vols. 1–3 (London:

Church Missionary Society, 1899–1916); Peter Beyerhaus and Henry Lefever, "Henry Venn of the Church Missionary Society," in *The Responsible Church and the Foreign Mission* (London: World Dominion Press, 1964), pp. 25–30; and especially Wilbert Schenk, *Henry Venn—Missionary Statesman* (Maryknoll, N. Y.: Orbis, 1983).

41. Ajayi, "Henry Venn and the Policy of Development," in Kalu, *History of Christianity in West Africa,* pp. 64, 65.
42. On the early and controversial application of the evolving tenets of British theological liberalism within the African mission arena, see below on Bishop J. W. Colenso. Also Owen Chadwick, *The Victorian Church,* vol. 2 (New York: Oxford University Press, 1970), pp. 58, 90–97.
43. William Knight, *Memoir of Henry Venn,* pp. 282–287. Quoted in Lynch, "Native Pastorate Controversy," p. 271. See also E. A. Ayandele, *The Missionary Impact on Modern Nigeria, 1842–1914,* p. 182, and Ajayi, "Henry Venn and the Policy of Development," p. 65. Both Geiss and Langley contend that Venn's "sympathy for Africans dated back to his childhood at Clapham Common, when he used to play with the children of the African Academy from Sierra Leone." Geiss, *Pan-African Movement,* p. 51; Ayandele, *Missionary Impact,* p. 180.
44. Ajayi, "Henry Venn and the Policy of Development," in Kalu, *History of Christianity in West Africa,* p. 65. It has been noted by numerous scholars that Venn's progressive mission theory was shared by his American counterpart, Rufus Anderson, secretary of the American Board of Commissioners for Foreign Missions (ABCFM) from 1826–1866. It appears, however, that Anderson's mission theory was more limited than Venn's. For a comparison of Venn's and Anderson's mission theories, see Ajayi, "Henry Venn and the Policy of Development," p. 74. On Anderson, see Forman, "History of Foreign Mission Theory," pp. 77–79, and Clifton J. Phillips, *Protestant America and the Pagan World: The First Half-Century of the American Board of Commissioners for Foreign Missions, 1810–1860* (Cambridge: Harvard University Press, 1969), p. 253.
45. Agricultural, industrial, and vernacular education were key components of the pedagogical reform advocated by Venn. Lynch, "Native Pastorate Controversy," p. 271, and Ajayi, "Henry Venn and the Policy of Development," pp. 70–71.
46. Lynch, "Native Pastorate Controversy," pp. 270–292. In recognition of Venn's importance, Blyden wrote to him in 1872, "I trust that God may spare your life and strength, especially for his African work. Dark will be the day for Africa when the active influence of Henry Venn is removed from the African culture—the Chariot of

our Israel and the horseman thereof." Ayandele, *Missionary Impact,* p. 83.

47. Ajayi notes that "Venn's principles became an important strand in the thinking of early West African nationalists." Ajayi, "Henry Venn and the Policy of Development," p. 73. See also Ayandele, *Missionary Impact,* pp. 180, 182–183.

2

The Sierra Leone Matrix

The presence of Orishatukeh Faduma in Sierra Leone was directly related to the historical forces and ideals that inspired the founding of the colony. His parents, John and Omolofi, were victims of the slave trade–inspired strife that ravished their Yoruba homeland throughout most of the nineteenth century.[1] Taken as captives of war, they were sold to Portuguese slave traders and were enroute to the New World slave markets when rescued in mid-Atlantic by a contingent of the British antislavery squadron.[2] Instead of being resettled in Sierra Leone, as was the usual fate of recaptives, they were transported to British Guiana (Guyana) as part of the British policy of "free labour" recruitment from West Africa.[3] In this British colony located on the northeastern coast of South America they joined other West Africans as indentured workers on the colony's coffee and sugar cane plantations.[4]

Under the influence of Wesleyan missionaries, John and Omolofi converted to Christianity before the birth of a son in Demerara on September 15, 1857.[5] In keeping with accepted missionary custom, the father, who upon conversion took the name John and the surname Davis for the family, provided their new son with a similarly appropriate "Christian name." The infant who later became known as Orishatukeh Faduma was christened William J. Davis in honor of a "Welsh missionary."[6]

Faduma spent the first years of his life in British Guiana, which had a strong Yoruba presence dating from the introduction of enslaved West Africans in the seventeenth century.[7] Before the end of his first decade, however, he and his family became part of the migratory movement of Africans in the West Indies and South America back to their ancestral land.[8]

Once in Sierra Leone, the family settled in the village of Waterloo. In this rural village, founded in 1819 along the colony's eastern mountains, John became a successful farmer and Faduma grew to young adulthood.[9] Although founded for the purpose of Christianizing and "civilizing" recaptive Africans, Waterloo nurtured a vibrant religious and cultural pluralism. It included more than seventeen distinct tribal groups whose cultural and religious traditions held their own against the forces of western evangelization.[10] Thus in Waterloo Faduma became an "eyewitness" to the peculiar strengths and weaknesses of Islam, West African traditional religions, and the various Christian denominations that sought to supplant them and one another.[11]

By the early1870s Wesleyan missionaries has established a school in Waterloo.[12] Presumably, it was at this institution that Faduma began to develop the academic skills, interests, and contacts that eventually placed him among Sierra Leone's Creole elite. In fact Waterloo, with its heritage of religious, political, and cultural independence ("rebelliousness," according to some European missionaries), nurtured a number of West African notables.[13] Beneath its rural and rustic veneer, the village was a pluralistic, dynamic, and stimulating environment that left its stamp on Faduma and other "favorite sons."[14]

In 1876 Faduma, then nineteen, moved from Waterloo to Freetown. This was a most propitious time to migrate to the "Athens of West Africa," as Freetown was sometimes styled.[15] Between 1871 and 1873 the city served as the home base for Edward Blyden, who was then well on his way to being acknowledged as the most articulate and brilliant defender of the African race.[16] Born in St. Thomas, Blyden migrated to the fledgling nation of Liberia in 1850 after being refused a theological education in the United States because of his race. In Liberia he completed his secondary education and began the intensive study of history, religion, culture, theology, and languages that earned him distinction as one of the most gifted black intellectuals of the late nineteenth century.[17] Although initially employed as a Presbyterian missionary and principal of the Presbyterian School in Liberia, Blyden became increasingly critical of the Eurocentric bias of Christian missions and missionary education in West Africa.[18] As did Henry Venn, he rooted his reformist and progressive missiological and pedagogical theories in the belief that Africans had unique talents and gifts that they should be free to develop and realize in both church and school.[19]

Blyden's increasingly strident critique of traditional mission practices and indiscriminate Europeanization, coupled with his assertion of African pride and identity, struck a responsive chord among young Creoles of Sierra Leone who were increasingly apprehensive about their declining status in the eyes of their European mentors and models. Rather than being hailed for their successful adoption of British culture and Christianity, they found themselves more and more the object of ridicule and criticism for "aping" Europeans.[20]

Blyden's developing racial, pedagogical, and missiological theories offered some measure of relief from the Creoles' painful and bewildering alienation. His presence in Sierra Leone stoked the embers of Creole racial and ecclesiastical self-consciousness and helped induce the "native pastorate controversy" that raged in Sierra Leone from 1871 to 1874. Under Blyden's influence, the demands of the Creole clergy and their lay supporters included the call for the formation of an independent, nonsectarian African Church and secular university. Both were to be staffed by Africans and oriented toward the goal of African cultural and ecclesiastical independence.[21]

Blyden articulated the popular rationale for their desire for self-determination. He argued that Africans should control both church and school—the two most potent agencies through which Western culture was being disseminated. Thus in correspondence with Pope-Hennessy, the Governor of Sierra Leone, Blyden called for both ecclesiastical and pedagogical reform. Demonstrating the critical historical consciousness central to his developing theological and missiological critique, Blyden argued that imported European creeds "rest on certain deep convictions which are present to the consciousness of the people among whom they arose," but that such "European formularies unmodified" should not be imposed upon Africa:

> They are constructive as records of religious growth and development in Europe and may be of great suggestive use in guiding us in the development of the African Church. . . . But it is evident that to make these creeds in all their details, authoritative in Africa, the intellectual and spiritual growth of the people must be checked or distorted by the introduction of the bitterness of theological rancour, and the harshness of conflicting sects.

The key institutional prescription for the "free and healthy development" of both Christianity and civilization in Africa was thus the development of a secular university freed from the warping influence of religious dogmatism as fostered by existing missionary institutions such as the Church Missionary Society's Fourah Bay College. Blyden noted that:

> The presence of such an institution with able African teachers brought, if necessary, from different parts of the world—even a Negro Arabic Professor from Egypt, Timbuctoo or Fatah—would have great influence in exposing and correcting the fallacies upon which our foreign teachers have proceeded in their utter misapprehension and, perhaps, contempt of African character.[22]

Another milestone in the emergence of nationalist and Pan-Africanist sentiment in Sierra Leone occurred in 1872 when Blyden and Sierra Leone's clerical nationalists established a journal provocatively entitled *The Negro*. Though short-lived, *The Negro* provided Blyden and his supporters with a medium to foster racial pride and to critique western missiological and pedagogical practices. Moreover, a Pan-African agenda was proclaimed in its first issues, in which it was noted that *The Negro* was intended "to represent and defend the interest of that peculiar type of humanity known as the Negro, with all its affiliated and collateral branches, whether on this continent or elsewhere."[23]

With Blyden's return to Liberia in 1873, *The Negro* ceased publication. Moreover, an alliance of British missionary and government agencies circumvented most of the demands made by Africans during the native pastorate controversy. Among the few concessions made by this alliance of ecclesiastical and colonial officials was the affiliation of Fourah Bay College with Durham University in England. It was, however, a concession that did not significantly alter perceptions by Blyden and his supporters of the College as being "too clerical, foreign and elitist."[24]

A related development, but of more immediate significance for young Faduma, was the establishment of Wesleyan Boys High School in 1874 under the direction of the Reverend Joseph Claudius (J. C.) May. Born in Freetown in 1845 of a liberated Yoruba who became a Wesleyan minister, May aborted a promising business career to become a minister and educator. He completed his education at Borough Road School and Wesley College in Taunton, England, under the sponsorship of the London Committee of the Wesleyan Church. Upon his return to Sierra Leone in 1871, he and his younger brother, Cornelius, became enthusiastic supporters of Blyden.[25] The brothers assisted Blyden with the founding of *The Negro,* and in 1884 Blyden returned the favor by assisting J. C. May in the establishment of the *Sierra Leone Weekly News*.[26] This wide-ranging weekly became a major conduit of Blyden's ideas and writings to the West African community.[27] Moreover, from 1882 to 1888, the enterprising and energetic J. C. May also monitored and influenced the Sierra Leone religious community through publication of the *Methodist Herald*.[28]

Despite his skills as minister and publisher, J. C. May made his most significant contribution to the West African community as an educator. As founder of Wesleyan Boys High School and its principal for 28 years (1874–1902), May trained generations of young men drawn to him and the school from throughout West Africa.[29] They eventually formed an elite association of "old boys" who shared a common allegiance to the school, to Principal May, and to their race. Included among his students were future West African Nationalists and Pan-Africanists such as J. E. Casely Hayford, T. Hutton-Mills, William B. Euba.[30]

Faduma's contacts with Principal May were especially intimate, and possibly date from May's efforts between 1871 and 1874 to organize and improve Wesleyan village schools in the colony.[31] Faduma's migration to Freetown in 1876 resulted in his boarding with May and serving as "parlour and kitchen boy" while attending classes at Wesleyan Boys High School.[32] This arrangement, known as the "ward system," was an informal continuation of the tradition of apprenticeship whereby rural youths boarded as servants in Creole households while ostensibly gaining an education or vocational skills.[33] This tradition also functioned as an important means by which rural youth were socialized in the manners and values of the Creole elite. It thus provided access to the status, privileges, and responsibilities of Creoledom.[34] While the "ward system" too often degenerated into an exploitative relationship akin to domestic slavery, it occasionally developed into a close "family relationship."[35] It was the latter relationship that developed between Faduma and J. C. May.

From May, who had been heavily influenced by Blyden, Faduma acquired many of the values and practices that shaped his later life and work. In a filial tribute delivered at the end of the century, Faduma declared his indebtedness to May:

> Brought from rustic life and placed under his care during my teens . . . . The master-hand which moulded my life for future work was Mr. May's. What I acquired afterwards were the finishing touches. The bold, rough outline . . . was laid out by him. There are principles and habits I have imbibed from him which have helped to give me a strong backbone in life—they are prayerfulness, carefulness in details, economy, race pride, self-respect, simplicity, total abstinence from strong drink . . . . When the history of West Africa is written, prominent among those who have helped to shape its destiny will be Principal May.[36]

Despite Blyden's increasingly strident warning that the education of African youth in Europe was counterproductive and debilitating, study in England, and especially a degree from a British University, remained a valued attainment in Sierra Leone. Indeed, it virtually guaranteed the holder membership among the elite of Creole society.[37] It was a distinction that Faduma would acquire. Having rapidly progressed under May's tutelage from student to teacher at Boys High School, Faduma won first prize "in a competitive scholarship of nine subjects."[38] This prize enabled him to depart Sierra Leone in1882 to attend his mentor's alma mater, Wesley College in Taunton, England.[39] Although a church-affiliated college, Wesley afforded Faduma, and several generations of West African Wesleyans, an educational curriculum and environment that was broader and less conservative than that of Fourah Bay College, which, despite its affiliation with Durham University, remained essentially a mission training institution.[40]

Of more importance was Faduma's decision to continue his education in the less restrictive and more cosmopolitan environment of the University of London. The product of the long controversy over religious and secular education in Britain, the University of London was established in the 1820s as a secular institution that required no religious tests and sought to keep theology out of a curriculum rooted more in the "new science than in the old humanities."[41] During Faduma's matriculation its curriculum reflected this agenda and the myriad changes induced within the pedagogical arena by the new scientific and intellectual currents of the late Victorian era.

In a tribute that illuminated his rationale for attending the University of London, Faduma noted the importance of its founding and the significance of efforts to ensure that it would be free from the stagnating influence of religious control and "imbued with the modern spirit":

> The older universities of England required a religious test and closed their doors for centuries against those who did not and would not subscribe to it. When London University was granted the charter, a new life and inspiration came upon English intellectual life. Without any religious test, men and women drank from the fountain of knowledge, including Jews and Mohammedans.[42]

By the time he matriculated at the University of London, Faduma was also aware of the challenges that the new scientific, academic and intellectual currents associated with Darwinism posed for the British academic and ecclesiastical establishments.[43] Since the publication of *Essays and Reviews* in the late 1850s, the British ecclesiastical and academic establishments had been embroiled in controversy over the compatibility of the findings of Darwinism, geology, anthropology, comparative religion, and biblical criticism with the "truths" of Christianity.[44] A series of heresy trials exacerbated the controversy as ecclesiastical defenders of orthodoxy sought to purge liberals from church and university. The controversy would not take a decisive turn until the publication of *Lux Mundi* by the adherents of an influential and liberal "broad church party" in 1889.[45]

During the course of Faduma's British sojourn, public awareness of the missiological implications of the wider controversy was heightened by the publicity occasioned by the death of Bishop Colenso in the early summer of 1883. In 1853, Colenso, as Bishop of Natal, had sought to advance the missionary effort in southern Africa by translating the Scriptures into Zulu. However, he became increasingly dissatisfied with traditional biblical interpretations and doctrines. Influenced by the work of British liberals such as Frederick Denison Maurice and continental biblical scholars such as Abraham Kuenen, Colenso produced a controversial series of critical biblical studies. Such works emanating from the pen of an Anglican bishop in a mission post provoked successful efforts by the defenders of orthodoxy to have Colenso removed from his see for denying truths "precious to the sinner's hope of salvation."[46] Colenso's painful public ridicule as "the bishop who went out to convert the heathen and came back converted by the heathen" suggested the profound and troubling implications that the new intellectual, scientific, and academic currents held for the ecclesiastical establishment and the mission enterprise.[47]

Sierra Leone and other Europeanized West African religious communities had not proved impervious to the new scientific, intellectual, and academic currents, nor to the controversy that accompanied them. Ecclesiastical and educational leaders such as J. C. May had been educated in Britain during the height of the controversy. The controversy touched others, laity and clergy, through religious journals and newpapers. Indeed, Sawyerr's Bookstore on Water Street in Freetown provided ready access to the flood of British publications inspired by the controversy. Consequently, the parishioner of James Johnson who "had his faith shaken by reading *Essays and Reviews*" was only one of a number of West Africans who had their conventional Christian convictions challenged by the era's new academic, scientific, and intellectual currents.[48]

Although Faduma expressed disappointment and disillusionment with the religious and moral climate of Victorian England, controversy related to the impact of evolutionary thought and its corollaries did not have any apparent negative effect on his academic efforts. The *Sierra Leone Weekly News* proudly communicated his academic success and projected it for emulation by the colony's youth:

> At the recent Intermediate Arts Examination of the University of London . . . Mr. William J. Davis [Faduma]—formerly a pupil of the High School . . . and subsequently one of its junior teachers—was one of the successful candidates. We believe this is the first instance of a native of this colony successfully passing the Intermediate Arts Examination . . . generally admitted as the most difficult in the British Empire. Mr. Davis [Faduma] we believe has the congratulations of every Sierra Leone resident and we hope others ere long will follow in his footsteps.[49]

In his agitation for a secular African university during the native pastorate controversy, Blyden argued that "pride of race" and "race feeling" were undermined when African youth were "sent for education from Africa to Europe."[50] Loss of racial pride and identity were not, however, by-products of the British education of J. C. May, nor of Faduma or his West African classmates at Wesley College and the University of London, John Mensah Sarbah and William B. Euba.[51] Their study in England not only heightened their racial pride and consciousness, but also fostered a critical perspective toward European cultural and religious influences in West Africa.

During the course of their studies the three West African youths were acutely aware of the less favorable perceptions of Africa and Africans that were gaining sway in Victorian England.[52] A resurgent racism, given new scientific and academic legitimacy by misapplication of the Darwinian thesis, supported the myth of African inferiority and justified the "scramble for Africa" by European imperialists.[53] This new pseudoscientific racism made the British sabbatical that had been so highly coveted by an earlier generation of Creoles far less pleasant for their generation. Fewer West Africans returned with starry-eyed ideals of Britain and her aims in Africa.[54] Indeed Sarbah, Euba, and Faduma returned to

West Africa with a heightened appreciation for African culture and a growing dissatisfaction with various European influences in West Africa.

Sarbah returned to the Gold Coast in 1887 after completing his legal studies at the University of London. He became the first Gold Coaster admitted to the English Bar and used his legal talents and training to defend African institutions, customs, and lands from European political, economic, and religious encroachment. In 1889 he organized the Fanti National Society, the first formal institutional resistance to "the demoralizing effect of certain European influences" on Fanti culture. Sarbah's efforts also included the publication of two influential studies and defenses of Fanti culture, *Fanti Customary Laws* (1897) and *Fanti National Constitution* (1906). His efforts earned him esteem as one of the "fathers of Ghanaian nationalism."[55]

Although Sarbah retained a Wesleyan Methodist affiliation throughout his life, it was not the pious Eurocentric missionary Methodism of his father's generation. While he did not engage in a blanket condemnation of the mission enterprise, he called for a mission policy that would be more sensitive to and aware of African customs and laws. European missionaries, he argued, should be more critical of their own cultural institutions before engaging in wholesale condemnations of African institutions that they did not understand.[56]

Similar sentiments inspired the subsequent life and work of William B. Euba. Born in Lagos of Yoruba parents, and a former student of May's at Boys High School, Euba returned to Nigeria, where he became a controversial Wesleyan minister and educator. His efforts to synthesize aspects of traditional African culture and institutions with Christianity resulted in growing tensions between himself and more traditional Wesleyan missionaries. He eventually became active in such nationalist and Pan-African organizations as the National Congress of British West Africa and the Lagos branch of Marcus Garvey's Universal Negro Improvement Association.[57]

Faduma's subsequent activities paralleled those of Sarbah and Euba. On his return to Sierra Leone in1885, he was hailed as the first West African to "successfully pass the intermediate B.A. at London University."[58] He rejoined May's staff at Boys High School and rapidly began to distinguish himself not only as a gifted teacher of mathematics and the "higher classics," but also as a committed and progressive community activist.

Despite having attained the credentials and status that guaranteed membership among Sierra Leone's Creole elite, Faduma began to give evidence of both "race feeling" and disillusionment with the European values and customs that had come to be intimately associated with Creole society.[59] In 1886 he demonstrated a growing pride and interest in his African heritage and ancestral roots with the publication in the *Methodist Herald* of "A Tale of Egba Land." This tale, narrated by Faduma in verse, was reportedly told to him by his father and included the revelation that the family's pre-Christian name was Faduma:

> My sire is Faduma of pure and noble line,
> An Egba of the Egbas a race renown'd and fine
> My sires were great warriors who wielded well the sword
> Who brav'd both heat and cold, yet ne'er complained a word.[60]

While illustrating Faduma's pride in and appreciation of his Yoruba (Egba) antecedents, the tale also reflected the tendency toward romanticization that many westernized Africans exhibited as they attempted to minister to a battered racial pride and identity.[61]

The racial pride and nationalist sentiment that Faduma and a small group of his fellow Creoles demonstrated in Sierra Leone received encouragement from Blyden, who had returned to the colony in 1885. The decade that had intervened since his earlier stay in Sierra Leone served to increase Blyden's doubts about the efficacy of Eurocentric Christian theology, missiology, and pedagogy in West Africa. Additional study had also heightened his appreciation of indigenous African culture and the salutary impact of Islam upon it.

Blyden advanced his provocative views in his magnum opus, *Christianity, Islam, and the Negro Race,* which was published in 1887, two years after Faduma's return to Sierra Leone.[62] This momentous and controversial work consisted of articles that Blyden wrote over a span of two decades. They reflect the theological, missiological, pedagogical, and ideological concerns and insights that marked Blyden's transition from an Old School Presbyterian minister and missionary to the foremost African critic of traditional western theology and missiology. The final stage of this transition occurred in 1886 when he demitted his Presbyterian ordination in order to become a "Minister of Truth."[63]

Although it is impossible to categorize with certainty the theological posture of the eclectic Blyden, these articles and later works indicate the broadly liberal direction of his theological as well as his missiological development.[64] A conservative, Calvinistic theological posture is evident in his early correspondence and publications.[65] By the 1870s, however, engaged in extensive biblical, historical, linguistic, theological, and comparative religious studies, Blyden had moved some distance from his traditional theological roots.[66] This shift is reflected not only in his renunciation of his ordination but also in *Christianity, Islam, and the Negro Race* and in his last major publications.[67]

In many of his post–1880 writings, Blyden articulates many of the classic tenets of the theological and missiological liberalism developing in progressive Protestant circles during the last half of the nineteenth century. His incorporation of evolutionary concepts, nonsectarian emphasis, use of the perspective and methodology of comparative religion, emphasis on personalism, awareness of the ethnic, cultural, and historical accruements of Christianity in the course of its development, call for a progressive and "liberal" pedagogy, efforts to appropriate modern scientific tenets and methodologies in the study of religion and culture, and the use of critical linguistic skills in the exposition of the Bible were being concurrently advocated by the formulators of Protestant liberalism.[68]

Unfortunately, the work entitled *Comparative Theology,* which Blyden began writing in 1908, four years before his death, was never completed.[69] It would have been helpful in accurately discerning Blyden's mature theological posture. Ironically, in his last major work, *African Life and Customs* (1908), Blyden argued that Africans had no need for European theological formulations:

> From our standpoint, we do not believe that Africa needed the theological interference of Europe, for the Theology of Europe is derived from the conceptions of Roman, Celt and Teuton, which have modified the Semitic ideas promulgated in the Bible. . . . Theology is our conception of and our attempt to describe the Being worshipped, Who has no name. What He is to one race, He is not in every respect to another.

The theological enterprise, he argued, was alien to the African religious consciousness: "The African does not attempt to formulate a Theology. He says, as the Psalmist did, 'Such knowledge is too wonderful for me; I cannot attain unto it.'"[70] Whatever may have been the accuracy of Blyden's assessment of the religious sensibilities of the "native" African, it is clear that it had little relevance for himself and other westernized Africans who by conversion and education had become thoroughly entangled in the maze of Western theology, ideology, and culture.

Few West Africans moved as far along the path of theological liberalism as did Blyden. However, with his pioneering efforts to employ the findings of modern scholarship, he played a major role in fostering a critical perspective toward traditional evangelical theology, missiology, and pedagogy that would lead Faduma and others to the threshold of theological liberalism.[71]

Sierra Leone's centennial provided Faduma and a small number of his colleagues with the occasion to offer a prescription for the sense of alienation and cultural strain increasingly prevalent among the younger generation of Creoles. Having attributed their dilemma to the perversion of their true racial personality by means of an indiscriminate Europeanization, they instigated a cultural reform movement that aimed to foster attitudes and practices more attuned to their African heritage and identity.[72] The movement offered an overt challenge to religious and cultural convictions long fostered and cherished in church, school, and society.

It was in accord with the goals of the reform movement that Faduma, on August 5, 1887, announced his change of name from William J. Davis to the "purely native name Orishatukeh Faduma."[73] Although Faduma was not the only member of the reform movement to reject his European baptismal name in favor of a name deemed more appropriate to his African heritage, he became the focus of much of the subsequent criticism and controversy.[74] Apparently his choice of a name explicitly associated with his Yoruba religious heritage and his prominence in the community comprised, for Creole conservatives, a double affront.[75] A letter to the editor of the *Sierra Leone Weekly News* by a critic who identified himself as "Sententia" expressed both the confusion and concern of Creole traditionalists:

> Sir,—The total change of name by Mr. W. J. Davis, Senior Resident Tutor of the Wesleyan High School . . . has furnished food for thought in this community. Mr. Davis's intelligence as a scholar, and position as a teacher, at once drew attention to his action in this matter . . . . Mr. Davis's objective in changing his name is not publicly made known; rumour says that he desires to be as much native as possible. In connection with a gentleman of his position, it may not be uninteresting to know the reasons for the change . . . .

Of special concern, noted "Sententia," was the derivation and meaning of Faduma's new name:

> Now, Mr. Editor, the most important feature in the matter is the meaning of the new name—for all native names especially Aku ones, have some signification. ORISHATUKEH FADUMA, the first appears to be composed of the two words in Aku, Orisha an idol, and Tukeh smiles, conveying the meaning that the idol god of the Akus, Orisha smiles. Faduma appears to be composed of the word Ifa and idol, dun, is sweet, ma or moh to know, signifying that the idol god of the Akus, Ifa is sweet to know.

"Sententia" concluded:

> Unless these names had been given to Mr. Davis, by his parents, and despised in his ignorance, but valued in his intelligence he may be regarded as guilty of great indiscretion in his selection.[76]

Another interpretation of Faduma's name, and a more positive assessment of his motives, was provided by a Freetown correspondent of the *Sierra Leone Weekly News:*

> ORISHATUKEH FADUMA. The first of these names is a contraction of the AKU word:—Orisha-otu okeh, the literal translation of which, is—"The god Orisha has loosed the bag." It is generally given, in its contracted form, to the one, whose mother or grandmother had long been asking for a child.

. . . Ifaduma of Faduma has its translation into English, in words to this effect:—"The worship of Ifa is pleasing to me" . . . . There are, of course, many things to be said pro and con in respect of any reasons which the senior tutor of the Wesleyan High School might advance, for thus forsaking his Welsh name of Davis, for that of the Aku one I have just been speaking about. But diverse as are our opinions in the matter, we cannot for a single moment deny the fact, that Faduma . . . has occupied a most prominent position among the enlightened "sons of the soil," in that he was the first to put into a practical shape, the mature convictions of his enlightened views.[77]

Explicitly involved in the controversy that raged as a result of Faduma's "great indiscretion" were fundamental missiological, theological, ideological, and pedagogical issues that increasingly troubled the West African Christian community. Central among them was the issue of indigenization: to what extent were Christianity and the mission enterprise, including their educational component, adaptable to the African culture and heritage, and to what extent did Africans have to reject their cultural heritage and identity in order to become Christian and "civilized"?

These issues were explicitly addressed by another member of the reform movement, Kufileh Tubohku (Tuboku-Metzger). Of Yoruba (Aku) heritage, Tubohku grew up in Kissy village and was baptized Albert Emerich Metzger in honor of his father's German missionary pastor. Trained in theology, with an Honours Licentiate awarded in 1881 from Durham University through its Fourah Bay affiliation, he served briefly in the Niger mission of the Church Missionary Society before becoming disillusioned and entering government service in 1885. In 1887 he joined the cultural reform movement and changed his name to Kufileh Tubohku.[78]

In a lengthy defense of the goals of both the reform movement and Faduma, who was being held up "as an object of censure, regarded by others as eccentric, and made by others the butt of a mighty ridicule," Tubohku thoroughly rejected the prevailing assumption that Christianity and the trappings of European culture "hang together as cause and effect, as root and branch."[79] He noted:

Some have censured Faduma and taken objection to the name because he had been well known from his birth as William J. Davis, and had been so baptized. These have regarded it as sacrilege for one to touch or change his baptismal name, which in their idea is like renouncing the Christian faith . . . . Others have ridiculed the name from an idea that it is harsh to the sensibilities of a refined ear, and from an idea that a mere European name of whatever nationality, bespeaks progress in civilization. These are of opinion that Faduma has lowered himself in the standard of civilization by renouncing a civilized European name for an uncivilized (?) Negro name, and has thereby descended to a lower caste in humanity. Whilst others, who would have otherwise commended, have nevertheless condemned him from

> a religious scruple, because the name Orishatukeh Faduma is connected with two Heathen Divinities in the Yoruba or Aku country, viz. Orisha and Ifa. The last have given out that Faduma in adopting this name gives preference to heathenism and shows his connection with, and belief in it.

Such sentiments, argued Tubohku, were erroneous in the extreme and the result of a century of faulty education and civilization:

> Every thinking man is forced to admit in spite of himself that the moral result of the English education and civilization we have received . . . is everything but satisfactory. For in Church, in State, and in social life, we feel ourselves to be forced out of the groove which is free and natural to us, vainly striving after what is most unlike ourselves and foreign to our tastes. We have received an education and a civilization that have instilled into us an element of doubt as to our own capacity and destiny, that have implanted in us falsehoods about ourselves, which instead of producing in us self-respect, efficiency, and self-reliance, with a sense of our own individuality—the outcome of a correct education—have rendered us self-detractors, self-depreciators, distrustful of our own possibilities, striving to escape from our own individuality if possible, contemptuous and doubtful of every native element, and indifferent to everything of our own originality.

Echoing Blyden, he contended that the true aim of education and civilization was "to ennoble not to detract, to strengthen not to weaken, to support not to destroy race individuality . . . to bring to prominence every latent and native power in an individual or a race."

Tubohku also reminded Faduma's detractors of their ancestral heritage and customs:

> Those who censured Faduma for changing a name by which he had been known from his birth, should remember that every one of our Liberated Negro Parents had a name given him in the land of his nativity by which he was called and known from his birth up to the time he arrived in the land of his exile. He had a name full of meaning, and explaining his family connection, the manner of his birth, and any peculiar circumstances attending it:—a name significant of the religious ideas of his parents and preserving a tribal or racial individuality. When transported through the baneful traffic of the Slave Trade to this land, that name was exchanged for a foreign one as void of meaning and insignificant to him, as his native name was full of meaning and significance.

Over the years this mistaken and indiscriminate Europeanization had been continued and perpetuated in almost every arena of Sierra Leone life:

> It is a great pity and much to be lamented that after one hundred years of civilization we cannot boast of any thing peculiar to us. The dress, the

name, the language we use, and even our very habits and thoughts are all foreign—European—with scarcely any regard to, or provision for local circumstances . . . . It is nought but a profound and crass ignorance that thinks a man who would be civilized must forsake all that belongs and is natural to him, in exchange for what is foreign and unnatural.

In specific reference to Faduma's critics, he charged:

It is the most fantastic fancy, the highest folly next to insanity that ridicules a man and thinks that he has descended in the standard of humanity and civilization, because he studies the surrounding circumstances of his being, adopts a name that describes his birth, parentage and history, and a dress more suitable to his convenience and constitution. Such a thought rather shows the false idea the thinker entertains of himself and his destiny, his ignorance of what is true civilization . . . .

Although the mission enterprise had contributed to the lamentable conditions in Sierra Leone, Tubohku argued that it was not Christianity per se that created the problems but rather an ignorance and misinterpretation of Scripture and doctrine. Both, he argued, testify to a Christianity that did not rob converts of their individuality by demanding that they indiscriminately forfeit their cultural heritage in favor of another. Contrary to the prevailing practices of Christian missionaries and converts, he called for a distinction to be made between the essentials of Christianity and the "incidental rites" that were not central to it. He argued that on the basis of such a distinction "Faduma cannot be religiously or otherwise regarded as renouncing his Christian baptism because he renounced his baptismal name which was a thing incidental and not necessary to give his baptism a full being, (vide Hooker, Book V)."[80] Finally, he contended that Scripture itself supported and ultimately vindicated Faduma's choice of names:

No one who reads the Scripture carefully and classically, and reflects intelligently on what he reads can condemn Faduma for the connection of his name with heathen divinities. In the New Testament we find retained amongst the early Christians such names as Dionysius and Areopagite derived from the Greek, Seus, (Latin Jupiter), genitive Dios, and Ares (Latin Mars), and Apollos, Hermes (Latin Mercury) Persis, Olympas, &c., (Romans chap. xvi); and all these are significant names connected with the most prominent Olympian divinities,—names which the bearers had before their conversion to Christianity.

Tubohku concluded his defense with the argument that Faduma, rather than being condemned, "should be highly commended" and encouraged in his efforts at advancing true Christianity and "genuine civilization" in Sierra Leone:

> Well may we express a desire that Faduma may exert a widespread influence over the youthful minds under his control by impressing upon them the obligation of studying only what is suited to the necessities of our country and the development of our race—a study that produces such minds that will triumph by intelligence and perseverance over the contemptuous indifference of our own people, and overcome the scorn and opposition of the enemies of our race.[81]

Despite Tubohku's apology and defense, Faduma's name continued to be a source of derision and criticism. Faduma himself, as a matter of principle, refused to respond to his detractors. Years later, when questioned about his refusal, he pointed out that by his continued use of his new name he was offering his most effective reply and rebuke to his critics.[82]

Amid continued controversy, Faduma persisted as an active participant in the cultural reform movement. The same sentiments that induced his change of name inspired his membership in the "Dress Reform Society." This society sought to redress another constant reminder of their European cultural dependency by attempting to establish a form of dress more culturally and environmentally appropriate for West Africans than the standard Victorian attire—the "Religion of the Frock Coat and Tall Hat"—which many Creoles associated with the attainment of Christianity and civilization.[83] In mid-December 1887 members of the Dress Reform movement hosted a meeting at Wilberforce Memorial Hall. Prominent among those in attendance were Edward Blyden, James Johnson, and J. C. May.[84] In their presence, Faduma joined with other members of the society in modeling a loose-fitting tunic and gown worn over knee breeches that they hoped would replace European attire and become the standard dress of Sierra Leone.[85]

Their efforts received the encouragement, though not the imitation, of their distinguished guests. James Johnson, the Anglican cleric of Yoruba descent and nationalist orientation, noted that their efforts represented "a distinct and decided advance in the state of society" in Sierra Leone. They were, he advised, "moving in the right path" because as black men they could not make themselves white men and "aping after them was injurious. . . and detrimental to the race." Johnson also recounted his painful experiences of the futility of such imitative efforts, noting how "small" he felt at Church Missionary Society functions in England where Indians, Chinese, and Japanese were garbed in their national costumes, he alone "the only foreigner in English dress, a sort of nondescript personality apparently without a nationality of his own."[86] While similar testimonies were forthcoming from Blyden and other guests, it was the chairman of the Dress Reform Society, J. H. Spain, who best articulated the broader implications and importance of their efforts. He asserted that although "the matter of dress . . . was no doubt a little one . . . the principle involved in it was a great one for it was nothing less than striving after independence in a small way, a principle which . . . deserved encouragement and success." This nationalist and Pan-African sentiment was echoed in J. C. May's *Methodist Herald,* where it was suggested that the society "could become more and more the rallying point for all who long for and are zealous for the independent national existence of Africa and the Negro."[87]

Another facet of the cultural reform movement, one which also bore the imprint of Blyden's influence, was the formation of a missionary society whose evangelical policies and practices would be consistent with the goals and ideals of the broader reform effort. In aiming to avoid many of the ills associated with traditional mission efforts, the society sought to foster a positive racial and cultural identity among both Creole missionaries and Sierra Leone's aboriginal population. Thus in his defense of Faduma and the cultural reform movement, Kufileh Tubohku warned his fellow Creoles of the dangers of perpetuating among their aboriginal brethren the misinformed beliefs regarding Christianity and civilization that they and their parents had too readily adopted. These beliefs, he argued, were responsible for their own "crab-wise progress, morally, physically, and politically." Consequently, he advised that if they were to be successful in missionizing efforts among their aboriginal brethren "it must not be according to foreign methods or our own particular whims and tastes, but according to the instinct, nature, and customs of the people independently."[88] Two years later Tubohku continued his call for something other than traditional missionary efforts as he addressed a cross-section of Sierra Leonean clergy assembled in Freetown's Zion Chapel African Methodist Episcopal Church. He informed his audience that they had been called together for "a missionary meeting different and unlike others" that they "have been accustomed to attend." They had assembled not "to listen to a report of the doings and trials of a missionary society whose missionaries are laboring in a particular field" or "to know what annual subscriptions have been raised, how much has been expended, and what is the debt or balance in hand at the end of the society's year according to general custom." Rather, they had come together to make a break with "faulty" and "stereotyped" mission practices and policies, and to formulate both a new organization and "new methods" of evangelical outreach. This new mission effort was to be propagated as a "progressive science," drawing on the most progressive and modern mission theories of the era. It was also to be rooted in a firsthand study of the beliefs and customs of both the Islamic and aboriginal populations of Sierra Leone. The rationale for such a radical alteration in mission policy and strategy was to be found in changed historical "circumstances" and a new awareness of and respect for "native tradition":

> [T]he circumstances under which Christianity was introduced to our parents and under which they received and embraced it are quite different from the circumstances under which we have to introduce it to our neighbouring brethren. The days when everything was taken for granted are past and gone. . . . It is quite otherwise now. We have now to carefully study the people we wish to evangelize and approach them with a civility in accordance with their native tradition.[89]

It is of significance that the key figure in this proposed progressive mission venture—"the man for the occasion"—was the A.M.E. missionary John Richard Frederick.[90] His presence in the colony was indicative of the growing interest in African missions by the A.M.E. Church.[91] This increasing evangelical zeal was articulated in the Bishop's Address to the 1884 General Conference of the A.M.E. Church: "The time has fully come for us to enter more largely upon the work of extending our church into foreign fields . . . . Let us seek to plant firmly the banner of the African Methodist Church upon the ramparts of the forts of the [pagan] enemy on the shores and in the hearts of Africa."[92]

Less than a year later an opportunity to concretize this missionary zeal was afforded the A.M.E. Church by the proposal of the trustees of Freetown's Zion Chapel for "union or amalgamation."[93] In response the A.M.E. Church dispatched Frederick to Sierra Leone. Once in Sierra Leone, Frederick, who was of Afro-Caribbean heritage, successfully negotiated the incorporation of Zion Chapel into the A.M.E. Church.[94] If developments and sentiments related to the cultural reform movement were a factor in the establishment of the A.M.E. presence in Sierra Leone, then the choice of Frederick as the A.M.E. missionary to Sierra Leone appeared fortunate. Both he and Zion Chapel members became actively involved in the reform movement. Thus at the December 1887 meeting of the Dress Reform Society, Frederick was "enthusiastic in his expression of sympathy" for its goals.[95] Partial explanation lies in the fact that Frederick had become an enthusiastic disciple of the movement's catalyst—Edward Blyden.[96]

The A.M.E. presence in Sierra Leone provided Faduma with not only the personal acquaintance of another progressive, race-conscious minister, but also an awareness of an African-American ecclesiastical institution that appeared to embody the ideological, ecclesiastical, and missiological tenets espoused by himself and the members of the reform movement. His initial perception of the A.M.E. Church was also influenced by his subscription to the *A.M.E. Church Review*.[97] Established by the General Conference of the A.M.E. Church in 1884 as the literary and scholarly supplement to the *Christian Recorder*, the *Review* advertised itself as "the recognized organ of the race . . . which no man or woman of the race of the least scholastic attainment can afford to do without."[98]

During its first four years, the *Review* rapidly cultivated a readership among the aspiring African-American middle class and intelligentsia and reflected the broadly informed, though conservative, theological posture of its founding editor, Benjamin T. Tanner. Educated at Avery College and Western Theological Seminary, Tanner sought to keep his readers abreast of the issues of the era that affected the Church and the broader African-American community.[99] David Wills observed that under Tanner's leadership the *Review* paralleled

> . . . both the reviews published by the major white denominations and the leading journals of opinion in the country at large. Like the former, it carried numerous articles on religious and ecclesiastical topics e.g., the theories of the Biblical critics, the nature of baptism, the proper role of clergy, the missionary movement and so forth . . . [I]t also gave considerable attention to social and political issues—particularly as these related to American blacks—and published a considerable amount of poetry and fiction. Its early contributors, moreover, included in addition to prominent clergymen in the A.M.E. Church many of the leading figures in black America as a whole . . . . Tanner himself supplied numerous learned book reviews and a running critical commentary on the contents of over a dozen other journals ranging from the *American Antiquarian* and the *Oriental Journal* to the *North American Review.*[100]

Moreover, Tanner's qualified commitment to evangelical Pan-Africanism was also reflected in his editorials and his selection of contributors. Prominent among its foreign contributors was Edward Blyden, whom Tanner described to his readers as "the one Negro of standing in the English world of recognized scholarship."[101] In the pages of the *Review,* Blyden's *Christianity, Islam, and the Negro Race* was extensively reviewed and publicized. Tanner himself informed his readers: "The facts which Mr. Blyden presents . . . are not to be denied. . . . We would wish that the men who shape the destiny of Christendom, each one and all, would possess themselves of this volume . . . ."[102]

It may well have appeared to Faduma that the theological and ideological goals of the A.M.E. Church, as exemplified by Frederick and the *Review,* were not unlike those which he and other reformers were attempting to actualize in Sierra Leone.[103] In addition to providing Faduma with access to the social, theological, missiological and ideological concerns of both the African-American and the broader American community, the *Review* also provided his initial contacts with the hierarchy of the A.M.E. Church. In 1887 he wrote to Tanner, who would soon be elected bishop, informing him that "through Dr. Blyden, a veritable friend of the Negro, your *Church Review* came into my hands. A Negro indeed, of unmixed blood, I feel proud that there is existing today a *Review* such as yours. I shall always read it with pleasure." In the same tone of racial pride, Faduma made an important announcement:

> Since I ordered for the *Review* I have undertaken a very important change. I have had it advertised in our local papers that my name, which formerly was W. J. Davis, is now to be called Orishatukeh Faduma. . . . Will you, therefore, be kind enough to send the A.M.E. *Church Review* to O. Faduma, 1st B.A. (London). The High School, Freetown, Sierra Leone.[104]

Finally, he asked Tanner, "Will you, dear Mr. Editor, accept contributions from me either in verse or prose?"[105] An affirmative answer resulted in Faduma becoming an important contributor to the *Review*.[106]

Faduma's contributions to the *Review* drew him firmly into the intellectual and ideological orbit of the A.M.E. Church and the wider African-American Christian community. He also attempted to use the *Review* as a forum to counter the negative stereotypes of Africa and Africans prevalent within the African-American religious community. Among his initial literary contributions were efforts at poetry entitled "A Ballad of Egba Land" and "In Memoriam the Centenary of Sierra Leone."[107] The latter work introduced Faduma to the readers of the *Review* as "A Native African" and in tortured lines illustrated the early synthesis of racial pride and religious faith that characterized his life and work. It also reflected Faduma's explicit rejection of religious-based fatalism and his sensitivity to the deleterious impact that such doctrines were having on Africa and Africans:

> A hundred years with howling beasts of prey
> And numerous foes to intercept our way;
> Through customs strange destructive to the race,
> And dire doctrine launched at our face:
> That Africa's land is doomed by iron fate
> And hoary Noah's unrelenting hate.
> Besotted men and blind who do declare
> That our sad state to mend we cannot dare.
> With trembling eyes we read thy will, O Lord,
> And see the rise of Ethiopia in thy Word.[108]

Another *Review* article, entitled "Thoughts for the Times," provided Faduma with a forum from which to address the broader and more substantive issues and implications related to the failure of the Sierra Leone community to support the goals of the collapsing reform movement.[109] Faduma thoroughly analyzed the malaise that was afflicting Sierra Leone and suggested a prescription indicative of his future vocational plans and ideological commitments. He found, as had Tubohku and Blyden, that the roots of the malaise were to be found in the system of faulty education—"defective training"—initially fostered in Sierra Leone by the European mission societies but now perpetuated by the Creoles themselves. It was a pedagogy, he charged, that bred "laziness," "superficiality," "pessimism," and ultimately "a chilling paralysis" that leaves its recipient "unable to swim against the current of his life." With implied reference to the painful ridicule experienced by himself and fellow members of the reform society, Faduma pointed out that such an education "makes men content to be made tools for the destruction of others . . . parasites, incapable of ameliorating their own unfavorable environments and those of their neighbours, incapable of working out the salvation of their race, and resigned to an invisible and invincible fate."[110] In such a superficial and fatalistic environment, it was not surprising that "Words memorized and glibly spoken tickle the ear and gain popular applause, whilst little actions, requiring a world of thought where they are performed, are sneered at and pooh-poohed."[111]

Faduma insisted that the antidote for this malaise was a progressive and expansive Pan-African–oriented pedagogy that encouraged men "to think for themselves." It was only such training that could produce the leaders needed as future rulers of "Church and country." Africans everywhere, he insisted, need leaders who are "receptive, originative, productive and capable to do some small good for the amelioration of their race," to help raise it "from degradation and oppression" and "place it on a lofty pedestal," thereby "convert[ing] the calumny of our detractors to praise and admiration."[112] Reflecting the dedication, independence, racial pride, and faith that would characterize his later life and work, Faduma wrote:

> Every man apart from and united with others has some work to perform towards the upbuilding of his race; this work he alone or he united with others can do and is peculiarly fitted to do. The fact that he is alone to attempt the difficulty ought not to paralyze his efforts if he remembers that there is an invisible Almighty power before and behind him who approves of his actions and is ready to support his feeble hands.

He drew upon biblical and historical examples as he admonished his readers, "Let not any consideration which is unjust deter you from pursuing the right . . . . Let not the thought of your insignificance paralyze any healthy and noble action of yours":

> It was through Moses, a man of slow speech and wanting in words . . . that the Almighty wrought the deliverance of His people from Egyptian bondage . . . . It was through David, the shepherd boy, that the mighty giant of Gath was felled to the ground . . . . A good thing it was that David did not allow his short-sighted brethren to discourage or de-individualize him—it would have been a woeful day for the Israelites . . . . In an age when . . . English society was rotten to its very core . . . arose one John Wesley holding the torch of reform—not without persecutions and misunderstandings—and kindling a religious fire in England which shall not be put out.

> In every age there have been special men, individual men to be guiding stars to their people; they must at any cost do the will of Him that sends them. Woe to them if they allow themselves to be frightened by any power inferior to God's and so neglect the important work they must as individuals perform. Let every individual, then, see that the work he undertakes be undertaken in the right spirit. Let him have God continually, guiding and controlling all his thoughts, and in spite of discouragements, in spite of his own feebleness, he may help to benefit his race and his country.[113]

Two years later Faduma left Sierra Leone to visit the United States. Although he claimed that the purpose of his visit was "to observe school methods and the Negro," perhaps more accurate was Cornelius May's insistence that Faduma departed Sierra Leone in hopes of finding "some wider field where he could find himself free to study and express himself without let or hindrance." He hoped to find in the United States the freedom to realize that "unselfish individuality" for the race that had been stifled and ridiculed in Sierra Leone.[114]

Notes

1. J. F. A. Ajayi and R. S. Smith, *Yoruba Warfare In The Nineteenth Century* (Cambridge: Cambridge University Press, 1964); Peterson, *Province of Freedom,* pp. 45–47; Fyfe, *History of Sierra Leone,* pp.136–176.
2. Orishatukeh Faduma, "An African Background," *Mission Herald* 44 (Sept./Oct., 1940): 19.
3. On the British policy of settling recaptives in the West Indies to provide an ostensibly "free labour" force after the Emancipation Act of 1834, see J. U. J. Asiegbu, "British Slave Emancipation and 'Free' Labour Recruitment from West Africa, 1840–1861," *Sierra Leone Studies* 26 (Jan. 1970): 37–47.
4. Faduma, "An African Background," p. 19.
5. Ibid. *Eighth General Catalogue of the Yale Divinity School Centennial Issue,1822–1922* (New Haven: Yale University, 1922), p. 323. Faduma's Chicago Theological Seminary Transcript records his year of birth as 1860. His death certificate lists his year of birth as 1857. Chicago Theological Seminary Transcript of Orishatukeh Faduma, June 1927; "Certificate of Death" of Orishatukeh Faduma, North Carolina Board of Health, Bureau of Vital Statistics, #2708, issued 11 Feb. 1946.
6. "My View of Things," Freetown Correspondent, *Sierra Leone Weekly News,* 20 Aug. 1887; Kufileh Tubohku, letter to the editor, *Sierra Leone Weekly News,* 24 Sept. 1887.

7. On British Guiana, which became Guyana with the granting of independence in May 1966, see Raymond T. Smith, *British Guiana* (London: Oxford University Press, 1962); Michael Swan, *British Guiana: The Land of Six Peoples* (London: H.M.S.O., 1957); A. J. Seymour, *Cultural Policy in Guyana* (Paris: United Nations Educational, Scientific and Cultural Organization (UNESCO), 1977), pp. 11–15. On British policy in Guyana related to Sierra Leone, see Fyfe, *History of Sierra Leone,* pp. 219, 230; Peterson, *Province of Freedom,* p. 222. On ethnic, cultural, and religious pluralism in Guyana, see Leo A. Despres, *Cultural Pluralism and Nationalist Politics in British Guiana* (Chicago: Rand McNally and Co., 1967).
8. Fyfe, *History of Sierra Leone,* p. 321. Faduma was reportedly seven years old when he and his family migrated to Sierra Leone. See Thomas Yenser, ed., *Who's Who In Colored America* (New York: The Author, 1933), p. 178.
9. Rina L. Okonkwo, "Orishatukeh Faduma: A Man of Two Worlds," *Journal of Negro History* 68 (Winter 1983): 24; Peterson, *Province of Freedom,* pp. 84–86, 93, 192–193.
10. Peterson, *Province of Freedom,* pp. 93–95, 212–215, 235; Fyfe, *History of Sierra Leone,* pp. 233–234.
11. Orishatukeh Faduma, "Success and Drawbacks of Missionary Work in Africa by an Eye-Witness," in Bowen, *Africa and the American Negro,* pp. 125–136.
12. Fyfe, *History of Sierra Leone,* p. 254.
13. Peterson, *Province of Freedom,* pp. 212–217, 220–224; Fyfe, *History of Sierra Leone,* pp. 305, 436, 444, 460, 499, 536.
14. "Waterloo Descendants Association," *Sierra Leone Weekly News,* 14 July1923.
15. Cyril P. Foray, *Historical Dictionary of Sierra Leone* (Metuchen, N.J. and London: Scarecrow Press, 1977), pp. 75–76.
16. Lynch, *Blyden,* pp. 54, 248.
17. Ibid., pp. 4, 13–14.
18. Ibid., pp. 13–14, 18–19.
19. Ajayi, "Henry Venn and the Policy of Development," pp. 63–75; Lynch, "The Native Pastorate Controversy," p. 277. See also Edward W. Blyden, "Mohammedanism in Western Africa," *Methodist Quarterly Review* (Jan. 1871), and "Mohammedanism and the Negro Race," *Fraser's Magazine* (Nov. 1875). Both are reprinted in *Black Spokesman: Selected Published Writings of Edward Wilmot Blyden,* ed. Hollis Lynch (London: Frank Cass & Co.,1971), pp. 271–294.
20. Spitzer, *Creoles of Sierra Leone,* pp. 9–50, 108–111.
21. Blyden argued that the key institutional prescription for the "free and healthy development" of both Christianity and civilization in

Africa was the development of a secular university freed from the warping influence of religious and cultural dogmatism as fostered by existing missionary institutions such as the Church Missionary Society's Fourah Bay College. Lynch, "The Native Pastorate Controversy," pp. 270–292.

22. Correspondence from Blyden to Governor Hennessy, 6 Dec. 1872 and 11 Dec. 1872, in Lynch, *Black Spokesman,* pp. 226–229.
23. Lynch, *Blyden,* pp. 93–94.
24. Peterson, *Province of Freedom,* p. 285; Lynch, *Black Spokesman,* p. xxiii.
25. On Wesley College, the alma mater of a number of prominent West Africans, see Fyfe, *History of Sierra Leone,* pp. 287, 350, 407, 423–24. On May see Foray, *Historical Dictionary,* p. 138.
26. Fyfe, *History of Sierra Leone,* p. 464; Foray, *Historical Dictionary,* p. 138.
27. Fyfe notes that "*The Sierra Leone Weekly News,* with Blyden as a regular contributor, tended to approve anything distinctively African, and deplored slavish imitation of European ways." Fyfe, *History of Sierra Leone,* p. 496.
28. Ibid., p. 465.
29. May is described as a stern disciplinarian and "an erudite and passionate teacher." The curriculum of Boys High School was weighted towards classical studies: Latin, Greek, French, ancient history, and English. There was also an attempt to include practical disciplines such as algebra, geometry, and physical science. Akintola J. G. Wyse, *H. C. Bankole-Bright and Politics in Colonial Sierra Leone, 1919–1958* (Cambridge: Cambridge University Press, 1990), p. 8.
30. "The Wesleyan High School Semi-Jubilee Celebration," *Sierra Leone Weekly News,* 20 May1899; Lynch, *Blyden,* p. 244.
31. Foray, *Historical Dictionary,* p.138.
32. Orishatukeh Faduma, "An Old Boy's Tribute to Principal May," *Sierra Leone Weekly News,* 10 July 1899.
33. Fyfe, *History of Sierra Leone,* pp. 182–183, 270; Peterson, *Province of Freedom,* p. 153; Cohen, *Politics of Elite Culture,* p. 226.
34. Spitzer, *Creoles of Sierra Leone,* p. 15; Cohen, *Politics of Elite Culture,* pp. 128–129, 225–226; Arthur T. Porter, *Creoledom: A Study of the Development of Freetown Society* (London: Oxford University Press, 1963).
35. Fyfe, *History of Sierra Leone,* pp.182, 251.
36. Faduma, "An Old Boy's Tribute."
37. Letter from Blyden to William Grant, Freetown, 22 May 1872, quoted in Lynch, *Black Spokesman,* pp. 223–224. On the impor-

tance of an English education see Spitzer, *Creoles of Sierra Leone,* p. 15 and Peterson, *Province of Freedom,* pp. 284–286.

38. Yenser, *Who's Who In Colored America,* 1941–1944, p. 64.
39. Ibid.
40. On the importance of Wesley College, which would later become Queens College, see F. L. Bartels, *The Roots of Ghana Methodism* (Cambridge: Cambridge University Press, 1965). Also Peterson, *Province of Freedom,* p. 285; Lynch, *Black Spokesman,* p. xxiii; and Eric Asby, *Universities: British, Indian, African: A Study in the Ecology of Higher Education* (London: Weidenfeld and Nicolson, 1966), pp. 147–169.
41. Howard Cline Barnard, *A History of English Education From 1760,* rev. ed. (London: University of London Press, 1961), pp. 83–87.
42. Ibid., pp. 135–143; O. Faduma, "African Negro Education," *Sierra Leone Weekly News,* 10 Aug. 1918.
43. For Faduma's expression of disillusionment with the formal and conservative religious climate of Victorian England, see Orishatukeh Faduma, "Where is Virtue?" *A.M.E. Church Review* 8 (Apr. 1891): 430–431.
44. Owen Chadwick, *The Victorian Church,* vols. 1 and 2, 2nd ed. (London: Adam and Charles Black, 1972); Clement C. J. Webb, *A Study of Religious Thought in England from 1850* (Oxford: Clarendon Press, 1933); L. E. Elliott-Binns, *English Thought,1860–1900: The Theological Aspect* (London: Longmans, Green and Co., 1956); Bernard M. G. Reardon, *Liberal Protestantism* (Stanford: Stanford University Press, 1968); Otto Pfleiderer, *The Development of Theology in Germany Since Kant and Its Progress in Great Britain Since 1825,* trans. J. F. Smith (London: Swan Sonnenschein and Co., 1890).
45. Chadwick, *The Victorian Church,* vol. 2, pp. 101–111. See also James R. Moore, *The Post-Darwinian Controversies: A study of the Protestant Struggle to Come to Terms with Darwin in Great Britain and America, 1870–1900* (Cambridge: Cambridge University Press, 1979).
46. Francis P. Weisenburger, *Ordeal of Faith: The Crisis of Church-Going America, 1865–1900* (New York: Philosophical Library, 1959), p. 218.
47. Chadwick, *Victorian Church,* vol. 2, pp. 58, 90–97. Ironically, in an 1866 letter to William Gladstone, Blyden commented on the "Vagaries of Dr. Colenso." Letter to the Right Hon. William E. Gladstone from Monrovia, Liberia West Africa, 3 Feb. 1866 in *Selected Letters of Edward Wilmot Blyden* ed. Hollis Lynch (Millwood, N. Y.: KTO Press, 1978), p. 69.
48. Spitzer, *Creoles of Sierra Leone,* pp. 24–25. Fyfe, *History of Sierra Leone,* p. 351. I. Tufuoh, "Relations between Christian Missions, Eu-

ropean Administrators, and Traders in the Gold Coast, 1828–1874" in *History of Christianity in West Africa,* ed. O. U. Kalu, p. 228. See also Spitzer, *Creoles of Sierra Leone,* pp. 127–128.

49. Editorial, *Sierra Leone Weekly News,* 6 Sept. 1886.
50. Letter from Blyden to William Grant, Freetown, 22 May 1872, quoted in Lynch, *Black Spokesman,* pp. 223–224.
51. Ibid.
52. On this change, see Curtin, *Image of Africa;* Spitzer, *Creoles of Sierra Leone,* pp. 45–69, 151.
53. Spitzer, *Creoles of Sierra Leone,* pp. 45–46.
54. Peterson, *Province of Freedom,* pp. 284–286; Spitzer, *Creoles of Sierra Leone,* p. 15. See Faduma's critique of the religious and moral climate of England in "Where Is Virtue?" Almost fifty years later, Faduma recalled the fear and fascination evoked by his dark skin. O. Faduma, "Africa the Unknown," *Mission Herald* 43 (Nov./Dec. 1939): 20.
55. S. R. B. Attoh-Ahuma, *Memoirs of West African Celebrities With Special Reference to the Gold Coast* (Liverpool: Phillips, 1925); John Mensah Sarbah, *Fanti Customary Laws* (London: William Clowes and Sons, 1897); John Mensah Sarbah, *Fanti National Constitution* (London: William Clowes and Sons,1906); Geiss, *Pan-African Movement,* pp. 70–73.
56. Harris W. Mobley, *The Ghanaian's Image of The Missionary: An Analysis of the Published Critiques of Christian Missionaries 1897–1965* (Leiden: E. J. Brill, 1970), pp. 128–129, 100; also Sarbah, *Fanti National Constitution,* pp. xvi–xvii, and Sarbah, *Fanti Customary Laws,* p. 41.
57. Ayandele, *Missionary Impact,* pp. 271–278; also Langley, *Pan-Africanism And Nationalism in West Africa, 1900–1945: A Study in Ideology and Social Classes* (Oxford: Clarendon Press, 1973), pp. 92, 185, 190.
58. Yenser, *Who's Who In Colored America,* p. 64; Okonkwo, "Man of Two Worlds," p. 25. Correspondence from the Registry and Paleography divisions of the University of London confirms Faduma's matriculation in June 1883 and his passing of the Intermediate Arts Examination in 1884. However, no record has been located that confirms that he was awarded a degree by the University of London. Letter from Simon Bailey, Paleography Room, University of London Library, 4 Mar. 1985; also letter from Mrs. A. M. Amos, Central Registry, Academic Division, University of London, 20 Feb. 1985. Okonkwo, "Man of Two Worlds," p. 25.
59. Spitzer, *Creoles of Sierra Leone,* p. 15; Peterson, *Province of Freedom,* pp. 284–286; Cohen, *Politics of Elite Culture,* pp. 128–129, 225, 226.

60. O. Faduma, "A Tale of Egba Land," *Methodist Herald* 25 Aug., 8 Sept. 1886). An edited version of this poem was published in the *A.M.E. Church Review*. See O. Faduma, "A Ballad On Egba Land," *A.M.E. Church Review* 5 (5 July 1888).
61. Spitzer, *Creoles of Sierra Leone,* pp. 120–224.
62. Edward W. Blyden, *Christianity, Islam, and the Negro Race* (London: W.B. Whittingham and Co., 1887). The book was favorably reviewed in religious journals on both sides of the Atlantic. One reviewer noted, "I am not sure but that Dr. Blyden's book, *Christianity, Islam, and the Negro Race,* may not yet prove the greatest contribution of the age on the gigantic subject of Christian Missions." Among those who commented favorably on the work were David Swing, the Presbyterian liberal; Rev. Cannon Isaac Taylor, the Anglican missiologist and Islamic scholar; and Dr. Benjamin Tanner, editor of the *A.M.E. Church Review.* Edith Holden, *Blyden of Liberia: An Account of the Life and Labors of Edward Wilmot Blyden, LL. D. As Recorded in Letters and in Print* (New York: Vintage Press, 1966), p. 597–599. Lynch, *Blyden,* p. 76.
63. Lynch, *Pan-Negro Patriot,* pp. xv–xvi.
64. Blyden's mature theological development reflected the self-study that characterized his scholarship in so many other areas. His rudimentary theological training began when he was a youth in St. Thomas, under the direction of John Knox, a Presbyterian minister educated at Rutgers Theological College. Blyden later continued his studies in Liberia under the direction of the Reverend D. A. Wilson, a graduate of Princeton Theological Seminary. His request for admission to Rutgers Theological College was denied because of his race. Later requests to the Presbyterian Board of Foreign Missions for assistance to study at one of the theological colleges in the United States went unheeded. Thus Blyden had neither the benefits nor the liabilities of a formal and systematic theological education. Ibid., pp. 4–13; Holden, *Blyden,* pp. 19–22, 29–30.
65. Thus in 1866 Blyden would allude to "the vagaries of Dr. [Bishop] Colenso" with a quote from Dante's Inferno. Letter from Blyden to the Right Hon. William E. Gladstone, 3 Feb. 1866, quoted in Lynch, *Selected Letters,* p. 71.
66. Lynch, *Blyden,* pp.18–19, 46–47, 54–83.
67. See Edward Wilmot Blyden, *African Life and Customs* (London: Phillips, 1908).
68. In his 1891 address, "The Aims and Methods of a Liberal Education for Africans," Blyden quoted the British Darwinians T. H. Huxley and Herbert Spencer. He also quoted from a work entitled *Christianity and Science* (New York, 1875) by the Harvard professor Andrew P. Peabody. *Blyden, Christianity, Islam, and the Negro Race,*

pp. 77, 84, 90. After an initially negative response to Darwinism, Peabody sought to reconcile Christianity and the new scientific currents of the era. See Francis P. Weisenburger, *Ordeal of Faith,* pp. 63, 68. Peabody also served as President of the Board of Trustees of Donations for Education in Liberia from 1876 to 1885. Holden, *Blyden,* pp. 284, 458, 515. In 1890 Blyden became an honorary member of the American Society of Comparative Religion. Lynch, *Blyden,* p. 82. On the emergence of Liberal Protestantism, see Bernard M. G. Reardon, *Liberal Protestantism* (Stanford: Stanford University Press, 1968), pp. 9–65. Blyden was forced by illness to decline an invitation to give a paper on comparative religion at the Columbian Exposition at Chicago in 1893. Holden, *Blyden,* p. 646.

69. Holden, *Blyden,* p. 848.
70. Blyden, *African Life and Customs,* pp. 63, 64.
71. Of special significance was Blyden's influence on Reverend Majola Agbebi, James Johnson, Abayomi Cole, and John R. Frederick. Lynch, *Blyden,* pp. 98, 219, 238–240, 242, 245–246, and Spitzer, *Creoles of Sierra Leone,* pp. 73–74, 111–123. This analysis finds support in the work of William R. Hutchison, who suggests a number of factors that appear to have been important for the rise and spread of American theological liberalism. Many of these factors appear to have been operative in the Sierra Leone context. Key among these was "cultural strain," defined as "the upsetting or rending of those patterns of meaning around which individual men have constructed their lives," and the presence of a "catalytic agent"—a "somewhat heretical or freethinking" individual—who served to emphasize the degree of cultural strain and dysfunction. Faduma and a growing number of Sierra Leone Creoles, finding themselves rejected by the Europeans whom they had idealized and emulated and equally marginal in terms of an African folk culture and heritage, were under intense "cultural strain." In this context Blyden clearly played the role of "catalytic agent." See William R. Hutchison, "Cultural Strain and Protestant Liberalism," *American Historical Review* 76 (Apr. 1971): 386–411. Also Spitzer, *Creoles of Sierra Leone,* pp. 108–122.
72. Spitzer, *Creoles of Sierra Leone,* pp. 106–108.
73. "An Important Notice," *Sierra Leone Weekly News,* 5 Aug. 1887. Faduma noted that his choice of a sire name was based on the recent discovery that his "father's native name was Faduma." The factors that inspired his choice of a new first name that had obvious reference to the Yoruba religious pantheon remains a mystery. The Review in Foreign Lands, letter from Faduma to Tanner dated 20 Aug. 1887, in *A.M.E. Church Review* 4 (5 July 1888).
74. Among the Creoles who joined Faduma in reforming their names were A. E. Metzger (Kufileh Tubohku), O. T. George (O. T. Nana),

Claude George (Esu Biyi), Isaac Augustus Johnson (Algerine Kefallah Sankoh), and Africanus Matthew Goodman (Eyahjemi Moondia). Spitzer, *Creoles of Sierra Leone,* p. 117. For similar expressions of cultural nationalism in other parts of West Africa during this era, see Ayandele, *Missionary Impact,* pp. 257–259, 254–255.

75. On the development of attitudes that would give rise to this controversy, see Ayandele, *Missionary Impact,* 242–245; Spitzer, *Creoles of Sierra Leone,* pp. 45–50, 108–111.
76. Letter to the editor by "Sententia," *Sierra Leone Weekly News,* 20 Aug. 1887.
77. Freetown Correspondent, "My View of Things," *Sierra Leone Weekly News,* 20 Aug. 1887.
78. Kufileh Tubohku, letter to the editor of the *Sierra Leone Weekly News,* 24 Sept. 1887. Cyril P. Foray, *Historical Dictionary.*
79. Gustav Warneck, *Modern Missions and Culture: Their Mutual Relations,* trans. T. Smith (Edinburgh: Gemmell, 1883), p. 6; Ayandele, *Missionary Impact,* pp. 242–243.
80. Richard Hooker was a famous sixteenth century theologian and apologist of the Church of England. The first five volumes of his *Treatise of the Laws of Ecclesiastical Polity* were published between 1593 and 1597. Patrick Collinson, *The Elizabethan Puritan Movement* (Berkeley and Los Angeles: University of California Press, 1967), pp. 430–431.
81. Tubohku, *Sierra Leone Weekly News,* 24 Sept. 1887.
82. "Departure of Professor O. Faduma," Editorial, *Sierra Leone Weekly News,* 12 Sept. 1908.
83. Spitzer, *Creoles of Sierra Leone,* pp. 117–119.
84. "The Dress Reform Society," *Sierra Leone Weekly News,* 17 Dec. 1887.
85. Spitzer, *Creoles of Sierra Leone,* pp. 118–119.
86. "The Dress Reform Society." On James Johnson and his often ambivalent response to this situation, see Ayandele, *Missionary Impact,* and E.A. Ayandele, *Holy Johnson: Pioneer of African Nationalism, 1836–1917* (New York: Humanities Press, 1970). See also Johnson's sympathetic analysis of the religion of the Yoruba in his *Yoruba Heathenism* (Exeter: J. Townsend, 1899) and *The Relation of Mission Work to Native Customs* (London, 1908). On Johnson's influence on Faduma see Langley, *Pan-Africanism and Nationalism,* p. 50.
87. "The Dress Reform Society;" *Methodist Herald* (21 Dec. 1887); Spitzer, *Creoles of Sierra Leone,* p. 118.
88. Tubohku, letter to the editor, *Sierra Leone Weekly News,* 24 Sept. 1887.

89. Toboku-Metzger, "Missionary Effort," *A.M.E. Church Review* 6 (July 1889).
90. Ibid.
91. The major catalyst was Bishop Henry M. Turner. See Edwin S. Redkey, "Bishop Turner's African Dream," in Burkett and Newman, *Black Apostles,* pp. 227–246.
92. Williams, *Black Americans,* p. 46.
93. Zion Chapel was originally affiliated with the Countess of Huntington Connection. Ibid., pp. 46–47; Geiss, *Pan-African Movement,* p. 141; Josephus R. Coan, "The Reverend John Richard Frederick—Pioneer Missionary to Sierra Leone," *A.M.E. Church Review* 102 (1987), pp. 36–42.
94. In 1897 Frederick withdrew from the AME Church and led his congregation into affiliation with the British Wesleyan Methodist Church. Lynch, *Blyden,* p. 219; Fyfe, *History of Sierra Leone,* pp. 469, 532.
95. "The Dress Reform Society," *Sierra Leone Weekly News,* 17 Dec. 1887.
96. Much of the missiological, theological, and ideological agenda of the new mission society reflected the tenets set forth by Blyden in *Christianity, Islam, and the Negro Race*. Lynch, *Blyden,* pp. 245–246. In 1888 Frederick penned a defense of Blyden's missiology and refuted the charge that Blyden had "gone over to Mahomet." This defense, which reflected his own theological, ideological, and missiological debt to Blyden, was published in the *Christian Recorder*. John R. Frederick, "Has Dr. Blyden Gone Over to Mahomet?," *Christian Recorder* (12 Jan. 1888); Holden, *Blyden,* pp. 600–601. Frederick would conduct Blyden's funeral services in 1912. See Lynch, *Blyden,* pp. 245. The progressive nature of Frederick's own missiology was reflected in his instructions to missionary Moses D. Davis. Davis, whom Frederick recruited to establish an interior mission station at Ro Mango, was charged to respect, "love" and "study," and instill in the indigenous Africans "a spirit of independence." He was also warned to "avoid everything like interference with their long-established customs." Daniel A. Payne, *History of the A.M.E. Church,* ed. Charles Spenser Smith (Nashville: Publishing House of the A.M.E. Sunday School Union, 1891), pp. 489–490.
97. Letter from Orishatukeh Faduma to Dr. Benjamin Tanner dated 20 Aug. 1887 *A.M.E. Church Review* 4 (5 July 1888).
98. Walter C. Daniel, *Black Journals of the United States* (Westport, Conn.: Greenwood Press, 1982), pp. 27–32; *Christian Recorder* (15 Mar. 1888): 8.
99. David Wood Wills, "Aspects of Social Thought in the African Methodist Episcopal Church, 1884–1910" (Ph.D. diss., Harvard

University, 1975), pp. 94–96. See also William J. Simmons, *Men of Mark: Eminent, Progressive, and Rising* (Cleveland: George M. Revell & Co., 1887; reprint, New York: Arno Press and New York Times, 1968), pp. 985–88 and Richard Robert Wright, Jr., *The Bishops of the African Methodist Episcopal Church* (Nashville: Printed by the A.M.E. Sunday School Union, 1963), pp. 323–326.

100. Wills, "Aspects of Social Thought," p. 68.
101. Tanner, "Contributions," *A.M.E. Church Review* 5 (July 1888): 6.
102. Tanner, *A.M.E. Church Review* 4 (Oct. 1887): 216; Holden, *Blyden of Liberia,* p. 597.
103. Wills, "Aspects of Social Thought," p. 68.
104. *A.M.E. Church Review* 5 (July 5, 1888).
105. Ibid.
106. In the last edition of the *Review* under his editorial direction, Tanner included Faduma among those "scholars of the race" who "so nobly helped us make the *Review* what it is . . . ." Other included were Blyden and James Theodore Holly *A.M.E. Church Review* 5 (5 July 1888).
107. O. Faduma, "A Ballad on Egba Land," *A.M.E. Church Review* 5 (July 1888). "This was apparently a revised version of "A Tale of Egba Land," published earlier in the *Methodist Herald.* O. Faduma, "A Tale of Egba Land," *Methodist Herald* (25 Aug., 8 Sept. 1886).
108. O. Faduma, "In Memoriam the Centenary of Sierra Leone," *A.M.E. Church Review* 6 (Oct. 1889): 239–240.
109. O. Faduma, "Thoughts for the Times," *A.M.E. Church Review* 5 (Oct. 1888): 121–126.
110. Ibid., p. 123.
111. Ibid., p. 122.
112. Ibid., p. 124.
113. Ibid., pp. 125–126.
114. O. Faduma, "My Nigerian African Background," n.d., p. 4. This was apparently a draft of an "An African Background," later published in the *Mission Herald.* O. Faduma, "An African Background," *Mission Herald* 44 (Sept./Oct.1940):19–20. Cornelius May, "Professor O. Faduma BD," *Sierra Leone Weekly News,* 13 June 1908.

3

Faduma and the New Theology

When Faduma arrived in the United States in 1891 the nation was in the midst of intense social, economic, racial, and religious ferment.[1] Of particular concern for the American religious community were the increasing challenges of urbanization, industrialization, and the new scientific, intellectual, and academic currents that had earlier had an impact on the European and British religious communities.[2] America's preoccupation with the Civil War and its aftermath had delayed the full impact of these developments. But by the last decades of the century, the American religious community could no longer avoid the radical challenges posed by the various modes of Darwinism, the historical-critical method of biblical interpretation, the new findings of geology, and the comparative study of religion.[3]

The religious crisis spawned by these developments has occasioned studies that characterize this era as an "Ordeal of Faith," a "Spiritual Crisis," and a "Critical Period" for the American religious community.[4] Of the dilemma faced by the American religious community during this period, Arthur M. Schlesinger has noted:

> Perhaps at no time in its American development has the path of Christianity been so sorely beset with pitfalls and perils as in the last quarter of the nineteenth century. The validity of the Bible itself seemed at stake in the light of the new pronouncements of science and scholarship. Darwinism, the emerging science of biblical criticism, the increasing knowledge and study of other great religions—such threats to orthodoxy could not be ignored, yet how could they be met?[5]

Taking their cues from liberalizing currents long present in their own tradition and from philosophical and theological developments in Britain and Germany, a small but influential group of predominantly New England "pastor-theologians" began to formulate responses to the challenges posed by the new intellectual and academic currents.[6] They labored amid intense spiritual and intellectual anxiety induced by the need to be both "serious Christians and intelligent moderns." Their efforts to appropriate the findings and methods of the new scientific, intellectual, and academic developments resulted in the formation of a distinctively American version of Protestant liberalism.[7]

This new theological synthesis first gained explicit expression in 1879 in a book entitled *Old Faiths in New Light*. It was written by the Congregationalist pastor and theologian Newman Smyth.[8] In 1883 Theodore

Thornton Munger, Smyth's friend and fellow Congregational minister, wrote an essay entitled "The New Theology," which announced in no uncertain terms the existence of this new theological mood and movement.[9] Its defining theological and ethical beliefs, as well as its tenor and nuances, were delineated in Munger's manifesto. He noted that the "New Theology"

1. . . claims for itself a somewhat larger and broader use of reason than has been accorded to theology . . . .
2. . . seeks to interpret the Scriptures in what may be called a more natural way, and in opposition to a hard, formal, unsympathetic, and unimaginative way. . . .It holds profoundly to inspiration, but it also holds that the Scriptures were written by living men, whose life entered into their writings. . . . In brief, it reads the Scriptures as literature, yet with no derogation from their inspiration . . . .
3. . . seeks to replace an excessive individuality by a truer view of the solidarity of the race . . . . It turns our attention to the corporate life of man here in the world. . . . Hence its ethical emphasis; hence its recognition of the nation, and of the family, and of social and commercial life, as fields of the manifestation of God and of the operation of the Spirit; hence its readiness to ally itself with all movements for bettering the condition of mankind. . . .
4. . . recognizes a new relation to natural science. . . . It admits that science has anticipated theology in formulating the method of creation known as evolution, that it has corrected modern theology by suggesting a closer and more vital relation between God and creation, and so has helped it throw off a mechanical theory and regain its forgotten theory of the divine immanence in creation . . . .
5. . . offers a contrast to the Old [Theology] in claiming for itself a wider study of man. . . .
6. . . recognizes the necessity of a restatement of belief in Eschatology, or the doctrine of last Things . . . . It finds itself driven to such conclusions as these: namely, that every human being will have the fullest opportunity for attaining to the end of his creation as a child of God; that every human being will receive from the Spirit of God all the influence impelling to salvation that his nature can endure and retain its moral integrity; that no human being will be given over to perish while there is a possibility of his salvation. . . .

Munger concluded:

> Such are some of the features of this fresh movement in the realm of theology . . . . It makes no haste, it seeks no revolution, but simply holds itself open and receptive under the breathing of the Spirit that has come, and is ever coming, into the world.[10]

An impressive cadre of "pastor-theologians" similarly disillusioned with what was perceived as the archaic orthodoxy of their youth joined Smyth and Munger in the construction of this new theological synthesis. They were enthusiastic about the development of a more "progressive orthodoxy" that would affirm the central tenets of Christianity yet address the myriad challenges of the modern era. In numerous books, articles, and sermons, this group, which includes Egbert C. Smyth, George Harris, George A. Gordon, William Newton Clarke, Lewis French Stearns, Washington Gladden, William Adams Brown, and Lyman Abbott, popularized, defended, and gave definitive shape to the New Theology.[11]

The fact that not all of the formulators or subsequent adherents of the New Theology (or liberal theology, as it was later styled) interpreted and emphasized its characteristic tenets and concerns in the same way and to the same degree gave rise to different varieties of theological liberalism. The two major divisions were designated "evangelical liberalism" and "modernistic liberalism."[12] The latter term characterized the more radical group of liberals who built upon the original synthesis formulated by the founding generation of liberal theologians. More radical in their orientation, perspective, goals, and methodology, they sought a more conscious break with orthodoxy. Their normative points of departure for the theological enterprise were "the presuppositions of modern science, philosophy, scholarship, and social thought."[13]

The designation "evangelical liberal" has been applied to those liberals primarily determined to affirm historical, doctrinal, and ecclesiastical continuity. Their accommodationist attitude was reflected in the term "progressive orthodoxy," which they sometimes applied to their theological synthesis.[14] The adherents of this theological agenda dominated American theological liberalism. From its ranks came many "ethical-social" liberals who believed that "ethics, the Christian conscience, and the kingdom of God" should be moved to the fore as the subjects of preaching and theological construction."[15] These concerns would make this wing of liberalism the prime nurture of the social gospel movement. Under the prophetic and formative leadership of Washington Gladden and Walter Rauschenbusch, this movement committed evangelical liberalism's optimistic idealism, resources, and adherents to the goal of establishing the "kingdom of God in America" and extending that kingdom worldwide.[16]

A key component of liberal efforts to establish and extend the "kingdom of God" was the religious education movement. Like its theological counterpart, it appropriated the evolutionary theory and was open to the findings of the new academic disciplines and methodologies as it sought an accommodation with modernity.[17]

No figure better represents the fusion of evangelical liberalism and the progressive religious education movement than George Albert Coe.[18]

An evangelical liberal who had studied at the University of Berlin, Coe attempted to synthesize the theological and "intellectual tendencies that were most essential to the development of the new theory of religious education."[19] In response to those who suggested that the new religious and pedagogical ideals of the era were inherently incompatible, Coe argued: "if . . . we compare the ideals of the new education with those of progressive Christianity, we discover no such gulf as is commonly supposed." Both were "tending toward a higher unity."[20]

Convinced that "the kingdom of God constitutes the ultimate end of Christian education and that growth is the process of attaining maturity within that kingdom," Coe was committed to the establishment and extension of the American kingdom of God via a soteriologically directed pedagogy ("Salvation by Education").[21] As advanced by Coe, his students, and his colleagues in the Religious Education Association, the progressive education movement became an important component in liberal efforts to realize and extend their vision of the American kingdom of God.[22]

The primary vehicle for the worldwide extension of the liberal ideal of the kingdom of God was to be an enlightened and progressive mission enterprise rooted in a missiology contoured by the tenets and concerns of the New Theology. However, the New Theology's emphasis on the immanence of God, evolutionary development, optimistic view of history and humanity, progressive eschatology, and soteriology, when coupled with the perspectives and findings of the emerging disciplines of sociology, philosophy of religion, and especially comparative religion, radically challenged many of the traditional premises, policies, and practices of the Protestant mission enterprise.[23]

The discipline that provided the most cogent support for liberalism's progressive missiology was that of comparative religion. As defined at the turn of the century by one of its early adherents, comparative religion was "that science which compared the origin, structure, and characteristics of the various religions of the world, with the view of determining their genuine agreements and differences, the measure of relation in which they stand one to another, and their relative superiority and inferiority. . . ."[24] Although the antecedents of the discipline are numerous and lie far back in antiquity, its flowering in the nineteenth century, first in Europe and later in the United States, was directly related to the development of the new biblical and historical scholarship associated with the rise of theological liberalism.[25]

From inception, the missiological implications of the developing discipline's more positive appraisal of non-Christian religions had been noted by its founders and early supporters.[26] Monier-Williams, the French Sanskritist, made its missiological implications a major factor in his successful campaign to win the Boden chair of Sanskrit at Oxford

University.[27] Moreover, E. B. Pusey, leader of the Oxford Movement, viewed Max Muller's translation of the Vedas as "the greatest gifts which have been bestowed on those who would win to Christianity the subtle and thoughtful minds of the cultivated Indians." He informed Muller that his studies would "form a new era in the efforts for the conversion of India."[28] Muller himself was a proponent of the new discipline's appropriation in the formation of a new "scientific treatment of Christian missions."[29]

In the United States, a more positive perception of non-Christian religions had been pioneered primarily by Unitarians and Transcendentalists. The works of James Freeman Clarke, Ralph Waldo Emerson, Theodore Parker, and Samuel Johnson, influenced by European developments in the field of comparative religion, presented assessments of non-Christian religions and cultures that contrasted radically with the prevailing images presented in orthodox missiological and academic circles.[30] However, it was the emergence and flowering of the New Theology in the last quarter of the nineteenth century that provided the major conduit for the perspectives and findings of comparative religion within American Protestant missiological and academic circles.[31]

Comparative religion's growing influence in the United States was reflected in the establishment of the first American chair of comparative religion at Boston University in 1873 and the founding in 1890 of the American Society of Comparative Religion.[32] The new discipline's most significant institutional triumph occurred in 1893 with the holding of the World's Parliament of Religion in conjunction with the Chicago Columbian Exposition.[33] Envisioned and organized by the liberal Presbyterian minister John Henry Barrows, the Parliament drew representatives from many of the world's religious traditions.[34] It met for seventeen days under the motto, "Have we not all one father? Hath not one God created us?" and served in effect as "an object lesson in the comparative study of religions" for the American public.[35]

Among the participants were representatives of African and African-American religious communities. Edward Blyden, perhaps the foremost black adherent of the discipline of comparative religion, was unable to attend because of ill health. However, Bishop Benjamin W. Arnett, of the African Methodist Episcopal Church, attested to the significance of the Parliament and the theological and missiological impact of the new discipline. In his closing address before the Parliament, Arnett idealistically proclaimed:

> If the Parliament has done nothing more, it has furnished comparative theology with such material that in the future there will be no question about the nature and attributes of God. The great battle of the future will not be the Fatherhood of God, nor that we need a redeemer, mediator or a model

man between God and man, but it is to acknowledge the Brotherhood of man practically.[36]

While fostering a more positive perspective toward non-Christian religions, cultures, and their adherents, comparative religionists usually retained a western Christian outlook and supported evangelical liberals in their claim and belief that Christianity was to date "the highest revelation of God to man." They often viewed non-Christian religions as "stepping-stones" to Christianity and eventually to a Christian-based "world religion" in which their spiritual gropings and "higher" elements would be fulfilled.[37] One of the classic examples of this missiological use of comparative religion is evident in an article by John Buckham entitled "Christianity Among the Religions."[38] Buckham, who had been educated at Andover Theological Seminary and later taught theology at Pacific Theological Seminary, noted that the "study of Comparative Religion is revealing Christianity in a wholly new light." For Buckham and many of his liberal colleagues, there was little doubt that Christianity clarified and revitalized by the New Theology and the discipline of comparative religion would provide the foundation of the evolving "world religion."[39]

Appropriation of the findings and perspectives of comparative religion by theological liberals made the mission arena one of the major battlefields in the ensuing controversy between the proponents of liberalism and the defenders of orthodoxy. To the latter, liberalism's "mission apologetic," with its cultural and religious relativism, seemed to deny or minimize the exclusiveness and superiority of the Christian revelation and the civilization it produced. It also appeared to de-emphasize soteriological concerns in favor of sociological and humanitarian goals. Thus the forces of orthodoxy warned that liberal missiology threatened to "cut the nerve of mission" and undermine the enterprise at its very roots.[40]

Despite the prevailing assumptions of traditional religious historiography, which identifies African-American Protestants almost exclusively with religious conservatism and fundamentalism, it is increasingly apparent that Protestant liberalism and the developments associated with its emergence had a significant impact within the African-American community.[41] Even as the post-Reconstruction African-American religious community struggled in the face of a resurgent racism to marshal its limited spiritual and material resources, it was not immune or impervious to the pervasive currents that were forcing reassessment and realignment of the theological, pedagogical, and missiological praxis of mainstream evangelical Protestantism. In fact, an increased sense of religious and racial crisis provoked one of the most creative eras of theological and missiological ferment within the African-American religious community.[42]

While the vast majority of poorly educated African-American clergy and laity were ill-prepared and ill-disposed to adopt the theological and missiological tenets of Protestant liberalism, even in its most moderate form, a small though significant minority selectively and critically appropriated the tenets of theological liberalism. They attempted to forge a theology and missiology that would be consistent with the needs of the race as it entered fully into the corridors of modernity. Like their white counterparts—and perhaps with even more intensity, given the racial prescriptions under which they lived—they felt "the compelling demand that living faith come to terms with the modern world."[43] Included in this group were such well known clerical activists as Sutton E. Griggs, J. Milton Waldron, Jesse E. Moorland, Reverdy Ransom, Richard R. Wright, Jr., William H. Ferris, Hugh Henry Proctor, A. W. Upshaw, George E. Haynes, Gordon B. Hancock, Adam Clayton Powell, Sr., Alexander Walters, and Theophilus Gould Steward. Although major studies of the theological convictions of these figures have yet to be produced, there is ample evidence in their writings and activities to warrant confidence in labeling them evangelical liberals.

For example, Sutton E. Griggs, born in 1872, was educated at Bishop College and Richmond Theological Seminary en route to becoming a Baptist minister and author. According to S. P. Fullinwider, Griggs was "something of a religious modernist," and Wilson J. Moses notes that he "was steeped in the theories of Darwin and other evolutionary theorists—Benjamin Kidd, Piotr Kropotkin, and Herbert Spencer." Moreover, Moses observed that Griggs's novels represented "an attempt to create a humane theory of biological and social evolution within the framework of a national literature."[44] In his *Guide to Racial Greatness or the Science of Collective Efficiency,* Griggs quoted the architect of pedagogical liberalism, George Albert Coe, and made reference to theological liberals such as Lyman Abbott and Shailer Mathews.[45] A similar response to the liberal currents of the era is to be recognized in the life and work of J. Milton Waldron. Educated at Lincoln University and Newton Theological Seminary, Waldron became a Baptist minister, a member of the Niagara Movement and the American Negro Academy. He is described as one of the "religious radicals" of the era and a "modernist."[46]

A more restrained response to these currents is evident in the activities of the African Methodist Episcopal Zion Bishop Alexander Walters. Walters was extremely active in the social and political affairs of the African-American community. In 1898 he played a key role in reviving the Afro-American Council and two years later chaired the first Pan-African Conference, held in London.[47] His progressivism was not, however, limited to secular spheres. In the late 1880s and 1890s he was actively involved in the struggle between "conservatives and progressives" within the A.M.E. Zion Church. He confessed to being among the handful of "progressives" prodding the denomination to "give up" her position of "ultra-conservatism and assume a progressive attitude."[48]

Black liberals such as Congregationalists Hugh Henry Proctor, George Edmund Haynes, and Jesse E. Moorland were members of predominantly white denominations that were on the cutting edge of the growing liberal influence within American Protestantism.[49] Many also attended liberal-oriented colleges, universities, and seminaries associated with these denominations. Of special importance were liberal-oriented institutions such as Yale, Harvard, Chicago, Boston, Andover, and Union. Theological education at these institutions was of major influence in shaping the theologies and ministries of black liberals such as Hugh Henry Proctor, Adam Clayton Powell, Sr., and William H. Ferris.[50] Born in 1874, Ferris was educated at Yale University, Harvard University, and Harvard Divinity School. Randall Burkett notes that "essentially Ferris accepted a social Darwinist conception of the evolution of society, though this was substantially modified by his wide reading of German philosophers and theologians . . . as well as the American John Fiske."[51] In his major work, a two-volume treatise entitled *The African Abroad, or His Evolution in Western Civilization: Tracing His Development Under Caucasian Milieux,* Ferris confessed his faith in a liberal divinity who "speaks in not uncertain tones in the common sense and conscience of mankind . . . and who manifests himself in the laws of reason."[52]

An education in liberal institutions in the United States and abroad was decisive for Richard R. Wright, Jr. Born in 1878, he was educated in the liberal environs of the Universities of Pennsylvania, Chicago, Berlin, and Leipzig en route to becoming a bishop of the A.M.E. Church. He became a major proponent of evangelical liberalism and progressivism within the A.M.E. Church and the wider African-American religious community.[53]

Another A.M.E. bishop and proponent of both theological liberalism and progressive social activism within the African-American religious community was Reverdy Ransom.[54] Ransom's pilgrimage to an acknowledged posture of evangelical liberalism was probably not unlike that of the majority of his fellow white and black liberals. Born in 1861, he was educated at Congregational-affiliated Oberlin and the A.M.E. Church's Wilberforce University.[55] Even as a student at Wilberforce, which he entered in 1881, Ransom was aware that he held "heretical" theological beliefs. In his autobiographical reflections, he confessed:

> I could not then, as I cannot now, accept the Doctrine of the trinity as it was taught. Our teacher in theology . . . was so orthodox that to him the science of evolution was anathema. He repudiated the science of geology and held literally to the account of creation as set forth in the book of Genesis. My heretical views, which I tried not to disclose in the classroom, more than once involved me almost up to the point of suspension . . . . As I went forward in my studies, there were so many of the doctrines that I did not and could not accept, that I was assailed by doubts concerning my call . . . . But

> finally, the Bible itself, together with a wide range of reading and the knowledge that these doctrines were man-made, gave me both confidence and courage to obey and follow the inner voice.[56]

The pervasive influences of Darwinism, higher criticism, and related currents also made their way into the general population of the African-American community by way of other educational institutions, which African-Americans attended with greater frequency during this era. Many of these schools were affiliated with liberal denominations and staffed by men and women who were themselves products of liberal educational and ecclesiastical institutions. For example, the American Missionary Association (AMA), sponsored by Congregationalists, supplied funds and staff for schools that provided a significant proportion of black secondary and college-level education in the South.[57] Thus James McPherson points out that in the 1890s Atlanta University, an AMA-sponsored institution, included among its faculty "graduates of Harvard, Yale, Andover, Williams and Oberlin; [Moreover] President Horace Bumstead . . . had studied in Germany as well as at Yale and Andover."[58] This "heritage of liberal Christianity" in AMA schools has also been noted by Clifton H. Johnson.[59] While matriculation at such institutions did not ensure that alumni became liberals, it did ensure that many were at least exposed to the tenets and influences of theological liberalism.[60] Moreover, the influence of such institutions was magnified as their graduates often returned to historically black religious and educational institutions to pursue their ministerial and teaching careers.

Another important but overlooked conduit of liberal influences within both the African and diaspora African communities were the "colored" and international divisions of the Young Men's Christian Association (YMCA) under the leadership of black theological liberals such as Jesse E. Moorland.[61] The YMCA's religious and theological impact on a developing Pan-Africanist is noted in the biography of Ras Makonnen.[62] Born in Guyana (British Guiana), Makonnen traveled to the United States in 1927 to further his education.[63] The progressive "nonconformist" religious and social thought of the YMCA appealed to Makonnen, who became a "Y" secretary. He recalled that the "Y" also attracted the "new black intellectuals" trained in the new disciplines such as sociology. Many of them, he observed, "had been to white theological seminaries, and got away from the emotionalism of the Negro Baptists towards the reason of the Presbyterians. They were professionals and to them their work in the 'Y' was the same philosophy that underlay Christian socialism." The "Y," he noted, operated with a "new theology" that ensured that its concern "wasn't only religion" nor "provincial." In fact, "the Galilean was used as the example of the man who went beyond his own tribal background to assist his fellowmen, bringing men from their provincial outlooks to a broader view."[64] According to Makonnen, the YMCA "helped . . . to portray in a most dramatic manner the role of Christ in the modern world."[65]

Black religious journals such as the *A.M.E. Church Review,* the *A.M.E. Christian Recorder,* and the *National Baptist Magazine* also attest that the scientific and intellectual currents which gave rise to Protestant liberalism were filtering into the African-American and West African religious communities from a variety of sources and provoking a variety of responses.[66] The *A.M.E. Review,* for example, under the editorial direction of Benjamin T. Tanner (1884–1888) and his immediate successors, Levi J. Coppin (1888–1896), H. T. Kealing (1896–1912), and Reverdy Ransom (1912–1924), exposed its readers to the major tenets of liberalism and the controversies they provoked within their own and the wider religious community.[67] Neither the editors nor contributors of articles to the *Review* were disinterested spectators as they commented on most of the disputed theological and missiological issues of the era.

The numerous articles and editorials related to these issues illustrate the growing tensions between the defenders of orthodoxy and the proponents of liberalism in the A.M.E. Church and the wider African-American religious community. Within the A.M.E. Church, orthodox forces were led primarily by Tanner, Levi Coppin, and Jabez P. Campbell. The small cadre of liberally inclined clergy and laity were led by Theophilus Gould Steward and A. W. Upshaw.[68] While black conservatives invoked orthodox interpretations of Scripture and theology, Steward and the budding cadre of liberals embraced a cautious, critical, and at some points ambiguous appropriation of the tenets of theological liberalism. Tanner articulated the theological agenda for both groups as he noted in 1888 that "the time has come for the Negro and even all the colored races of the earth, to conduct a theology for themselves."[69] Primarily because of Tanner's intellectual leadership between 1884 and 1893, the A.M.E. Church fostered "a greater range of theological discussion than at any previous period in its history."[70]

One of the earliest defenses of black orthodoxy from the assaults of liberalism came from the pen of Bishop Jabez P. Campbell in an 1884 article entitled "A Scriptural View, or The Statement Concerning Paradise That Was Lost Regained." In this work Campbell, who enjoyed the reputation of a theological scholar within the A.M.E. Church, reasserted that Moses was the author of the Pentateuch and defended the literal accuracy of the Genesis account of creation and humanity's fall. He argued that the

> creation and the six periods of development in it are facts and not fancies of the human brain. Eden and the garden planted by the hand of God in it, is truth, not fiction. God, man, creation, Eden, the Garden of Eden, the tree

> of life, and the tree of the knowledge of good and evil, the man, the woman and the serpent are real entities, and not personified objects and things which have no real existence.[71]

A year later, James A. Handy presented a less dogmatic though no less orthodox refutation of Darwinism in an article entitled "The Mystery of Man." Drawing upon the supportive conclusions of an earlier generation of orthodox scientists, Handy affirmed that "geology, ethnology and the natural history of man bear ample testimony of the truth of the Mosaic statement as recorded in the book of Genesis."[72]

The equally controversial findings of the historical-critical method also occasioned heated discussion in the pages of the *Review*. In repudiation of liberal efforts to appropriate the new biblical insights, the defenders of orthodoxy affirmed scriptural authority and Divine Inspiration. In an 1888 article entitled "Biblical Criticism," James Theodore Holly, the first black Episcopal bishop of Haiti, rejected liberalism's "hypercriticism" as "a mere literary recreation, or intellectual speculation."[73] Tanner also denounced the "Higher Criticism" and "portrayed the German higher critics as descendants of the defeated skeptics of earlier ages."[74]

Also under debate were theological and missiological concerns such as the nature and meaning of Christian eschatology and soteriology. Even the issue of future probation, which was racking Congregationalism, found its advocates and detractors among the contributors to the *Review*.[75] Similar responses were evoked by the findings and conclusions of comparative religion. In an 1887 article entitled "Comparative Religion," George William Cook drew on the new discipline to expound on a wide range of world religions. Consistent with the liberal appropriation of the discipline, he concluded that "whatever diversity there may be in detail of religions, their ultimate purpose is the same—to worship God. It is a question of how, not of intentions. Sift the ancient systems and study the modern, and you find in them all the universal fact of reverence to God, the Father Almighty, Maker of heaven and earth."[76]

In 1887 Tanner wrote one of the most extensive apologies of Protestant orthodoxy published in the *Review*.[77] In an article entitled "The Origin of Man," he rejected the claims of the evolutionary theory and the historical-critical method while defending the divine authority of Scripture and the orthodox interpretation of humanity's origins. In response to what he viewed as the confident and expansive claims of "Mr. Darwin" and "Mr. Huxley," Tanner vigorously declared:

> [T]he grounds upon which they propose to erect so vast a superstructure will in the end prove to be so much quicksand. We have no idea that their present seeming solidity will be maintained all the way through. On the contrary, we have no doubt that the day will come when science itself will

openly confess that this structure now so reassuring will become a mere seam altogether too thin and uncertain to stand upon, much less to build. Wherefore this confidence of ours? The answer we make is: Wherefore this doubt of the world—the Bible-reading world we mean? Can evolution be accepted as true and the character of the Bible be maintained? We frankly answer: No.[78]

In response to contentions by the defenders of orthodoxy that the findings of the Darwinian thesis, the historical-critical method, and comparative religion were incompatible with Christianity, the proponents of black liberalism defended their appropriation of modern theories and attitudes as consistent with the essentials of the faith. In an article published in the *Review* in 1887 and entitled, "Heaven and the Divinity as Seen by the Poets," Charles A. Johnson drew on the writings of Theodore Munger to defend the compatibility of evolutionary theory with Scripture and the doctrine of immortality:

Evolution, in some of its teachings, may mislead some into the belief that an existence immortal is impossible, since the evolutionist theory of creation in some parts seems contradictory to the Bible and the utterances of the Divinity. Yet evolution and the [Christian] Faith mutually agree. Rev. T. T. Munger, in the *Century* of May, 1886, gives a thorough discussion of evolution and the Faith, and shows conclusively to an active mind that the Divinity does exist behind the evolutionist theory, and, therefore, there must be an Immortality . . . . "Evolution," says Mr. Munger, "not only perfects our conception of the Unity of God, but it strengthens the argument from design, by which His goodness is proved."[79]

Two years later the Reverend A. W. Upshaw invoked the writings of Lyman Abbott to defend the "New Theology" and its synthesis of "Reason and Revelation":

Among the most advanced thinkers of the present day a "New Theology" is gaining acceptance. It sacrifices nothing of dogma or orthodox theological formulae, but claims to interpret them in greater harmony with the nature and character of God. Dr. Lyman Abbott says, in a recent article, where he makes a lucid and able statement of the "New Theology": "It believes that it is necessary to understand the writers in order to understand their writings. It subjects the Bible to the same kind of literary investigation to which it would subject any other literary collection. It expects a progressive revelation from Moses to John and looks for a higher conception of God and of redemption in Paul's Epistles than in the Levetical code . . . . We must expect a clearer revelation of God in the New Testament than in the Old—a better understanding of His will and purpose in John and Paul than in Moses or David—above all, we shall be very sure that, whatever the voice of God seemed to say to the old Hebrews, God can never contradict himself, and it is far more probable that they misapprehended his

> meaning than that the spiritual consciousness of the Christian Church, quickened into life by this very book, itself can be wholly wrong."

Johnson concluded with the assertion that "These ideas are based upon what must be accepted as the true inspiration as set forth by the New Theology against the inspiration of diction of the Old School."[80]

The responses of both black liberals and conservatives to the new scientific, academic, and intellectual currents of the era were rooted in racial as well as religious concerns. Liberals optimistically believed that these currents offered the most constructive foundation for a theology, pedagogy, and missiology that would meet the needs of the race as it entered the corridors of modernity. Meanwhile, defenders of orthodoxy discerned a linkage between these developments and the resurgence of racism and imperialism.[81]

Tanner feared that the Darwinian theory and the new biblical criticism as employed in the liberal assault upon Scripture and traditional Christianity would be employed to deny the humanity and rights of the black race. In works such as *The Negro's Origin* and *The Descent of the Negro* (1898), he vigorously defended the scriptural account of the race's humanity and origins.[82] Thus, he concluded the latter work with the assertion:

> The Negro is a man. He is of Adam. He is of Noah. The Negro is a brother, and will be until science can demonstrate the Bible is no more than a fable—that Moses made mistakes, and that the divine Son of God with men hitherto supposed to be inspired, endorsed them.[83]

Black defenders of orthodoxy also observed that despite the New Theology's ethical commitments, many of its white adherents failed to confront the racism and imperialism that paralleled its rise to influence.[84] Moreover, both racism and imperialism seemed to find not only acceptance but also spokespersons among the followers of the New Theology. Alfred Moss observed that "though they produced a number of creative theological reconceptualizations, and were, at times, perceptive and courageous in tackling some sources of social injustice, these religious liberals were unable to transcend the orthodox racism of the day."[85]

Representative of the racial attitudes that the tenets of liberalism could evoke both in the United States and in the mission arena was the Congregationalist minister, Josiah Strong. Although an adherent of the New Theology and a leader in the development of the social gospel, Strong was also an advocate of the era's increasingly less benign racialist and imperialistic attitudes. In works such as *Our Country: Its Possible Future and Its Present Crisis* (1886), *The New Era, or The Coming Kingdom* (1893), and *Expansion Under New World Conditions* (1900), he "advanced his message of an inevitable worldwide Christendom under the stewardship of the Anglo-Saxon race and civilization."[86] Convinced that the Anglo-Saxon race was "destined to dispossess many weaker races, assimilate others and mold the remainder, until . . . it has Anglo-Saxonized mankind," Strong felt that he could discern "the final competition of the races," for which the Anglo-Saxon was being tutored:

> Then this race of unequal energy . . . the representative, let us hope, of the largest liberty, the purest Christianity, the highest civilization—having developed peculiarly aggressive traits calculated to impress its institutions upon mankind, will move down upon Mexico, down upon Central and South America, out upon the islands of the sea, over upon Africa and beyond. And can anyone doubt that the result of this competition of races will be the "survival of the fittest?"[87]

That black proponents of theological liberalism were neither slavish imitators of their white colleagues nor oblivious to the glaring deficiencies of the New Theology is evident in the theological writings of Theophilus Gould Steward. Steward produced a number of articles and books that illustrate both his critical appropriation of the tenets of theological liberalism and his explicit rejection of racism and imperialism advocated by fellow liberals such as Strong.[88]

Steward, one of the increasing number of blacks attending predominantly white seminaries during this era of theological ferment, studied at Protestant Episcopal Divinity School in Philadelphia from 1877 to 1880. Of his theological studies, he recalled, "Here many of my erroneous notions were corrected. I found the professors . . . ripe in scholarship, and profoundly Christian."[89] His graduation in 1880 at the head of his class evoked the following praise from the school's dean:

> In the senior class, Mr. Steward, a minister of the African Methodist Episcopal Church, who now completes his full three years' course with us has particularly distinguished himself. His essays are of the very highest order, both for style and for philosophical and theological accuracy . . . . I have had few men under my instruction, in any classes, who have so thoroughly mastered the subjects and system of Christian theology as Mr. Steward has.[90]

Steward brought his theological training to bear on the issues of the era. Though he had commented earlier on the "very able scientific lectures" of Thomas Huxley, his sustained reflections on the evolutionary thesis and its impact on the authority and "credibility" of Scripture were presented in *Genesis Re-read, or The Latest Conclusions of Physical Science, Viewed in Their Relation to the Mosaic Record*.[91] His cautious appropriation of the perspective and central tenets of evangelical liberalism is apparent throughout this work. His apologetic intent was confessed in its preface:

> Without pronouncing finally upon the subject of evolution, the writer of this book believes that the Mosaic record, while surely teaching a direct creation, also allows for orderly development and hence does not regard the evidence of evolution as in any way affecting the credibility of the Bible.

Citing as corroborating evidence the works and words of James McCosh, president of Princeton University and one of the earliest proponents of the compatibility of the evolutionary thesis and Christianity, Steward concluded:

> Evolution has been examined, its depths have been sounded, and no response has come forth inconsistent with the declaration that in the beginning God created the heavens and the earth. All the talk about "physiological units," "molecular motion," "natural selection," is so manifestly talk about what is secondary, that it of necessity implies an originating power—a living force, a divine and evolutionary cause.[92]

Despite his adherence to the perspective and tenets of theological liberalism, Steward was explicit in his rejection of both racism and imperialism. His most significant work in this regard was the eschatologically focused *The End of the World; or Clearing the Way for the Fullness of the Gentiles*.[93] His vision of "The New Era" and "the coming kingdom" was radically different from that of Strong. It marked not the triumph of Anglo-Saxonism and Anglo-Saxonized Christianity envisioned by Strong, but rather God's judgment upon Anglo-Saxons for having undermined Christianity's quintessential universalism by having imprisoned it within a racial tribalism that made it in effect "a white man's religion." With explicit rejection of Strong's triumphant Anglo-Saxonism, Steward insisted, "It is not Saxonism that is to become universal, but Christism . . . Saxonism must utterly and signally fail, in order that Christ may be all in all."[94]

In reference to Steward's contribution to the theological ferment within the A.M.E. church during this era, David Wills concluded:

> Steward not only explored a more liberal approach to theology, but also employed that refashioned theology to articulate a new sense of black destiny. . . . [His] work was the primary indication during these years of the potential importance for the [A.M.E.] church's ongoing task of cultural formation of an emerging theological elite able to relate theological reflection and social criticism.[95]

As a subscriber to the *Church Review,* Faduma was aware of the theological ferment within the A.M.E. Church and the wider American religious community. Moreover, his "Thoughts for the Times" article calling for the development of a progressive, race-conscious pedagogy and missiology verifies that as early as 1888 he had joined the debate concerning the theological, pedagogical, and social implications of the new scientific and intellectual currents.[96]

Documentation which might attest to the exact nature of Faduma's relationship with the A.M.E. Church during this period is unavailable. Langley contends that prior to his departure for the United States, Faduma had become a member of the A.M.E. Church presumably though its Freetown mission under the leadership of Reverend John R. Frederick.[97] However, Faduma makes no mention of formal membership in either his autobiographical sketches or later writings pertaining to the A.M.E. Church.[98] Nevertheless, his itinerary upon arrival in the United States, which included a stay in Philadelphia where the headquarters of the Church was located, subsequent employment at an A.M.E. school, and attendance at the Church's annual convention, suggests that he had either established some type of formal affiliation with the A.M.E. Church or was contemplating such affiliation. Such a relationship might have been mutually beneficial. It would have provided the A.M.E. Church with evidence of the success of its new mission in Sierra Leone. It would have provided Faduma with membership in a church that appeared, at least from a distance, to epitomize the tenets of racial pride, ecclesiastical independence, and progressivism that he held dear.[99]

A more tangible benefit of Faduma's relationship with the A.M.E. Church was his employment at Kittrell Normal Institute. This A.M.E. institution, located thirty-seven miles north of Raleigh, North Carolina, was founded in 1886 as an institute "for training teachers and making skilled workmen." It advertised itself as offering "good discipline and careful teachers" as well as "special inducements to young ladies and gentlemen who wished to fit themselves for life's work."[100]

Faduma's employment at Kittrell afforded him his first opportunity for prolonged interaction with African-American students and teachers. In the spring of 1891 Faduma, by then serving as assistant principal at Kittrell, employed the pages of the *Christian Recorder* to report on the institution and his experiences there. While lauding the school as "second to none of its kind in the State, both from an intellectual and moral standpoint," his inherent evangelical Pan-Africanism and his role as a conduit of that sentiment to the African-American community were reflected in his observation that Kittrell's staff was of such "ability and Christian moral character" as to induce his wish that they might "be transferred to Africa, their ancestral home."[101]

Despite the congenial relationship that Faduma had early on shared with the A.M.E. Church, he apparently became increasingly disillusioned with it in particular and the African-American church in general.[102] Perhaps his perception of the A.M.E. Church as a progressive institution compatible with his own theological and ideological sentiments waned somewhat as he became a closer observer of its internal dynamics. His evolving liberalism may also have been a source of discomfort amid increased conflict between defenders of orthodoxy and proponents of liberalism within the A.M.E. Church.[103]

Faduma's spiritual and theological restlessness appears to date at least from his British sojourn. This restlessness was evident in a poem submitted to the *Review* from Kittrell in the spring of 1891. Entitled "Where Is Virtue?", the poem was an autobiographical account of his quest to find spiritual and ethical certainty amid the worldliness, materialism, and religious hypocrisy of the Gilded Age. It suggests that for Faduma the necessary prescription was not to be found amid the relics of institutional orthodoxy or sectarianism.[104]

No doubt, Faduma's spiritual and ecclesiastical restlessness were factors in his subsequent decision to enroll in Yale Divinity School, where he began preparation for the Congregational ministry. However, a more significant clue to his vocational decision and institutional preference is provided by Faduma in an article entitled, "Thoughts for the Times, or The New Theology."[105] Published in the A.M.E. *Review* before his arrival in the United States, the article placed Faduma firmly in the midst of the theological controversy within the A.M.E. Church and the wider American religious community over the tenets of the New Theology. It was one of the first sustained assessments of the New Theology by an African and was recognized as such by a review originally published in the *Boston Herald* and subsequently reported in the *Christian Recorder:*

> A curiosity is a paper by a native African, Orishatukeh Faduma, on "Thoughts for the Times," by which he means the new theology. This is the first time that a critic of the new theology has turned up from the dark continent, and is a curious and significant paper. When a native can write like this on subjects in which he has been obliged to educate himself, it means that we are to say nothing more against the intelligence of the African race.[106]

While correct in noting the historical significance of Faduma's efforts, the reviewer's condescension disclosed his failure to appreciate and understand the sophistication and depth of Faduma's theological agenda. Analysis of Faduma's critique of certain elements of the New Theology did not, as implied by the reviewer, entail his rejection of it. Rather, his comments on the controversial issues of evolution, the historical-critical method, comparative religion, missions, the historical development of Christianity, and his insistence upon the ethical and practical dimensions of Christianity suggest that his theological orientation lay among the ranks of evangelical liberals. The article is also indicative of the manner in which black liberals selectively critiqued and appropriated the tenets of liberalism to further their own racial and religious agendas. Faduma's efforts in this regard placed him at the forefront of the small cadre of persons of African descent who acted as mediators of the new theological synthesis to the wider African and diaspora African communities.

Consistent with efforts by evangelical liberals to "seek rapprochement with science," Faduma opened his article on the New Theology by identifying theology as "the science of religion," which "like other sciences [is] progressive," as evidenced by the development of its "new Truths" from the elaboration and transformation of "old ones."[107] Although conservatives generally disregarded the importance of this developmental process and therefore regarded "science" as "antagonistic to religion," Faduma argued that "true science" and "true religion" could never be in opposition:

> The seeming conflict between them is a conflict between the old theology and the new—a conflict between the old systems of thought and the new. The Christian world of the nineteenth century is having a fuller conception of God and humanity, as well as of the physical world, than it did in past centuries. If Knowledge is progressive—as indeed it is—our ideas which are its bases admit of progression, be they ideas about the Creator or His creatures.

Faduma warned that "The Church gains not a whit by placing herself in direct conflict with science" because "Science is not per se an enemy of religion." Moreover, he claimed that the Bible itself was "the most scientific book on earth," a fact little realized "because it does not indulge in scientific technicalities."

At the root of the theological conflict between liberals and the conservatives, Faduma discerned a faulty understanding of the progressive nature of Christianity and theology:

> The Great Teacher says, "I come not to destroy, but to fulfill." To the conservative mind this fulfilling of the old often appears as an introduction of a new element that is opposed to the former, and thus he ignorantly and needlessly places himself in the way sword in hand to defend the so-called old paths. In reality the new is the old fulfilled. It is the old path reconstructed, cleaned out and widened. He who refuses to acknowledge theology as thus progressive naturally becomes an opponent to any new discovery of Christian thought and activity, and allows no more light than what he himself saw when first he caught a glimpse of its rays . . . . If the physicist by continual study and investigation can discover new facts about matter, why may not the seeker after Divine truth, aided and guarded by the Holy Spirit, be gratified with a fuller knowledge of the Divine Will and a better knowledge and appreciation of His love?

On the related dispute over the use of higher criticism in the study and interpretation of Scripture, Faduma pointed out that "Interpretation of Scriptural truths once considered perfect and final, will often in our

Christian and intellectual progress be found out to be partial." He insisted, however, that the findings of the new biblical scholarship should not be allowed to distract from the deeper significance and meaning of Scripture:

> It is of small account that we have mastered all the schools of New Testament criticism, that we can place every incident in its right setting, and give the true interpretation of every text: our real lesson is what we find at the heart of the Gospel of Christ, and is recorded for us in the imagery of the Baptism, the Temptation, the Transfiguration and the Cross, telling how that living touch with the Eternal made the Man of Nazareth a messenger to all souls from the Most High, speaking as Son of Man to all the sons of Men.

Faduma was keenly aware of the New Theology's emphasis on the historical development of Christianity and the missiological implications of its incorporation of the findings of comparative religion. In reference to the latter, he quoted from an article entitled "Our New Attitude Toward the World Religions," published in the June 1890 issue of the *Unitarian Review*.[108] He found additional support for the New Theology's emphasis on the historical development of Christianity and its universal adaptability in an article published in the *Homiletic Review* that referred to a lecture by Professor Auguste Sabatier, one of the major formulators of a "thoroughly liberalized Protestantism," on "The Inmost Life of Dogmas and the Power of Evolution."[109] Sabatier, explained Faduma, "shows that dogmas are not dead, but that they live and grow." Moreover, "Christianity itself, he claims, has followed the law of adaptation. It was Hebrew in Palestine; in passing into the Hellenic world it received a Greco-Roman coloring."[110]

In Sabatier's contentions, and in the New Theology in general, Faduma found theological and historical rooting for a missiology that supported the adaptation of Christianity to meet the racial and cultural idiosyncrasies of non-European peoples. It also provided theoretical and theological support for the reforms demanded in the West African matrix by Blyden, Henry Venn, and the cultural reform movement.[111] Thus from a position firmly rooted in theological liberalism, Faduma could echo Blyden in asserting:

> The fundamental principles of Christianity will ever remain the same, while in their application to meet the necessities of the human race, adaptation is a desideratum. This is as fair as it is scientific. Upon the Hebrew mind, there is and ought to be a Hebrew coloring; upon the Negro mind, a Negro coloring; upon the European mind, a European coloring."[112]

The missiological implications of this position became foundational to Faduma's subsequent efforts to develop a mission theory and policy sensitive to the ethnic, racial, and cultural propensities of non-European peoples and consistent with his own developing ideology of evangelical Pan-Africanism.[113]

Although insistent that the new theoretical and scientific advances were not to be ignored, Faduma nevertheless argued that the New Theology must not be consumed with theory at the expense of practical application.[114] With his insistence that praxis was the decisive test of the New Theology, Faduma embraced the fundamental tenets of the "ethical-social" wing of evangelical liberalism, which included social gospel leaders such as Washington Gladden and Walter Rauschenbusch. Their "primary interest was in relating the Christian message to the ethical and social needs of men in the modern world." Religion and theology was for them "primarily a practical concern . . . centered in the moral life."[115] They shared Faduma's contention that

> The substance of Christ's teaching is "Love to God and man"; "on these two commandments hang all the law and the prophets." If the Fatherhood of God and the brotherhood of man are not practically demonstrated in our every-day life, in our social, political and religious environments, our religion is a farce, our metaphysical speculations on the attributes of the Deity a nonsense, and ourselves a huge deception of the name Christian.[116]

Faduma also shared with fellow evangelical liberals the optimistic and idealistic belief that the New Theology heralded the advent of the "kingdom of God" on earth. Even from a distance, he claimed to discern evidence of this development in America:

> Christian America of today compared with what it was a hundred years ago is manifesting signs of progress. The Fatherhood of God and the brotherhood of man, in spite of political hate and ecclesiastical pride, are being better, though slowly understood, because her conceptions of God are being elevated and the teachings of His words are being better grasped . . . .

It was a combination of optimism, idealism, and naiveté that led Faduma to affirm, in spite of the era's increasing racism and imperialism, that the New Theology was "destined to uproot American prejudice against the Negro, elevate and purify the State, the Church, conquer Anglo-Saxon haughtiness, and make all nations confess that 'God is no respecter of persons.' "[117] Thus, unlike Tanner and other black conservatives who were fearful of the racial as well as the religious implications of the new sciences and theology, Faduma readily, though critically, appropriated them and proclaimed that they exposed the old scientific and theological props of racism and inferiority as "pseudo-science" and "pseudo-theology."[118]

He concluded this historic article with a ringing endorsement of the New Theology as the needed prescription for the world's ills:

> Without this New Theology our multiplication of churches at home and foreign lands serves only as fuel for the wrath of God . . . . What the world needs today, I repeat and emphasize, is a New Theology, a new creation, a new method of life, a new order of thought . . . . It is needed in the schoolroom . . . in the State and society, where the imbibed principles should become practical realities; and the Church, the visible representative and living exponent of truth. When these separate departments shall be infused with this new truth and new life . . . the world will see what it has not yet been privileged to see—a new North and a new South, a new spiritual Church and a new America in a spiritually new world—and men shall behold in living reality what the divine John saw in his apocalyptic vision—"A new heaven and a new earth."[119]

Faduma's enrollment in Yale Divinity School and his decision to prepare for the Congregational ministry were fully consistent with the convictions expressed in his "Thoughts for the Times" articles. Not only was Congregationalism fast becoming "the most fertile soil for liberalism," but the predominately Congregationalist Divinity School and its immediate environs, with Theodore Munger and Newman Smyth pastoring neighboring churches on the New Haven Green, were primary breeding grounds of the New Theology.[120]

As a student at the Divinity School from 1891 to 1894, Faduma studied under scholars who labored constructively and effectively to reconcile the old faith and the new scholarship.[121] Among his professors were George E. Day, George Park Fisher, Samuel Harris, Lewis O. Brastow, George B. Stevens, Edward L. Curtis, and Frank Chamberlain Porter. They all sought to clarify the issues and challenges presented to their respective disciplines by the new scientific and intellectual currents.[122] The work of Franklin C. Porter, holder of the Winkley Chair of Biblical Theology and "the very epitome of the prevailing liberalism," was of particular importance. He and the other professors named above were specifically referred to by Faduma fifty years after his graduation as having "left behind them and in my life memories which are indelible."[123]

Sharing Faduma's immersion in the liberal climate of Yale and New Haven was a small group of African-American students, which included Hugh Henry Proctor, Bernard Tyrell, and Thomas Nelson Baker.[124] Faduma joined them in a quartet that sang "Negro melodies" in churches throughout New England and performed on at least one occasion at the Divinity School commencement exercises.[125]

Perhaps most prominent among Faduma's African-American classmates was the Tennessee-born and Fisk-educated Hugh Henry Proctor.[126]

Proctor recalled that the Divinity School provided a congenial environment for students of color: "although there were many students from the South, one's color counted nothing against one, and nothing in one's favor."[127] The professors of his day, he noted, were "Giants." His autobiography contained recollections of

> Professor Harris who had written a number of books on the self-revelation of God . . . . Professor George B. Stevens, an authority on the New Testament, and a man of great humanity. Professor Curtis [who] drilled us in the roots of Hebrew, and gave us insight into the genius of the Hebrew mind. Professor Frank Porter [who] spoke authoritatively on the Old Testament. President Dwight who lectured on John. Dr. Day who was the dean at the time . . .[and] Professor George Fisher [who] lectured from his own books in church history.[128]

Moreover, Proctor recalled that at Battell Chapel and local churches "presided over by Munger and Smyth . . . Phillips, Twitchel [Twichell], Luckey, and Mutch," students had the opportunity to hear some of the "ablest preachers of the country."[129]

Proctor also documented the theological and pedagogical transition taking place at the Divinity School during their enrollment:

> Before going to Yale I had heard much of the Yale theology but when I got there I could find no particular brand. A new type of teaching had come into vogue. The professor did not try to put over any particular theory. It was the endeavor to make the men think out things for themselves and to come to their own conclusions. In the classroom there was the freest opportunity for discussion. On graduation day we were told by one of the professors in the graduating address: "Young men, we have taught you nothing; we have showed you where the ore is. Go, dig for yourselves."[130]

For Proctor, Faduma, and a number of their classmates such as Edward Scribner Ames, the ore mined would be of liberal grade and their tools the methodologies and insights of comparative religion, biblical criticism, philosophy of religion, and sociology.[131]

During Faduma's and Proctor's years at Yale, the faculty added a number of courses to the traditional curriculum. These courses reflected the impact that the new scientific and academic currents were having within seminaries throughout the nation.[132] In their first year a course in "Social Ethics" was added which examined the relations of classes in society, socialism, communism, and the labor question.[133] In the Fall of 1892 a course on "The Religious and Theological Conditions in Germany" was offered "by Dr. Stuckenberg, pastor of the American Church in Germany."[134] Its purpose was to inform students of current theological trends in Germany.[135] And of particular emphasis were the writings and thought of two of the foremost figures of German liberalism—

Albrecht Ritschl and Adolf von Harnack.[136] Stuckenberg's theological orientation was apparent as he informed students that

> the Germans above others, have cultivated the historic sense. They have applied the genetic method to the study of theology, laying stress upon primitive Christianity. They seek to make theology a part of that organism of thought which embraces all sciences. Seeking thus to go back to beginnings and to justify theology before other sciences, new paths have been entered, new positions taken.[137]

Although Yale Divinity School did not establish a chair of missions until 1906, neither faculty nor students were impervious to the mission fervor of this era.[138] George E. Day, Faduma's instructor in Greek and Hebrew, was actively laying the foundations for a chair in missions with his collection of the volumes which eventually formed the core of the Day Mission Library.[139] Of particular importance for Faduma was the introduction into the curriculum of courses in missions in both 1891 and 1892. The 1892 course, entitled "Modern Missions in the East," was taught by the Congregationalist missionary and liberal mission theorist, Edward A. Lawrence.[140] Its goal was to foster "more intelligent ideas on missions" among "the men of the seminary."[141] Faduma's mature missiology would draw heavily on the progressive missiological principles emphasized by Lawrence.[142]

Faduma himself noted both the missionary temper of the era and the controversial changes that such courses and the disciplines associated with them were fostering in the mission arena. He observed in 1895:

> [We] are now living in an age of intense missionary activity. . . . Missionary work is no longer tentative. It has become a serious study, a science for all. Throughout the larger universities of the land are to be found volunteer bands, and chairs on the philosophy of religion and comparative religion, besides annual lectures on missions from returned missionaries. Men and women are not expected to rush heedlessly into the foreign field; they are giving an intelligent study to their prospective fields of labor.[143]

The relationship between Congregationalism, the New Theology, and liberal missiology had not gone unnoticed by Faduma. During his period of study at Yale, the decisive battle within Congregationalism over the missionary implications of the New Theology was taking place.[144] In 1893 the struggle ended in victory for the forces of liberalism when the American Board was reconstituted to "become a denominational agency and therefore came to reflect the more liberal opinions that had gained ascendancy in the denomination."[145] Consequently the Congregational mission enterprise, and eventually those of other American denominations, would be more open to the new insights afforded by the currents of the modern era.[146] The challenge and dilemma that these insights subsequently entailed for the proponents of a liberalized mission enterprise led William R. Hutchison to characterize their missiological agenda as "The Liberal Search for An Exportable Christianity." He argued that liberals

> articulated a program—or at least a coherent and connected set of attitudes—that was prophetic of twentieth-century changes in mission theology throughout the mainline Protestant denominations. The program for which they contended entailed the search for a quintessential Christianity suitable for export; the conversion of the idea of Christian finality into an almost purely ethical conception; a professed devotion to the ideal of establishing native churches free of Western control; a questioning of the right of Western Christendom to lecture the rest of the world; and a steady assertion that it was the old theology, not the new, that threatened to "cut the nerve of missions."[147]

The fact that liberalized Congregational missiology was far from free of the less savory attitudes and policies of its orthodox predecessor is vividly apparent in the racial and cultural chauvinism manifest in the works of Josiah Strong.[148] However, the mission writings of George A. Gordon, while reflecting "traces of the traditional condescension toward non-Christian people," also illuminated the radically altered perceptions, policies, and ideals that theological liberals could bring to bear upon the mission enterprise.[149] Gordon, who was born in Scotland and educated at Bangor Theological Seminary and Harvard University, explicitly rejected the racial and religious chauvinism advanced by both conservatives and fellow liberals such as Josiah Strong.[150]

As early as 1887, Gordon labeled the theology and missiology of conservatives "a libel upon Christian ethics and a stupendous insult to the church of Christ."[151] The mission enterprise, he insisted, could no longer be rooted in the theology and scholarship of traditional evangelical Protestantism.[152] Gordon warned:

> The missionary enterprise has transcended the conception in which it originated: it has led the church that inaugurated it into a new world; it has been fruitful of ideas and feelings beyond all expectation; and today is largely a stupendous pedestal in the air, waiting for the new conception of the mission of God in Christ to be put under it as adequate and everlasting support.[153]

It was manifest to Gordon that the "new conception" of the mission enterprise was to find its support and foundation in liberal theology. In a sermon delivered in 1895 before the newly reconstructed and liberalized American Board, he presented his vision of the new missiology and the theological, methodological, and scriptural norms that undergirded and shaped it.[154] Drawing upon his awareness of the historical development of Christianity and his related belief that Christianity could and should be stripped of its accumulated cultural and ethnic baggage, Gordon rejected the cultural imperialism and racism of both Strong and the traditionalists. In language and tones reminiscent of both Blyden and Henry Venn, he asserted:

> We prize our idea of the gospel, but we must never make the mistake of supposing that our ideas are the gospel . . . . We are not under any obligation to export our entire body of belief. There is no particular call for our church polity, our special theology, or the traditions of our Christian life. These are not wanted; if sent they would prove unsuitable. . . . All attempts to export systems of theology must fail. They will be tolerated by no people having in them a spark of original genius. Contrasted previous civilizations and the total diverse character of inheritance and environment will forever make impossible the domination of one division of humanity by the rigidly formulated mind of another.[155]

Faduma was not oblivious to the potential and promise that liberal missiology held for the African mission arena. He would draw upon it as he attempted to reconcile theological liberalism with an emerging Pan-African consciousness and ideology.[156]

The academic and intellectual skills that Faduma demonstrated as a student in Sierra Leone and England were also evident at Yale. His academic success was noted by Yale's faculty and his classmates. In a recollection that alluded to the era's resurgent pseudo-scientific racism, Hugh Henry Proctor noted with pride: "[A]lthough his [Faduma's] parents were natives taken right from the bush, he was one of the brightest men in the class of over thirty coming from the picked universities of the world. He upset all the theories of the phrenologists and ethnologists."[157]

Faduma's efforts to appropriate the potentially rich harvest of liberal theology and scholarship were reflected in a number of articles published in the *A.M.E. Church Review* during his matriculation at Yale.[158] His familiarity with the new methods of biblical scholarship was displayed in an exegetical work published in 1894.[159] In this article, entitled the "Pastoral Epistles," he joined the debate among biblical scholars such as Alford, Lightfoot, Schaff, Neander, Bauer, Eichorn, Holtsmann, Pfleiderer, and Renan regarding the "authenticity" and purpose of the "pastoral epistles."[160]

Faduma was also especially interested in the missionary methods and tactics reflected in the pastoral epistles. Thus, he informed his readers that as "the missionary epistles of Paul" they were "valuable to Christendom on account of the strictly missionary character of their contents."[161] In a later work, he explained that they presented the historical and scriptural brief by which the "controversy" was settled "once for all whether Christianity was to be a racial or a universal religion."[162]

Faduma's acceptance and appropriation of the theory of evolution in the formation of his progressive Pan-African missiology was also apparent during this era.[163] In confronting the hotly debated issue of evolution's compatibility with the scriptural account of creation, Faduma, consistent with his liberal evangelical orientation, affirmed the scriptural legitimacy of the evolutionary thesis.[164] In one of his most extensive discussions of this issue, Faduma explained with characteristic finesse:

> The writer of Genesis chapter 1 gave a pictorial representation of the Creation, including man, ending with a mechanical reproduction of Eve from man's ribs after God had put him into a deep sleep. But chapter 1 had already pointed out, in spite of the human language used, that creation, including man, was not mechanical but out of divine fiat, and evolutional. It is therefore left to the thinking student to judge between the evolutional process in chapter 1 and the mechanical in chapter 2 verses 7, 21, 23. The account in chapter 1 has appealed to my reason as the orderly process of creation.[165]

Faduma's similar efforts to appropriate the teachings and tenets of comparative religion were also illustrated. Two of his earliest works in this regard, published under the titles "Africa or the Dark Continent" and "Religious Beliefs and Worship of the Yorubas in West Africa," reflect the first of his numerous attempts to apply the findings of comparative religion in analysis and defense of his ancestral heritage.[166]

Faduma's labors to appropriate liberal scholarship were given additional impetus upon his graduation from the Divinity School in 1894 with "Honors" and a $400 scholarship, which enabled him to continue graduate studies at Yale University for an additional year. He spent the year studying Semitic languages and the philosophy of religion.[167] The latter was of growing importance in liberal missiology and would contribute to Faduma's efforts to forge a viable Pan-African missiology.[168]

An article published in 1896, entitled "Materials for the Study of the World Religions," illustrated his commitment to and thorough grounding in the philosophy and comparative study of religion.[169] After arguing that awareness of the Divine is basic to all humanity ("Man is so constituted that it would be necessary to invent a God if he were deprived of one") Faduma drew on both disciplines to defend the legitimacy of his ancestral religion:

> There is reality underlying all beliefs in a deity. Jupiter or Zeus is more than the sky, it represents a power behind the sky. Neptunus or Poseidon is more than a personification of water, it represents the power which imparts physical life. The Oludumare, Orisha, or Ifa of the Yorubas, and the Unkulunkula of the Zulus are not mere names or phantoms, they are gross representations of a blurred conception of a real God.

He argued:

> If you deny reality as underlying the conception of God in these ethnic religions, you are forced to deny the same of all religions, and in doing so you deprive them all of God. If the primary conception of God is a poetical figure to the pagan, it must be so to the Christian . . . . The idea of God, the religious sense, the moral sentiment are innate in man. They are not fictions of the mind, but grow with man's growth, and assume various forms according to his culture and development.

Reflective of his unwavering commitment to Christianity and typical of the way that evangelical liberals appropriated both disciplines, Faduma concluded:

> The Christian idea takes up all that is best in the ethnic and the revealed religions of the world. It is the progressive development of the ideas of God in all ages, and the latest and fullest revelation of God to man through Christ. It is essentially the religion of love.[170]

Faduma's passing of a rigorous ordination examination and subsequent ordination to the Congregational ministry in May, 1895 were further proof of his successful appropriation of the tenets and scholarship of evangelical liberalism.[171] Thirty years after the event, Faduma recalled a four-hour oral examination "before a Council of Congregational ministers, men of God, versed in theology, writers some of them on great themes in Ethics, Philosophy, and Religion."[172] Although unable to agree with them in all respects as to his understanding of Christianity and Scripture, he nevertheless gave "satisfactory reasons" and "was accepted as a fit candidate for the Congregational ministry."[173] Of his theological posture at the time, Faduma recalled, in a statement that reflected the broad-based and eclectic stance characteristic of evangelical liberalism, that he was "in some respects an Arminian, in other respects a Calvinist, and a Puritan in theology."[174] Faduma's liberal theological inclinations were also illustrated in his reply to a complex question asked him by the examination council:

> I shall never forget one question which was orally put to me, "Do you believe in prayer? Do you believe God answers prayer, and all prayers?" This three-fold question, I answered separately. The first two affirmatively, the last negatively. But asked a distinguished questioner "does not your negative answer contradict Christ who said, 'If ye shall ask anything in my name, I will do it.'" (John 14:14 and John 16:18); I replied anything and whatsoever are limited by the phrase "in my name," which means in accordance with my moral character. So that if I should ask God to do what is not right He will not do it. Some of the prayers of David are not consistent with what I understand God's character to be. He believed God would answer all he asked for in the destruction of his enemies but I do not.

However, Faduma disagreed with the suggestion that such prayers be eliminated from the Bible. Consistent with the position taken by most evangelical liberals, he insisted that they "remain as showing the beginning or infancy of religious thought in Judaic religion as compared with its development in Christianity. The mistakes of David are recorded, not for our imitation but for correction and instruction in right living."[175]

By 1895 Faduma had completed his studies at Yale. Yearning to return to Africa to apply his liberal missiology, he submitted an application to the newly reconstituted American Board. Ironically, the Board, citing financial constraints, was unable to provide Faduma, undoubtedly one of the best prepared of its foreign missionary candidates, with an appointment.[176] Thwarted in his efforts to obtain a missionary appointment to serve among his brethren in his ancestral home, Faduma made the fateful decision to cast his lot with the American Missionary Association and its missionary and educational efforts in the American South. He became in effect an African missionary to rural-based African-Americans.

Notes

1. Aaron Ignatius Abell, *The Urban Impact on American Protestantism 1865–1900* (Cambridge: Harvard University Press, 1943); David M. Reimers, *White Protestantism and the Negro* (New York: Oxford University Press, 1965) and Henry F. May, *The Protestant Churches and Industrial America* (New York: Harper & Row, 1949).
2. Bernard M. G. Reardon, ed., *Liberal Protestantism* (Stanford: Stanford University Press, 1968), pp. 9–65.
3. Bert James Loewenberg, "Darwinism Comes to America, 1859–1900," *Mississippi Valley Historical Review* 28 (Dec. 1941): 339–368, and Ferenc Morton Szasz, *The Divided Mind of Protestant America, 1880–1930* (University, Ala.: University of Alabama Press, 1982), pp. 1–41.
4. Francis P. Weisenburger, *Ordeal of Faith: The Crisis of Church-Going America, 1865–1900* (New York: Philosophical Library, 1959); Paul A. Carter, *The Spiritual Crisis of the Gilded Age* (De Kalb: Northern Illinois University Press, 1971); Arthur M. Schlesinger, Sr., "A Critical Period in American Religion, 1875–1900," in *Religion in American History: Interpretive Essays,* ed. John M. Mulder and John F. Wilson, (Englewood Cliffs, N.J.: Prentice-Hall, Inc., 1978), pp. 302–317.
5. Schlesinger, "A Critical Period," pp. 302–303.
6. Lloyd J. Averill, *American Theology in the Liberal Tradition*

(Philadelphia: Westminster Press, 1967), pp. 30, 34, 49–54; William R. Hutchison, *The Modernist Impulse in American Protestantism* (Cambridge: Harvard University Press, 1976), pp. 1–110.

7. Harry Emerson Fosdick, *The Living of These Days* (New York: Harper & Brothers, 1955), p. vii. H. Shelton Smith notes that these formulators of the new theological synthesis "took seriously (though not uncritically) the Darwinian theory of evolution, and they endeavored to harmonize their theological conceptions with that theory as fully as possible consistent with maintaining the essential elements of the Christian faith." H. Shelton Smith, *Changing Conceptions of Original Sin: A Study in American Theology Since 1750* (New York: Charles Scribner's Sons, 1955), pp. 164–166.
8. Smith, pp. 168–171; Newman Smyth, *Old Faiths in New Light* (New York: Charles Scribner's Sons, 1879).
9. Smith, pp. 166–168; Hutchison, *Modernist Impulse,* pp. 95–99; Theodore T. Munger, *The Freedom of Faith* (Boston: Houghton, Mifflin and Co., 1883), pp. 11–44.
10. Munger, "The New Theology," quoted in Robert R. Mathisen, ed., *The Role of Religion in American Life: An Interpretive Historical Anthology* (Lanham: University Press of America, 1982), pp. 252–258. A broader and more contemporary profile of the defining characteristics of the New Theology is provided by Lloyd Averill, *American Theology,* pp. 69–94.
11. A number of the members of this group studied in Germany, where they were influenced first-hand by major formulators of European liberalism such as the philosopher Rudolf Hermann Lotze, the theologian Albrecht Ritschl, and the church historian Adolf von Harnack. Hutchison, *Modernist Impulse,* pp. 122–132; Averill, *American Theology,* pp. 30–49; and Reardon, *Liberal Protestantism,* pp. 9–65. On Egbert C. Smyth, George Harris and the impact of developments at Andover Seminary on the development of the New Theology, see Daniel Day Williams, *The Andover Liberals: A Study in American Theology* (New York: King's Crown Press, 1941). On other members of this group, see Hutchison, pp. 76–184; Averill, pp. 151–155; and Smith, *Changing Conceptions,* pp. 164–197.
12. Kenneth Cauthen, *The Impact of American Religious Liberalism* (New York: Harper & Row, 1962), pp. 26–37. Robert T. Handy, "Fundamentalism and Modernism in Perspective," *Religion In Life* (Summer 1955): 386–393.
13. Cauthen, pp. 29–30; Ahlstrom, *A Religious History,* pp. 782–783.
14. Cauthen, p. 27.
15. Cauthen, pp. 33–34; Ahlstrom, *Theology in America,* p. 70.
16. On the relationship between the New Theology and the Social

Gospel Movement, see Ahlstrom, *Theology in America,* pp. 73–77; Charles H. Hopkins, *The Rise of the Social Gospel in American Protestantism, 1865–1915* (New Haven: Yale University Press, 1940). On the formative role played by Washington Gladden and Walter Rauschenbusch, see Robert T. Handy, *The Social Gospel in America, 1870–1920: Gladden, Ely, Rauschenbusch* (New York: Oxford University Press, 1966). For the American liberal conception of the "kingdom of God" and its coming to the fore as a focus of their ministerial, social, and missiological efforts, see Ahlstrom, *Theology in America,* pp. 69–71, and H. Richard Niebuhr, *The Kingdom of God in America* (1937; reprint, New York: Harper & Row, 1959), pp. 161–163, 184–198.

17. H. Shelton Smith, "Christian Education," in *Protestant Thought in the Twentieth Century: Whence and Whither?* ed. Arnold S. Nash (New York: Macmillan, 1951), pp. 225–246.
18. William R. Hutchison, ed., *American Protestant Thought: The Liberal Era* (New York: Harper & Row, 1968), p. 117.
19. Smith, "Christian Education," p. 230; Hutchison, *Modernist Impulse,* pp. 155–164.
20. George Albert Coe, *The Religion of a Mature Mind* (Chicago, 1902), pp. 299–302, quoted in Smith, "Christian Education," p. 231–240. See also George A. Coe, *Education in Religion and Morals* (New York: Fleming H. Revell Co., 1904), and *A Social Theory of Religious Education* (New York: Charles Scribner's Sons, 1917).
21. Smith, "Christian Education," pp. 234–235. See Coe's essay entitled "Salvation by Education" in Coe, *Religion of a Mature Mind,* pp. 293–396.
22. Smith, "Christian Education," p. 229. Also see Stephen A. Schmidt, *A History of the Religious Education Society* (Birmingham, Ala.: Religious Education Press, 1983).
23. William Hutchison has provided perhaps the most focused analysis of the changes fostered in American missiology by Protestant liberalism. See his studies entitled *The Modernist Impulse in American Protestantism* (Cambridge and London: Harvard University Press, 1976); *American Protestant Thought: The Liberal Era* (New York: Harper & Row, 1968); and especially "Modernism and Missions: The Liberal Search for an Exportable Christianity, 1875–1935" in *The Missionary Enterprise in China and America,* ed. John K. Fairbank, (Cambridge and London: Harvard University Press, 1974), pp. 110–131. On the dilemma that this posed for the American proponents of liberal missiology, see Hutchison, *Modernist Impulse,* pp. 112–144, 258–261, and "Modernism and Mission." On the continuation of this dilemma and controversy into the twentieth century

and its impact, see report of Laymen's Foreign Missions Inquiry Commission of Appraisal, *Re-thinking Missions: A Laymen's Inquiry After a Hundred Years* (New York: Harper, 1932) and Lyman Van Law Cady, "The Liberal Attitude Toward Other Religions," in *Liberal Theology: An Appraisal. Essays in Honor of Eugene William Lyman,* ed. David E. Roberts and Henry P. Van Dusen (New York: Charles Scribner's Sons, 1942), pp. 137–150. For the revision that this dilemma provoked in the mission theory of a major European proponent of Protestant liberalism, see the writings of Ernst Troeltsch, especially *The Absoluteness of Christianity and the History of Religions,* trans. David Reid (1901; reprint, Richmond, Va.: Knox Press, 1971), and "The Place of Christianity Among the World-Religions," in *Christian Thought: Its History and Application,* ed. Baron F. von Hugel (London: University of London Press, Ltd., 1923). For an analysis of the development of Troeltsch's mission theory and controversy with Gustav Warneck, Germany's foremost missiologist, see Moses Moore, "Ernst Troeltsch and the Problem of Christian Missions," unpublished paper, December 1979. On Troeltsch, see also John Powell Clayton, ed., *Ernst Troeltsch and the Future of Theology* (Cambridge: Cambridge University Press, 1976); Benjamin Reist, *Toward a Theology of Involvement: The Thought of Ernst Troeltsch* (Philadelphia: Westminster Press, 1966); and Stephen Neill, *A History of Christian Missions* (Baltimore: Penguin Books, 1973), p. 455.

24. Louis H. Jordon, *Comparative Religion: Its Genesis and Growth,* p. 63, quoted in Sharpe, *Comparative Religion: A History,* pp. xxii.
25. Neill, *A History of Christian Missions,* p. 455. Sydney Ahlstrom, *The American Protestant Encounter with World Religions* (Beloit, Wisc.: Beloit College, 1962); Mircea Eliade and Joseph M. Kitagawa, eds., *The History of Religions* (Chicago: University of Chicago Press, 1959), pp. 2–5; Weisenburger, *Ordeal of Faith,* pp. 109–116; Cauthen, *Impact of American Religious Liberalism,* pp. 8–9.
26. Cauthen, *Impact,* p. 9; Chadwick, *The Victorian Church,* vol. 2, pp. 35–39.
27. Charles Long, *Significations,* pp. 15–16.
28. Letter from Pusey to Max Muller, 2 June 1860. Quoted in Chadwick, *The Victorian Church,* vol. 2, pp. 36–37.
29. Olav G. Myklebust, *The Study of Missions in Theological Education: An Historical Inquiry into the Place of World Evangelization in Western Protestant Ministerial Training with Particular Reference to Alexander Duff's Chair of Evangelistic Theology,* vol. 1, (Olso: Egede Institute, 1955), pp. 307, 351.
30. Ahlstrom, *American Protestant Encounter.* See also James Freeman Clarke, *Ten Great Religions: An Essay in Comparative Theology*

(Boston: Houghton, Mifflin, 1871, 1883); Eliade and Kitagawa, *The History of Religions,* pp. 1–5; and Forman, "A History of Foreign Mission Theory," in *American Missions in Bicentennial Perspective* ed. R. Pierce Beaver (South Pasadena, Calif.: William Carey Library, 1977), pp. 69–79.

31. Foreman, "A History of Foreign Mission Theory," pp. 86–87; Weisenburger, *Ordeal of Faith,* pp. 109–116; Ahlstrom, *American Protestant Encounter;* Szasz, *Divided Mind of Protestant America,* pp. 10–14; and Eliade and Kitagawa, *The History of Religions,* pp. 1–5.
32. Ahlstrom, *American Protestant Encounter*. Weisenburger, *Ordeal,* p. 112. See also Jerald C. Brauer, "General Editor's Preface" and Joseph M. Kitagawa, "The History of Religions in America," in *The History of Religions,* ed. Eliade and Kitagawa, pp. vii–x; 1–30.
33. Szasz, *Divided Mind of Protestant America,* pp. 11–14.
34. Weisenburger, *Ordeal,* p. 115.
35. *Public Opinion,* 16 (1893): pp. 5–6. Quoted in Szasz, *Divided Mind of Protestant America,* p. 12. Ahlstrom notes that "never before or since has the science of religion received such wide attention in the United States . . . . Indeed, for the study of world religions the Parliament of 1893 serves as a kind of landmark or watershed." Ahlstrom, *American Protestant Encounter.* See the illuminating discussion of this Parliament in Martin E. Marty's, *Modern American Religion: The Irony of It All, 1893–1919* (Chicago and London: University of Chicago Press, 1986), pp. 18–19, 21–22, 195–196.
36. John Henry Barrows, ed., *The World's Parliament of Religions* (Chicago: Parliament Publishing Company, 1893), vol. 1, p. 130. See also Charles Spencer Smith, *A History of the African Methodist Episcopal Church,* vol. 2 (Philadelphia: Book Concern of the A.M.E. Church, 1922; reprinting, New York: Johnson Reprint Corporation, 1968), pp. 197–198. Also significant for both groups was the Congress on Africa held in conjunction with and in the spirit of the Parliament. See Esedebe, *Pan-Africanism,* pp. 45–46.
37. Cauthen, *Impact,* pp. 8–9; Weisenburger, *Ordeal,* pp. 114–116; H. Shelton Smith, Robert T. Handy and Lefferts A. Loetscher, *American Christianity,* vol. 2, 1820–1960 (New York: Charles Scribner's Sons, 1963), p. 301.
38. John W. Buckham, "Christianity Among the Religions," *The Hibbert Journal* 7 (Oct. 1908/July 1909): 513–21. Quoted in Smith, Handy, and Loetscher, *American Christianity* vol. 2, pp. 302–306.
39. Ibid.
40. Daniel Day Williams, *Andover Liberals,* pp. 64–67, 71–77, 86–87; Smith, *Changing Conceptions of Original Sin,* pp. 164–197. Paul Varg, *Missionaries, Chinese, and Diplomats: The American Protes-*

tant Missionary Movement in China, 1890–1952 (Princeton: Princeton University Press, 1958), 68–74. For the sociological emphasis within missions, see especially James S. Dennis, *Christian Missions and Social Progress: A Sociological Study of Foreign Missions* (New York: Fleming H. Revell Company, 1897); David Everett Swift, "Conservative Versus Progressive Orthodoxy in Latter Nineteenth Century Congregationalism," *Church History* (Mar. 1947): 21–31; Hutchison, *Modernist Impulse,* pp. 134–144, 258–261; Hutchison, "Modernism and Missions," pp. 110–131.

41. The few exceptions include Thomas F. Gossett, *Race: The History of an Idea in America* (New York: Schocken Books, 1965), pp. 144–176; Ronald C. White and C. Howard Hopkins, *The Social Gospel: Religion and Reform in Changing America* (Philadelphia: Temple University Press, 1976), pp. 93–96, 101–113; and Carter G. Woodson, *The History of the Negro Church* (Washington, D.C.: The Associated Publishers, 1921), pp. 224–289. See also S. P. Fullinwider, *The Mind and Mood of Black America: Twentieth Century Thought* (Homewood, Ill.: Dorsey Press, 1969), pp. 26–27.
42. See, for example, Woodson's long-neglected chapter on "Progressives and Conservatives," in *The History of the Negro Church,* pp. 224–289; and Wills and Newman, *Black Apostles at Home and Abroad,* pp. 23–24.
43. Cauthen, *Impact,* p. 5. Note the expression of these sentiments by leading liberals such as Henry Churchill King and Harry Emerson Fosdick. Henry Churchill King, *Reconstruction in Theology* (New York: Macmillan, 1901), p. v, and Harry Emerson Fosdick, *The Living of These Days* (New York: Harper Brothers, 1956), p. vii.
44. Fullinwider, *Mind and Mood,* pp. 73–74; Moses, *Golden Age,* pp. 27, 171–172. See also Griggs's autobiography, *The Story of My Struggles* (Memphis, 1914).
45. Sutton E. Griggs, *Guide to Racial Greatness, or The Science of Collective Efficiency* (Memphis: National Public Welfare League, 1923), pp. 38, 214. See also the complementary work entitled *Kingdom Builder's Manual Companion Book to "Guide to Racial Greatness"* (Memphis: National Public Welfare League, 1924). Both books were designed to show "the direct connection between [the] . . . findings of science and the teachings of the Bible." Griggs, *Kingdom Builder's Manual,* p. 10. On Griggs, see also Hugh M. Gloster, "Sutton E. Griggs, Novelist of the New Negro," in *The Black Novelist* ed. Robert Hemenway (Columbus, Ohio: Charles E. Merrill Publishing Co., 1970), pp. 4–22.
46. Fullinwider, *Mind and Mood,* pp. 47, 63.
47. Meier, *Negro Thought,* pp. 130, 172; Geiss, *Pan-African Movement,* pp. 182–190; George Mason Miller, "'A This Worldly

Mission': The Life and Career of Alexander Walters (1858–1917)," Ph.D. diss., State University of New York at Stony Brook, 1984.

48. Alexander Walters, *My Life and Work* (London and Edinburgh: Fleming H. Revell Company, 1917), pp. 141–142.
49. See Hugh Henry Proctor, *Between Black and White: Autobiographical Sketches* (Boston: Pilgrim Press, 1925). Samuel K. Roberts has noted that the Fisk, Yale, and Columbia University-educated Haynes was "squarely within the liberal tradition of American Protestantism." Samuel K. Roberts, "George Edmund Haynes: Advocate for Interracial Cooperation," in Burkett and Newman, *Black Apostles,* p. 114. On Jesse E. Moorland, see Alfred A. Moss, Jr., *The American Negro Academy: Voice of the Talented Tenth* (Baton Rouge and London: Louisiana State University Press, 1981), pp. 117, 133–134, 142–146, 159, 164–165, 223–224, 245, 261; Boris, *Who's Who,* p. 145.
50. On Powell, see Meier, *Negro Thought,* p. 221, and especially Adam Clayton Powell, Sr., *Against the Tide: An Autobiography* (New York: R. R. Smith, 1938).
51. Randall K. Burkett, *Black Redemption: Churchmen Speak for the Garvey Movement* (Philadelphia: Temple University Press, 1978), p. 65.
52. William H. Ferris, *The African Abroad, or His Evolution in Western Civilization: Tracing His Development under Caucasian Milieux,* vol. 1 (New Haven: Tuttle, Morehouse and Taylor Press, 1913), p. 416. Also see Moses, *Golden Age,* p. 212; Fullinwider, *Mind and Mood,* pp. 22–25, and below, chapter 8.
53. On Wright, who in 1933 became a bishop of the A.M.E. Church, see Yenser, *Who's Who,* p. 589; Wills, "Aspects," p. 230; and Richard R. Wright, Jr., *Eighty-seven Years behind the Black Curtain: An Autobiography* (Philadelphia: Rare Book Company, 1965).
54. On Ransom, who later became the editor of the *A.M.E. Church Review* (1912–1924), organized the Institutional Church and Social Settlement in Chicago in 1900, and in 1930 would be the major catalyst in the establishment of the Fraternal Council of Negro Churches, see Calvin S. Morris, *Reverdy C. Ransom: Black Advocate of the Social Gospel* (Lanham: University Press of America, 1990). Also see below, chapter 8, and Fullinwider, *Mind and Mood,* pp. 36–46.
55. On liberal influences at Oberlin and especially the role of its President, Henry Churchill King, see Szasz, *Divided Mind,* pp. 5, 34; Weisenburger, *Ordeal of Faith,* pp. 79, 152, 184–186. On the origins and tradition of Wilberforce, see Daniel A. Payne, *History of the African Methodist Episcopal Church,* ed. C. S. Smith (Nashville: Publishing House of the A.M.E. Sunday School Union, 1891; reprint, New York: Johnson Reprint Corporation, 1968), pp. 422–425, 428–438, 443–447.

56. Reverdy C. Ransom, *The Pilgrimage of Harriet Ransom's Son* (Nashville: A.M.E. Sunday School Union, n.d.), pp. 38, 86–87, 93.
57. On the influence of Congregationalism and the AMA, see A. Knighton Stanley, *The Children Is Crying: Congregationalism among Black People* (New York: Pilgrim Press, 1979); James McPherson, *The Abolitionist Legacy: From Reconstruction to the NAACP* (Princeton: Princeton University Press, 1975), pp. 207–210; Wesley A. Hotchkiss, "Congregationalists and Negro Education," *The Journal of Negro Education* (Summer 1960): 289–290; Joe M. Richardson, *Christian Reconstruction: The American Missionary Association and Southern Blacks, 1861–1890* (Athens and London: University of Georgia Press, 1986).
58. McPherson, *Abolitionist Legacy,* p.182.
59. Clifton H. Johnson, *Our American Missionary Association Heritage* (New York: Division of Higher Education and American Missionary Association of the United Church Board for Homeland Ministries, 1967), p. 40; Stanley, *Children,* pp. 39–48.
60. McPherson, *Legacy,* pp. 148–149; Knight, *Children,* pp. 50–58. See also W. E. B. Du Bois's account of the impact that Fisk University had upon his religious development. W. E. B. Du Bois, *Dusk of Dawn: An Essay toward an Autobiography of a Race Concept* (1940; reprint, New York: Schocken Books, 1968), pp. 32–33. See also Reverdy Ransom's remembrance of his school days at Wilberforce and Oberlin. Ransom, *Pilgrimage,* pp. 33–34 and Reverdy Ransom, *School Days at Wilberforce* (Springfield, Ohio: New Era, 1890).
61. On the impact of the YMCA and these leaders, see Woodson, *History of the Negro Church,* pp. 250–251, 286, and Meier, *Negro Thought,* pp. 133, 232, 271. Also Roberts, "George Edmund Haynes," pp. 112–113.
62. Ras Makonnen, *Pan-Africanism from Within,* ed. Kenneth King (Nairobi, London, New York: Oxford University Press, 1973).
63. Makonnen's baptismal name was George Thomas Nathaniel Griffith. Makonnen, *Pan-Africanism from Within,* p. ix.
64. Ibid., pp. 45, 47, 77.
65. Ibid., p. 41, 43. On Makonnen's YMCA and later Pan-African activities, see Makonnen, *Pan-Africanism From Within,* pp. ix–xi, 41–51, 105–283; Geiss, *Pan-African Movement,* pp. 387–390, 401, 406, 423; George Padmore, *Pan-Africanism or Communism* (New York: Doubleday and Co. 1971), pp. 124, 133, 152.
66. David Wills, "Aspects," pp. 88–158 and James Melville Washington, *Frustrated Fellowship: The Black Baptist Quest for Social Power* (Macon, Ga.: Mercer Press, 1986), pp. 184, 192–193, 212–213.
67. Wills, "Aspects," pp. 89–158. Fullinwider, *Mind and Mood,* pp. 33–46. See, for example, Coppin's comments on the case of the Presbyterian biblical scholar Charles Briggs of Union Theological

Seminary. Levi J. Coppin, "Editorial," *A.M.E. Church Review* 10 (Oct. 1893): 203; *A.M.E. Church Review* 8 (July 1891):110–111; *A.M.E. Church Review* 9 (Apr. 1893): 425. The precedent was set by Tanner, who consistently monitored the issues addressed in many of the nation's religious journals. Wills points out that Tanner "noted and commented upon the contents not only of the various Methodist periodicals but also of *Wide Awake, The Chautauqua, The Gospel in All Lands, The Pulpit Treasury, The Homiletic Review, The Baptist Quarterly Review, The Andover Review, The Unitarian Review, The Universalist Quarterly Review, The Catholic World,* and *St. Joseph's Advocate.*" Wills, "Aspects," p. 91. Wills also observes that largely because of Tanner's intellectual leadership, between 1884 and 1893 the A.M.E. Church fostered "a greater range of theological discussion than at any previous period in its history." Wills, "Aspects," pp. 89–92.

68. Ibid., pp. 88–136.
69. Benjamin T. Tanner, "Editorial," *A.M.E. Church Review* 4 (Apr. 1888): 457, quoted in Wills, "Aspects," p. 128.
70. Wills, "Aspects," p. 90.
71. Jabez P. Campbell, "A Scriptural View, or The Statement Concerning Paradise That Was Lost Regained," *A.M.E. Church Review* 1 (July 1884):12.
72. James A. Handy, "The Mystery of Man," *A.M.E. Church Review* 2 (July 1885): 20.
73. James Theodore Holly, "Biblical Criticism," *A.M.E. Church Review* 4 (Apr. 1888): 367. On Holly, see David M. Dean, *Defender of the Race: James Theodore Holly, Black Nationalist Bishop* (Boston: Lambert Press, 1979).
74. Benjamin T. Tanner, "The Higher Criticism," *A.M.E. Church Review* 10 (July 1893): 115. Quoted in Wills, "Aspects," p. 89.
75. On soteriology, see Benjamin T. Tanner, "The Freeness of Salvation," *A.M.E. Church Review* 5 (Apr. 1889): 426, and Wills, "Aspects," p. 107. On the future probation issue and Congregationalism, see David E. Swift, "Conservative versus Progressive Orthodoxy in Latter Nineteenth Century Congregationalism," *Church History* 16 (Mar. 1947): 22–31; Williams, *Andover Liberals,* pp. 65–67, 71–77, 86–87, 183; Henry L. Phillips, "Probation," *A.M.E. Church Review* 3 (April 1887): 35–56; W. H. Coston, "Is the Doctrine of Universal Immortality Christian? Does It Prohibit Crime?" *A.M.E. Church Review* 4 (Apr. 1888): 376–382.
76. This article was originally presented as his Master's Oration at Howard University. George William Cook, "Comparative Religion," *A.M.E. Church Review* 3 (Jan. 1887): 277–282. See also Moss, *Academy,* pp. 119, 216, 251, and Wills, "Aspects," p. 106.

77. Benjamin T. Tanner, "The Origin of Man," *A.M.E. Church Review* 4 (Oct. 1887): 203–213.
78. Ibid., pp. 204–213.
79. Charles A. Johnson, "Heaven and the Divinity as Seen by the Poets," *A.M.E. Church Review* 4 (July 1887): 527. Note also the sympathetic treatment of evolution by Henry L. Phillips in "Alfred Russell Wallace, LL.D., F.L.S., Etc., On Darwinianism," *A.M.E. Church Review* 6 (Oct. 1889): 161–165.
80. Reverend A. W. Upshaw, "Reason and Revelation," *A.M.E. Church Review* 5 (Apr. 1889): 327–328. Note also Upshaw's critical appreciation of the discipline in "Biblical Criticism," *A.M.E. Church Review* 8 (Oct. 1891): 198–201. Fullinwider, *Mind and Mood,* pp. 34–35.
81. Faduma, "Thoughts for the Times, or The New Theology," *A.M.E. Church Review* 7 (Oct. 1890): 139–145; Wills, "The Double Crisis of Black Christianity;" Moss, *Academy,* pp. 5–10; George M. Frederickson, *The Black Image in the White Mind: The Debate on Afro-American Character and Destiny, 1817–1914* (New York: Harper & Row, 1971), pp. 198–319; Gossett, *Race,* pp. 176–197; and Rayford W. Logan, *The Betrayal of the Negro from Rutherford B. Hayes to Woodrow Wilson* (New York: Collier Books, 1965), pp. 242–274.
82. Benjamin T. Tanner, *The Negro's Origin, And Is the Negro Cursed?* (Philadelphia: A.M.E. Book Depository, 1869); Benjamin T. Tanner, *The Descent of the Negro* (Philadelphia: A.M.E. Publishing House, 1898).
83. Tanner, *The Descent of the Negro.*
84. As interpreted by men such as Thomas Dixon, Jr., "one of the leading advocates of the social gospel" and also one of the era's most notorious literary racists, the tenets of both the New Theology and the social gospel provided a veneer of scientific and theological respectability for an overt racism. On Dixon, who authored such racist works as *The Leopard's Spots* and *The Klansmen* and inspired the making of "The Birth of a Nation," see A. R. Allen, "Thomas Dixon, Jr. and Political Religion: From Social Reformer to Racist," *Foundations: A Baptist Journal of History and Theology* 14 (Apr./June 1971): 136–152. For a broader interpretation of the Social Gospel Movement and its impact on both blacks and whites, see Ralph E. Luker, *The Social Gospel in Black and White: American Racial Reform, 1885–1912* (Chapel Hill and London: University of North Carolina Press, 1991).
85. Moss, *Academy,* p. 8 and Wills, "Aspects," pp. 124–125, 127. See also Glenn R. Bucher, "Social Gospel Christianity and Racism," *Union Seminary Quarterly Review* 28 (Winter 1973): 146–157; Thomas Gossett, *Race: The History of an Idea in America* (New

York: Schocken Books, 1965), pp. 144–197, and Luker, *The Social Gospel in Black and White.*

86. Josiah Strong, *Our Country: Its Possible Future and Its Present Crisis* (New York: Baker and Taylor, 1886); Josiah Strong, *The New Era, or the Coming Kingdom* (New York, 1891); Josiah Strong, *Expansion under New World Conditions* (New York, 1900). The extent of the racism and imperialism present in the thought and writings of Strong has induced a long, ongoing discussion. Dorothea R. Miller has been one of the defenders of Strong against charges of racism and imperialism. Dorothea R. Miller, "Josiah Strong and American Nationalism: A Reevaluation," *The Journal of American History* 53 (June 1966/67): 487–503. See also Ralph E. Luker, "The Social Gospel and the Failure of Racial Reform, 1877–1898," *Church History* 46 (Mar. 1977): 80–93.
87. Strong, *Our Country,* pp. 175, 178.
88. See Theophilus Gould Steward, *Fifty Years in the Gospel Ministry: From 1864 to 1914* (Philadelphia: A.M.E. Book Concern, 1921). See also Wills, "Aspects," pp. 98, 108–9, 113–123; Frank Lincoln Mather, ed., *Who's Who of the Colored Race: A General Biographical Dictionary of Men and Women of African Descent* (Chicago: Memento Edition, Half-Century Anniversary of Negro Freedom in the United States, 1915), p. 253.
89. Steward, *Fifty Years,* p.182.
90. These sentiments were echoed in a testimonial signed by the entire faculty. Ibid.
91. Steward, *Fifty Years,* pp. 157–166; Theophilus Gould Steward, *Genesis Re-Read, or The Latest Conclusions of Physical Science, Viewed in Their Relation to the Mosaic Record* (Philadelphia: A.M.E. Book Room, 1885).
92. Steward, *Genesis Re-Read,* p. 248. He quotes McCosh's *Christianity and Positivism* (New York, 1871), originally presented as a series of lectures at Union Theological Seminary. For an analysis, see Stow Persons, "Religion and Modernity, 1865–1914," in *The Shaping of American Religion,* ed. James Ward Smith and A. Leland Jamison (Princeton: Princeton University Press, 1961), pp. 376–379. Also see James McCosh, *The Religious Aspects of Evolution* (1888; reprint, New York: Charles Scribner's Sons, 1890).
93. Theophilus Gould Steward, *The End of the World, or Clearing the Way for the Fullness of the Gentiles* (Philadelphia: A.M.E. Book Rooms, 1888).
94. Steward, *The End of the World,* pp. 120–123, 135. For Steward's explicit reference to and rejection of Strong's *Our Country,* see *The End of the World,* pp. 73, 122–125; also Wills, "Aspects," pp. 117–120, 122–123.
95. Wills, "Aspects," p. 123.

96. Faduma, "Thoughts for the Times," *A.M.E. Church Review* 4 (Oct. 1888): 121–126.
97. Langley, *Ideologies of Liberation* (London: Rex Collings, 1979), p. 188.
98. See, for example, O. Faduma, "My Nigerian African Background," Yale Divinity School Alumni File.
99. Okonkwo, "Man of Two Worlds," p. 26; O. Faduma, "The A.M.E. Church and Kittrell Normal Institute," *Christian Recorder* (16 Apr. 1890): 289.
100. Smith, *History of the African Methodist Episcopal Church,* pp. 57–59.
101. Faduma, "The A.M.E. Church and Kittrell," p. 289.
102. See Orishatukeh Faduma, *The Defects of the Negro Church,* American Negro Academy Occasional Papers No. 10 (Washington, D.C.: The American Negro Academy, 1904).
103. On the Black Church and ministry during this era, see Wills, "Aspects," and Meier, *Negro Thought in America.* For a critical appraisal, see E. Franklin Frazier, *Black Bourgeoisie: The Rise of a New Middle Class in the United States* (London: Collier-Macmillan, 1957), pp. 78–79. For a more contemporary view of ecclesiastical politics in the A.M.E. Church, see James Cone, *My Soul Looks Back* (Nashville: Abingdon, 1982), pp. 65–66, 85. Okonkwo reports that Faduma was in attendance at the 1892 General Conference of the A.M.E. Church held in Philadelphia. Okonkwo, "Man of Two Worlds," p. 26. If so, Faduma was probably an eyewitness to one of the most acrimonious general conferences held by the A.M.E. Church. See Smith, *History of the African Methodist Episcopal Church,* pp. 163–173.
104. Orishatukeh Faduma, "Where is Virtue?" *A.M.E. Church Review* 8 (Apr. 1891): 430–431. See also Paul A. Carter, *The Spiritual Crisis of the Gilded Age.*
105. Orishatukeh Faduma, "Thoughts for the Times, or The New Theology," *A.M.E. Church Review* 7 (Oct. 1890): 139–145.
106. "The A.M.E. Church Review," *Christian Recorder* (13 Nov. 1890): 3.
107. Faduma, "The New Theology," p. 139.
108. "Our New Attitude Toward the World Religions," *Unitarian Review* (June 1890), quoted by Faduma, "The New Theology," p. 144.
109. "The Life of Dogmas," *Homiletic Review* (May 1890), quoted by Faduma, "The New Theology," p. 142. Sabatier, of Strasbourg, articulated a position and methodology similar to those of Adolf von Harnack, the great German proponent of theological liberalism. On Auguste Sabatier and Adolf von Harnack, see Reardon, *Liberal Protestantism,* pp. 10, 31, 34, 44–58, 65, 163.
110. Faduma, "The New Theology," p. 142.

111. Ayandele, *Holy Johnson,* p. 342.
112. Compare with Blyden's "Christian Mission in West Africa," originally published in *Fraser's Magazine,* Oct. 1876, reprinted in Blyden, *Christianity, Islam, and the Negro Race,* pp. 46–70.
113. Faduma, "The New Theology," pp. 142–143.
114. Ibid., p. 139.
115. Faduma, "The New Theology," pp. 144–145.
116. Faduma, "The New Theology," p. 143.
117. Faduma, "The New Theology," p. 144. For a more realistic appraisal of America's racial situation during this era, see Logan, *The Betrayal of the Negro;* Moss, *Academy,* pp. 5–10; and C. Vann Woodward, *The Strange Career of Jim Crow* (New York: Oxford University Press, 1966).
118. Faduma, "African Negro Education," *Sierra Leone Weekly News,* 24 Aug. 1918.
119. Faduma, "The New Theology."
120. Ahlstrom, *Religious History,* pp. 775–776.
121. Buckham, *Progressive Religious Thought,* pp. 295–96, and Roland H. Bainton, *Yale and the Ministry: A History of Education for the Christian Ministry at Yale from the Founding in 1701* (New York: Harper & Brothers, 1957), pp. 169–195.
122. George Park Fisher was appointed the first Professor of Church History at Yale Divinity School in 1861. On his shift to a liberal theological posture, see Weisenburger, *Ordeal,* pp. 102–103; Bainton, Yale and the Ministry, pp. 189–190. Samuel Harris, Professor of Biblical Theology, was particularly concerned "with the question of revelation and the problem of knowledge within the sphere of religion." Bainton, *Yale and the Ministry,* pp. 169–70. George B. Stevens taught systematic theology, having "transferred from the field of New Testament." He had studied in Germany and emphasized the belief that the Bible contained more than one theology. His works include *The Pauline Theology* (1892), *The Johannine Theology* (1894), *The Christian Doctrine of Salvation* (1905), and *The Theology of the New Testament* (1899). Bainton, *Yale and the Ministry,* pp. 179–183. Edward L. Curtis stresses contextualism in the study of the Bible, insisting that "the Bible is an oriental book" and that to understand it one must be prepared to "wear the garb of the orient, and dwell beneath Syrian skies." Bainton, *Yale and the Ministry,* pp. 178–179. On Day, Brastow, and Porter, see below. It should be noted that William Rainey Harper served as a Professor in the biblical field from 1881 to his departure for the University of Chicago in 1890. Weisenburger, *Ordeal,* pp. 105–106.
123. Bainton, *Yale and the Ministry,* p. 219. See also Ahlstrom, *Religious History,* p. 776. Porter held the Winkley Chair of Biblical

Theology. His particular concern was with the question of ethics. Bainton, *Yale and the Ministry,* pp. 202, 225.

124. James M. Washington, "Pan-African Religionists at Yale University," an unpublished listing, n.d.
125. Hugh Henry Proctor, *Between Black and White,* pp. 41–42.
126. Ibid., pp. 95, 106–108; Knight, *Children,* pp. 84–85.
127. Proctor, *Between Black and White,* p. 40.
128. Ibid., p. 43.
129. Ibid., p. 45, and Weisenburger, *Ordeal,* pp. 11, 241. African-American churches in New Haven also hosted distinguished ministers during this era. Dixwell Avenue Congregational Church, formed in 1820, was being pastored by Albert President Miller, a Fisk University and Yale Divinity School graduate. See Moss, *Academy,* pp. 26–27, and especially Edward F. Goin, "One Hundred Years of Negro Congregationalism in New Haven, Connecticut," *Crisis* 19 (Feb. 1920):177–181.
130. Proctor, *Between Black and White,* p. 43.
131. Ames graduated in 1892 and would become a leader among the distinguished group of liberals at the Divinity School of the University of Chicago. Weisenburger, *Ordeal,* pp. 249–250; Hutchison, *Modernist Impulse,* pp. 177, 300–301, 304; and Cauthen, *Impact,* pp. 148, 155.
132. Hutchison, *Modernist Impulse,* pp. 113–122; Cauthen, *Impact,* pp. 4–5.
133. Bainton, *Yale and the Ministry,* p. 191.
134. "Lectures at Yale Divinity School," *The Congregationalist* 77 (17 Nov. 1892): 448. John H. W. Stuckenberg was a Lutheran minister, sociologist, social gospel activist, and pastor of the American Church in Berlin. His lecture series illuminates his role as a mediator of German theological thought within the United States and the many ways in which this thought was disseminated among seminary students apart from actual study in Germany. Hutchison, *Modernist Impulse,* p. 115.
135. Hutchison, *Modernist Impulse,* pp. 122–132; Averill, *American Theology,* pp. 30–34.
136. Reardon, *Liberal Protestantism,* pp. 20–48.
137. "Lectures at Yale Divinity School," p. 448.
138. Much of this fervor was associated with the Student Volunteer Movement then making its impact felt in the colleges and seminaries of the nation. Forman, "A History of Foreign Mission Theory," pp. 80–81.
139. George E. Day taught Greek, Hebrew, and Syriac. He started his mission collection in 1886. Bainton, *Yale and the Ministry,* pp. 176–178, 195.

140. Ibid. Forman points out that Edward A. Lawrence was "a promising young congregational minister who died at an early age after completing a trip around the world to study missions." Forman, "A History of Foreign Mission Theory," p. 89. On his progressive mission theory, see Edward A. Lawrence, *Modern Missions in the East: Their Methods, Successes, and Limitations* (New York: Harper & Brothers, 1895).
141. Bainton, *Yale and the Ministry,* pp. 176–178, 195.
142. See Faduma, "Success and Drawbacks to Missionary Work in Africa by an Eye-Witness" in Bowen, *Africa and the American Negro,* pp. 125–136.
143. Ibid., p. 125.
144. David E. Swift, "Conservative versus Progressive Orthodoxy in Latter Nineteenth Century Congregationalism," *Church History* 16 (Mar. 1947): 22–31, 209. The primary locus of this struggle between the proponents of liberal mission theory and the forces of orthodoxy was the American Board of Commissioners for Foreign Missions. Founded in 1810, the American Board functioned as the foreign mission arm of Congregationalism. From 1886 to 1893 it was embroiled in controversy as conservative members of its Prudential Committee, which ruled on foreign mission applicants, sought to reject candidates who gave evidence of having been influenced by the New Theology. Hutchison, *Modernist Impulse,* pp. 133–134; Varg, *Missionaries,* pp. 68–70.
145. Varg, *Missionaries,* p. 70.
146. Ibid., pp. 69–70; Hutchison, *Modernist Impulse,* pp. 145–155.
147. Hutchison, *Modernist Impulse,* pp. 133–134. See also William Newton Clark, *A Study of Christian Missions* (New York: Charles Scribner's Sons, 1900), and William R. Hutchison, "The Liberal Search for an Exportable Christianity," in *The Missionary Enterprise In China and America* ed. John K. Fairbank (Cambridge: Harvard University Press, 1976), pp. 10–131.
148. Hutchison, *Modernist Impulse,* pp. 133–134.
149. George A. Gordon, *The Christ of Today* (Boston: Houghton, Mifflin, 1895); George A. Gordon, *The Gospel for Humanity: A Sermon before the American Board of Commissioners for Foreign Missions, Delivered at Brooklyn, New York, October 15, 1895* (Boston: ABCFM, 1895); George A. Gordon, "The Missionary Motive and the American Board," *Christian Union* 35 (13 Jan. 1887): 17–19. William R. Hutchison argued that Gordon's writings on missions "prefigured the liberalism of the epochal Laymen's Inquiry on missions that appeared in 1932." Hutchison, *American Protestant Thought,* p. 97.

150. George A. Gordon, *My Education and Religion: An Autobiography* (Boston: Houghton, Mifflin and Co., 1925).
151. Gordon, "Missionary Motive," pp. 17–19. Quoted in Hutchison, *Modernist Impulse,* p. 137.
152. Gordon, *The Christ of Today,* pp. 20–21. Quoted in Hutchison, *American Protestant Thought,* p. 98.
153. Ibid., p. 99.
154. Gordon, "The Gospel for Humanity," quoted in Hutchison, *American Protestant Thought,* pp. 99–107.
155. Ibid., pp. 99–106.
156. See, for example, O. Faduma, "Religious Beliefs of the Yoruba People in West Africa," in Bowen, *Africa,* pp. 31–32.
157. Proctor, *Between Black and White,* p. 42. Although Proctor did not share Faduma's Pan-African orientation, he did believe that liberalism's potential affinity for development of positive ethnic manifestations of Christianity was second to none. Indeed, Proctor stressed the relationship between ethnicity and Christianity in his graduation address entitled "A New Ethnic Contribution To Christianity." Proctor noted that "In the historic development of Christianity, race and religion have had a reciprocal relation," and that "Every race that has embraced Christianity has brought to the system its own peculiar contribution." Proctor, *Between Black and White,* pp. 49–53.
158. See O. Faduma, "Africa or the Dark Continent," *A.M.E. Church Review* 9 (Jan. 1893): 1–8, and O. Faduma, "Religious Beliefs and Worship of the Yorubas in West Africa," *A.M.E. Church Review* 12 (July 1895): 150–158.
159. O. Faduma, "The Pastoral Epistles," *A.M.E. Church Review* 11 (Oct. 1894): 215–230.
160. Ibid., pp. 215–227. For a contemporary discussion of the authenticity of this material and a conclusion differing from Faduma's, see Wayne A. Meeks, ed., *The Writings of St. Paul* (New York: W.W. Norton & Co., 1972), pp. 132–148.
161. Faduma, "The Pastoral Epistles," pp. 215–227.
162. O. Faduma, *The Defects of the Negro Church* (Washington, D.C.: The American Negro Academy, 1904), p. 3.
163. See, for example, O. Faduma, "Materials for the Study of the World Religions," *A.M.E. Church Review* 12 (Apr. 1896): 461–473.
164. See, for example, Egbert Smyth's treatment of the Genesis account of creation in *Old Faiths in New Light,* pp. 138–50, 171–172. See also Lyman Abbott, *The Theology of an Evolutionist.*
165. O. Faduma, "The Faith that Is in Me," *Sierra Leone Weekly News,* 16 June 1923.

166. O. Faduma, "Africa or the Dark Continent," *A.M.E. Church Review* 9 (Jan. 1893): 1–8, and O. Faduma, "Religious Beliefs and Worship of the Yorubas in West Africa," *A.M.E. Church Review* 12 (July 1895): 150–158.
167. O. Faduma, "My Nigerian African Background," manuscript version in Yale Divinity School Alumni files, p. 4.
168. Ahlstrom, *Theology in America,* pp. 71–72; George F. Thomas, "The Philosophy of Religion," in *Protestant Thought in the Twentieth Century,* ed. Arnold Nash, pp. 73–101; Eliade and Kitagawa, *History of Religions,* pp. 4–6.
169. O. Faduma, "Materials for the Study of the World Religions," *A.M.E. Church Review* 12 (Apr. 1896): 461–473.
170. Ibid., pp. 461, 466, 470.
171. Okonkwo, "Man of Two Worlds," p. 26.
172. On the traumatic nature of this examination for some liberals who became unwilling victims of the defenders of orthodoxy, see Swift, "Conservative Versus Progressive Orthodoxy;" Hutchison, *Modernist Impulse,* p.134 and O. Faduma, "The Faith That Is in Me," *The Sierra Leone Weekly News,* 2 June 1923.
173. O. Faduma, "The Faith That Is in Me."
174. Ibid.
175. Ibid.
176. Joseph E. Roy, "Africa and America Illustrated: Their Mutual Relation of History and of Service," in Bowen, *Africa,* p. 223. See also "Rev. Orishatukeh Faduma," *American Missionary* 58 (Jan. 1904): 15.

4

West African Missionary to the American South

While "under appointment of the American Board to return to Africa as soon as the finances will allow," Faduma accepted "temporary assignment" with the American Missionary Association (AMA) "to work in the South among the lowly as a preparation for missionary work in Africa."[1] His initial assignment as superintendent of Peabody Academy and pastor of the Congregational Church at Troy, North Carolina, marked the beginning of what would be a thirty-nine-year tenure as an AMA missionary and educator.[2] Reversing the traditional flow and perception of the mission enterprise and the stereotypes that it engendered among both African-Americans and whites, Faduma served in effect as an African missionary to his "kith and kin" in the South.[3]

The first seventeen years of Faduma's work with the AMA were spent at Troy. He arrived there in the fall of 1895 with his new bride, Henrietta Adams, of Augusta, Georgia, and his assistant, Ms. Amanda Moore. Both women were graduates of AMA institutions (Atlanta and Fisk Universities) and well-prepared to assist Faduma in restructuring the Troy mission.[4] Since its founding in 1881 the mission had been staffed by whites, but in keeping with the AMA's accelerated policy of racial self-help, Faduma and his staff replaced the white workers and implemented "the new idea of starting for self-support."[5] Ironically, Faduma recalled that the most bitter opposition to their assignment to the formerly white post came not from local whites but from blacks who "excepting one deacon . . . all believed that a Negro was not sufficiently trained to be a leader in missionary work." Faduma attributed this attitude to "prejudice due to ignorance."[6]

Although Faduma described his post at Troy as being "absolutely rural," he explained: "While I had educational advantages in the North and could have stayed there, yet I saw that the bulk of my people lived in the South. I chose the South for my field of labor so as to be of use to my people."[7] The "largest portion," he noted, were "still living on the plantations, practically untouched by Christian influences of this century, living without God and not touched by our mission work."[8]

Faduma's acceptance of this post is also partially explained by his conviction that the policies of the AMA were in many respects compatible with his own racial and religious agenda. In an article written after his first year at Troy, he explained the attraction that both the AMA and

Congregationalism held for him. He believed the philosophy and policy of both to be consistent with his commitment to racial pride, independence, ethical activism, and progressivism:

> Foremost in the education of the Negro along the line of self-support is the American Missionary Association . . . . [T]he policy of the Association regarding self-help is not theoretical but practical . . . .The Association states in emphatic and unequivocal language its belief, founded on long experience, in an indigenous ministry. As Dr. Beard says: "Our general policy has been to prepare the race to save the race . . . ."

Faduma concluded by emphasizing that "the position taken by the American Missionary Association is the true one in preparing the people for self-support and thus toward the self-support of our churches."[9]

The roots of the AMA and its policy of racial self-help date from an alliance of black and white evangelicals concerned with racial uplift, anti-slavery action, and evangelical outreach in the 1840s.[10] Although the AMA had been founded as a home and foreign mission agency, the Civil War and its aftermath shifted its focus to the South and the newly freed slaves.[11] Thus in 1875 the AMA withdrew from all of its foreign mission fields, with the exception of the Mendi mission in Sierra Leone. The rationale for this exception lay in the conviction, later shared by Faduma, that mission efforts among West Africans and former slaves in the American South were intrinsically related: "The Association envisioned these two fields as part of one work. Blacks trained in AMA churches and schools could be used for the Christianization and transformation of their brothers and sisters in Africa."[12] While this vision continued to inform AMA policy, by 1883 "the increasingly pressing challenge" of the home mission field forced it also to withdraw from the Mende mission and to concentrate its resources on the religious and educational needs of the southern United States.[13]

The educational arena became an important component of AMA efforts at evangelical outreach. In the face of white resistance to black education it played a major role in founding, staffing, and funding black educational institutions at the primary, secondary, and collegiate level throughout the South.[14] By the period of Faduma's appointment, AMA institutions were generally providing the most progressive and often the only form of education available for many Southern blacks.[15] At the pinnacle of the educational system established and supported by the AMA were institutions such as Hampton Institute, Atlanta University, Tougaloo University, Straight University, Talladega College, and Fisk University. These institutions and their numerous "feeder schools" additionally served as the "embryo" of Congregationalism among African-Americans.[16]

The Troy mission post provided Faduma with a living laboratory in which to test his theological, missiological, and ideological commitments. But he was not to be a prisoner of his laboratory. Indeed, within a brief span of time he became an important public speaker on the interrelated problems of race, religion, and culture as experienced in the Southern and international mission arenas.

In December 1895, less than three months after settling in his mission post at Troy, Faduma traveled to Atlanta to address the Congress on Africa held in conjunction with the Cotton States and International Exposition. Sponsored by the Stewart Missionary Foundation, the Congress was an ecumenical affair that attracted a broad cross-section of participants of both African and European descent. All were concerned with the destiny of Africa and "the relation of the American Negro to the civilization and redemption of his fatherland."[17] Illustrative of the broad, progressive, and evangelical premise of the Congress were the opening remarks of its president, Wilbur P. Thirkield of Gammon Theological Seminary:

> This congress comes to take its place in the ever-widening plans of God for Africa . . . . We aim, therefore, to give the public clearer views of Africa and of the African movement. From a survey of the knowledge and experience gained in the last twenty-five years we should be able to deduce general principles and definite plans that may influence future work in the line of commercial, industrial, civilizing, and redeeming effort.[18]

The Congress was additional evidence of the growing interest in Africa during the last decades of the nineteenth century. It was, in fact, the second congress on Africa held in the United States during the first half of the 1890s. The first, held in Chicago in conjunction with the 1893 Columbian Exposition and the World's Parliament of Religion, was called "the World's Congress on Africa." It shared and advanced the generally liberal and progressive attitude that gave vision and substance to the Parliament of Religion. It also drew many of its participants and much of its audience from the Parliament.[19] Frederick Perry Noble, its major catalyst and organizing secretary, was an evangelical liberal with social gospel inclinations who envisioned the Congress as the missiological counterpart of the World's Parliament.[20] He and other organizers of the Congress solicited the findings and insights of the "world's most eminent men" in the fields of missions, science, politics, and education in response to the question: "Whether the methods and policies of modern African missions are what they ought to be."[21] Among the experts of African descent invited to participate were Edward Blyden, James Johnson, Booker T. Washington, Henry M. Turner, and Bishop Alexander Walters.[22]

Although the 1893 Congress did not live up to the expectations of its organizers, it nevertheless served to stimulate further an evangelical

Pan-African consciousness among some of its African-American participants. Thus in its aftermath Bishop Henry M. Turner reaffirmed an African kinship and committed himself to "now work for the cause of mission, as I never have before."[23] Moreover, the decidedly Pan-African tenor of the Congress prompted one Chicago newspaper to report:

> [T]his great congress was unquestionably one of the most notable convocations of recent years in any country. We have had pan-Presbyterian, pan-Methodist, pan-Anglican, pan-Missionary and pan-Congregational councils . . . . But none signified more than this pan-African conference.[24]

The 1895 Congress on Africa, as had its predecessor, served as stimulus and barometer of rising interest in Africa among both black and white Americans. Moreover, the two congresses were linked by an overlap of interests, concerns, and participants. This relationship was acknowledged at the opening ceremonies of the 1895 Congress when President Thirkield read to the participants a telegram from Frederick Perry Noble that expressed hope that the Congress might "advance Africa's annexation to Christ's kingdom."[25] Other participants or invitees to both congresses included Alexander Crummell, Henry M. Turner, and Edward Blyden.[26] Although unable to attend, Blyden addressed a letter that expressed his hope that it would be a significant conclave:

> The "Congress on Africa" at this time is most opportune. . . . I hope that the results of the congress upon the Negro population will be such as to lead them to take greater practical interest in the land of their fathers . . . [Y]our congress, I trust will be one of the providential agencies in the promotion of the magnificent work of Africa's regeneration.[27]

At the Congress, which was in session from December 13 to 15, Faduma joined the ranks of an impressive group of clergy, educators, politicians, scholars, and missionaries. The list of participants included Wilbur P. Thirkield, President of Gammon Theological Seminary; Bishop Isaac W. Joyce of the Methodist Episcopal Church; W. Y. Atkinson, Governor of Georgia; Cyrus C. Adams, editor of the *New York Sun;* Reverend R. S. Rust, Honorary Corresponding Secretary of the Freedmen's Aid and Southern Education Society of the Methodist Episcopal Church; John H. Smyth, ex-minister to Liberia; John Wesley E. Bowen, professor of Historical Theology at Gammon Theological Seminary; and T. Thomas Fortune, editor of the *New York Age*.[28] According to the *Atlanta Constitution,* the Congress "was probably the most distinguished gathering of learned men of both colors that has ever been assembled together within the history of the south."[29] With specific reference to the congress's African-American participants, it declared:

> There certainly has not been gathered in any other city a more august body of colored divines and men of brains and eloquence in their race . . . . Colored men of deep learning, who have thrown around them a luster that has commanded the admiration of the entire world of learning and to whom their race look for the deliverance of their benighted brethren beyond the seas. . . .[30]

Although the overall tone of the Congress was progressive, the many papers presented in its nine sessions reflect the varied, ambivalent and often contradictory opinions held on the topics of "Africa; The Continent; Its Peoples; Their Civilization and Evangelization," and "The American Negro; His Relation to the Civilization and Redemption of Africa."[31] With but few exceptions, the papers also reflected traditional evangelical theological and missiological perspectives. Among the few papers that broke most conspicuously with this tradition were two presented by Faduma.[32]

Faduma's first presentation was entitled "Religious Beliefs of the Yoruba People in West Africa."[33] In this extended and more scholarly version of his "Religious Belief and Worship of the Yorubas in West Africa," published earlier that year, Faduma explicitly drew upon his recently completed studies in comparative religion and philosophy of religion to argue for a more enlightened perspective on African religions and cultures. He opened his address by updating his audience on the significance of the contributions that religious scholars such as "Max Muller, [George] Rawlinson, and [Archibald H.] Sayce" had made to the contemporary understanding of the "evolution" of the major world religions.[34] Faduma noted, however, that such studies should not be limited in their application and scope to Western and Near Eastern religions—the so-called world religions. Rather, he argued, "The study of religion in all its forms ought to be important to the student of comparative religion."[35] He contended that such studies, if correctly applied, could also shed valuable light on the religions of Africa and their relationship to Christianity, and could ultimately assist in the process of evangelization. Then, as if to offer an example, he presented a critical yet "sympathetic" analysis of his ancestral religion.[36]

It was an appropriation and synthesis of theological liberalism and the new religious studies that induced Faduma to contend that the "superstition," "fear," and "idolatry" seemingly rampant in Yoruba religion should be understood as the Yoruba people "groping in the dark" in quest of the higher truths manifest in Christ and found ultimately in Christianity.[37] With support from *The Essential Nature of Religion* by James A. Picton, he contended that for them as for other members of the human family, "God is the fundamental conception . . . . We cannot deny to these people the possession of a religious or a moral sense. Both exist, though corrupted and distorted."[38]

With explicit reference to his postgraduate study at Yale University, Faduma noted that "the study of the philosophy of religion is bringing us nearer and nearer the truth that the conception of God is universal, and that it is only the "fool that saith in his heart there is no God." In concluding, he embraced and incorporated the insights expressed by the influential liberal Lewis French Stearns in his 1891 lectures on "The Evidence of Christian Experience":

> In this experience of God, every soul of man has a part. He is not far from every one of us; in Him we live and move and have our being. It is possible for every soul, however degraded, however ignorant and humble, to feel after Him and find Him . . . . The knowledge of God is common knowledge. However imperfectly and pervertedly men may hold it and express it, all have it, so that when the higher Christian truth comes to a soul, it does not come to one ignorant of God, but to one that, from its earliest days, has felt his presence and power.[39]

Faduma made the missiological implications of this thesis explicit in his second presentation before the Congress. In this address, entitled "Success and Drawbacks of Missionary Work in Africa by an Eye-Witness," he employed the perspectives of liberal theology and the findings of comparative religion and philosophy of religion to critique the mission enterprise as practiced in Sierra Leone.[40] Although exuberant about the new prominence given the scientific study and practice of missions, he warned that it was still too often hampered by serious "drawbacks" that were rooted in the spiritual, cultural, and ecclesiastical chauvinism of western missionaries.

First among these drawbacks was the attempt of missionaries to replace native languages with their own. "The African people," argued Faduma, "must hear the word of God in their own language." Although the European languages contained "treasures in philosophy and the natural sciences" and could be "valuable aids in the evolution of the native mind," they should not replace native languages:

> None of the European languages is poetic enough, none is as euphonious, none touches the tender cords of the soul and makes them vibrate in harmony with the music of heaven and the great heart of God, as the native language as spoken to a native. If God is to be seen, felt, and interpreted, let this be done by the eyes, the ears, and the understanding of the native.[41]

The second major drawback was "the inability of instructors to distinguish between the natural and unnatural in the life and thought of the native." Faduma lamented:

> Coming into contact with Christian converts, especially along the West Coast, one is pained to see too frequently, an exact reproduction of the white teacher. Native modes of thought, and all those peculiarities of language and manner which ought to differentiate one race from another, are suppressed. . . . [T]he general impression is, that in order to civilize and Christianize the African, he must be foreignized. Hence, one's native name, dress, and food must be changed in order that he may be ranked among the civilized portion of the community.[42]

With reference to the failure of the cultural reform movement that had drawn his participation and induced his change of name, he noted:

> We have had individuals point out these mistakes. Reforms have been started . . . but with little or no effect. Habit has become second nature . . . . But as one bad seed sowed generates more than one, so in Sierra Leone, the oldest of missionary fields in West Africa, and where this foreignizing process is carried to its utmost extent, it has been productive of much evil. It is already a maxim that everything which is white and foreign is necessarily good.[43]

The third drawback of missionary practice was an ecclesiastical paternalism that bred "parasitism," crushed "self-respect," and made men "become children . . . helpless sucklings":

> It wins thousands of adherents who are at best sycophants and cringers, men who will not dare express their thoughts for fear their missionary masters will be angry at them and cut off their means of living. Paternalism in the working of missions is rotten to its very core . . . .[44]

The failure of the mission enterprise to give adequate attention to "the industrial development of the natives" was listed as the fourth drawback hampering evangelical success. Faduma suggested that this represented "a blindness" to "the spirit of the age," which although "largely materialistic," was not "necessarily unspiritual:"

> The church, by failing to introduce and develop the industries in mission fields, seems to be unwilling to recognize God in matter. It seems to think that a man's development is complete when he is religious. It has failed to appreciate the fact that body and soul are linked together in this mundane system.

Thus, he declared, "the need of Africa is a rounded Christianity, not a spiritual, nor physical hypertrophy. The song of the church and of missions for the new century should be Christ, Tools and Man."[45]

The fifth drawback, that Faduma noted was the planting in Africa of "an adulterated Christianity, a Christianity corrupted by the vices of the foreigner, and the heathen environments of the native converts." He observed, however, that these tendencies were not exclusive to modern Christianity:

> Paul, the Christian apostle, was tinged with rabbinical thought. James was a Christian, but he leaned toward Judaism. Some of the Pauline epistles contain agnostic errors with which the air was charged, and which threatened to destroy the purity of Christian truth by amalgamating with it. Christian teachers in the early age of the Church, could not escape the infection of Platonic thought which is even traceable in our modern theology.[46]

The final drawback was "denomination[al] rivalry" which not only squandered the resources of the mission enterprise, but also "with its opposing creeds is confusing to the native mind." Faduma longed fervently for the end of such rivalry:

> It would certainly be a day of Pentecost to the Christian church when she can unite all her forces and do battle for the Lord; when narrow bigotry and religious intolerance will vanish . . when the disciples of Christ shall emphasize life and character in such a way that a man's creed does not become a hindrance to his usefulness; when societies will be large hearted enough to turn over their fields to others who can work them better . . . when there shall be a return to apostolic church government, and we shall hear, not of the *churches,* but the church in Egypt, the church in Sierra Leone, the church in Lagos, the church in Natal, the church in Gazaland.[47]

Having listed and analyzed the drawbacks of missionary practice in Africa, Faduma turned his attention to those developments that contributed directly and indirectly to missionary success. Foremost among them was "the school house." In addressing the complaint that it was a waste of money to train men and women who are never employed as mission agents, he pointed out that this was "a very selfish and narrow way of estimating success":

> Whether or not men are fitted in these schools for a preaching life, it will be found out on careful examination that these schools have furnished good leaven to native society . . . . Much more good than harm is done by education. It expands the intellect, and leaves men more prepared to receive the truths of Christianity. Christianity and the intellect are not enemies. They should never be divorced from each other.

Again he employed the findings and perspectives of comparative religion and the philosophy of religion as he argued:

> In the preparation of humanity for Christ the ancient nations of Egypt, Chaldea, Rome and Greece contributed. Philosophy, science and art have helped to expand men's minds; Plato, Seneca, Marcus Aurelius and Aristole, heathen though they were, uttered truths which were not antagonistic,

> but preparatory to Christianity . . . . Christianity did not spring into the world of a sudden. In this work of the expansion of the intellect, the schools are doing much indirectly to make the gospel intelligible to the native mind.[48]

In conclusion, Faduma argued that the only overall prescription for missionary success in Africa was the encouragement of those developments that furthered the indigenization of Christianity:

> Let us have a Christian life and thought expressed in Africa, not after the manner of a Frenchman, an American, or Englishman, but assimilated into African. Let Christianity planted in Africa become native to the soil, growing from within and without, but losing none of its manhood and inherent vitality. I believe in race variety and development. If the Christian religion is not the white man's religion, but the religion of Jesus Christ, having life to support every race, let it have a trial on these ethnic races . . . . Every race has a peculiar contribution to make to the sum total of spiritual and moral life. Christianity has not reached its highest achievement until all the races of mankind have brought in their contribution to the foot of the cross.[49]

Faduma's progressive missiological and pedagogical insights were well received by the Congress. He reportedly "delighted" those in attendance with his "two profound dissertations."[50] In addition, extensive excerpts of his addresses and a photograph were published in the *Atlanta Constitution*.[51] His missiological insights and credentials were also noted before an international audience when the editors of the *Missionary Review of the World,* one of the foremost missiological journals of the era, praised his presentations as "the excellent views of one of the most highly and broadly cultured natives concerning missionary work."[52]

Despite the positive reception given his addresses at the Congress on Africa and his exceptional qualifications as a foreign missionary, Faduma continued to be frustrated in his efforts to gain appointment to an African mission post. However, as an evangelical Pan-Africanist, he valued his work as an AMA missionary among African-Americans as an important alternative and complement to work among Africans on the Continent. Moreover, his role as an African missionary to African-Americans was noted with pride and amazement by his friends in Sierra Leone with whom he kept in contact via the *Sierra Leone Weekly News*.[53] The irony of Faduma's reversal of traditional mission practice and strategy induced Cornelius May to editorialize: "It is interesting to note that in this remarkable case matters have been reversed, and Africa has given one of her sons to carry literature and learning to the house of bondage and oppression."[54]

Since Faduma perceived that the problems of evangelization, education, and racial development among diaspora Africans were not unlike the problems faced by indigenous Africans, Troy and the surrounding community functioned as a laboratory in which to assess and propagate his Pan-African missiology and pedagogy. Thus in 1902 he informed his West African friends of his continued efforts at "disseminating" his "race ideas . . . in the schoolroom, the press and pulpit."[55]

In his 1890 article on the New Theology Faduma expressed his optimistic conviction that the New Theology was "destined to uproot American prejudice against the Negro, elevate and purify the state, the church, [and] conquer Anglo-Saxon haughtiness . . . ."[56] However, during the course of his seventeen-year ministry at Troy, Faduma found himself experiencing and chronicling the resurgence of a more virulent racism in church, state, and society.[57]

As early as 1898 Faduma described himself as a "philosopher" of the race problem. To further this agenda he became a member of the American Academy of Political and Social Science.[58] His membership reportedly provided him with "opportunities . . . to exchange views with American and European scholars on the Negro as a body politic and social."[59] In 1902 he informed his friends in Sierra Leone that he was "here fighting the foe on his own ground with his own tools of precision."[60] These "tools of precision" consisted of his appropriations of liberal theology, comparative religion, biblical criticism, and the philosophy of religion. To these he soon added the perspective and findings of sociology which was rapidly becoming a popular discipline for the study of race relations and the "Negro Problem."[61]

Faduma's encounter with the race problem was not merely theoretical. By 1902 he had made the decision to become a naturalized citizen of the United States. In explanation, he confessed, "My racial group was considerably handicapped. In order to feel and suffer as my people felt and suffered, I made up my mind to become a naturalized citizen under the Stars and Stripes of the United States of America. I was willing to pass through the stings of Southern segregation."[62]

Faduma's attention to racial development and the increasingly intransigent problem of racism in its various modes was reflected in many of his sermons and writings during this era. Exemplifying his effort and perspective was a sermon on "Racial Destiny" delivered in 1902 to the Colored Women's Christian Temperance Union Convention.[63] Taking for his text Psalm 68:31, the "Ethiopian prophecy" long drawn upon for inspiration and legitimation by black evangelicals and Pan-Africanists, Faduma insisted that the African race "has a distinct and peculiar mission or message to the world."[64] He also reminded his audience of the debt that the world already owed to Africa:

> Without the nurture of Africa, Judaism and Christianity could not exist. Insomuch as Mohammedanism is an offshoot of Judaism we may safely say

> that these great religions with their commanding personalities—Moses, Christ and Mohammed who have morally transformed the world are indebted to Africa. Princes shall come out of Egypt. . . .[65]

One of Faduma's most comprehensive efforts to address the wider problematic of race, religion, and culture was presented in 1907 in an address entitled "Christian Missions among Less Developed Races."[66] Here he underscored his belief that there was an intrinsic link between his work as a missionary in the American South and the broader foreign mission enterprise, especially as it pertained to Africa. He also explicitly applied the evolutionary theory to racial development and missionary expansion.

Like a number of his African-American contemporaries such as Reverdy Ransom and W. E. B. Du Bois, Faduma attempted to divorce the evolutionary theory from its most racist implications and incorporate it as part of an apologetic and defense of the African race.[67] Since the evolutionary process had guided the historical development of Christianity among Western nations, he insisted that "the same laws of evolution are applicable to the operations of Christian missions among the less developed nations of the world."[68] Crucial to the success of the mission enterprise was an awareness that all races and nations passed through stages of evolution. In the first stage, "the period of childhood . . . men are merely receivers and imitators" and "are eager to adopt indiscriminately what is laid before them." In the second stage men "begin to investigate and are eager to know the whys and wherefores of things." This was a "critical" stage because here the recipient also begins to challenge and criticize the plans of the missionary and educator. The latter may in turn "become impatient and through ignorance of psychological laws of growth condemn and discourage the precocious native mind." Faduma noted that if "at any time a double portion of the Holy Spirit and the spirit of wisdom, humility and tolerance are needed, it is at this stage." The final stage was that "of manhood." At this stage "the mind is now ready to assimilate what is best for its growth. It is able to cast off and retain by being able to discriminate between the necessary and the accidental, between the true and the spurious."[69]

A key component of this evolutionary process was a proper education. In partial explanation of his own linkage of pedagogy and missiology, Faduma noted that "it is by a process of education that each [race] is expected to find out what its distinctive mission or destiny is." Thus he insisted:

> The work of Christian missions includes the education of the native mind in such a way that the native can see the truth whenever it is presented to him. Every nation has an individuality of its own which must be cultivated and transferred to another age to be increased or diminished. The right kind of education enables one to know when to add or subtract from this individuality.

It is a "sorry process of education," he noted, "which leaves the learner a man of no country, a non-descript, or a mere imitator, a civilized or religious monkey."[70] This pedagogical model had significant implications for the indigenization of Christianity:

> There is much in religion which is external and accidental, and may be dispensed with or be changed according to climate and temperature. The creeds, vestments, liturgies, and architecture of the West are the result of Western thought and life, and may not be needed in the East, because they do not express the thought and life of the East. Only those should be retained which are an expression of the life, thought and experience of the learner.[71]

Furthermore, Faduma noted, "It should not be expected that there would be the sameness in form between Japanese and American Christianity or between African and Anglican Christianity" since "Race individuality impresses itself upon Christianity wherever it is presented." Thus contrary to the expansive claims made by his fellow liberal missiologist Josiah Strong, Faduma argued that the "destiny of the African or the Japanese as any other nation is not in the hands of the Anglo-Saxon, but is in God's keeping.[72] It was this ultimately inexorable process of race individuality that made empty "the boastful dream of politicians to Europeanize, Russianize, Germanize, or Anglo-Saxonize dependent nations." In response to the cultural and racial chauvinism explicit in the claim that it was "their mission . . . to Westernize ethnic nations in thought, manners, social customs, names, dress, church liturgy, and architecture," Faduma charged:

> It is when this political idea of Westernizing the world is injected into Christianity that we have a confusion of ideas between civilization and Christianity . . . . It is well for all Christian missionaries to efface themselves as English, German or American, and abolish the idea of Anglo-Saxonizing, Germanizing, or Americanizing native peoples. The kind of supremacy needed for native people is neither Anglo-Saxon, nor Teutonic, it is the supremacy of Christ . . . . We plead for the opportunity to be given Christianity to do its own work, and the backward nations to develop unfettered.[73]

Faduma observed that a prime example of failure to heed the developmental process was in South Africa. There European chauvinism and fears led to the suppression of the Ethiopian movement—a movement that he described as "epochal in the religious history of South Africa" and "the greatest movement undertaken by natives for their development."[74] The result:

> Native independence in ecclesiastical matters, which the philosophy of missions has proved to be the best for all people, has been rudely shaken,

> and the native is now forbidden to exercise control in his own church, but must be led and controlled by a white missionary. In South Africa it is either a white leader for the native or no church.[75]

He warned his predominantly black audience of "Congregational workers" that this development had serious implications for their own status and mission efforts in the South. "This convention," he admonished, "will be negligent of its duty if it fail[s] to catch the significance of this downward tendency in the history of Christian missions in Africa, a tendency calculated to paralyze the growth of native churches and encourage infidelity and skepticism in the minds of educated natives."[76]

Faduma also cautioned of the missiological consequences of increasing racism in the United States:

> Every wrong done by the more advanced to the less advanced nation creates one more barrier to the progress of Christianity . . . . The wrong treatment of the Negro, Chinaman, Japanese, or Filipino in Christian America affects Christianity here and in their ancestral homes. Christianity is on trial. Not only men, but religions must also be tested by their fruits. . . . Every act of social and political injustice dealt by the white man to the Chinese, Japanese, Negro, Filipino, or Cuban in the United States is known and resented by their brothers in China, Japan, Africa, Philippine Islands, and Cuba.[77]

Conversely:

> One of the quicker and best ways to reach these different peoples in foreign lands is to treat them in a Christ-like manner here at our doors. Each one is already a missionary for good or evil. "For as much as ye have done it unto one of the least of these my brethren, ye have done it unto me," says Christ.[78]

Although this address was delivered before a Southern black audience, the editors of the *Missionary Review of the World* deemed his message worthy of an international audience. A condensed version of the address, along with a biographical sketch of Faduma, was published in their June 1907 edition.[79]

Despite being stationed in rural North Carolina, Faduma managed to maintain contact with the broader intellectual and academic communities, not only through his published writings, but also through his membership in organizations such as the American Academy of Political and Social Science and the American Negro Academy (ANA).[80] His membership in the latter organization was of special importance because it facilitated his contact and discourse with the African-American intelligentsia. It also provided him with an important forum from which to project his liberal-oriented evangelical Pan-Africanism.[81]

Established on March 5, 1897, under the guiding impetus of the Episcopalian minister and former African missionary Alexander Crummell, the ANA was defined by its constitution as "an organization of authors, scholars, artists, and those distinguished in other walks of life, men of African descent, for the promotion of letters, science, and art." It aimed also "to aid, by publication, the dissemination of truth and the vindication of the Negro race from vicious assaults."[82] Faduma's nomination and election to the ANA in 1899 with the endorsement of Crummell, Albert P. Miller, William H. Ferris, John Albert Johnson, and Levi J. Coppin linked him with an impressive group of black scholars, educators, and clergy. Moreover, a number of its members, such as Albert P. Miller, John W. E. Bowen, William H. Ferris, Theophilus Gould Steward, Alexander Walters, and Jesse E. Moorland, were of progressive or liberal theological orientation.[83]

It was as a participant in the activities of the ANA that Faduma presented two of his most controversial papers. At its 1902 meeting, which had as its theme "The Religion of the Negro," he read a paper entitled "The Defects of the Negro Church."[84] In this controversial presentation, he roundly critiqued the African-American Church and its clergy from a liberal theological perspective, which he projected as both normative and prescriptive.[85]

Faduma opened with the disclaimer that he was "compelled to use the surgeon's knife . . . with the utmost sympathy and with a view to heal" and that "the defects of the Negro Church are found more or less in churches of other races."[86] Listed first among these "defects" was "the tendency to lay stress on outwardness rather than inwardness." This, he warned, fostered worldliness and made "religion a puppet show."[87] In a passage that perhaps explained his estrangement from the African Methodist Episcopal Church, Faduma offered a stinging rebuke to both "worldliness" and ecclesiastical politics:

> The world spirit is in the churches and has taken hold of our ministry. . . . [W]orldliness follows when desire for position or recognition in the church overcomes the desire to save men, and when the ordinary tricks of politics are resorted to in order to gain church distinction. . . . [T]he more elaborate the organization of a church is, the larger the number of preferments to offices and greater the opportunity given to office seekers to make these the first things . . . . [T]oo much organization in the church leads to too much officialism and worldliness for "where the carcass is, there will the vultures be gathered together."[88]

The second alleged defect was of special significance to Faduma. It was the "neglect of rural communities" where, he noted, "eighty to eighty-five percent of the race is to be found." While acknowledging factors that accounted for this neglect—among them a lack of funds and the "repulsiveness of rural districts on account of inadequate protection and little justice given to the Negro"—he nevertheless charged that the result had been the "paganization of Christianity":

> One of the saddest things that has happened to Negroes in our rural districts is the presentation to them of Christianity in a crude, uncouth, and distorted form. It is a form of Christianity with the Christ left out. The songs of the church, its prayers and experiences are there but in a mutilated form, divested of their spiritual significance. . . . In Africa, Christianity is displacing paganism, in rural America paganism is displacing Christianity. . . . [89]

Faduma's cultural and theological biases were again exposed as he alleged that the third defect of the Negro Church was the lack of "scholarship and culture" of its ministry.[90] As a consequence hermeneutics, theology, and ethics suffered:

> It follows as a matter of course that where the ministry is [uneducated and] uncultured, the interpretation of the word of God suffers. . . . [The black minister] believes too much in the non-essentials of religion, his heaven and hell are too much in the distant future . . . . The new heaven and the new earth which John saw and the new Jerusalem coming down from God to man are antipodal to his conceptions. His God is seen going up to some cloudless region instead of coming down to tabernacle with men . . . . His sermons feed the feelings but neglect the intellect and will, they tickle the ear and subordinate truth to eloquence . . . . He pursues his beaten path along the old ruts of ecclesiasticism. He believes in a revelation which is non-progressive and whose distinctive feature is sameness for all times . . . . His theology is in the main denominational and is like the laws of the Medes and Persians which admit of no change. His mind does not discriminate between the *ipse dixit* of the Almighty and external matters relating to dogma. In the pulpit he lacks decorum, deep spirituality, and contemplation. His oratory is thunderous, too physical, and lacks grace and beauty.[91]

"The leader of a people," insisted Faduma, "must be a man of broad culture, wide sympathies, and in touch with all the varied interests of the people." Moreover, such a leader must be abreast of contemporary social, scientific, and intellectual developments and have at his command the modern findings of comparative religion as well as literature and history:

> It is not enough to be able to read the Bible or pass an examination in denominational theology. The modern teacher and preacher of today must be acquainted with the humanities. If not a scientist, he must know the trend of scientific thought and its relation to the Bible. The best poetry of nations should be at his command. . . . [T]he masterpieces of the world's best prose writers, the history of art, the study of the philosophy of history, and the too neglected study of the history of ethnic religions must be in his possession, not simply in the library of his home but in the library of his mind.[92]

Morever, Faduma contended that in order to end "the reducing of the Bible to a Fetish," African-American clergy needed to cultivate an appreciation of modern methods of biblical interpretation.

The final defect alleged by Faduma was "excessive emotionalism in worship":

> Paradoxical as it may seem, in religion the Negro's emotions constitute his strongest as well as his weakest point . . . [H]is defect is not that he is emotional, but that he is excessively so. Like other races in their childhood, he is a bundle of feelings. He does not think after God, he does not will after God, but he feels after God.[93]

Ironically, Faduma's controversial critique represented one of the earliest efforts to apply the perspectives and findings of comparative religion and philosophy of religion to "Negro religion." Faduma was conscious of this as he noted:

> There are some general facts in connection with the philosophy of religion which are often overlooked in the study of Negro religion . . . . There is nothing new in the religion of the Negro. He is by no means a peculiar man from a religious standpoint. The physical contortions and gyrations noticed in his Christian worship are as old as the history of religion itself if not older than it. In his worship we may see things which are found in the heathen rites of the native African, in the Bacchanalia of the Greeks, among the Sali or dancing priests of the Romans and among the Carybontes.[94]

Faduma concluded his paper with a call for the type of education that would produce a balance between emotion and reason:

> What is needed for the proper religious development of the Negro is education, not repression or subjugation of his feelings. . . . . [T]he Negro needs more thought in his religion, but religion is not all thought. To have a proper balance in religion as in every-day life, the faculties of thought, feeling, and volition must be present, distributed in fair proportions. When reason is overfed in the exercise of religion, the result is a dry and barren rationalism. When the emotions are overfed, the result is a wild and sickly sentimentalism, a neurotic religion.[95]

The executive committee of the ANA conceded that Faduma's paper was a scholarly and generally accurate analysis of the Black Church. Nevertheless, they were hesitant to publish it among the Academy's occasional papers.[96] Their reluctance was apparently rooted in their fear that the paper would be viewed as an attack on the Black Church and its clergy by the Academy. Finally, in 1904, upon recommendation by ANA President Archibald Grimke, the controversial paper was published as the Academy's Occasional Paper number 10.[97] In the aftermath of its publication, the clerical reaction feared by the Academy's executive committee did not materialize. However, "the paper seems to have generated public interest for several years" and continued requests for it resulted in several reprints.[98]

Faduma's critique of the Black Church and ministry was not the last that the ANA would entertain and publish. In 1909 it published an essay written by the Congregationalist minister, Jesse E. Moorland entitled *The Demand and the Supply of Increased Efficiency in the Negro Ministry*. Though less acrimonious than Faduma's, it was a similarly liberal-based and biased critique that called for extensive reform of the Black Church and its clergy.[99] Moorland argued, as had Faduma, that it was only a comprehensive and liberal education that would increase the "efficiency" of the black ministry:

> The Negro minister ought to be the best trained man among us in order that he may be able to assume his rightful place as a leader of the people. The training needed for the ministry of today must be comprehensive and practical . . . [W]hat we need today for our ministers is a training which will put them in possession of the knowledge of human society just as it is.[100]

The traditional seminary curriculum, he argued, was neither "calculated" nor structured to prepare ministers to address and respond to the problems of the modern era, since it contained little "that inspires men with the gravity of the problems of human society in the beginning of the twentieth century." Moorland's social gospel inclinations were evident as he noted: "Too many times in our seminaries men speculate about theories of salvation and various other things labeled doctrines, which are of little or no value to men whose business it is to bring the Kingdom of Jesus on earth as it is in heaven."[101] Much more relevant, he suggested, was the new curriculum being instituted at two of the nation's foremost liberal seminaries, Yale Divinity School and Chicago Theological Seminary. It was a curriculum designed "to emphasize the relation of the minister to the problems of modern society, giving special attention to Christian sociology, ethics, and methods of Christian activity." Thus Chicago, he noted, had expanded its curriculum to include courses in "the psychology of Christian living, religious pedagogy, evangelism, missions, Christian sociology and citizenship."[102]

While calling upon other seminaries to follow the model of Yale and Chicago, Moorland was aware of the problem faced by the vast majority of the black clergy who had no access to seminary training. For them, he recommended a program of independent study and a basic reading list heavily weighted with liberal authors, themes, and issues:

> Every preacher should own, read, and ponder the following books and extend his reading as he may see fit: "The Social Crisis" by Rauschenbusch

> . . . ; "The Social Message of the Modern Pulpit" by Brown . . . ; "The Religion of a Mature Mind" and "The Spiritual Life" by Coe . . . ; "The Psychology of Religion" by Starbuck . . . ; "Elements of Sociology" by Giddings . . . ; and Proceedings of the Religious Education Association.[103]

Moorland's paper apparently encountered little difficulty en route to publication by the ANA and was issued in 1909 as Occasional Paper number 13. Less successful was a second paper that Faduma presented before the Academy in 1908. This paper, entitled, "Social Problems in West Africa From the Standpoint of an African," reflected Faduma's growing appreciation and toleration for indigenous West African cultural institutions and their importance for the indigenization of Christianity.[104] It also reflected the continued influence of Edward Blyden. In his 1895 article entitled "Success and Drawbacks of Missionary Work in Africa by an Eye-Witness," Faduma had denounced polygamy and listed the effort to "introduce polygamy into the church" as a blatant example of "the commingling of heathen and Christian conceptions" that gave rise to "Christianity heathenized" and "adulterated."[105] But in 1908 he argued before the Academy that polygamy was one of the indigenous West African institutions with which Christianity must be willing to coexist. It is not incidental that his new appreciation of polygamy coincided with the extended defense of polygamy and other aspects of African culture presented by Blyden in his 1908 publication entitled *African Life and Customs.*[106]

John W. Cromwell, one of the founding members and guiding lights of Academy, noted the impact of Faduma's paper. It was, he reported, "a revelation to many for the scholarship shown and the novelty of the arguments in behalf of polygamy for the West African."[107] A similar assessment was made by two Howard University scholars, Kelly Miller and Charles C. Cook.[108] Nevertheless, the paper radically challenged the Victorian conventions of many ANA members and was considered too controversial for publication. Alfred A. Moss concludes that despite the "acknowledged . . . scholarship of the author, this was not enough to allay the fear that publication would have a negative effect on the image of the academy and black intellectuals."[109]

The more tolerant and appreciative attitude that Faduma expressed toward polygamy and other aspects of indigenous West African culture at the 1908 meeting of the ANA may have also been directly influenced by his visit to Sierra Leone in the summer of 1908. This trip, which extended from June 24 to September 12, was Faduma's first visit to his homeland since his departure for the United States in 1891. The announcement of his impending return was published in the *Sierra Leone Weekly News* and elicited additional insight regarding Faduma and the developments that had induced his departure.[110] After reviewing Faduma's early life and schooling, both in Sierra Leone and England, Cornelius May reported that upon his return from London in 1885 and resettlement into the Sierra Leone Community:

> [Faduma's] views of life were meanwhile developing and latent ideas of his race were asserting themselves and found practical expressions in words and deed, which resulted in his being regarded as before his time, and many did not hesitate to express disapproval with some of his views. This led Faduma to direct his attention to some wider field where he could find himself free to study and express himself without let or hindrance.[111]

Thereupon, explained May, Faduma "sailed for America and . . . was not there long before his scholarship was acknowledged and accepted. [There] he found ample scope for the development of his ideas . . . ."[112]

Contrary to May's assessment, Faduma confessed that he had not found unbridled freedom for the development of his thought and ideas in America. Although he lectured Sierra Leone audiences on a broad range of subjects, including agriculture, industrial education, domestic relations, "the sacred and literary use of the Bible," and "the origins and growth of Christianity," his primary topic was race relations in the American South.[113] In various discussions of this topic, Faduma revealed the extent to which racism had circumscribed his life and work in the South over the course of the previous thirteen years. Contrary to his optimistic prophecy racism and prejudice had not yielded to the idealistic vision and ministrations of the New Theology.[114] His writings and lectures clearly reflect the degree to which racism and prejudice mitigated the theology of progressivism, self-help, and racial pride that he sought to share with his students, parishioners, and the wider African-American community.

Ironically, Faduma's strategy for engagement and encounter with the white South can best be described as accommodationist.[115] As early as 1898 he confessed that he was becoming more "conservative" on the issue of race.[116] Echoing Booker T. Washington, whom he held in high esteem, Faduma conceded:

> By an unwritten law in American society, the Negro's status is fixed. No legislation can give him social recognition. Unfortunately there is a confusion in men's minds between equality of rights and social equality. Politicians have helped to bring this confusion. There is no law to make one man, be he white or black, the social equal of another.[117]

By 1902 he had also disavowed any interest in Southern politics. However, during his 1908 tour, Faduma presented a humorous and illuminating account of his early efforts to exercise his electoral rights despite the infamous literacy test used to deny the vote to Southern blacks. As recounted by a correspondent to the *Sierra Leone Weekly News:*

> [M]en were "plucked" by the hundred. Graduate or no graduate, professor or no professor, after reading and transcribing a short paragraph the Yankee tyrant-examiner would turn you down as "illiterate." But in Faduma's case, either he was one too many for the examiner, or the latter still had some soul left in him. After our countryman had finished his task the registration officer said to him;—well I guess you will do"; and requesting the candidate's name, when he was told, he said:—How do you spell it?"[118]

In the course of his 1908 lectures on "Life in the United States," Faduma further revealed how he managed to live and work among white Southerners and even win their respect and admiration. He confessed:

> I have been working in North Carolina these thirteen years and Southern men have recognized my work. They come to my school and see what I am doing and once in a while, a distinguished white man would come to my house. All over the country white men who know me give me the greatest respect.[119]

The price of this respect was often feigned acceptance or total accommodation to the social customs and racial proscriptions of the white South. Something akin to the latter is revealed in Faduma's description of his role as a member of the Troy Board of Education:

> A few years ago when a Board of Education was formed at Troy, the white people put me on that board. In other parts of the country the coloured members of the board would act on the law, visit the white schools and speak with the white lady teachers but I did not do anything like that. I told the Board of Education that as much as public opinion was against the Negro posting himself into these places although the law gave him authority to do so, I would rather have the privilege of visiting the Negro schools: they agreed to it and we had no trouble.[120]

In his 1904 critique of the "Negro Church" Faduma listed among its "defects" the failure to supply an adequate ministry to the rural South. Yet his testimony of the constant circumspection occasioned by the racism and racial proscriptions and mores of the rural South—an ever present need to exercise "thoughtfulness and commonsense" in dealing with whites—explained in part why better-educated black clergy eschewed life and work in rural areas of the South.[121] In this environment Faduma confessed that even the reception and reply to a letter from a white woman entailed caution and anxiety: "If I had a letter from a Southern white lady I would not answer the letter myself but would ask my wife to do the answering because I did not know whether some one had prompted that white lady to write me a letter so as to bring trouble upon me."[122]

The attitudes Faduma encountered among Southern whites and the dubious nature and success of his efforts to gain their respect and support is further illustrated by the response of Sam Smitherman to a questioner sent out as part of a study of "Southern Whites and the Negro Church."[123] Smitherman, a white resident of Troy, reported that the influence of black churches and ministers in Troy was "as a whole bad," with the sole exception of Faduma and his ministry: "We have one good, honest and reliable Negro preacher in our community, and he is trying to raise the standard of living among his race. . . . The Negro preacher that I refer to is O. Faduma." Unmindful of the fact that Faduma's education probably exceeded that of himself and most residents of Troy, Smitherman added:

> Everyone that is acquainted with the Negro race knows that a Negro is better off without an education than he is with one, for when he has an education he begins to feel then to want to do some mischief. He will either go to preaching or stealing or both. Of course there are some better than others.[124]

Faduma's responses to the racial and social prescriptions of the South appear to be patterned after the "commonsense philosophy" employed by Booker T. Washington in his public interaction with whites. But Faduma's appreciation of Washington was also rooted in his conviction that Washington's emphasis on racial self-help and industrial education was compatible with his own Pan-African missiological and pedagogical paradigm.[125] Thus in what amounted to a broader conceptualization of Washington's program of industrial education, Faduma noted:

> The agitation for industrial education has done much good in that it has corrected a tendency among the college-bred to ignore the trades. Tuskegee has some of the best equipped scholars directing her industrial work. Yet emphasis must be laid on an intelligent industrial education . . . . The industrial education of the Negro to be of much value to him and his employers must be intelligent, from the writing of a book to the baking of a biscuit, from the building of a palace to the ironing of clothes. It must be superior to that of the mule. It is a great power when it is infused with the life which comes from religion and vitalized with a spiritual force.[126]

It was such a program broadly conceived that Faduma attempted to develop at Peabody Academy in Troy. Of his program and its rationale, Faduma explained:

> The industrial problem is a great one in the South, as we all know, and touches the Negro in many points. In our missionary school we are solving it in a practical way . . . . We are, however, more interested in making men rather than mere farmers or artisans; women rather than mere cooks or teachers . . . . However important the head, the heart, and the hands are, each does not make a man when it is not correlated with the rest.[127]

In 1912, on the verge of terminating his seventeen-year assignment as an African missionary to African-Americans, Faduma chronicled

"Church and School at Troy." He began with the mission's establishment in 1881 under the Reverend William Harmon Ellis, an 1874 graduate of Williams College who was "buffeted and ridiculed because he was a 'nigger' preacher and teacher," and concluded with his own tenure as its first nonwhite superintendent. Over the course of his tenure, he and his assistants had successfully raised "the standard of the school from an Elementary to a Normal and Industrial Institute" which now sent out students to Talladega and other colleges.[128] The broader impact and significance of his success at Troy is perhaps best reflected in the fact that "about 90 percent of the teachers" in Montgomery County were products of Peabody Academy.[129] Though proud of his successes at Troy, Faduma was increasingly disappointed by the manifest failure of the New Theology to successfully confront Southern racism and usher in "the kingdom of God" in America as he had naively predicted more than twenty years earlier. Sobered by his experiences in the South, he would find in the Back-to-Africa Movement of Chief Alfred Sam a new vehicle and locus for his mature and chastened evangelical Pan-Africanism.

Notes

1. "Rev. Orishatukeh Faduma," *American Missionary* 58 (Jan. 1904): 15. Joseph E. Roy, "Africa and America Illustrated: Their Mutual Relation of History and of Service" in Bowen, *Africa,* p. 223; Orishatukeh Faduma, "Some of My Experiences in the Southland," *The Expected* (July 1943): 9.
2. Letter from Faduma to Dean Luther A. Weigle, Yale Divinity School Alumni File.
3. "Reverend Orishatukeh Faduma," *Sierra Leone Weekly News,* 2 Aug. 1902. Faduma was not the first African to serve in this capacity with the AMA. Barnabas Root and Thomas DeSaliere came into contact with the AMA through its Mendi Mission in West Africa. Both came to the United States to complete their education and subsequently taught in AMA institutions in the South. Root attended Knox College and later earned a Bachelor of Divinity degree from Chicago Theological Seminary. Before returning to Africa in 1874, he was an instructor of Hebrew at Straight University and pastored the AMA church at Montgomery, Alabama. Tucker was educated at Oberlin College and Straight University Law School. He later became president of Florida State Normal College. Richardson, *Christian Reconstruction,* p.193. Faduma eventually became acquainted with the most famous African educator in the South, Dr. Kwegyir Aggrey. Mrs. Abna Aggrey Lancaster, daughter of Dr. Aggrey, reported that Faduma had been a friend of her father's and that he vis-

ited their home in Salisbury, North Carolina. Telephone interview with Mrs. Abna Aggrey Lancaster, 18 Jan. 1984. On the remarkable career of this important Gold Coast-born educator and missionary statesman, see Edwin W. Smith, *Aggrey of Africa: A Study in Black and White* (New York: Doubleday, Doran & Co., 1929).

4. Faduma, "Some of my Experiences," p. 9. In 1907 "Mrs. H. R. Faduma" is listed as secretary and treasurer of the North Carolina Women's State Organization of the AMA. *American Missionary* 61 (Jan. 1907): 32; Faduma, "My Nigerian African Background," p. 4. Typed manuscript located in Yale Divinity School Alumni File, published in revised form as "An African Background," *Mission Herald* 44 (Sept./Oct. 1940): 18–20.
5. Faduma, "Some of My Experiences," p. 9; O. Faduma, "Church and School at Troy, N.C." *American Missionary* 66 (July 1912): 225.
6. Faduma, "Some of My Experiences," p. 9.
7. Faduma, "Church and School at Troy, N.C.," p. 225; Orishatukeh Faduma, "Life in the United States of America, "*Sierra Leone Weekly News,* 1 Aug. 1908.
8. Orishatukeh Faduma, "A Negro Upon Self-Help and Self-Support," *American Missionary* 50 (Sept. 1896): 279.
9. Ibid., pp. 276–279.
10. Bertram Wyatt-Brown, *Lewis Tappan and the Evangelical War Against Slavery* (New York: Atheneum, 1971), pp. 205–220; Augustus Field Beard, *A Crusade of Brotherhood: A History of the American Missionary Association* (Boston: The Pilgrim Press, 1909; New York: Kraus Reprint Co., 1970).
11. Joe M. Richardson, *Christian Reconstruction: The American Missionary Association and Southern Blacks, 1861–1890* (Athens and London: University of Georgia Press, 1986).
12. Stanley, *Children,* p. 59.
13. Beard, *Crusade,* p. 480.
14. Ibid., pp. 146–147.
15. McPherson, *Legacy,* p. 182. For a more focused study of the origins of the AMA and its work among African-Americans, see especially Clifton H. Johnson, "The American Missionary Association, 1846–1861: A Study of Christian Abolitionism," Ph.D. diss., University of North Carolina, 1959, and Richard Bryant Drake, "The American missionary Association and the Southern Negro, 1861–1888," Ph.D. diss., Emory University, 1957.
16. Beard, *Crusade,* p. 139; Stanley, *Children,* pp. 45–46. Statistics reveal that the vast majority of AMA graduates chose to pursue their ecclesiastical vocations and lives within historically African-American denominations. However, statistics do not reflect the full impact of the AMA and Congregationalism within the

African-American community. Professor Kelly Miller explained that "the result is seen rather in the intellectual and moral uplift than in religious proselytism. The real advantage consists largely in the reflex influence upon the [black] Methodist and Baptist denominations." H. Paul Douglass, *Christian Reconstruction in the South* (Boston: Pilgrim Press, 1909), p. 159.

17. "Opening Remarks" by President W. P. Thirkield of Gammon Theological Seminary, in Bowen, *Africa,* p. 14. A concern to develop both informed mission policies and personnel for the evangelization of Africa had been the guiding rationale for the founding of the Stewart Missionary Foundation for Africa in 1883 by Reverend W. F. Stewart of the Northern Methodist Episcopal Church. Through its headquarters at Gammon Theological Seminary, the Foundation sought "to encourage thought and investigation, spread intelligence and stimulate personal and property consecration among American Negroes for missionary work in Africa." Bowen, *Africa,* p. 10.
18. Ibid., p. 13.
19. Frederick Perry Noble, *Africa at the Columbian Exposition* (Chicago: Newberry Library, 1893). See also "Progress of the Kingdom: Africa in the Columbian Exposition," *The Congregationalist,* 8 Dec. 1892; Esedebe, *Pan-Africanism,* pp. 45–46; Redkey, *Black Exodus,* pp. 141–142; and Frederick P. Noble, *The Chicago Congress on Africa,* pp. 280–281.
20. For Noble's social gospel inclinations, see Luker, "The Social Gospel," pp. 84–85, and Luker, *The Social Gospel in Black and White,* pp. 34–35, 37, 39–40, 48–49. For some indication of his theological orientation and approach to Scripture, see his pamphlet entitled *The Bible as Literature: An Oration to the Research Club, Spokane, April 13th, 1914* (Spokane, Wash.: The Research Club, 1914).
21. Noble, *Africa at the Columbian Exposition,* pp. 9, 13–14.
22. Ibid., pp. 16, 10–11; Esedebe, *Pan-Africanism,* p. 45.
23. Turner, *Voice of Missions* (Oct. 1893): 2. Quoted in Williams, *Black Americans,* p. 52. See also Frederick P. Noble, "The Chicago Congress on Africa," *Our Day* 12 (Oct. 1893): 284.
24. Esedebe, *Pan-Africanism,* p. 46; Noble, "The Chicago Congress on Africa," p. 313.
25. "Minutes of the Congress," Bowen, *Africa,* p. 227. Although unable to attend, Noble submitted a paper that was read before the Congress by Reverend Joseph Roy. Roy was a district secretary of the AMA and had served as chairman of the 1893 congress. Bowen, *Africa,* pp. 219–225.
26. Bowen, *Africa,* pp. 195–198, 229.
27. Edward Blyden, "Letter of Greeting and Commendation," Bowen, *Africa,* p. 16.

28. Bowen, *Africa,* pp. 227–235.
29. "Congress on Africa," *Atlanta Constitution,* 14 Dec. 1895.
30. "Ethiopia's Hand . . . The Congress on Africa," *Atlanta Constitution,* 14 Dec. 1895.
31. Bowen, *Africa,* pp. 11, 160.
32. For another example of this break with traditional missiology, see John H. Smyth, "The African in Africa and the African in America," in Bowen, *Africa,* pp. 228; 69–83.
33. Orishatukeh Faduma, "Religious Beliefs of the Yoruba people in West Africa," Bowen, *Africa,* pp. 31–36.
34. On Muller, see above. George Rawlinson (1812–1902) was a scholar of ancient Eastern religions. He authored such works as *The History of Ancient Egypt* (New York: Dodd, Mead and Co., 1882) and *The Religions of the Ancient World, Including Egypt, Assyria and Babylonia, Persia, India, Phoenicia, Etruria, Greece, Rome* (London: The Religious Tract Society, 1882). Archibald Henry Sayce (1854–1933) was also a student of ancient Eastern religions and cultures and in 1887 gave the Hibbert Lecture on "The Origin and Growth of Religion as Illustrated by the Religion of the Ancient Babylonians."
35. Faduma, "Religious Beliefs," p. 32.
36. Ibid.
37. Ibid., 33.
38. Ibid.
39. Ibid. Quoted from Lewis French Stearns, *The Evidence of Christian Experience: Theistic Philosophical Presuppositions* (New York: Scribners, 1890). See also Williams, *Andover Liberals,* p. 42.
40. Faduma, "Success and Drawbacks of Missionary Work in Africa by an Eye-Witness," Bowen, *Africa,* pp. 125–136.
41. Ibid., p. 126.
42. Ibid., pp. 126–127.
43. Ibid., pp. 127–128.
44. In support of this critique Faduma drew on the missiological writings of E. A. Lawrence, who taught the course on missions during Faduma's second year of study at Yale Divinity School.
45. Faduma, "Success and Drawbacks," p. 30.
46. Ibid., p. 131
47. Ibid., p. 132.
48. Ibid., pp. 133–135. It was this progressive and liberal pedagogical paradigm that Faduma further developed and employed during his years as a missionary educator in both the United States and West Africa.
49. Ibid., p. 128.
50. J. E. Roy, "Africa and America Illustrated," Bowen, *Africa,* p. 223.

51. *Atlanta Constitution,* 15 Dec. 1885.
52. Editorial, "Addresses on the Congress on Africa," *Missionary Review of the World* (19 Sept. 1896): 693.
53. In 1902 Faduma informed Cornelius May that "In this strange land the *Sierra Leone Weekly News* is my father and mother. Without it I shall be homesick." Editorial "Reverend Orishatukeh Faduma," *Sierra Leone Weekly News,* 2 Aug.1902.
54. Ibid.
55. Ibid.
56. Faduma, "The New Theology," p. 139.
57. On the resurgence of racism during this era, see Logan, *Betrayal of the Negro;* Moss, *Academy,* pp. 5–10. For developments in North Carolina see Eric Anderson, *Race and Politics in North Carolina, 1872–1901* (Baton Rouge and London: Louisiana State University Press, 1980).
58. Faduma became a member of the Academy in 1897. Editorial, "Africa and America," *Sierra Leone Weekly News,* 24 Dec. 1898.
59. Ibid.
60. Editorial, "Reverend Faduma," *Sierra Leone Weekly News,* 2 Aug. 1902.
61. In 1898 Faduma informed Cornelius May that he had become "very much interested in the science of sociology." Editorial, "Africa and America," *Sierra Leone Weekly News,* 24 Dec. 1898. On the increased importance of sociology in the study of "The Negro Problem," see John H. Bracey, Jr., August Meier, and Elliot Rudwick, eds., *The Black Sociologist: The First Half Century* (Belmont, Calif.: Wadsworth Publishing Co., 1971), and James E. Blackwell and Morris Janowitz, eds., *Black Sociologists: Historical and Contemporary Perspectives* (Chicago: University of Chicago Press, 1974), pp. 73, 74.
62. Faduma, "Some of My Experiences," p.10.
63. Faduma, "Race Destiny: The Race Problem from a Negro's Viewpoint," *Sierra Leone Weekly News,* 2 Aug. 1902, and Orishatukeh Faduma, "An African Speaks on Negro Problem," *Sierra Leone Weekly News,* 9 Aug. 1902.
64. On the significance of this text, which predicted that "Princes shall come out of Egypt and Ethiopia shall soon stretch forth her hands unto God," see Geiss, *Pan-African Movement,* pp. 133–134, and Raboteau, *Black Destiny.*
65. Faduma "Race Destiny," p. 3.
66. Faduma, "Christian Missions Among Less Developed Races," *American Missionary* 61 (Jan. 1907): 69–74. See also his 1902 address, "The Problem of Race Development," delivered at commencement exercises at the Deaf, Dumb, and Blind Institution for

the Education of Negro Children, in Raleigh, North Carolina. Orishatukeh Faduma, "An African Speaks on Negro Problem," *Sierra Leone Weekly News,* 9 Aug. 1902.

67. See Calvin S. Morris, *Reverdy C. Ransom, Black Advocate of the Social Gospel* (Lanham, University Press of America, 1990), pp. 46–51; W. E. B. Du Bois, "The Conservation of the Races," in *Negro Social and Political Thought, 1850–1920,* ed. Howard Brotz (New York: Basic Books, 1966), pp. 483–492.
68. Faduma, "Christian Missions Among Less Developed Races," p. 70.
69. Ibid.
70. Ibid.
71. Ibid.
72. Ibid.
73. Ibid., pp. 71–72.
74. Ibid., p. 72. "The Ethiopian movement" was the South African wing of a broader movement for cultural and ecclesiastical independence. It arose in South and Central Africa at the end of the nineteenth century. For a discussion of its origins and significance for the Pan-African and mission movements, see Esedebe, *Pan-Africanism,* p. 23, and especially Geiss, *Pan-African Movement,* pp. 132–159; also Bengt Sundkler, *Bantu Prophets in South Africa* (London: Oxford University Press, 1964), pp. 53; and Shepperson, "Pan-Africanism," pp. 4–5. On related movements in West Africa, see James Bertin Webster, *The African Churches among the Yoruba 1888–1922* (Oxford: Clarendon Press, 1964); Sanneh, *West African Christianity,* p. 126; and Ayandele, *Missionary Impact,* pp. 177–179, 235–238.
75. Faduma, "Christian Missions," pp. 72–73.
76. Ibid., p. 73.
77. Ibid., p. 74.
78. Ibid.
79. Orishatukeh Faduma, "Christian Missions among Less Developed Races," *Missionary Review of the World* 20 (June 1907): 453–455.
80. On the American Negro Academy, see Alfred A. Moss, Jr., *The American Negro Academy: Voice of the Talented Tenth* (Baton Rouge and London: Louisiana State University Press, 1981).
81. Its African-American membership included such figures as Alexander Crummell, W. E. B. Du Bois, Francis J. Grimke, William H. Crogman, Alexander Walters, John W. Cromwell, Albert P. Miller, and Levi J. Coppin. The African component of the Academy included corresponding members such as Edward Blyden, Samuel Lewis, and Joseph E. Casely Hayford of West Africa, James Theodore Holly of Haiti, and Duse Mohamed Ali of London. Moss, *Academy,* pp. 19, 26–31, 79, 80, 127–128.

82. Ibid., pp. 1–2.
83. Ibid., p. 73.
84. Moss, *Academy,* p. 89.
85. Faduma's critique also reflected in its main outline the spiritual and cultural chauvinism of the AMA relative to the Black Church and its clergy. On this issue and the problem it posed for both parties, see Richardson, *Christian Reconstruction,* pp. 143–159, 259. See also Joe M. Richardson, "The Failure of the American Missionary Association to Expand Congregationalism among Southern Blacks," *Southern Studies* 18 (Spring 1979): 55–64. Harlan P. Douglass cites Faduma as an example of the "cultured Negro minority" who had become "fully abreast with American civilization" by having "affiliated themselves with the northern denominations which have done the most for Negro uplift and education." Douglass also noted that these churches "constitute but two percent or less of the Negro church membership of America," and yet their power and influence was "disproportionate" to these statistics. But this pioneer in the sociological study of religion also observed that the churches of this select group had their peculiar weaknesses and temptations. They lacked contact with the community, and the masses, in turn, denounced them as "stuck up." Douglass, *Christian Reconstruction in the South* (Boston: Pilgrim Press, 1909), p. 58.
86. Orishatukeh Faduma, *The Defects of the Negro Church,* American Negro Academy Occasional Papers No. 10 (Washington, D.C.: American Negro Academy, 1904), p. 1.
87. Ibid., pp. 4–5.
88. Ibid., pp. 12–13.
89. Ibid., pp. 6–7
90. Ibid., p. 8.
91. Ibid., pp. 11–12.
92. Ibid.
93. With reference to a study that claimed to show a relationship between the emotive level of worship, denominational affiliation, and insanity, Faduma suggested that he "should not be surprised that there were fewer maniacs among Presbyterians and Congregationalists than among Baptists and Methodists." Ibid., pp. 14–16.
94. Ibid., pp. 15–16.
95. Ibid., 17. The liberal-oriented Religious Education Movement provided the progressive pedagogical paradigm envisioned by Faduma as corrective of these defects. Its tenets and adherents were shaping the curriculum of ministerial education in a number of the nation's leading seminaries. On the Religious Education Movement, see Smith, "Christian Education," 225–246, and Coe, *Religion of a Mature Mind.* On changes in the nations' leading seminaries see Jesse

E. Moorland, *The Demand and the Supply of Increased Efficiency in the Negro Ministry,* American Negro Academy Occasional Papers, No. 13 (Washington, D.C.: American Negro Academy, 1909).

96. Moss, *Academy,* p. 151.
97. Ibid., pp. 151–152.
98. Ibid. Faduma's essay on the Black Church was only one of a number of controversial critiques of the Black Church published during this era. In 1886 Francis J. Grimke, the venerable Princeton-educated Presbyterian minister, published a critique entitled "The Defects of Our Ministry and the Remedy." In 1890 Booker T. Washington authored a critique entitled "The Colored Ministry: Its Defects and Needs." This critique instigated a divisive and long-running controversy within the black community. See Francis J. Grimke, "The Defects of Our Ministry and the Remedy," *A.M.E. Church Review* 3 (Oct. 1886): 154–157, and Booker T. Washington, "The Colored Ministry: Its Defects and Needs," *Christian Union* (14 Aug. 1890). On the wider dimensions and implications of this controversy, see Louis R. Harlan, *Booker T. Washington: The Making of a Black Leader, 1850–1901* (New York: Oxford University Press, 1972), and Louis R. Harlan, ed., *The Booker T. Washington Papers,* vol. 3 (Chicago: University of Illinois Press, 1974), pp. 71–75, 97–98, 108–109, 114–115, 199.
99. Moorland, *Demand.* Moorland was born in 1863 in Coldwater, Ohio. He graduated from the theological department of Howard University and in 1906 was granted the Doctor of Divinity degree. In 1907 he was elected a trustee of Howard University. He served as General Secretary of the "Colored" Y.M.C.A. and was involved in missionary work in North Carolina and Virginia. Boris, *Who's Who in Colored America,* p. 45.
100. Moorland, *Demand,* p. 9.
101. Ibid., p. 10.
102. Ibid.
103. Ibid. Walter Rauschenbusch, *Christianity and the Social Crisis* (1907; reprint, New York: Harper & Row, 1964). The author of "The Social Message of the Modern Pulpit" was the liberal evangelical, Charles R. Brown; on George Albert Coe and the Religious Education Association, see Smith, "Christian Education," and above, Chapter 3. On Edwin D. Starbuck and the influence of the psychology of religion among liberals see Smith, Handy, and Loetcher, *American Christianity* vol. 2, p. 429 and Edwin D. Starbuck, *Psychology of Religion* (New York, 1899). On Giddings, see Franklin Henry Giddings, *Elements of Sociology: A Textbook for Colleges and Schools* (New York and London: Macmillan, 1898).
104. Moss, *Academy,* pp. 160–161.

105. Faduma, "Success and Drawbacks," p. 131.
106. Blyden, *African Life and Customs.*
107. Moss, *Academy,* p. 161.
108. Ibid., pp. 160, 162–166. Charles C. Cook was an instructor in English at Howard University. In 1899 the Academy published his comparative study of the Negro problem as its fourth Occasional Paper. Charles C. Cook, *A Comparative Study of the Negro Problem,* American Negro Academy Occasional Papers No. 4 (Washington, D.C.: American Negro Academy, 1899); see Moss, *Academy,* p. 31.
109. Moss, *Academy,* p. 160. For the broader discussion and implications of the polygamy issue during this era, see Webster, *The African Church among the Yoruba.*
110. Editorial, "Principal O. Faduma, B.D.," *Sierra Leone Weekly News,* 13 June 1908.
111. Ibid.
112. Ibid.
113. See "Professor Faduma at Hastings," *Sierra Leone Weekly News,* 25 July 1908, and "Rev. O. Faduma at Wesley Church," 11 July 1908.
114. Faduma, "The New Theology."
115. This posture has often been associated with Booker T. Washington. On the complexity of Booker T. Washington and his stratagem for survival and success in the South, see Louis R. Harlan, *Booker T. Washington: The Making of a Black Leader, 1856–1901* (New York: Oxford University Press, 1972).
116. Editorial, "Africa and America," *Sierra Leone Weekly News,* 24 Dec. 1898.
117. "An African Speaks on Negro Problem," *Sierra Leone Weekly News,* 9 Aug. 1902.
118. Rambler, "Rambling Talks," *Sierra Leone Weekly News,* 10 Sept., 1915.
119. O. Faduma, "Life in the United States of America," *Sierra Leone Weekly News,* 1 Aug. 1908.
120. Ibid.
121. Faduma, *Defects,* p. 6.
122. Faduma, "Life in the United States," p. 3. Faduma's concerns and fears were not without substance. McPherson reports violence directed at both black and white AMA missionaries. McPherson, *Legacy,* pp. 174–183.
123. This study was directed by W. E. B. Du Bois and sponsored by Atlanta University. Its findings would later be published in *The Negro Church.* William E. B. Du Bois, ed., *The Negro Church: Report of a Social Study Made under the Direction of Atlanta*

University, Together with the Proceedings of the Eighth Conference for the Study of the Negro Problem, Held at Atlanta University, May 26th, 1903 (Atlanta: Atlanta University Press, 1903), pp. 164, 168–169. See also H. Paul Douglass, *Christian Reconstruction,* p. 158.

124. Ibid.

125. In 1912 Faduma praised Washington as "the apostle of industrialism and commonsense philosophy which has won him and his race international fame." In the same article he described W. E .B. Du Bois as "the sociologist and clear-cut thinker, breaker of false images set up in the popular mind against the Negro," and the recently deceased Edward Blyden as "the foremost African scholar, philosopher, and race prophet." Editorial "Vale! Longum Vale!" *Sierra Leone Weekly News,* 20 July 1912; 13 July 1912.

126. Faduma, "Negro Problem," p. 3.

127. Faduma, "Church and School," pp. 226–227.

128. Ibid.

129. Ibid.

5

Faduma and the Back-to-Africa Movement

On July 13, 1912, an editorial in the *Sierra Leone Weekly News* announced that Faduma, in "need of rest through change," was leaving Troy in order to become Dean and Professor at the National Religious Training School at Durham, North Carolina.[1] Letters of introduction and recommendation indicate that he departed Troy with "the respect, good-will and esteem" of both the Congregational Church and the local community.[2] The recommendation of Troy attorney Charles A. Armstrong, however, is suggestive of the tension and ambiguity experienced by Faduma during the course of his seventeen years at Troy. After professing to have known Faduma personally for over fourteen years and having had "frequent opportunities of forming estimates of his character as an educator, citizen, and uplifter of his race," Armstrong proclaimed that Faduma had "shown himself to be just what a high toned colored man should be in the position he occupied in order to gain the respect and esteem of the white and colored people among whom he lived and labored." He added: "During his seventeen years of labor in this town he has helped his people wonderfully; teaching them by precept and example to live sober, steady and industrious lives; and has always done everything in his power to foster kindly feelings between the white and colored people of this section."[3]

In an article written after his departure from Troy, Faduma himself reflected upon the high cost of black survival in the United States. He charged that:

> In the United States Anglo-Saxon teaching on race ideals is that all race varieties other than his are inherently inferior and dependent . . . . In state, church, and society, the idea is put into practical operation in such a way that the best in the Negro is treated as filthy rags. In the Southern states particularly, the idea is enforced by means of the *argumentum baculinum*—brute force—and all kinds of class legislation which the imagination can devise.

The impact upon blacks was spiritually as well as physically debilitating: "The result is a dwarfing of Negro manhood and womanhood, a dwarfing of the Negro soul. There are millions of Negroes in the United States who are labouring under this oppression, but, like dumb dogs, cannot bark, because if they bark the result is more oppression, with considerable suppression." No doubt with painful reflection upon his own accommodation to Southern racism, he added: "The Negro cannot successfully speak his mind in the South. He must follow the *Zeitgeist,* the spirit of the times in the South, to be popular and agreeable . . . he is unable to interpret the Negro soul. He is trained to be a stage player, whose truths are masked."[4]

By the summer of 1913 these conditions led Faduma to migrate to Boley, Oklahoma, where he joined other similarly disillusioned African-Americans in the Back-to-Africa Movement of Chief Alfred Sam. Having long nourished the dream of a selective black return to Africa, he became an enthusiastic and important recruit of this Pan-African–oriented commercial, missionary, and emigrationist venture, which foreshadowed the more widely known movement headed by Marcus Garvey.[5]

It was neither incidental nor accidental that Boley and other black enclaves in Oklahoma became the primary matrix of the "African Movement." In the aftermath of Reconstruction some Southern blacks sought immediate relief from increasing white repression by migrating to Africa. Others migrated to the newly opened and sparsely settled Indian and Oklahoma territories.[6] Most of the latter hoped simply to be free of racial repression. Others such as Edwin P. McCabe cast their trek in nationalist and Pan-African dimensions. They envisioned black migration into the new territory as an opportunity to shape the destiny of the entire race. Hence McCabe worked tirelessly to have Oklahoma territory admitted to the union as a state governed entirely by African-Americans.[7] There blacks would exercise the political, economic, and social rights increasingly denied them in the North as well as the South and eventually achieve "racial self-fulfillment."[8] As late as 1905 the *Indianapolis Freeman* defended and encouraged this vision: "The more we think about the subject the more we are convinced that it is not only possible, but it would be an easy matter for the colored people to make Oklahoma and Indian territory a state under their own control and management, where all the opportunities of any other American would be theirs."[9]

A similar desire for local self-government and racial self-fulfillment occasioned the founding of predominantly black townships such as Boley. The popular story of its founding in 1903 was widely publicized by Booker T. Washington, who attributed its existence to an argument between whites over the self-governing capabilities of blacks.[10] By 1905 Boley was thriving as an all-black town and projecting itself as evidence that the race was capable of self-determination and self-government. Boley's local newspaper, the *Progress,* regularly offered a racial challenge and appeal to Southern blacks: "Now is the time for you to come . . . and help prove to the Caucasian race and not only the Caucasian race but the world that the Negro is a law-making and law-abiding citizen, and help us solve the great racial problem that is now before us."[11] In nationalist tones it inquired:

> What are you waiting for? If we do not look out for our own welfare, who is going to do so for us? Are you always going to depend upon the white race to control your affairs for you? Some of our people have had their affairs looked after by the white man for the past 30 years, and where are they today? They are on the farms and plantations of the white men . . . with everything mortgaged so that they cannot get away and forever will be so long as they are working upon their farms and trading in their stores.[12]

When Oklahoma achieved statehood under white political domination, the dream of racial self-fulfillment nourished by blacks in Boley and other parts of Oklahoma rapidly became a racial nightmare. As whites in surrounding communities consolidated their power and privileges by intimidation, violence, and fraud, the black vision of a racial utopia in Oklahoma collapsed.[13] Blacks who had fled the deep South and entered the territory with unbridled optimism reached new depths of despair as there seemed no way to escape racism and oppression in the United States. Even the once optimistic *Progress* bitterly inquired, "Is there no spot where the Negro can escape the slime, froth, and derision of our superiors, who feast and grow fat on prejudice?"[14] For many of the disillusioned

> one reasonable possibility remained. They could migrate once more to a place where they might hope to gain strength, power and complete freedom. They could leave behind the unyielding pressure of the American racial code and migrate to a new continent where they would be accepted unquestionably as equals. They could go to Africa.[15]

This option was far from novel. Since the eighteenth century, the prospect of blacks' returning to Africa had been roundly debated, and some had even made the grand exodus. It had always been, however, during periods of the most intense persecution that significant numbers of blacks seriously viewed a return to Africa as a solution to their own and Africa's problems.[16] It was at such a historical juncture that Faduma and many of Oklahoma's blacks became enthusiastic participants in the Back-to-Africa Movement led by Chief Alfred Sam. Redkey notes that "Chief Sam could hardly have found a state more hospitable to his scheme. In 1913 most of the Blacks in Oklahoma had come from other states in their search for land and security. When Oklahoma proved to be just another Southern state in racial matters, the Blacks were . . . disillusioned and candidates for emigration."[17]

Chief Alfred Charles Sam, the self-styled and popularly acclaimed "Moses" of this intended exodus, was born in 1879 or 1880 on the Gold Coast. His father, desiring that Sam become a missionary and teacher, arranged for him to be educated in mission schools staffed by the Basel Evangelical Mission.[18] Presumably at these schools, Sam was indoctrinated in the theological and missiological tenets of evangelical pietism rather than liberalism.[19] Though of a deep religious nature, Sam expressed more immediate interest in material rather than spiritual matters. At an early age he became involved in the rubber export trade and began developing plans for establishing an American-based transatlantic trading company.[20] On July 15, 1911, his plans took concrete form with the chartering of the Akim Trading Company in New York.[21] The company, headquartered in Brooklyn with Sam as President, reportedly had assets of over $600,000.[22]

An explicitly Pan-African consciousness and agenda was expressed in the company's prospectus and articles of incorporation. It not only claimed to be "the first Negro corporation ever conceived amongst the race," but also offered shares at half price to people of African descent as an inducement to help "the civilized Negro" meet his responsibility "to develop Africa."[23] The major proponent of this synthesis of Pan-African concern with commercial interest was Sam, who, upon his return to West Africa, began acquiring land for the resettlement of diaspora Africans.

It was through newspaper advertisements such as "Agricultural Lands in Africa and How to Obtain Them," that Sam and the Akim Trading Company came to the attention of black Oklahomans inquiring about migration to West Africa.[24] Subsequent correspondence between Sam and Dr. P. J. Dorman of Mantee, Oklahoma, and Professor J. P. Liddell of Weleetka, heightened Sam's Pan-African and commercial interest. Upon receiving affirmative responses from Gold Coast chiefs about the availability of additional land for the settlement of African-American colonists, he sailed for the United States.[25]

Upon his return to the United States, Sam severed relations with the Akim Trading Company and on March 21, 1913, established the Akim Trading Company, Ltd.[26] With an emphasis on facilitating the emigration of African-Americans to West Africa, the new company exhibited a distinctly Pan-African focus. Indeed, Sam claimed that this venture would fulfill his long-held dream of returning to Africa his "wandering black brothers in America."[27] The company's articles of incorporation and its ambitious prospectus sought to encourage "the emigration of the best Negro farmers and mechanics from the United States to different sections in West Africa." It listed among its goals the establishment of a college of agriculture and industry in all the trades of manufacturing and agriculture," as well as the development of "hotels, restaurants, bath houses, theaters, or other places of amusement."[28]

By the summer of 1913 Sam was in Oklahoma, where his commercial and Pan-African interests merged with evangelical fervor, convictions, and symbols. Consequently, the Back-to-Africa Movement was infused with a strong evangelical component and dynamic. Meetings to sell stock in the new company quickly and invariably took on the character and tone of revival camp meetings with hymns, prayers, and the invocation of appropriate biblical symbols, imagery, and narratives.[29] In these meetings Sam, a "low brown man" of five feet, six inches and 160 pounds with a less than imposing voice and oratorical skills, found himself cast as the black Moses sent by God to deliver African-Americans from New World bondage to the West African Canaan.[30]

Sharing the evangelical orientation of the majority of blacks attending his meetings, Sam rapidly developed the charismatic and evangelistic skills with which he reportedly worked his supporters up "to a semi-religious frenzy."[31] Even in Sam's absence, however, the "typical meeting" of the movement was described as "a passionate affair, with broad, inspiring camaraderie, racial consciousness, and sense of religious duty and mission."[32] In keeping with this emphasis, Sam claimed a missionary purpose for the movement: "I am a Christian myself, though not all of my people are. The 'Back Home' movement has for its goal not only the development of the Gold Coast, but the Christianizing of all those who do not love the Lord."[33]

The exact nature of the religious and missionary impetus and focus of both Sam and the movement was complicated by Sam's relationship with the predominantly white "Holy Ghost and Us Society." This little-known "fundamentalist utopian sect," with holiness and pentecostal proclivities, originated in the charismatic leadership of Frank W. Sanford.[34] Born in Bowdoin, Maine, in 1862, Sanford attended Bates College and Cobb Divinity School. Cobb, however, refused to grant him a degree because of his eccentric spiritual inclinations, which included conversations with God.[35] In 1893 he founded the Holy Ghost and Us Society and established its Zion called Shiloh in the Androscoggin Valley of Maine.[36] As the sect flourished at Shiloh, Sanford and his followers founded a Bible and Missionary Training School and purchased a fleet of ships intended to extend his message and movement worldwide. West Africa became a focus of these efforts.[37]

There are divergent accounts of Sam's initial encounter with the sect, but they all agree that at some point he became a convert and visited its headquarters in Maine during his 1911 and 1913 trips to the United States.[38] Subsequently, the sect's leaders encouraged and assisted Sam in his commercial and Pan-African endeavors. The sect apparently viewed the African Movement as a means of advancing its own evangelical interests and concerns in West Africa.[39] As the African Movement matured, however, racial, ideological and theological tensions increasingly strained the relationship between the two movements and eventually undermined chances for a cooperative interracial evangelical venture.[40]

Whatever may have been the motives of Sam and his fellow members of the Back-to-Africa Movement, it clearly offered Faduma the opportunity to actualize his liberal-rooted Pan-Africanist missiology and pedagogy in the African context. He joined the movement expecting to become the principal of its proposed College of Ethiopia. This institution was to be modeled after Booker T. Washington's Tuskegee Institute.[41] Thus on December 12, 1913, Faduma penned the following letter to Booker T. Washington from Knoxville, Tennessee:

> My Dear Sir: I have been recently elected Principal of the College of Ethiopia in the Gold Coast, West Africa. After ten years of teaching in the High School of Sierra Leone, West Africa and three and a half years of study in the University of London, England, I took the full divinity course in Yale University where I graduated in 1894 with a post-graduate course in 1895. I have since been Principal of Peabody Academy in Troy, N.C. for seventeen years under the American Missionary Association. Before leaving the United States I desire to visit your school and to have an opportunity of studying the plans and methods of its industrial features. My plan is to introduce as much as possible industrial education and am interesting Negro farmers and toolmen to go with me and form Christian industrial settlements. Such practical demonstration in my opinion will do more in hastening the industrial development as well as Christian [development] of West Africa. I should like to be in your school for five days' thoro[ugh] examination of your methods and will appreciate all the help you and your faculty can give me to facilitate my work.[42]

Presumably Faduma's interest in exporting to West Africa the Tuskegee model of industrial education and development induced an affirmative reply from Washington, who was usually critical of the "back to Africa" efforts of African-Americans.[43] If so, Faduma would have been only one of a number of missionary educators who visited Tuskegee in the hope of applying its educational principles among the colonized peoples of Africa, Asia, and the Caribbean.[44] In fact heightened interest by both European missionaries and colonial officials induced Washington to host the International Congress on the Negro at Tuskegee in 1912.[45] In attendance were delegates from twenty-one foreign countries representing twelve different religious denominations and twenty-five missionary societies.[46] Washington viewed the conference as having two objectives: (1) "to inform leading missionary and colonial educators about the methods of Tuskegee," and (2) to see to what extent these methods "can be applied to the problem concerning the people in countries that are peopled by the darker races."[47] However, in spite of their conservative tenor, both the conference and Washington's pedagogical model stimulated Pan-African sentiment.[48]

The Pan-African implications of Washington's pedagogical model were not lost on Faduma. Thus in 1914 he wrote: "One of the most remarkable things in Tuskegee Institute is that the greatest industrial school in the world for Negroes has not a single white man in its faculty . . . [There] the Negro boy and girl receive direct inspiration from Negro instructors, a principle which is highly commendable from a standpoint of philosophy and psychology."[49]

While Sam was the acknowledged leader of the African Movement, it was Faduma, in the role of ideologue and theologian, who articulated to American and West African audiences the movements rationale, goals, and significance. His efforts served as a stimulus for nationalist and Pan-African sentiments in West Africa that were eventually given institutional focus with the formation of the National Congress of British West Africa.[50]

In a series of articles published in West African newspapers, Faduma thoroughly explained the history, impetus, and goals of the movement.[51] Not surprisingly, he cast the movement firmly in the historical and theological framework of liberal theology and evangelical Pan-Africanism. However, few members of the African Movement shared his sophisticated Pan-African vision. Even fewer shared his liberal theological and missiological orientation.[52]

In explaining to his West African comrades the immediate impetus of the movement and its attraction to Oklahoma's blacks, Faduma evoked the memory and sentiments of Bishop Henry M. Turner (whom he incorrectly reported as deceased):

> Oklahoma is one of the worst of the mob-ruling states in the South . . . . It is the home of grafters, grabbers, and cut-throats; the land where the native Indian and the Negro have been and are still robbed of their property; where the White mob take the law into their hands and hang and shoot down Negro men, women, and children without fear of compunction; a land of blood and moral darkness; a very hell on earth. To understand the eagerness of the Negro to escape from Oklahoma to anywhere in West Africa, where they have been taught and told that life is sacred, one must visit this portion of the world . . . . It was the late Bishop H. M. Turner, a man of indomitable courage and sensitive soul, who in a fit of desperation said, "Better to live in hell than in the Southern states." It is a seemingly exaggerated statement, but it contains more truth than exaggeration. It is the outburst of an overburdened soul over the woes of his race.[53]

Faduma was quick to point out that the African Movement was "not a new movement." The nineteenth-century migratory efforts of Paul Cuffee, whom he identified as the "son of a West African Negro," and those of other African-Americans, as well as "Nova Scotians and Maroons from British Guiana, Jamaica, Trinidad, and other West India Islands . . . [and] Brazil" were evoked as proof that "There was always a feeling among Negroes in the new world to return to Africa, their motherland." The current effort was only the latest manifestation of the "home instinct" which was "one of the deepest and most permanent in man." It was an instinct

> intensified when a man like the American Negro is deprived of his civil and political rights, butchered, burned, ostracized, his women corrupted and no law to protect them because of their color . . . when the best of his race is "Jim Crowed" and public opinion is powerless to prevent it . . . when he lives in communities where might means right and religion itself is flouted. Under conditions as these, "there is no place like home."

Adding religious and theological warrant, Faduma asserted that "this instinct was of Divine origin," and as such:

> No law or customs should be tolerated which curtail it. No religion, call it by whatever name you please, is worth considering which directly or indirectly condones the suppression of the home instinct . . . . As long as the world lasts, and God is God, man will have these longings. . . . They may be smothered for a while, but the breath of the infinite will rekindle the dying embers and the real man will ultimately emerge crying out again and again. . . .The Negro, stolen and forced away from his ancestral home, is longing to return home, and will continue to long. The African movement is a movement looking towards home. If the home movement is a fraud, then home itself is a fraud, nature a fraud, and the God of nature the biggest fraud.[54]

Among the "leading ideas" of the African Movement Faduma listed "Race, Patriotism, and Individuality." He believed that these too had theological and religious warrant. Reflecting his synthesis of the concept of African personality as formulated by Blyden and the liberal concept of Personalism, Faduma insisted that American racism should be rejected because it resulted in the "dwarfing of the Negro soul" and hampered the full development of his racial and divine personality.[55] According to Faduma, the African Movement held "that every man in a race has a soul, a divinity that is never satisfied until it finds its true self." As African-Americans were unable to realize that respected and inner divinity in the United States, it was therefore a divine commandment that they go elsewhere. He explained: "If the Negro in the United States cannot find himself as a distinct and respectable species side by side with the Anglo-Saxon, the feeling is growing that he should go anywhere to find himself. Those among them who think that Africa, their ancestral land, is the place, are uniting for strength to settle there gradually. 'Who would be free themselves must strike the blow.' They are now striking for race individuality."[56]

The second leading idea and impetus of the movement was an expansive and service-oriented "missionary spirit." But this was not to be confused with the often narrow and self-serving spirit of traditional mission efforts: "The African movement is missionary and stands for service to others . . . . The missionary spirit, the spirit which is willing to give what one has for another's good, the spirit which loves the other man as one loves himself, is one of the inspiring motives of the movement." However, Faduma contended that full development of this missionary spirit was impossible in the United States because "Pharisaic Christianity hedges the Negro on all sides and leaves little room for his normal development." The African Movement offered a corrective which included ecclesiastical independence:

> The African movement realizes that a man cannot expand spiritually until he is allowed spiritual freedom. The Negro's present environment does not encourage the highest type of spiritual freedom. Believing that the best inspiration to any race must be found within the race, and that true development must come from within and not external and accidental, it seeks to encourage a self-governing Negro church.[57]

The third shaping idea of the African Movement was "Industrial Development." Although rooted in an ideological awareness that "to be industrially developed is to be industrially independent," it too had theological and scriptural warrant:

> The divine command given to man as he came forth out of the hands of the Creator was, "Be fruitful and multiply, and replenish the earth and subdue it". . . .In order to "subdue the earth" . . . to have dominion over matter, man must be spiritual. Every conquest of nature is brought about by the highest nature in men. Until the Ethiopian's highest nature is developed, he cannot subdue the earth.[58]

Unfortunately, he noted, neither the development of the "Ethiopian's highest nature" nor subsequent fulfillment of this "divine command" could be fully realized in America, where restrictions "of the most repressive kind" were "increasing ad infinitum." These restrictions were so strong as to undermine even the industrial program of Booker T. Washington: "Already there is an industrial problem. Every Negro industrially trained meets with it in competition: the boycott of the white union labour. He must submit to industrial drudgery in many cases or get out of the field. . . .The young men and women of the race are asking whether their industrial training is to be a waste."[59] Africa, Faduma insisted, was the place where the spiritual, intellectual, and physical dimensions of "the Ethiopian" would be fully matured and harnessed in a program of industrial development that would both uplift the race and meet the divine command.[60] The African movement, proclaimed Faduma,

> now takes the initiative to welcome our industrially trained men and women of African ancestry to become pioneers and cross the Atlantic to

> Africa, their ancestral land . . . .The African movement believes in business in religion and religion in business. It is an appeal to the business men and business instinct of the race to expand their horizon and organize to exploit the land of their ancestors and not allow foreigners to take it all. It is an appeal to all the Negro industrial schools of the United States to have an eye on Africa, where their graduates can have a profitable employment and direct all kinds of industry in a modern way. It is voicing the cry of Ethiopia's sons and daughters in Africa to those in the United States to come over and help develop the land for Africa and the world . . . . The American Negro must now learn to regard himself as one of the internal forces for Africa's regeneration.[61]

Even as Faduma offered his historical, theological, and ideological justification of the movement and its goals, considerable domestic and international opposition to it developed. In Oklahoma skeptics accused Sam of being a fraud and a swindler.[62] Faduma, however, suggested that other issues and factors motivated the opposition. In recounting Sam's initial visits to Oklahoma, he observed: "Opposition set in and was encouraged by the bankers, owners of plantations and sawmills . . . who depend on the labour of the people for their support. Scenes of opposition, persecution, and prosecution followed in quick succession, but were met calmly and in a Christian spirit by the Chief whose form of Christianity proved superior to that of his opposers."[63]

Although the movement had a decidedly religious ethos and enlisted the support of Faduma and ministers of varied theological and ecclesiastical persuasions, it nevertheless encountered considerable resistance from other black ministers. At Boley, where Sam arrived as his guest, Faduma recalled:

> Pastor Hubbard, of the A.M.E. Church advised Mayor Powell of the town not to allow the Chief to stay because he was stirring the populace and was an enemy to Christianity. Another ecclesiastic of the same grade openly advised flogging and violent expulsion. Not only in Boley, but elsewhere, the chief priests and scribes, AS IN DAYS OF YORE, MISLED THE PEOPLE and told infamous lies against the character of the chief. The fear of losing their congregation, who were inclined to go to Africa, their ancestral land, and the desire of these priests and scribes to stay in the United States, impelled them to violate every law of Christian charity and sell their honour to other citizens to prosecute the Chief.[64]

A series of arrests and a trial ensued. The latter, according to Faduma, completely vindicated Sam and the movement of charges of fraud:

> The following important facts were proved to the satisfaction of the court: (1) That the person called Chief Sam was in reality a chief of the Akim Tribe of the Gold Coast, West Africa. (2) That he was invited by Dr. Dor-

> man and Professor Liddell of Ok[lahoma] to visit the Negroes of that State and to help to devise plans for their return to their ancestral land. (3) That the Akim Trading Company, Limited, of which Chief Sam is president, is a chartered corporation under the laws of the state . . . . (4) That in public meetings no attempt was made by the Chief to mislead the people by misrepresentation of conditions in West Africa.

Faduma optimistically reported that as a result of the trial "the once skeptical mind was convinced and finally converted to the movement. The total effect. . . on the popular mind was to create a larger following for the movement than would otherwise have been."[65]

By January 1914 Sam had raised enough capital to purchase a ship for $69,000. The ship, christened the *Liberia* in an elaborate ceremony at Galveston, Texas, was to serve as the flagship of the Ethiopian steamship line. However, this development, instead of dissipating skepticism, attracted more serious and concerted opposition to the movement.[66] Faduma bitterly lamented:

> It would seem as if every success in the movement made its enemies more bitter and determined to upset it. The lying secular press became more lying and devilish, and was powerful to influence some of the religious press against it. Prominent Negroes who were opposed to it used every means to influence State as well as Federal Government and the British Government against it.[67]

Among the "Prominent Negroes" opposed to the movement was W. E. B. Du Bois. Although committed to the Pan-African cause and one of its major proponents and activists throughout the first half of the twentieth century, Du Bois was not supportive of the Back-to-Africa emigrationism strategy espoused by either Chief Sam or his immediate successor, Marcus Garvey.[68] The *Crisis,* edited by Du Bois, "warned its readers against 'Chief' Sam and his African schemes."[69] Ironically, it also published accounts of the racial climate in Oklahoma that explained why so many of its black residents were eager supporters of Sam's "schemes." A 1914 editorial quoted extensively from a letter that exposed the economic motive at the heart of much of Oklahoma's racial repression:

> In no state in the Union have Negroes been robbed, actually robbed with impunity and openly, as in this state, and today white men are worth millions who have built up their fortunes by thievery. Practically all the rich oil fields in the state were originally the property of Negroes. When the restrictions preventing the sale of freedmen's lands were removed by Congress in 1908, it was the signal for wholesale robbery of these freedmen's lands, and the white guardians of Negro minors sold their . . . [holdings] for a mere pittance and in turn shared in the fortunes made from oil found on the lands sold.[70]

Criticism of Sam's movement also came from outside the United States. Duse Mohamed Ali, the "half Sudanese, half Egyptian" Pan-Africanist and editor of the *African Times and Orient Review,* was also critical of the African Movement. He interjected what proved to be a prophetic note of political realism as he assessed Sam's plans to settle African-Americans on the Gold Coast:

> All the lands in that British colony are tribal lands, which can neither be sold nor given away by the chiefs . . . . I'm sure that even if the British government allowed them to have their own towns, it would not permit them to set up a form of government. It would be disastrous if these people were induced to go to Africa and find themselves stranded.[71]

Ali's critical notice of Sam's movement was of particular historical importance because one of his "office boys" was the young Jamaican, Marcus Garvey. Garvey, observed Langley,

> would draw more ambitious, albeit equally unrealistic, conclusions from Chief Sam's African Movement . . . . His Black Star line was . . . [to] attempt the same venture as Chief Sam's Ethiopian steamship line, just as his Universal Negro Improvement Association is reminiscent of Sam's African Movement. What Sam initiated at the beginning of the Great War Garvey enlarged and publicized with greater effect at the end of that war.[72]

Initial opposition to the African Movement also came from West Africans.[73] T. Hutton Mills of Sierra Leone characterized it as "venturesome and foolhardy," while the editor of the *Gold Coast Leader* warned: "We have heard before of Mr. Alfred C. Sam and we would advise coloured folks in America not to take him and his scheme of 'Back to Africa' seriously." It hastened to add, however, Pan-African sentiments that foreshadowed its later support of the movement:

> We would welcome our coloured American brethren as traders, agriculturists, and mechanics, but they must know clearly the conditions they are coming to meet. Our climate is as bad for coloured Americans as it is for white men, and our Anopheles and Stegomyiae may play as much havoc with the constitution and system of American negroes as they do with Europeans and other white races. This our coloured American brethren must clearly understand.[74]

The African Telegraph and Gold Coast Mirror was critical of both the movement and Faduma's involvement in it. It charged that "The African Movement as a business proposition is hopeless, and the whole scheme a delusion and a snare." Faduma, it observed, was "unpractical and visionary," and "like all other dreamers and patriots, obsessed by his fixed idea . . . saw in Sam's commercial scheme the materialization of his [own] dreams."[75]

More serious still, and with unexpected ramifications for subsequent Pan-African and Pan-West African developments, was the active opposition of the British Colonial Office.[76] Seeking to "nip the movement in the bud," it quickly labeled "the whole thing a fraud" and requested United States officials "to do all in their power to stop the movement."[77] In an effort to comply, U.S. Post Office authorities engaged in an extensive investigation of the movement on suspicion that Sam had used the postal service to engage in a "fraudulent scheme."[78] Upon the failure of this investigation to find corroborating evidence, British officials attempted to withhold the *Liberia*'s registration papers.[79] Only after a three-month delay, during which Sam vigorously insisted upon his "rights as a British subject," were the necessary papers and authorization granted.[80]

Meanwhile, in West Africa, the Gold Coast Legislative Council, upon instruction from the British Colonial and Foreign offices, suspended Standing Orders to approve at one sitting "the Regulation of Immigrants Ordinance" which required new immigrants to make a "security deposit" of twenty-five pounds.[81] It was evident that this ordinance, which defined the deposit as reparation insurance, was directly inspired by the African Movement. Its rationale lay in the assessment by British officials that the movement was "made up of unreliable, undesirable, half-fed men and women, the ragamuffins of Negro society, who must ultimately depend upon the Government of Gold Coast for their daily support."[82]

The initial response of Sam, Faduma, and their West African brethren to the opposition of the colonial administration was characterized by a mixture of tolerance and idealism rooted in their belief in British "fair play" and "justice."[83] Faduma noted publicly that "it had been the boast and pride of every African in the United States that Great Britain's representatives were men above popular prejudice, men swayed by reason rather than by feeling, men who stood as a stone wall on the side of law and order."[84] Thus he predicted that "when the truth is known" about the slandered and misrepresented men and women of the movement, "their African kinsmen and the British Government, their political protector" will "give them such a welcome . . . as the world has never witnessed." He concluded, "unless we are mistaken in our knowledge of the moral fibre of the British Government, of the true patriotism of the natives of the Gold Coast, and of the ultimate triumph of justice, we fully expect a right appraisal by them of this movement."[85]

When the Liberia finally set sail July 3, 1914 for the Gold Coast with Sam, Faduma, and approximately 60 delegates, West African perceptions of the African Movement and British opposition to it were being revised in light of a heightened Pan-African and Pan-West African consciousness.[86] The *Gold Coast Leader,* which had earlier expressed skepticism regarding Sam and the movement, now directed its criticism at the activities of British colonial officials. It warned:

> [I]t is one thing to condemn the business tactics of Chief Sam, and quite another thing to put difficulties in the way of American Negroes coming to this country to settle. The Government appear to us to have confused both issues, and have allowed themselves to be driven into an action in the matter which thoughtful natives must condemn . . . . After all this country is ours . . . . It is putting a strain on our endurance for the Government to place, as they have done, difficulties in the way of American Negroes, our own kith and kin, seeking a livelihood in our country. There is no ordinance in the colony preventing the entry of white men into the country. The Regulation of Immigrants Ordinance (No. 4 of 1914) is, in our opinion, a class legislation, specifically directed against black men, and our chiefs and people should see to it that that particular legislation is expunged from the statute book of the colony.

In even more strident tones of Pan-Africanism, the editorial reminded its readers that

> . . . thanks to God, and the good sense of our fathers, we have not bartered the ownership of our lands to our white rulers who under the inscrutable decree of Providence have come to our country to seek a livelihood, and to guide us in the path of progress and civilization. As the price of their guidance, our white rulers fill their pockets with most of the good things that our land produces, and readily fill the pockets, too, of their own white sons, their own kith and kin, from whatever part of the world they come. We bear all this with patience; it is, however, adding insult to injury for white men not only to grudge us the crumbs that fall to us as our share . . . [but] deliberately attempt to prevent men of our own colour from seeking to earn a livelihood in our own country.[87]

Among the factors inducing West Africans to change their perspective on both the African Movement and governmental opposition to it were Faduma's extensive apologies published in West African papers. In an extensive series of articles on the Movement, he insistently cast it within the context of Pan-African and Pan-West African consciousness as espoused by the recently deceased Blyden.[88] Thus he underscored "Race Patriotism" as the major tenet of the movement and emphasized that it was even reflected in the makeup of the ship's crew: "[E]very officer in the ship, except two wireless operators, was of African extraction. Members of the crew were from the United States, West Africa, Cape de Verde and the West Indies." Alluding to the Ethiopian prophecy in Psalm 68: 31, he noted that they were "a fair representation of Ethiopia reaching out in the spirit of adventure for the development of Africa."[89]

As the *Liberia* made scheduled stops in Havana, Barbados, and Cape St. Vincent, en route to the Gold Coast, Faduma kept his West African readers informed of Africa's disapora presence. In Havana he reported encounters with Afro-Cubans "who were proud of the movement, and prouder to own Africa as their motherland." He was also delighted to reveal the discovery of a Yoruba "kinsman" who remembered bits of sentences used by his deceased father.[90]

The political and economic implications of the African Movement, and expressions of support for it from a growing chorus of West Africans increasingly irritated British colonial officials. As the ship arrived at Maio to take on a cargo of salt, it was seized by the British cruiser *Victorian,* impounded, and towed to Freetown, Sierra Leone. British officials disingenuously explained the seizure as a "war precaution" made necessary by the presence aboard the "Liberia" of a German-made wireless.[91]

The *Liberia's* forced detention in Sierra Leone occasioned the first of the delegates' many celebrations of welcome from West Africans. It was doubly fitting, given the historical significance of Sierra Leone, that at the Freetown service the "Venerable Patriot" Bishop James Johnson delivered the official welcome address. With equal parts of racial and religious pride, Johnson hailed Sam as "the Moses of the African movement" whom God "has raised up to help to bring back African Israel to their own home from the foreign land which had been to them a land of bondage." He welcomed the delegates as "Brethren," "members of one and the same ancient Negro stock," as well as "fellow believers in Jesus; fellow followers and disciples of the World's Redeemer." In an additional expression of evangelical Pan-Africanism, he informed the delegates of the expansive hopes that the movement instilled in the West African community:

> We discern in you those who are evidently intended by God, the Father of all, to be with us fellow missionaries and fellow workers for the up-building of our desolated Aboriginal homeland, the repeopling of it, the regenerating of West Africa religiously, intellectually, morally, socially, and otherwise.[92]

Faduma contended that this and subsequent meetings of welcome in Sierra Leone, one of which was held in his native village of Waterloo, "abundantly proved," that the "Sierra Leone public was in hearty accord with the movement," and that "blood is thicker than water."[93]

On January 2, 1915, the *Liberia* was released by British authorities. It had suffered the confiscation of its wireless and a twenty-eight day uncompensated and unexplained detention. And as it proceeded to the Gold Coast, Sam and the delegates were notified by British authorities of the Gold Coast immigration ordinance that required twenty-five pounds from each delegate. This requirement further depleted the severely limited reserves of the movement. Faduma bitterly characterized the required payment as an "exorbitant, unnatural and prohibitive sum which every African must regard as 'blood money.' Sold into bondage and taken by force to an unnatural home *for money,* yet cannot return except *for money.* This is the kind of advanced ethics with which we are confronted in the twentieth century, this the result of the progress in morality which the Anglo-Saxon has evolved in the year of the world 1915."[94]

As he elaborated upon the factors that influenced the Legislative Council of the Gold Coast "to pass in haste" such an unprecedented ordinance, Faduma drew parallels between the Council's discriminatory actions and those of Southern whites. In fact, he charged that the Council was "suffering from Americanitis":

> In several of the Southern States in the United States of America, in order to discourage and exclude their Negro citizens from the privileges of voting, laws were made limiting votes to those who could read and write the Constitution . . . [similarly] the Gold Coast Colony is suffering from Americanitis, in that by virtue of her superior power she is using questionable methods in the regulation of immigration. The persecuting and hounding process adopted to regulate the immigration of American Negroes and the conspiracy behind the process, is altogether un-English. It is American, because it overrides the law and creates prejudice against good government.

He concluded with the observation that "It will be shown in due time how the 'Ordinance to make provision to regulate the immigration of persons not born in any part of West Africa' is in its practical effect an ordinance to prevent it."[95]

By 1915 both the Freetown and Gold Coast press had become fervent supporters of the African Movement and joined Faduma in expressing disillusionment with the colonial government's paternalistic and heavy-handed response to it. In the wake of the controversy elicited by the movement, they also began to express nationalist and Pan-Africanist concerns and speculated "on the possibility of launching a Pan-West African movement for political and other reforms."[96] The Pan-African and Pan-West African implications of African-American emigration were clearly noted by the *Sierra Leone Weekly News.* After pointing out that the African-American delegates and supporters of the movement "had stretched their hands across the Atlantic from America to us in Africa, from one side of the Atlantic to the other," it editorialized, "If we give them a grip . . . and let the Blacks in America unite with those in West Africa as one people, this would evoke a force which nothing can resist. *L'union fait la force.*"[97]

In January 1915 the *Gold Coast Leader* also cast the movement in the historical and ideological context of both Pan-Africanism and West African nationalism. It warned British authorities that "any harsh steps taken against the pioneers of this important movement will be sure to meet the resentment of enlightened West African opinion." It added:

> We ask those in authority to regard the movement as actuated by the highest impulses that can move humanity, and no matter what flaws there might be in details, to respect the wishes of a people who are yearning to receive back their exiles long lost to home and peace . . . . Nor is there any harm in recording the fact that this African movement is not a new-fangled notion that has been sprung upon the attention of West Africa. Those acquainted with West African history do know that this is a purposeful idea which has been realized by years of preparation. Our dreamers dreamt dreams. They foresaw a day when the Afro-American laden with the good things stored from the land of his exile, would seek to place them upon the lap of Africa . . . . Advanced people may watch the scene with amusement. They may discredit it. They may even discourage it. But we are persuaded that no amount of ridicule or persecution is going to turn this African movement back . . . . For it goes without saying that movements of this sort are rare in the history of humanity, and that this one may be the beginning of great things for West Africa.[98]

In a subsequent article the *Gold Coast Leader* charged that British actions against the movement were "causing dissatisfaction, if not uneasiness" among Gold Coast residents. It inquired:

> What has Chief Sam done to merit all this opposition from the British Government? What has he done to warrant the seizure of his ship and the blasting of the hopes of numbers of American and African Negroes who were looking forward to the unfolding of his patriotic ideas and the working of his scheme? The man has been thoroughly examined and his good faith searchingly investigated; a procedure which we joined in advocating at the beginning, and now that no fault has been found in him nor anything fraudulent in his scheme why should the British Government continue their opposition against him? An undertaking like Chief Sam's could be immense benefit to us natives of British West Africa; it could be the means of leading us to that higher state of civilization . . . and for the fullest realization by us of the benefits of British citizenship. Why should our rulers be afraid of a project like that of Chief Sam and his band of American Negroes. . . ?[99]

Amid such controversy the long-delayed arrival of the *Liberia* and its delegates to the Gold Coast took place on January 13, 1915. An account of the "remarkable welcome accorded Sam and the delegates at Salt Pond" was recorded by Faduma, who described it as both a cultural and spiritual triumph: "The variegated native costumes and the beating of native drums made the occasion peculiarly native, while the ringing of church bells gave an air of sanctity to the gathering, and was in keeping with the idea of the African Movement, namely, that it is a divine and therefore sacred movement."[100]

The formal reception, held on the following Friday and attended by "Ohin Kurantsin III, and Elders and Representatives of all the religious denominations in town," was described as "a feast of reason" during which the "lost chord in the African's national life" was "found." Sam's response was in his native language and reemphasized both the Pan-African and religious dimensions of the movement. After recounting the hardships that the movement faced, he "thanked heartily the Kings, Chiefs and people of Gold Coast for the warm reception given him and their relatives, who for more than three centuries were absent from their African home through no fault of theirs." Despite his detractors and critics, he "felt he had accomplished a divine mission" and that his "success so far was due to Him who had entrusted so great a mission to his frail self."[101]

Sam also called upon the assembled chiefs to exert pressure on the colonial government for reform of the immigration ordinance:

> The legislation which the Government has introduced by requiring £25 from each immigrant is prohibitive. I hope the chiefs and the country at large will see that a reform be made, so that what is drastic in it will be struck out, and the best of our lost kinsmen will be encouraged to return to develop the land of their ancestors. These Negroes are not strangers, and should not be considered strangers. They and their forebears were taken away by force from home, and there are now some of them anxious to return home. The land is as much theirs as yours. God has preserved you to take care of the land till their return.[102]

Sam's remarks before the welcoming assemblage were followed by those of various delegates. Of particular significance were the well-received comments of three of the women delegates who emphasized that the elevation of women of African descent was a vital component of the movement. Faduma reported that Mrs. Hall, "President of the Women's Clubs in the United States," delivered a speech that "electrified the audience." She noted that she and the women of the African movement "had come to build up, not to destroy, to save, not to break to pieces what was good in native social life." Their goal was "to contribute towards elevating the social and moral condition of the native African women who were like other women in other parts of the world." And although their influence "would be gentle, sympathetic and silent" it would nevertheless "have an upward tendency."[103] Mrs. W. H. Lewis, "General Secretary of the Women's Clubs in the United States," suggested a still more progressive agenda as she emphasized that "there would be no true progress which left out the uplifting of women." Hence, "the women of the African Movement stood shoulder to shoulder with all other agencies at work for the uplifting of the family life of the native African."[104] Finally, Mrs. Stewart, "Secretary of one of the Clubs," and the oldest female delegate on board the *Liberia,* firmly cast their projected efforts in Pan-African context: "We, the women of African descent, though born in the United States, are in supreme love with Africa, the home of our ancestors. We have never regarded ourselves as aliens . . . . We have come to lock hands with you, native chiefs and representatives, to build up a great civilization."[105]

More impressive still was the welcoming ceremony for Sam and the delegates held the following month at Suedro. Before the aged King Omanhim Kofi Ahin Kora and his court, an inspired Sam again repeated the history of the movement, its goals, and the opposition arrayed against its success. He now attributed governmental opposition to the movement to monopolistic commercial concerns: "Certain commercial firms, dreading native competition and fearing that the incoming of the American negro would introduce intelligent labour among natives, had for selfish purposes skillfully used the British Government and the local government as cat's-paws to cripple their efforts."[106] After noting increasing difficulties that the movement was experiencing and attacks upon his own integrity, he added:

> Having no ulterior motive than that of developing my native land through her own sons . . . I have no apology to make to you or the world for inaugurating this patriotic and industrial movement. If I have made any mistakes they are not intentional, they are defects of the head rather than of the heart.

He concluded with a formal request that the delegates and their successors be accepted as returned brothers and sisters:

> Venerable Omanhin, Chiefs and representatives of the people, receive this day these few delegates, who are only a small part of over ten million, bone of your bone and flesh of your flesh . . . . They are willing to live and die with you. They are willing to share with you all they have learnt best in the white man's civilization, and hope your family instinct, your sense of devotion to your country, will compel you to throw your arms around them.[107]

The reception at Suedro marked the zenith of the African Movement. Of its significance, Faduma optimistically and romantically predicted:

> [T]his day will long be considered by the delegates as epochal; an important stage in the history of the African Movement. . . . It will be the beginning of the reversal of judgement on the movements of the African pioneers. Instead of considering them as hot-headed enthusiasts, dreamers of the impossible, void of reason, undesirables, incapables, the ragamuffins of society, they will begin to consider them as lovers of freedom and country, who are ready to conquer or die for their God-given rights. They will begin to consider them as men who are daring enough to pursue the right in the face of difficulties, who have won the right to live because they are not afraid to die.[108]

During his travels with Sam and his fellow delegates to Appausa, in the interior of the Gold Coast, Faduma found much that was encouraging to his perception of the goals and ideals of the African Movement. At Nsuaem "the most civilized and up-to-date town between Salt Pond and Apurri," he was impressed with its well-equipped school that had an industrial education curriculum under the headmastership of a native. Consistent with his commitment to coeducation, Faduma's only criticism of Nsuaem's school was its practice of gender discrimination: "The one great drawback all along the line is the absence of girls from the schools, due to the fact that the natives of the interior, unlike those along the coast, do not consider female education necessary in their social regime."[109] He was especially thrilled by the performance of indigenous music ("native soul music"). Contrasting it to the "imitative" Europeanized music often heard on the coast, he proudly noted: "[T]he writer has heard rendered the most classical music of England, Germany and Italy. He has listened to symphonies which were soul enrapturing, but he cannot forget the peculiar feelings which swept over his soul at the rendition of this native Fanti music. If he did not dance with his feet, he did in his soul."[110]

By early spring, however, neither Sam nor his fellow delegates shared the confidence in the movement that Faduma continued to project before the West African community in his articles. Most of the delegates had been disappointed by the conditions under which they were expected to live at Appausa. They were unaccustomed to native food and found their dwindling resources inadequate to provide them with western provisions. A few weakened and succumbed to the demanding environment.[111] Adding further aggravation to their increasingly dire situation was the continous stream of restrictions colonial officials leveled against Sam and the movement.[112]

Throughout the spring and summer of 1915 the difficulties afflicting the African Movement increased. By late summer Faduma's articles on the all-but-collapsed movement were consumed with explanations of the myriad problems that beset their "Herculean" enterprise. "The wonder," he exclaimed, "is that Chief Sam and the movement . . . are still in existence, and the S.S. 'Liberia' has weathered the storms and bullets of the public as no modern dreadnoughts have been able to withstand."[113] His comments proved premature. The fate of the movement was soon sealed by the seizure of the *Liberia* by government officials for unpaid debts.[114]

With the collapse of the movement in September, most of the delegates made arrangements for an ignominious return to the United States. Faduma, however, resettled in Sierra Leone.[115] Undaunted, he continued to function as ideologue and theologue of the collapsed movement. Having envisioned so much for the movement, he refused to accept its failure in any ultimate sense.

In a series of reflections on "The Perils of Pioneering," he drew parallels between the African Movement and other pioneering movements that had prematurely been dismissed by their detractors as failures.[116] After reminding his readers that "there is no crown without its cross, no rose without its thorns, no life without death," he recounted the difficulties of other "unfortunate pioneers," such as Columbus, DeSoto, Balboa, Magellan, and Sir Walter Raleigh. Their experiences served to point out that "the path to success and glory is not often strewn with roses." Consequently, if the black race desired to achieve true manhood it too had to accept the risks of pioneering:

> There are no difficulties which the American or African Negro will meet in pioneering which white peoples have not met in a more terrible form. Now is the time for us to prove our manhood. Let the African and the Negro scattered over the world begin to read history and its philosophy with a purpose. Let him study the history of civilization and the evolution of European peoples, catch the inspiration and develop the energy to do for his own people what the white people did and are doing for their own. This is not a time for a life of ease . . . . In this tedious and often perilous task of developing Africa by Africans, "He that loseth his life shall find it. He that seeketh to save his life shall lose it."[117]

Though few of his fellow delegates seemed at this point inclined to agree, Faduma argued that even death in Africa for a worthwhile cause was better than life in the southern United States:

> It is certainly better for American Negroes to die of African fever in the effort to contribute to Africa's development, than to be riddled by the bullets of the white mob who control the local governments of the United States. It is better to help to civilize Africa, where even among the most pagan and naked tribes there are laws protecting female chastity, than to live among the domineering white men of the southern States, where a beautiful black girl finds it difficult to escape from their hawkish grasp. It is better to live even among Pagans, where the majority respect their laws and life is secure, than to be in a country where only the minority are law keepers as in the southern States. Africa is not the land of immortals. The right kind of people die here only once as in other parts of the world. Only "cowards die many times before their death."[118]

Faduma insisted that the inability to aim at high ideals, not failure to accomplish them, was the crime. His continued commitment to theological liberalism was reflected in his contention that even God had failed to realize perfection in the creation of humankind: "In the great archetypal thought of the God of the universe, man was to be sinless and a perfect image of Him. Even Deity failed to realize his ideal. Man is a failure though not a complete one." Consistent with his appropriation of the evolutionary thesis, he contended: "Man is still in the making and an every day making. Evolution is a process, not a finality. Deity has not given up but continues making men."[119] In a more comprehensive theological exposition of this thesis, Faduma argued:

> The making of man is a process. God has not finished his work of making him. He is making him every day and epoch. Failure is involved in the process because man is a moral being . . . . He does not cease making and remaking them because he has failed to realize his purpose in them. If God so fails why should man. . . cease trying. . . . There is a cosmic process through which man must pass before his evolution is attained. He must achieve success through experience gained by repeated failures, downfalls, and uprisings . . . . There are failures worth making and are better than so-called successes that have no high ideal behind them. Not failure but low aim is crime.[120]

Faduma emphasized that Pan-African history was interwoven with "Sacred History" as he responded to those who viewed the collapsed movement as "a delusion and a snare," and himself as an "impractical" dreamer and "visionary." Pan-African visionaries such as his old schoolmate, "John Sarbah of the Gold Coast," his mentor, "Blyden of Liberia," and by implication, Chief Sam, were likened to Abraham and Moses:

> The first pioneer recorded in Sacred History was Abraham who left home for a land in which he had not a foot of ground, going he knew not where. A senseless idiot, a visionary, our modern critics would call him . . . . Moses was dominated by a great idea, the emancipation of Israel. Had he been living in our modern twentieth century with its overpowering materialism, had he been a subject of Great Britain, he would be in prison, considered a stupid maniac . . . convicted of manslaughter and criminal negligence . . . . He died without a realization of his cherished idea, a failure. But Providence used Joshua to carry out to a successful end what the leader failed to effect. The idea of Moses was carried out in piece meals. Most of the ideas of the World's thinkers are carried in the same way. In many cases they are mere projectors and injectors of ideas to be worked out by future generations.

Thus Faduma reminded his readers that although men may die, ideas and movements do not:

> "Crush the movement, nip it in the bud," we hear from high authority. How can you successfully crush the idea of human progress and emancipation? Is not liberty, is not the emancipation of the soul an instinctive and natural idea? You may retard its progress, but you cannot annihilate the idea. Truth, as an idea, though crushed to earth will rise again. This power of resurrection which is given it by the Almighty cannot by any subterfuge or circumvention in politics be taken away. *Governments and individual interests may be mighty, but God is Almighty.*"[121]

In his final articles on the African Movement Faduma engaged in more than romantic ideological and theological rationalizations. He also presented an objective analysis of the many administrative failures that beset the African Movement. He acknowledged that much of the difficulty faced by the movement and its delegates would have been less traumatic if there had been: (1) a smaller number of delegates designated to make the initial voyage of the movement; (2) better provisions made for their upkeep during their stay in the colony; (3) better cooperation sought with the leaders of the country, especially the Gold Coast Aborigines Rights Protection Society and through them the gaining of introduction to the Governor of the Colony; and (4) a thorough organization of the Akim Trading Company, Ltd., in keeping with the requirements of modern business practices.[122] Despite acknowledging errors in judgement and planning, Faduma insisted that no assessment of the movement could ignore or minimize the impact of the active opposition of British officials.[123] And although the African Movement had been undermined by faulty planning and powerful opposition, Faduma noted that the continued oppression of African-Americans in the United States would inevitably give rise to other Back-to-Africa Movements: "When a house is on fire men take unusual risks to save their lives. Some will fling themselves over high elevations while the few are deliberate and cautious in their methods of escape."[124]

Even in the face of the obvious failure of the African Movement, Faduma continued to nourish and pass on to younger generations the ideals and vision that inspired it. His efforts are strikingly illustrated by a sermon entitled "The Man of Dreams," that he delivered in Freetown to the 1916 graduating class of Albert Academy.[125] In a masterful exposition of Genesis 37:5, 19–20, recounting the story of the "dreamer" Joseph, Faduma encouraged his young audience to dare to dream and to pursue their dreams despite obstacles and painful ridicule.[126] Although he made no direct reference to the African Movement, it is obvious that the ill-starred movement and his relationship with it provided the immediate inspiration for his choice of text and sermon. Moreover, in the course of his forceful homily, Faduma in effect gathered up the tattered dream and vision of the African Movement and flung them into the future with the hope that they would be realized by a later generation.

His prophetic exposition was given wider audience when the sermon was published in the April 1916 issue of the *Sierra Leone Outlook*. Introductory comments from the editor suggest that Faduma had suffered no great loss of personal status or prestige in Sierra Leone as a result of his association with the African Movement:

> We take pleasure in publishing the sermon delivered to the students of Albert Academy by Rev. O. Faduma . . . . It has the proper ring and strikes to

> the heart of the matter. Professor Faduma is a man of wide experience and an illustration of what a man can accomplish when he puts the Kingdom of God first in his life. Whenever and wherever he speaks he has a message—some truth or principle which he is ready to proclaim.[127]

The editor concluded with the wish that Faduma "be used abundantly in our Colony and Protectorate to arouse young men and quicken them to more splendid endeavor for the master." His wish was to be granted. Over the course of the next eight years, Faduma would indeed contribute "abundantly" to educational, religious, and political developments in Sierra Leone and wider British West Africa.

Notes

1. Editorial, "A Broken Column," *Sierra Leone Weekly News,* 13 July 1912. The National Religious Training School was established in 1910 by James E. Shepard. Shepard, a black Baptist minister, has been described as "an acute interracialist." In 1923 the state of North Carolina took over the institution and after a number of name changes it became North Carolina Central University. Gavins, *Perils and Prospects,* pp. 106, 119, 137; John Hope Franklin, *From Slavery to Freedom: A History of Negro America,* 5th ed. (New York: Alfred A. Knopf, 1980), p. 405. Apparently Faduma did not accept this position. No mention is made of it in later summaries of his teaching appointments.
2. Testimonials were presented by the moderator and secretary of the North Carolina Conference of Congregational Churches, the County Superintendent of Public Instruction, the County Superintendent of Schools, and Troy's mayor. The latter hailed Faduma as "truly one of our country's greatest and best men in the broadest sense of these terms." Editorial, "The U.M.C. and Professor Faduma," *Sierra Leone Weekly News,* 25 Sept. 1915.
3. Ibid.
4. O. Faduma, "What the African Movement Stands For," *African Mail,* 25 Sept. 1914.
5. During his first year in the United States, Faduma called for selective African-American emigration to Africa. O. Faduma, "The A.M.E. Church and Kittrell Normal Institute," *Christian Recorder* (16 Apr. 1890): 289. On the similarities and parallels between the African movement and Garvey's Universal Negro Improvement Association, see J. A. Langley, "Chief Sam's African Movement and Race Consciousness in West Africa," *Phylon* 32 (Summer 1972):164–178, also Robert A. Hill, ed., *The Marcus Garvey and*

Universal Negro Improvement Association Papers, vol. 1 (Berkeley: University of California Press, 1983), pp. 536–547; also vol. 2, pp. 122–123.

6. Redkey, *Black Exodus,* pp.1–23, 99–100; William E. Bittle and Gilbert L. Geiss, *The Longest Way Home: Chief Alfred C. Sam's Back-to-Africa Movement* (Detroit: Wayne State University Press, 1964), pp. 20–24.
7. Redkey, *Black Exodus,* p.100; Bittle and Geiss, *Longest,* p. 25.
8. William E. Bittle and Gilbert L. Geiss, "Racial Self-Fulfillment and the Rise of an All-Negro Community in Oklahoma," *Phylon* (First Quarter, 1957): 247–260.
9. *Indianapolis Freeman,* 29 July 1905. Quoted in Bittle and Geiss, *Longest,* p. 25.
10. Booker T. Washington, "Boley: A Negro Town in the West," *The Outlook* 96 (Jan./Apr. 1908): 28–31; Bittle and Geiss, *Longest,* p. 26.
11. Bittle and Geiss, *Longest* p. 29.
12. Ibid., p. 30.
13. Ibid., pp. 33–67.
14. Ibid., p. 29.
15. Ibid., p. 67.
16. Redkey, *Black Exodus;* Floyd J. Miller, *The Search for a Black Nationality: Black Emigration and Colonization, 1787–1863* (Urbana: University of Illinois Press, 1975).
17. Redkey, *Black Exodus,* pp. 292–293. On the earlier tradition of African migration from Oklahoma and the Midwest, see Bittle and Geiss, *Longest,* pp. 42–48, and Redkey, *Black Exodus,* pp. 99–126, 249–251.
18. Bittle and Geiss, *Longest,* pp. 70, 195; "'Chief Sam' and the Negro Exodus," *The Literary Digest* 48 (Mar. 1914): 647; Hill, *Garvey Papers,* vol. 1, p. 536.
19. Reardon, *Liberal Protestantism,* pp. 9–48; Averill, *American Theology in the Liberal Tradition,* pp. 30–49.
20. Bittle and Geiss, *Longest,* pp. 70–71; Hill, *Garvey Papers,* vol. 1, pp. 536–537.
21. Bittle and Geiss, *Longest,* p. 71.
22. Ibid.
23. Ibid.; Hill, *Garvey Papers,* vol. 1, p. 537.
24. Ibid., p. 538.
25. Ibid.
26. Ibid.; Bittle and Geiss, *Longest,* pp.71–73.
27. Bittle and Geiss, *Longest,* p. 72; "Negro Exodus," *Literary Digest,* p. 647.
28. Articles of Incorporation, Akim Trading Company, Ltd. Quoted in Bittle and Geiss, *Longest,* p. 72.

29. Ibid., pp. 74, 79–80.
30. Ibid., p. 70.
31. Ibid., p. 167.
32. Ibid., p. 79.
33. Interview published in *New York World,* 8 Mar. 1914. Quoted in Bittle and Geiss, *Longest,* p. 123.
34. Hill, *Garvey Papers,* vol. 1, p. 537; Bittle and Geiss, *Longest,* pp. 128–129.
35. Bittle and Geiss, *Longest,* pp. 128–129.
36. Ibid. Sanford's link with the Pentecostal movement is noted by Robert Mapes Anderson, who points out that among the visitors to Shiloh in 1900 was Samuel Parham. Parham, along with a number of his followers, spent about six weeks studying at Shiloh and was "impressed" enough to imitate Sanford's "Shiloh techniques" at his own "College of Bethel" in Topeka, Kansas. Robert Mapes Anderson, *Vision of the Disinherited: The Making of American Pentecostalism* (New York and Oxford: Oxford University Press, 1979), pp. 50–51.
37. Bittle and Geiss, *Longest,* pp. 128–130; Hill, *Garvey Papers,* vol. 1, pp. 537–538; Anderson, *Vision,* p. 50.
38. Hill, *Garvey Papers,* vol. 1, pp. 537–539; Bittle and Geiss, *Longest,* pp. 128, 132.
39. Bittle and Geiss, *Longest,* pp. 130–132; Hill, *Garvey Papers,* vol. 1, pp. 538–543.
40. Bittle and Geiss, *Longest,* pp. 135–140, 142.
41. Okonkwo, "Man of Two Worlds," p. 27.
42. O. Faduma, letter to Booker T. Washington, 12 Dec. 1913. Booker T. Washington Papers, Manuscript Division, Library of Congress, Washington, D.C.
43. "Digest," Booker T. Washington Papers, Manuscript Division, Library of Congress, Washington, D.C.; Redkey, *Black Exodus,* pp. 231, 253–254; Louis R. Harlan, "Booker T. Washington and the White Man's Burden," *American Historical Review* 71 (Jan. 1966): 441–67. No evidence of Washington's reply or Faduma's visit to Tuskegee has been found.
44. The World Missionary Conference that met in Edinburgh in 1910 recommended that missionaries to Africa study the Tuskegee/Hampton educational system. Kenneth King, *Pan-Africanism and Education: A Study of Race Philanthropy and Education in the Southern States of America and East Africa* (Oxford: Clarendon Press, 1971), pp. 15–16.
45. Robert E. Park, "The International Conference on the Negro," *Southern Workman* 41 (June 1912): 347–352; Geiss, *Pan-African Movement,* pp. 218–220.

46. King, *Pan-Africanism and Negro Education,* p. 16; editorial, "The International Conference on the Negro," *The Southern Workman* 41 (June 1912): 322–323. Geiss notes that "in conformity with his whole temperament, Booker T. Washington avoided political themes such as racial questions and nationalism in his invitation, and concentrated upon the educational activities of 'missions and governments.'" Geiss, *Pan-African Movement,* p. 219. Harlan notes, "The conference involved the same ambiguity of relationship to the blacks and whites that was evident in his other African activities and his role in American society." Harlan, "White Man's Burden," pp. 464–465.
47. Park, "The International Conference on the Negro," pp. 348–350.
48. This contention is supported by the fact that a letter was addressed to the conference from the Gold Coast nationalist and Pan-Africanist J. E. Casely Hayford. Blyden also commended the conference by letter. Harlan points out that "A curious anomaly of the Washington Papers is his friendly correspondence with most of the leaders of African nationalism. There is no evidence, however, that he encouraged or even clearly understood their nationalistic and Pan-African views." Washington also refused invitations to the earlier Pan-African conferences. Harlan, "White Man's Burden," pp. 460, 464–465; also Shepperson, "Negro American Influences," pp. 310–311. Langley describes the 1912 conference as a "small-scale Pan-African conference." He notes the importance of the attendance of Henry M. Turner, the leading proponent of missionary Pan-Africanism, and contends, "In fact, the conference showed Booker T. Washington not as an isolationist leader which his rivalry with Du Bois led observers to think he was, but as one whose approach to racial solidarity was based on political realism and a preference for technical and educational development of Africa." Langley, *Pan-Africanism and Nationalism,* pp. 32–33.
49. O. Faduma, "What the African Movement Stands For," *African Mail,* 2 Oct. 1914.
50. Langley, "Chief Sam's African Movement," and *Pan-Africanism and Nationalism,* pp. 50–54.
51. O. Faduma, "What the African Movement Stands For," *African Mail,* 25 Sept. 1914.
52. Despite Faduma's efforts to cast the African Movement within the context of theological liberalism, it drew much of its spiritual and theological impetus from the traditional black evangelicalism that he had roundly denounced in his 1908 paper, "The Defects of the Negro Church." Perhaps the failure of a more "rational," intellectual, and decorous evangelical liberalism to effect significant change in American society fostered an increased appreciation of the more emotive and less rationalistic religiosity of the Black

Church tradition. See Orishatukeh Faduma, "Growing Interest in West Africa," *Sierra Leone Weekly News,* 18 Feb. 1915. For Faduma's later and more comprehensive appraisal of African-Americans and their religion, see O. Faduma, "Negro Development—Its Phases," *Sierra Leone Weekly News,* 24 Sept. 1921.

53. Ibid. Although ill for some time, Turner did not die until 1915, at the age of 82. Redkey, *Black Exodus,* pp. 7–9.
54. Ibid.
55. On Personalism, see Cauthen, *American Religious Liberalism,* pp. 61–83, 180, 191. Faduma, who employed Blyden's concept of an "African Personality" as a key component in his Pan-African ideology, also found liberal theology's emphasis on the importance of personality congenial and supportive. He was convinced of the divine origin of the "African Personality," and perceived racism as a sin because it hampered its full development. Orishatukeh Faduma, "What the African Movement Stands For," *African Mail,* 25 Sept. 1915. On Blyden and the "African Personality," see Lynch, *Blyden,* pp. 54–55, 61–62, 65, 191, 216, 237, 239, 240, 244, 352.
56. Ibid., pp. 521–522.
57. Ibid., p. 522. The call by the African Movement for a "self-governing Negro church" must have presented Faduma with a dilemma. Although a supporter of ecclesiastical nationalism and Ethiopianism he, unlike other ecclesiastical nationalists such as Majola Agbebi and his old schoolmate William Euba, did not make a decisive break with Congregationalism in favor of African or African-American ecclesiastical affiliation. Perhaps the key to this apparent paradox lies in his failure to discover an African or African-American denomination as supportive of his liberal theological, missiological, and pedagogical convictions as was Congregationalism. See Orishatukeh Faduma, "Christian Missions among Less Developed Races," *American Missionary* 61 (Jan. 1907): 71–72.
58. O. Faduma, "What the African Movement Stands For," *African Mail,* 2 Oct. 1914.
59. Ibid.
60. This was to be the task of the Ethiopian Institute, the African-based Tuskegee that he planned to establish.
61. Ibid.
62. Faduma confirmed that "there had been many Fakirs traveling through the country under the title chief" and that in the course of his own lecture tours throughout the state, he too had been viewed with suspicion. Orishatukeh Faduma, "The African Movement," *African Mail,* 20 Nov. 1914; Faduma, "Some of My Experiences," p. 9.
63. Orishatukeh Faduma, "The African Movement," *African Mail,* 20 Nov. 1914.
64. Ibid., pp. 73–74.

65. Ibid., p. 74.
66. Bittle and Geiss, *Longest,* pp. 86, 91–94, 99. Faduma, "The African Movement," *African Mail,* 27 Nov. 1914.
67. Faduma, "The African Movement," *African Mail,* 27 Nov. 1914.
68. He also became increasingly critical of the evangelical missionary movement that had actually nurtured, and indeed continued to provide, much of the ideological impetus for the Pan-African movement. Most students of Pan-Africanism note that Du Bois's Pan-African consciousness and race ideology were probably influenced by his study in Germany, where he "may have been exposed to the current race theories and Pan-German strands of thought." However, far less attention has been given to the implications of his possible exposure to currents of theological liberalism then prevalent in the German academic community. Du Bois's subsequent critique of traditional evangelical missiology and theology suggests the need for a closer study of the possible influences of these theological currents and influences upon his Pan-African ideology and activities. Langley, *Pan-Africanism and Nationalism,* pp. 59–70, 72; William E. B. Du Bois, *Dusk of Dawn* (New York: Harcourt Brace, 1940); Williams, *Black Americans,* p. 172; Harold R. Isaacs, "Du Bois and Africa," *Race* (Nov. 1960): 3–23.
69. "Migration and Africa," *The Crisis: A Record of the Darker Races* (June 1914): 75.
70. "Robbery," *Crisis,* (Feb. 1914): 175.
71. Quoted in Bittle and Geiss, *Longest,* pp. 101–102.
72. Langley, "Chief Sam's African Movement," p. 168. See also Hill, *Garvey Papers,* vol. 1, p. 536.
73. Langley, "Chief Sam's African Movement," p. 167.
74. "A 'Modern Moses,'" quoted in Langley, "Chief Sam's African Movement," p. 168.
75. "Alfred Sam's Repatriation Scheme, an Examination," *African Telegraph and Gold Coast Mirror,* Dec. 1914. Quoted in Okonkwo, "Emergence of Nationalism," p. 106.
76. Faduma, "The African Movement," *African Mail,* 27 Nov. 1914.
77. Langley, "Chief Sam's African Movement," p. 166.
78. Faduma characterized the investigation as "one of the most thorough any company could be subjected to. It was a continuous investigation of every phase of the movement . . . . [f]or the detection of anything fraudulent. Finally all investigation ceased and the post office department threw up its hands." Faduma, "The African Movement," *African Mail,* 27 Nov. 1914.
79. Faduma, "The African Movement," *African Mail,* 4 Dec. 1914.
80. Ibid. Sam argued that "If he was a British subject, then he was entitled under treaty to have the protection of Great Britain over his ship. If he was not a British subject, then Great Britain had misled

him and his tribe as being under her protection." Faduma, "The African Movement," *African Mail,* 27 Nov. 1914.

81. Langley, "Chief Sam's African Movement," p. 167.
82. Langley, "Chief Sam's African Movement," p. 167; Faduma, "The African Movement," *African Mail,* 4 Dec. 1914.
83. Faduma, "The African Movement," *African Mail,* 27 Nov. 1914.
84. Ibid.
85. Faduma, "The African Movement," *African Mail,* 4 Dec. 1914.
86. Langley, who has closely examined British governmental papers related to the rise of Pan-Africanism and nationalism in West Africa, makes a convincing case for the impact that the movement had on the development of both. Langley, "Chief Sam's African Movement," and *Pan-Africanism and Nationalism,* pp. 41–58.
87. "American Negroes and the Gold Coast," *Gold Coast Leader,* quoted in *African Mail,* 5 June 1914.
88. Blyden died on February 7, 1912, in Sierra Leone and was buried there. Langley, *Pan-Africanism and Nationalism,* pp. 110–112; Lynch, *Blyden,* p. 250; and Hollis R. Lynch, "Edward W. Blyden: Pioneer West African Nationalist," *Journal of African History* 6 (1965): 373–88.
89. Faduma also indicated that the agenda and involvement of the Holy Ghost and Us Society had not completely coincided with the broader Pan-African agenda of the African Movement. Of the religious character of the "Kingdom Crew," which had helped outfit the ship and prove it seaworthy, he noted that "The peculiarity of the Kingdom Crew was their distinctively missionary spirit. Every member of the crew was a Christian, and attended religious exercises twice a day . . . to which everyone in the ship was invited. Their Christian character was outstanding . . . . They would have been willing to take the ship to and back from West Africa had the people as a whole wanted them to do so, and had Providence willed it." Faduma, "The African Movement," *African Mail,* 4 Dec. 1914.
90. Faduma, "The African Movement," *African Mail,* 12 Mar. 1915.
91. Bittle and Geiss suggest that "this clearly improbable accusation was doubtless a cover-up for continued British concern over the landing of the Negroes on the Gold Coast, and may simply have been a last minute attempt to prevent the ship from ever reaching that colony." Bittle and Geiss, *Longest,* pp. 182, 233–234.
92. "The Afro-Americans at Victoria Park," *Sierra Leone Weekly News,* 23 Jan. 1915; Faduma, "The African Movement," *African Mail,* 22 Jan. 1915.
93. Faduma, "The African Movement," *African Mail,* 10 Sept. 1915.
94. Faduma, "The African Movement," *African Mail,* 12 Mar. 1915.
95. Faduma, "The African Movement," *African Mail,* 10 Sept. 1915.

96. Langley, "Chief Sam's African Movement," pp. 173, 175.
97. *Sierra Leone Weekly News,* 16 Jan. 1915. Quoted in Langley, "Chief Sam's African Movement," p. 173.
98. Editorial, *The Gold Coast Leader,* 23 Jan. 1915. Quoted in Langley, "Chief Sam's African Movement," p. 174. Langley reports, "At the end of January, the *Leader* again claimed that the whole of British West Africa was unanimous on the idea of the African Movement and that Africans in the four colonies would not tolerate official opposition to 'this patriotic movement.'" *The Gold Coast Leader,* 30. Langley, "Chief Sam's African Movement," p. 174. The *Leader* also acknowledged Faduma as "a man of distinguished parts, a writer and a thinker of no mean order, and . . . one of our own." "Arrival of Chief Sam and his party in the Gold Coast," *African Mail,* 26 Feb. 1915.
99. "Chief Sam and His Mission," *African Mail,* 12 Feb. 1915.
100. Faduma, "The African Movement," *African Mail,* 19 Mar. 1915.
101. Ibid.
102. Ibid.
103. Ibid.
104. Ibid.
105. Ibid.
106. Sam added that the same forces "had attempted to influence the native press, but failed, and would fail, so long as there was a spark of loyalty and patriotism in the native." Faduma reported that Sam's hour-long speech was "dignified, forceful, and statesman like . . . full of inspiration and pathos, patriotic to its very core" and "the best" he had "ever heard fall from his lips." Faduma, "The African Movement," *African Mail,* 7 May 1914.
107. Ibid.
108. Ibid.
109. Faduma, "The African Movement," *African Mail,* 27 Aug. 1915.
110. Ibid.
111. Faduma also confessed that his situation had been very different from those of the other delegates. He was well known throughout British West Africa and his friend on the Gold Coast had "been profuse in giving him creature and other comforts." Also of importance was his cultural adaptability whereby "among the Fantis he became a Fanti without prejudice to his health." Orishatukeh Faduma, "The African Movement: Its Ideas and Methods," *Sierra Leone Weekly News,* 2 Oct. 1915.
112. Langley, "Chief Sam's African Movement," p. 175.
113. O. Faduma, "The African Movement," *African Mail,* 13 Aug. 1915.
114. Langley, "Chief Sam's African Movement," p. 175.

115. Faduma, "The African Movement," *African Mail,* 20 Aug. 1915; *Marcus Garvey Papers,* vol. 1, pp. 463–464.
116. Faduma, "The African Movement: Its Idea and Methods," *Sierra Leone Weekly News,* 2 Oct. 1915; Orishatukeh Faduma, "The African Movement: The Perils of Pioneering—A Parallel," *Sierra Leone Weekly News,* 11 Sept. 1915.
117. Faduma, "The African Movement: The Perils of Pioneering."
118. Ibid.
119. Ibid.
120. O. Faduma, "Not Failure But Low Aim Is Crime," *Sierra Leone Weekly News,* 29 Mar. 1919. Quoted in Langley, *Ideologies of Liberation,* pp. 195–202.
121. Faduma, "The African Movement: The Perils of Pioneering."
122. See Faduma, "The African Movement: Its Ideas and Methods." Also Langley, "Chief Sam's African Movement," p. 177.
123. Faduma, "The African Movement: Its Ideas and Methods."
124. Ibid.; Langley, " Chief Sam's African Movement," pp. 177–178. Faduma's assessment proved to be prophetic of the response only five years later of the African-American masses to the "Back-to-Africa" efforts of Marcus Garvey and his Universal Negro Improvement Association.
125. Albert Academy was established in 1904 by the United Brethren in Christ (U.B.C.). It aspired "to give such a comprehensive preparation to each student, that, whether he goes out as a preacher, teacher, professional man, or tradesman, he will be a factor in the extension of Christ's church in Africa." *Sierra Leone Outlook* 7 (Dec. 1916): 20; Orishatukeh Faduma, "The Man of Dreams," *Sierra Leone Outlook* 7 (Apr. 1916): 3–8. The introduction to this sermon reported that Faduma had been awarded a doctorate and Okonkwo indicates that this honorary degree was granted by Livingstone College. However, correspondence with Livingstone officials and archivists has revealed no evidence of the issuance of this degree. Faduma does not refer to this degree in later reports of his life, work, and education. "A Helpful Sermon," *Sierra Leone Outlook* 7 (Apr. 1916): 9; Okonkwo, "Man of Two Worlds," p. 26.
126. The text as quoted by Faduma read: "And Joseph dreamed a dream and he told it his brethren; and they hated him yet the more . . . And they said one to another, Behold the dreamer cometh. Come now therefore, and let us slay him and cast him into some pit, and we will say some evil beast hath devoured him. And we shall see what will become of his dreams." Faduma, "The Man of Dreams," p. 3.
127. "A Helpful Sermon," *Sierra Leone Outlook* 7 (Apr. 1916): 9.

6

Liberal Theologue of West African Pedagogical and Political Reform

The development and implementation of an educational philosophy and curriculum that would facilitate the entrance of Africans and diaspora Africans into the corridors of modernity was a central concern for Faduma and other Pan-Africanists.[1] It had been a focus of Faduma's efforts in North Carolina and he had envisioned realization of his Pan-African pedagogy in the African Movement's proposed College of Ethiopia.[2] With the collapse of the African Movement, however, Faduma was faced with the task of attempting to implement his reformist pedagogical theories within existing educational institutions in Sierra Leone. It was a task further complicated by the traditional missionary and colonial orientation of most of these institutions.

Immediately after his arrival in Sierra Leone, Faduma, once hailed as one of the colony's most gifted young instructors, accepted the first of a series of educational appointments.[3] His initial appointment was as principal of the United Methodist Church Collegiate School. Two years later he was appointed to the colony's Education Committee.[4] The following year he accepted government employment as Inspector of Schools, tutor of teacher training, and officer in charge of the model school.[5] In each of these positions and in numerous addresses and articles on education and educational theory, Faduma advocated and attempted to implement pedagogical reforms that adapted African education to the developments and requirements of the modern era while retaining a sensitivity to African history and culture.[6] Thus at the Collegiate School, Faduma, with the assistance of "a brilliant" young African teacher, "overhauled" its "work" and introduced vernacular instruction, the study of science, and subjects such as Negro history, Arabic, and African folklore.[7] With these efforts and his defense of them, he assumed a leadership role in the long-running and intensifying controversy over the proper education of Africans and other colonized peoples.[8]

A fundamental component of Faduma's reformist pedagogy was his synthesis of liberal theological tenets and progressive educational theories with his Pan-African ideological concerns. This synthesis was illuminated in a series of articles on "African Negro Education" written by Faduma and published in the *Sierra Leone Weekly News* in 1918. He called for "scientific" and "eclectic education" for the African because "in an age of scientific progress it is dangerous to cling tenaciously to any one system of thought."[9] Characteristically, his reformist pedagogy was modeled after the New Theology. Since "true theology is the sum of all theologies and refuses to be denominational," educational methods should "not be hide-bound but should be the product of all that is best in present day methods." Thus Faduma argued that

> Pestalozzi, Froebel, Herbart, Comenius, Montessori and many other leaders of educational methods need careful study but not wholesale adoption. Each of them needs careful pruning and intelligent sifting, an addition here and a subtraction there . . . . [I]t is a Procrustean system of education which tolerates no change of methods or procedure. When new and fresh facts are discovered, our old conclusions must be changed. It is here that the too conservative mind, club, state, or religious society becomes a stumbling block to progress and must be fought to a finish to prevent fossilization. . . .

The need for "judicious selection" in choice of educational methods was also necessary because "all flesh is not the same flesh." "Racial idiosyncracies" in particular necessitated modifications because "what suits the Chinaman may not suit the Englishman, and what suits the Englishman may not suit the African and so on." Faduma also argued, as had Blyden, that though the scaffolding of education might be laid by the foreigner, "the only true interpreter of the man African must be an African, one like himself with similar yearnings, hopes and aspirations."[10]

Explicit in Faduma's advocacy of liberal-oriented pedagogical reform was a critique and rejection of the basic theological and ideological premises of traditional missionary education in West Africa. While acknowledging the positive contributions missionary societies had made in laying the foundation for African education, he noted that their methods had been "nonscientific" and "the wonder is that much good had come out of such unscientific teaching."[11] It was evident to him, however, that mission education was increasingly unable to cope with the realities and needs of the modern era. Not only was it lacking in materials and resources, but it was also grievously hampered by sectarianism and "unable to meet inevitable conditions arising out of a population with different creeds."[12]

Faduma charged that the narrow dogmatic and sectarian perspective of traditional missionary education not only blinded teachers and students to many of the important scientific and intellectual developments, but also exacerbated differences among various segments of the African community. Moreover, its "dogmatic methods" of teaching fostered an intellectual and theological immaturity that Africa could ill afford in the modern era. Faduma's critique and rejection of the alliance of theological and pedagogical traditionalism is illustrated in his observation that:

> The obedient scholar swallowed everything and was considered smart in proportion to his quickness in reproducing. He was encouraged to be an imitator rather than a thinker and producer. His theology was one of memory rather than of life. One could reproduce Paley or Butler but had no opinion of his own on what they wrote. On questions relating to morals the text books decided everything and he dared not think differently for fear of being heterodox: "Hell is a dark and bottomless pit, full of fire and brimstone," was true in all its physical nakedness, and Heaven could only be reached after, never before death. Sin is a breaking of God's law, but never of Nature's law. This kind of dogmatic teaching has left its impress on the minds of natives and has become a huge incubus preventing progress.[13]

As a corrective of religious dogmatism and "sectarianism," Faduma advocated a greater role for the government in education. His call for "state education" was additionally based on the premise that it would focus the colony's limited resources on the educational welfare of all of its youth without consideration of gender or religious orientation.[14] Moreover, state sponsorship of free and compulsory education would permit inclusion of modern scientific, intellectual, and academic theories and inevitably contribute to the development of the modern democratic African state. Ironically, Faduma noted that valuable lessons were to be gleaned from the relationship between pedagogical and political developments in both the United States and Britain. Of particular importance was his perception of the political contribution made by his alma mater, the University of London. He noted that its founding under state control and its being free from religious tests had stimulated English intellectual life and the development of modern "Democratic institutions."[15]

Consistent with his call for state control of education in Sierra Leone and throughout West Africa, Faduma transcended the old evangelical Pan-African vision and paradigm that held as axiomatic the belief that its goals could only be realized in a "Christian state."[16] In contrast, he argued that the quest for "a sectarian state" was "out of place" among the democratic institutions required in the modern era—especially in Africa with its varied religious creeds.[17] Sectarian competition and restrictions, especially in the educational arena, had no place in the modern African state that he envisioned. Its educational system would be one that "has no religious bias, but respects the conscience of the Christian equally as that of a Mohammedan or Hindu."[18]

> Our conception of the modern state is such as to lead us to assert the following truths which may be regarded as axiomatic. 1. It is the duty of the State to educate its citizens. 2. It is the duty of the State to educate all its citizens. 3. It is the duty of the state in the education of its citizens to draw no line between Jew, Christian, Muslim, Heathen, etc., but to give equal opportunity to all.[19]

As envisioned by Faduma, church and state would be "separate and distinct in their spheres of influence, yet cooperative[,] . . . the state producing an orderly and intelligent citizenship, the Church using this orderly intelligence already prepared for her for the working out of the spiritual salvation of the people."[20]

Faduma's unwavering commitment to educational reform in the colony, coupled with his critique of mission education and his support of an increased role for the colonial government in the educational sphere, led to his appointment in 1917 to the colony's Education Committee.[21] His passionate commitment to pedagogical reform may also have precipitated his resignation in 1918 as principal of the United Methodist Church Collegiate School. In announcing his resignation, Faduma noted that it "had been communicated to him" that he should "not expect to be re-appointed Principal after the expiration of his term."[22] He was nevertheless convinced of the success of his reforms at the Collegiate School and later wrote, "as the result of this work, I can now point with joy to graduates and undergraduates of an English university besides a few trained teachers and men equipped for the gospel ministry."[23] His success, dedication, and influence were also confirmed by a letter from one of his former students to the editor of the *Sierra Leone Weekly News*. The letter, occasioned by Faduma's resignation, read: "Principal Faduma is a wonderful man in the sight of his students, the good he has done we do not think any other person will do for us. He was a father, mother, sister and brother to his scholars . . . . He introduced many good things and taught many students after school hours." [24]

The inability of the colony's Director of Education to find a European to fill the vacancy as Inspector of Schools resulted in Faduma's appointment as "Temporary Inspecting Officer."[25] In this new post, he continued his critique of the pedagogical status quo and the theological tenets undergirding it. He also found himself increasingly at odds with the racial attitudes of fellow members of the Education Committee, especially as these attitudes influenced policy decisions that perpetuated an inferior education for Africans. Such attitudes provoked Faduma to publicly rebuke a member of the Education Committee who dared to suggest that African students had little need for knowledge of modern science. Faduma explained his rebuke and expounded on the sentiments that inspired it in a series of articles on "The Study of Science in Elementary and Secondary Schools." In his introduction to this series, which was published in the *Weekly News,* Faduma confessed:

> I am prompted to write on the above subject because a member of the Education Committee seemed to think "that there was no great demand for this subject on the part of the pupils," and that there was "no object in view

> in acquiring a knowledge of science." I am glad no African teacher, I mean no Negro who is a teacher, has been heard to express similar views.[26]

The pertinent and relevant question, he insisted, was why African youth should be kept ignorant of the laws of biology, geology, and the operation of the world around them:

> Why should not the African boy or girl take interest in the life of a frog and watch its development from a tadpole ? . . . Why should school children be ignorant of the life of a butterfly and not follow up its gradual development? Why should they not know by sight and contact the life and habits of the honey bee, the wasp, the spider, and various species of ants? Why should they not observe the seed in the soil in all stages of its growth and development? Why should they be ignorant of the beginnings of life? Why should they see the heavens studded with stars, the sun and moon giving light without knowing their relation? . . . Can this be progress in a world of progress?[27]

In a follow-up series entitled "What the Study of Science Means," Faduma pursued the issue and was explicit about the religious as well as the educational significance of the modern study of science.[28] Of particular importance among its various branches were the "study of religion" and the modern study of geography. The former he described as "a science which systematizes the beliefs of peoples, primitive or otherwise, in God or gods, as well as their ideas on the origin of the world and its operations, the future life; the existence of spirits and demons and their influence over men."[29] Of the religious significance of the science of geography, which was not to be confused with "Geolatry," he noted:

> It makes us see God's earth in a new light, and helps us know our place in nature. . . . Many of the puzzling things in nature which the untutored Indian and his untutored African brother do not understand but which they regard as mysterious and miraculous, disappear, as mist before the noonday sun in the modern study of Physical Geography.[30]

In final reference to the sentiments that provoked his extensive apology, Faduma concluded:

> With the progress of modern Educational Science it is altogether ill-timed to say that there is no demand for the teaching of science among any class of African and especially in Sierra Leone. The work which Ruskin did in popularizing Art in England, and Huxley, science, can be done in any school room in Africa.[31]

Faduma noted, however, that the most important of the new sciences that the African needed in order to achieve self-knowledge and race-conscious development was "Negrology":

> [T]he African, the Negro, must be taught to know and respect himself. All other knowledge besides this self-knowledge must be supplementary. The first science he needs to know at once is Negrology. Materials for such a study are lying scattered and fragmentary waiting for the synthesist.[32]

Faduma also argued that the initial focus of the new educational curriculum should be the African environment. It was imperative that the African student have a thorough grounding in his own culture and history before turning to the study of Europe:

> In the study of Geography and History, the Senegalese, the Gold Coaster, the Yoruba should have an accurate knowledge of their respective countries, their customs, industries, plants and animals, before they are made to study the Geography and History of England or France. We should begin to study things near us and proceed to things far from us . . . . These are some of the changes which modern education has started. It is practical, scientific, and philosophical.[33]

The conviction that a modern, progressive, scientific, and race-conscious pedagogy was destined to be a key factor in the development of the "Negro" race was reiterated by Faduma in a series of articles on "Negro Development."[34] In this series he also fine-tuned the long-running debate between the proponents of "higher education for the Negro" and the supporters of "industrial education."[35] In response to those who were of "the opinion" that industrial education for blacks should not include intellectual and skilled training, Faduma asserted

> Industry of a high grade to which Negroes everywhere should aspire requires intelligence of a high order. To be a skilled farmer requires a thorough knowledge of insect, plant and cattle life . . . . To be a first-rate builder requires more than an elementary knowledge of mathematics, but also a knowledge of the science of architecture.[36]

Linking his argument to increased post–World War I economic concerns in West Africa, Faduma observed:

> We have already too much of Negro labour in Africa especially, which is profitless because not intelligent . . . . All labour, from the tilling of the soil to the baking of bread, from the writing of a book to the building of a house, must be directed and operated by intelligence. If Negro boys are to take much interest in farming they should have such an education as will help them grow their crops and make profits for themselves.[37]

In this series of articles on "Negro Development," Faduma again drew upon both the evolutionary theory and what he termed "race psychology." According to his Darwinian-influenced developmental theory, each race had its "periods of childhood, youth, and manhood." Although the majority of the black race was still in the earlier stages of development, a significant minority—a critical mass—had reached maturity and was poised to lead the majority into full manhood. Consequently, imitativeness was being thrown aside; self-assertiveness and independence of thought were now manifesting themselves. It was imperative that at this crucial stage the race be allowed to take its "natural path" to its own unique destiny in accordance with the "laws of evolution" and "race psychology." "The laws of racial growth," he contended, "must be obeyed if the race is to be preserved."[38] While acknowledging that, "there are thinkers who scorn the above idea and honestly believe that one race type can be fitted into another and be grafted like plants," Faduma again warned:

> If by a process of education you succeed in Anglo-Saxonizing or Gallicizing alien peoples a non-descript type is formed. We are strongly of the opinion that the identity and individuality of every race type should be kept intact and that all education to be worth much should be adaptive. If a man is five feet in height, it is absurd to dress him with a piece of cloth two feet long, then keep on chopping his legs to reduce him to the measure of the cloth. Instead of reducing him to a stump by the chopping method you need to add more to the cloth. There is often in Negro education a false measurement, a wrong standard of him as a man. The result is a form of education wholly Procrustean . . . . One of the greatest problems which modern civilization and modern education must solve is the upbuilding of the several race groups and the preserving of their individuality and identity in harmony with one another.[39]

Among the more controversial of Faduma's proposed educational reforms was his advocacy of the incorporation of Islamic subjects into the educational curriculum. Faduma's rationale was similar to that of Blyden, who pioneered this position. It was rooted in both a profound respect for Islam and its salutary impact on African life and culture and a view to achieving racial unity by bridging religious divisions between Muslims and Christians.[40] His sensitivity to Islam and the plight of its adherents was heightened by his early study of Arabic in Sierra Leone under Imam Alfa (Alpha) Omaru, one of the most widely respected leaders and scholars of the West African Islamic community.[41] An intellectual, missiological, and ideological interest in Islam continued during his study and work in the United States. Although this interest was reflected in a number of his pre-1914 articles and addresses, his major studies of the missiological implications of Islam in West Africa were published in 1914 and 1925 and entitled "Christianity and Islam in Africa" and "Christianity and Islam in Africa: A Native African's View of the Situation."[42] One of the theological pillars of his expansive pedagogy and his generally positive regard for Islam and other non-Christian religions was his liberal-influenced conviction that God is "the revealer of all truth, whether scientific, religious, social, mathematical [or] legal. Therefore all truth is divine whether uttered by a Christian, Mohommedan, Hindu or Pagan."[43]

Even more radical and controversial was Faduma's call for expanded educational opportunities for African women. His progressive posture on this divisive issue was also rooted in the tenets of theological liberalism and the progressive education movement, his personal experiences with co-ed education in the American South, and his marital relationship. During his 1908 lecture tour in Sierra Leone, he supported his call for greater educational and social opportunities for females by referring to the educational and professional attainments of his Atlanta University–educated spouse, who not only assisted him in church and school at Troy but also served as secretary and treasurer of the North Carolina Women's State Organization of the American Missionary Association.[44] Faduma also shocked his traditionally chauvinistic audience with the confession that "while my wife is going on with the breakfast, I run to the house and take broom and sweep. I not only sweep the house but make the bed."[45] His deeper sensitivity to the plight of women in both modern and traditional cultures is illustrated in his observation that "Neither the civilization found in primitive life, nor that found in modern advanced societies has yet been able to give a satisfactory solution to the marriage problem. Woman is still a slave in society, and often in its worst forms."[46]

In defense of the intellectual capabilities of women before an often skeptical West African audience, Faduma employed the same arguments that he directed against white educational theorists who questioned the intellectual capabilities of the black race. While acknowledging the social limitations imposed on women, he thoroughly rejected all theories of an inherent intellectual inferiority. Any apparent inferiority, he insisted, was the "result of environment and training": "In Africa where the African female is still limited to the study of the three R's her mentality is inferior to the male who is given the greater opportunity of the higher studies. But such superiority is only temporary and local, not inherent."[47]

The impact of Faduma's challenge to the prevailing sexual chauvinism in Sierra Leone and the theological and pedagogical beliefs undergirding it was expressed in a 1923 editorial on education in the colony. The author observed that prior to Faduma's vigorous efforts,

> [t]he tendency among us was to think that women were inherently inferior to men and that God had made them to be domineered by men. Our present system of education encouraged those ideas. Dr. Faduma contended and we believe still contends that either girls should have the full benefit of the Model School or be sent under Government expense not by twos and threes but not less than half the number of boys to the separate female schools

> in the Colony. We believe Dr. Faduma stood alone at the time in his co-educational idea.

The author added: "How can we have a cultured and civilized society without cultivated women? It is farcical to speak of *character building* without providing for the female in society along the same line."[48]

Among those most influenced by Faduma's Pan-African pedagogy, especially his enlightened emphasis on the capabilities of and opportunities for women, was the prominent Sierra Leone educator and Pan-Africanist, Adelaide Casely Hayford.[49] Rina Okonkwo observed:

> One sees the imprint of Faduma's educational ideas in Hayford's emphasis on the dignity of labor and interest in vocational and industrial education. Faduma may also have inspired Hayford's cultural nationalism by advocating the instilling of racial and national pride through education . . . . [and] convinced Hayford to travel to the United States to observe the new educational methods, and to raise funds.[50]

In assessing Faduma's position on women and women's issues relative to that of his Pan-African and nationalist counterparts, Okonkwo concluded, "In his ideas about women, Faduma stood alone among the Cultural Nationalists." On this issue, as so many others, "he was far ahead of his time."[51]

Faduma's interest and efforts in educational reform extended beyond the elementary and secondary school levels. His awareness of the need for reform at the collegiate level led him to advocate a modern and less sectarian curriculum at Fourah Bay College. He especially lamented the "absence of science and educational psychology" from its curriculum.[52] Little wonder, he observed, that "men of science" in West Africa "have been African lawyers and physicians, not theologians and schoolteachers."[53] Adaptation of his proposed reforms would redress this situation and allow the college to serve as the foundation of the modern West African University envisioned earlier by Blyden and his supporters.

Moreover, despite his critique of traditional missionary education and call for government control of schools, Faduma's missiological concerns remained intact. Pedagogical, missiological, and ideological concerns converged in his call in 1918 for the establishment of a "co-operative Missionary Training Institution" that would train Africans in modern religious and mission sciences. Not surprisingly, he envisioned "the study of Comparative Religion, the Philosophy of Religion, Anthropology and Race Psychology, and Religious Psychology" as critical components of its curriculum.[54]

Although Faduma was usually cautious of active participation in the political arena, his writings and activities relating to the African Movement and pedagogical reform in West Africa led to his involvement in the realm of colonial politics. As noted by Langley, the often romanticized and idealized Pan-African and Pan–West African sentiments expressed in his extensive writings as ideologue and theologue of the African Movement struck a responsive chord of latent "race consciousness" in British West Africa. Additionally, the heavy-handed response of the Colonial Office to the African Movement and its failure to address the postwar concerns of West Africans further stimulated and focused nationalist and Pan-Africanist sentiment.[55] The National Congress of British West Africa, which Faduma assisted in founding in 1920, represented the institutionalization of those sentiments and concerns.[56]

The roots of the Congress stretch far back into the nineteenth century-most directly to Blyden's dream of a united West African community "transcending tribal, religious, and possibly territorial divisions created by the colonizing powers."[57] Thus Hollis Lynch has called Blyden "the ideological father of the idea of West African unity."[58] It would be his ideological heirs, among them Faduma and especially J. E. Casely Hayford, who revived the idea and attempted to concretize it. While the more politically attuned Hayford—a Gold Coast lawyer, nationalist, and alumnus of Wesleyan Boy's High School—would take the actual lead in birthing and nurturing the Congress, Faduma's contributions were significant.[59] At the founding meeting of what would become the Sierra Leone branch of the Congress in early 1918, it was Faduma who seconded the major resolution that called for a West African conference preliminary to the formation of a West African Congress.[60] Reflecting his characteristic agenda and concerns, he noted, "Politics apart it would be excellent if doctors, lawyers, educationalists, agriculturalists, and merchants could meet with their *confreres* from other colonies, and exchange ideas with a view to mutual improvement."[61] Unable to attend the subsequent meeting of the Sierra Leone branch of the Congress, he submitted a paper suggesting a practical scheme of organization and was elected in absentia as a member of its Organizing Committee.[62]

Faduma's organizational scheme reflected not only his characteristic interests and concerns but also a measure of hard-headed realism gained during his experiences with the African Movement.[63] His elaborate organizational proposal suggested that the Congress should be composed of a variety of men—"practical men of affairs, workers and doers"—who would staff a series of "committees" and "departments of work." The latter would include a "Department of Political and Social questions" and an "Industrial Department." Moreover, he suggested that the Conference be inclusive of the concerns and institutions of the native population and culture:

> Native political and social institutions should be given their proper place in the conference, as the future of the race is involved. How far their institutions should give way to European ones, and how far the process of making black men white should be carried require thoughtful handling by our native thinkers.[64]

His elaborate organizational scheme provided additional stimulus for the Congress movement and won public endorsement from the *Gold Coast Independent:*

> We are in entire agreement with the Professor's suggestions, and the sooner they are acted upon throughout British West Africa, the better. The economic situation brought about by the world war now . . . ought to stimulate the best thought . . . . Let committees—practical, and not talking committees—be formed as early as possible in all the various towns . . . on the Sierra Leone model, and let us get to business at once.[65]

In the final months of 1918 Faduma also joined Casely Hayford in encouraging the formation of the Gambia branch of the Congress. The most immediate concerns of the Congress movement were reflected in their assurance to its local organizers "that the West African Congress was to secure for West Africa a recognition of those social, political, and national rights which the representatives of Great Britain in the colonies have not infrequently denied us."[66]

Faduma does not appear to have been among the delegates attending the inaugural session of the West African Conference that met in Accra in March 1920 and formally constituted itself as the National Congress of British West Africa.[67] Although it failed to adopt his proposed organizational scheme, he remained a supporter of its endeavors and activities. Among these was its controversial sponsorship of a delegation that subverted the colonial hierarchy by traveling to London to place West African grievances directly before the British public and governmental officials.[68]

In support of the short-lived activism of the Congress, Faduma evoked the spirit and tenets of theological liberalism as he explicitly rejected conservative theological tenets that he perceived as supporting quietism and the colonial status quo. With words that evoked memories of the ill-fated African Movement, he advised that

> holding of the arms and waiting for outside help and initiative will not give us the right kind of development which is needed. Race salvation must be ultimately worked from within. There is a theological conception that we are saved not by works but by favor. It may be applicable to the spiritual life. [But] this Protestant teaching which is in harmony with the teaching of St. Paul cannot be applied to our social and national life. Our social and

> national salvation must be worked out in fear and trembling under divine help and guidance . . . . We must be saved . . . not by favour but by our own desert . . . . We must know our rights and responsibilities and fearlessly shoulder both. The history of nations has clearly shown that there can be no real emancipation of a people until it emancipates itself. The chains which bind the hands and feet of the slave may be destroyed by legislation: not so those that bind the mind. The worst slavery is mental and spiritual.

He concluded:

> For these reasons we congratulate the leaders of the National Congress of British West Africa, in spite of preliminary blunders, for their success in brushing aside conventionalisms . . . and approaching at first hand the direct representatives of the British Empire . . . and laying before His Majesty the King the burdens of British West Africa. They have gone asking no favours from their governors but have demanded the rights of the people already guaranteed by the British constitution.[69]

"The success of this movement," he predicted, "will depend on the ability of the people of the Colonies of West Africa to see the great principles which underlie their development, to work for their attainment and pass over matters of less moment."[70]

The National Congress of British West Africa also provided Faduma with a sympathetic forum from which to project his Pan-African pedagogy. Failure of the colonial government to institute educational reforms that were long advocated by Faduma and others brought the issue of pedagogical reform to the forefront of the Congress's concerns. The subject had been comprehensively addressed at the founding meeting of the Congress with a resolution that called for "compulsory education" at the primary and secondary levels and the establishment of a National Educational Fund "to ensure the development of a National Educational Scheme . . . on national lines supported by the people." The capstone of its proposed reform was to be the establishment of the long-advocated West African University "on such lines as would preserve in the students a sense of African nationality."[71]

Educational reform that would enhance the national and racial consciousness of African students was also a priority at the second session of the Congress held, in Freetown, Sierra Leone, in 1923. In the Presidential Address before the assembled delegates, Casely Hayford reiterated its importance.[72] It was Faduma, however, who delivered the major address on "Education in British West Africa." In an hour-long presentation before delegates from throughout British West Africa he reiterated the basic tenets of his Pan-African pedagogy. After an extended discussion of his proposals, the Congress tended to him its appreciation and agreed to print and circulate his address.[73]

The Freetown session of the National Congress of British West Africa illustrates many of the deficiencies, difficulties, and contradictions under which the Congress movement labored throughout its tenuous existence. Among these was its lack of a functional organizational structure, its core conservatism, and perhaps most important, its inability to transcend its Creole class and religious orientation and be fully representative of the varied segments of the British West African population.

The inherently conservative and "constitutional" posture of the Congress was reflected in its constitution as ratified at the Freetown session. It declared that the "policy" and "aims" of the Congress

> shall be to maintain strictly and inviolate the connection of the British West African Dependencies with the British Empire, to maintain unreservedly all and every right of free citizenship of the Empire and the fundamental principle that taxation goes with effective representation . . . [and] to aid in the development of the political institutions of British West Africa under the Union Jack, so as eventually to take her place beside the sister nations of the Empire.[74]

It was this constitutional conservatism coupled with sentiments of West African nationalism that induced the Congress to disclaim any official relationship with the Pan-African movement led by W. E. B. Du Bois and especially the more controversial Pan-African efforts of Marcus Garvey and his Universal Negro Improvement Association (UNIA). Although both movements had supporters among members of the Congress, it officially declared:

> [T]he National Congress of British West Africa has never attempted to identify or even associate itself with any other movement in Europe or America. It has as a result of calm deliberation elected to work on absolutely independent lines, and has never thought it within its province to offer any opinion about any other movements, whatever their aim and policy may be.[75]

In an insightful critique of the fundamental conservatism of the Congress and its leaders, Langley makes an observation that also applied in large measure to Faduma. They were, he charges, essentially "petty-bourgeoisie nationalists":

> [I]n spite of all the race rhetoric they were essentially cooperationists with exceedingly limited political objectives, a sub-elite whose interests generally coincided with, and were in fact protected by, the foreign rulers they were agitating against. Although they claimed to speak in the name of "the people" the interests of the nationalist petty-bourgeoisie were not identical with those of the people; in fact, it was the contradictions within the colonial system itself that they sought to harmonize in order to protect

> and expand their own interests without upsetting the system; hence their constitutionalism and their recognition of the benefits of the *Pax Britannica*. Their Pan-Africanism apart, their main objective was the acquisition of representative institutions to protect their socio-economic interests and to enhance their opportunities in colonial society.[76]

Much of the elitist and conservative perspective of the Creole-dominated Congress can be attributed to the preeminent role played by Christian laity, clergy, and ideology. Although it reflected at points the growing impact of secular currents and less conservative theological tenets within West Africa, the Congress was a direct continuation of the older and more conservative tradition of evangelical nationalism and Pan-Africanism.[77] This tradition and its liabilities was alluded to in the founding year of the Congress by an article entitled "Nationalism in Church and State with Especial Reference to West Africa."[78] The author linked the contemporary manifestations of West African nationalism as reflected in both the political and religious realms to the legacy of Bishop James Johnson.[79] After noting the vital social and political functions played by the National Churches of Britain and Germany, the author called for a similar establishment of an African National Church. This nationalistically conscious Church was envisioned as the key to the Congress's succeeding in that "great task before it"—that is, "how to weld into one homogeneous whole that heterogeneous mass of polyglottic and diversified tribes constituting the Political [and Religious] communities of West Africa."[80]

The author's call for a solution based on the formation of a National West African Church that would function as the West African counterpart of the Anglican and Lutheran state churches was clearly not the unitive prescription for a religiously and culturally diverse West African population. His proposal highlights one of the major failings of the National Congress of British West Africa—its inability to transcend its conservative Christian orientation and attract a supportive constituency from other West African religious and cultural communities. Although some Muslims and traditionalists participated, the Congress was severely limited in its claims to legitimation and support by its failure to appeal successfully to non-Christian segments of the West African community, particularly the increasingly powerful and influential Muslim segment of the population.

Throughout the Congress's existence its leaders and members were predominantly mission school–educated Christian Creoles. The profile of the active membership of the Sierra Leone branch of the Congress was consistent with that of other branches of the Congress. It reveals "a preponderance of clergymen, lawyers, doctors, and journalists, together with a fair sprinkling of traders." Its leadership was "overwhelmingly middle-class Creole, with the exception of a few 'Creolized' Muslims."[81] However, this profile of the membership of the Sierra Leone branch of the Congress contrasted sharply with the 1911 and 1923 census returns that revealed an increasing predominance of "Mohammedan" and "Pagan" believers in the colony.[82]

The religious tone and temper of the Congress and the overwhelming dominance of the Christian perspective and tradition were starkly illustrated at its 1923 session. In anticipation of its opening, religious services were scheduled to be "held in every church, chapel and mosque throughout West Africa" in hope the that it could never be said "that the African could be so obsessed with world-glory and the pomp of power and prosperity as would lead him to eliminate the God-consciousness in him as the prime motive force of every successful endeavour."[83] However, the special commemorative service held on the opening day of the Congress (January 28, 1923) took place in Wesley (Methodist) Church and was "attended by representatives of all the Christian creeds and denominations in British West Africa." This ceremony, complete with Christian hymns composed for the occasion and a sermon by Reverend J. O. C. During based on the text "I appeal unto Caesar," climaxed when the African ministers in attendance united "in a great patriotic impulse by praying for God's blessing on the Congress."[84] While exhibiting an impressive degree of religious fervor and Christian ecumenism, this commemorative service was ill conceived to gain an enthusiastic response and support from the non-Christian segment of the West African population. Such political and religious insensitivity continually undermined the Congress's assertions that it represented "substantially the intelligentsia and the advanced thought of British West Africa, and . . . the bulk of the inhabitants of the various indigenous communities and with them claims, as sons of the soil, the inherent right to make representations as to existing disabilities, and to submit recommendations for the necessary reforms."[85] It also played into the hands of British officials who were engaged in efforts to ensure that the Islamic and traditional African communities would remain isolated from the Congress and thus provide them with a challenge to the Congress's claims of authority and legitimacy.[86]

It was a belated awareness of the difficulties that the predominantly Christian tone and character of the Congress posed for its success that inspired the formation of a "committee on prayer." The committee, which included one "Mohammedan member," was charged to discuss "whether there should be prayer" in the official functions of the Congress. It recommended that divine supplications at official functions be limited to "silent prayer."[87] However, the committee's recommendation evoked a discussion that further illustrated the controversial and divisive nature of the religious issue. It was finally resolved, "that the sessions should be opened and closed with prayer and that Christian ministers and Mohammedan priests should be asked to take part."[88]

However, a minority of committee members recommended "that as the Congress consisted of persons of different religious faith it would be fitting that no particular religious sect be allowed to obtrude its form of prayer . . . [upon] the religious susceptibilities of the others; every one shall in his own way offer prayer for the Congress before coming."[89]

Despite an increased sensitivity to the "religious issue," a Christian orientation and perspective remained dominant and normative as reflected throughout the third session of the Congress, held at Bathurst in 1926.[90] Like its 1923 forerunner, the Bathurst session "began with an impressive church service," and the offering of prayer in divine petition that the Congress might become "an effective instrument for the redemption and uplift of Africa."[91] However, at Bathurst the "religious issue" and corollary tensions between Christians and Muslims were especially acute. Langley notes that "religion was exploited by some of the leaders, thereby further weakening an already ineffective movement and leaving it completely to the tender mercies of the colonial bureaucrats."[92]

In the year prior to the Bathurst session of the Congress, Kobina Sekyi, the University of London-educated philosopher, lawyer, African traditionalist, and Congress leader, issued an apology for Africa's indigenous religions that challenged both Christian and Muslim nationalists. It also suggested again how divisive the "religious issue" could be even among those fervently committed to West African unity and cooperation. In *The Parting of the Ways,* Sekyi wrote:

> [I]t could not be disputed that our ancient religion was our national religion, and functioned well as such in the development of our well-built constitution . . . . Therefore those among us who have adopted one or other of the two main foreign religions that have been established in our midst, have to consider that, if they would be true patriots useful to their generation and those who will follow, it behoves them to examine the principles of their adopted faiths as to whether they can stand the test of tests . . . . In the present period of our development as a people, under the guardianship of a foreign ruling race . . . , it is important for us to know on what side the adherents of foreign religions among us will range themselves in the event of a conflict of interests, whether on the side of the state or *Oman* to which they belong or on the side of the foreign religion which they profess . . . . The development of foreign religions among us has proceeded long enough for us to draw conclusions as to the effect of such religions on our manhood as members of our race and our efficiency as patriots.[93]

The chronic inability of the Congress to resolve "the religious issue," and insistence on ceremonies that exacerbated it, continued to undermine the realization of its professed goal of a united West African community. As a result the Congress would remain vulnerable to charges of being nonrepresentative and illegitimate throughout the remainder of its existence.[94] The National Congress of British West Africa was not alone, however, in its failure to resolve "the religious issue." This issue and dilemma plagued other Pan-African movements and efforts throughout the pre-Manchester period and beyond.[95]

Faduma's direct and active involvement with the National Congress of British West Africa apparently ended with his return to the United States in September 1923 amid controversy directly related to his efforts at pedagogical and political reform.[96] Although both a product and perpetrator of many of the influences, frailties, and foibles that weakened the Congress, Faduma's contributions to the Congress, particularly in the realm of pedagogical reform, had been significant. Langley suggested that his contributions to the Congress would have been more significant if its leaders had adopted his more realistic and representative organizational scheme:

> Faduma's draft scheme was certainly both functional and idealistic and had the N.C.B.W.A. [National Congress of British West Africa] adopted such a scheme, perhaps with a few modifications, the movement would have been far more coherent, effective, and better able to refute the criticisms of the colonial office.[97]

Perhaps a more profound contribution by Faduma to the success of the Congress would have resulted from its adoption of his expansive liberal theology–rooted ecumenism and his related conviction that a modern, unified West African political entity could be realized only by efforts aimed at transcending rather than exacerbating the religious divisions among West Africans.[98] The incorporation and application of this ecumenical sensitivity and its political and pedagogical corollaries might have contributed significantly to the success of the Congress movement.

Between 1913 and 1923 Faduma had actively participated in two movements of Pan-African significance on both sides of the Atlantic. Although neither Chief Sam's Back-to-Africa Movement nor the National Congress of British West Africa were successful, both, as predicted by Faduma, proved to be important milestones in the evolution and maturation of Pan-Africanism. Moreover, Pan-Africanism as both idea and movement was being rapidly reshaped and redefined by the varied strands and currents of secularization during the interwar period. These currents and related developments would also have a profound impact on Faduma's theological and ideological orientation.

NOTES

1. King, *Pan-Africanism and Negro Education,* pp. 128–149. See also Edward H. Berman, *African Reactions to Missionary Education*

(New York and London: Teachers College Press, 1975), pp. ix–53; Esedebe, *Pan-Africanism,* pp. 32–193; Ashby, *Universities,* pp. 147–375.

2. Faduma, letter to Booker T. Washington, 12 Dec. 1913.
3. Letter to the editor by "Sententia," *Sierra Leone Weekly News,* 20 Aug. 1887.
4. Correspondence of Director of Education, No. 777/ED 122/17, 27 July 1917.
5. "The U.M.C. and Professor Faduma," *Sierra Leone Weekly News,* 25 Sept. 1915. Orishatukeh Faduma, "Sierra Leone Revisited," *American Missionary* 78 (Dec. 1924): 352.
6. Orishatukeh Faduma, "African Negro Education," *Sierra Leone Weekly News* 3 Aug. 1918; Orishatukeh Faduma, "Some Suggestions on Native African Education," *Sierra Leone Weekly News,* 11 Dec. 1915; Orishatukeh Faduma, "The New Education," *Sierra Leone Weekly News,* 8 Apr. 1916; Orishatukeh Faduma, "Industrial Education," *Sierra Leone Weekly News,* 29 Aug. 1908; Orishatukeh Faduma, "The Study of Science in Elementary and Secondary Schools," *Sierra Leone Weekly News,* 7 Oct. 1922.
7. Faduma, "Sierra Leone Revisited," p. 352.
8. King, *Pan-Africanism and Negro Education,* pp. 128–149. Brian Holmes, ed. *Educational Policy and the Mission Schools: Case Studies from the British Empire* (London: Routledge & Kegan Paul, 1967), pp. 1–45; Ashby, *Universities,* pp. 147–375.
9. Faduma, "African Negro Education," *Sierra Leone Weekly News,* 24 Aug. 1918; Faduma, "African Negro Education," *Sierra Leone Weekly News,* 3 Aug. 1918; Faduma, "African Negro Education," *Sierra Leone Weekly News* 31 Aug. 1918.
10. Faduma, "African Negro Education," *Sierra Leone Weekly News,* 31 Aug. 1918; The *Lagos Weekly Record* correctly deduced the source of much of Faduma's pedagogical thought. In commenting on one of Faduma's many articles on education it referred to him as "another Blyden," adding that "one could discern the Blyden spirit permeating the article from start to finish." "Editorial," *Lagos Weekly Record,* 27 July/4 Aug. 1918. Quoted in Langley, *Ideologies of Liberation,* p. 47.
11. Faduma, "Sierra Leone Revisited," p. 352.
12. Orishatukeh Faduma, "African Negro Education: Some Demands of Modern Education," *Sierra Leone Weekly News,* 10 Aug. 1918.
13. Faduma, "African Negro Education," *Sierra Leone Weekly News,* 17 Aug. 1918.
14. Faduma, "Lessons and Needs of the Hour," *Sierra Leone Weekly News,* 2 Nov. 1918.
15. Faduma, "African Negro Education: Some Demands of Modern Education," *Sierra Leone Weekly News,* 10 Aug. 1918.

16. See, for example, Alexander Crummell, *The Duty of a Rising Christian State* (1850). Quoted in Langley, *Ideologies of Liberation,* pp. 148–154. Also see St. Clair Drake, *The Redemption of Africa and Black Religion* (Chicago: Third World Press, 1970); Alexander Crummell, *Africa and America: Addresses and Discourses* (Springfield, Mass.: Wiley and Co., 1891); Alexander Crummell, *The Future of Africa* (New York: Charles Scribner, 1862); Robert G. Weisbord, *Ebony Kinship Africa, Africans, and the Afro-American* (Westport, Conn., and London: Greenwood Press, 1973).
17. Faduma, "African Negro Education: Some Demands of Modern Education," *Sierra Leone Weekly News,* 10 Aug. 1918.
18. Faduma, "Lessons and Needs," *Sierra Leone Weekly News,* 12 Oct. 1918.
19. Ibid.
20. Faduma, "African Negro Education," *Sierra Leone Weekly News,* 9 Nov. 1918.
21. Correspondence of Director of Education, No. 777/ED 122/17, 27 July 1917.
22. "United Methodist Church District Meeting," *Sierra Leone Weekly News,* 2 Mar. 1918.
23. Faduma, "Sierra Leone Revisited," p. 352.
24. "Resignation of Principal Faduma," letter to the editor from J. G. Keso-Bright, *Sierra Leone Weekly News,* 2 Mar. 1918.
25. Orishatukeh Faduma, "Letter to the Director of Education," 20 Feb. 1918. Correspondence of Director of Education C.S.O 2/25 1918.
26. O. Faduma, "The Study of Science in Elementary and Secondary Schools," *Sierra Leone Weekly News,* 7 Oct. 1922.
27. Ibid.
28. Faduma, "What the Study of Science Means," *Sierra Leone Weekly News,* 21 Oct. 1922.
29. Ibid.
30. Ibid.
31. Ibid. Faduma's insistence on the importance of science was also directly related to his perception of its relationship to Africa's industrial development. "A World of Industry," he proclaimed, "is introduced in a moment through the aid of science. The more scientific a people become, the more industrious they are." Faduma, "African Negro Education," *Sierra Leone Weekly News,* 3 Aug. 1918.
32. Langley, *Ideologies of Liberation,* p. 46.
33. Faduma, "What the Study of Science Means," *Sierra Leone Weekly News,* 21 Oct. 1922.
34. This series appears to have had its origins in Faduma's earlier writings on "Negro Development" which he hoped to "have published in book form." Editorial, *Sierra Leone Weekly News, 2* Aug. 1902.

See also Faduma, "The Problem of Negro Development," *Sierra Leone Weekly News,* 9 Aug. 1902.

35. The "cry against higher education for the Negro," he contended, was "not justified by the facts in the case either in Africa or in the United States of America." It had proved necessary for the "highest intellectual" development of the race and the training of its leaders. On the other hand, he noted that "the counter agitation for industrial education has done much good in that it has called attention to a *tendency* among the college-bred to ignore the trades." Moreover, he added, "it is gratifying . . .to note that Tuskegee Industrial Institute has some of the best equipped scholars before and since the industrial agitation." Faduma, "Negro Development—Its Phases," *Sierra Leone Weekly News,* 24 Sept. 1921.
36. Faduma, "Negro Development—Its Phases," *Sierra Leone Weekly News,* 1 Oct. 1921.
37. Ibid.
38. Faduma, "Negro Development: Its Periods of Growth and Danger in Education," *Sierra Leone Weekly News,* 22 Oct. 1921.
39. Ibid.
40. Blyden, *Christianity, Islam, and the Negro Race.*
41. This study preceeded his emigration to the United States. Orishatukeh Faduma, "My Nigerian African Background," and Edith Holden, *Blyden,* pp. 831, 839.
42. See Faduma, "Religious Beliefs of the Yoruba of West Africa," in Bowen, *Africa,* 31–36; Faduma, "Materials for the Study of World Religions," Orishatukeh Faduma, "Christianity and Islam in Africa," *African Mail,* May 22, 1914; Orishatukeh Faduma, "Christianity and Islam in Africa: A Native African's View of the Situation," *Missionary Review of the World* 48 (Nov. 1925): 865–868. See also Orishatukeh Faduma, "Khalil's Mohammedan Code from the French of N. Seignette," *Sierra Leone Weekly News,* 24, Dec. 1921; 14 Jan. 1922; 21 Jan. 1922.
43. Faduma, "Lessons and Needs," *Sierra Leone Weekly News,* 12 Oct. 1918.
44. *American Missionary* 61 (Jan. 1907): 32.
45. Faduma, "Industrial Education," *Sierra Leone Weekly News,* 29 Aug. 1908.
46. Orishatukeh Faduma, "Obligations of the Weak to the Strong," *Sierra Leone Weekly News,* 6 Dec. 1916. Quoted in Langley, *Ideologies,* pp. 193–195.
47. Orishatukeh Faduma, "How to Cultivate a Love for Reading," *Sierra Leone Weekly News,* 12 Aug. 1922; 19 Aug. 1922.
48. "Report of the Education Department VII," *Sierra Leone Weekly News,* July 28, 1923.

49. See Rina Okonkwo, "Adelaide Casely Hayford: Cultural Nationalist and Feminist," *Phylon* 42 (Jan. 1981): 41, and Adelaide M. Cromwell, *An African Victorian Feminist: The Life and Times of Adelaide Smith Casely Hayford, 1868–1960* (London: Frank Cass & Co. Ltd., 1986).
50. Okonkwo, "Adelaide Casely Hayford," p. 43. Her pedagogical concerns and efforts were similarly rooted in an awareness "that the education meted out to us had, either consciously or unconsciously, taught us to despise ourselves, and that our immediate need was an education which would instill into us a love of country, a pride of race, an enthusiasm for the black man's capabilities and a genuine admiration for Africa's wonderful art work." Quoted from Adelaide Hayford, "A Girl's School in West Africa," *Southern Workman* 55 (Oct. 1926): 450. On Faduma's support for Mrs. Hayford, see "The Proposed Girl's Vocational and Teacher's Training School," *Sierra Leone Weekly News,* 23 June 1923.
51. Okonkwo, "Man of Two Worlds," p. 33.
52. Faduma, "Sierra Leone Revisited," p. 352.
53. Ibid.
54. Orishatukeh Faduma, "Drawbacks and Successes of Missionary Work in Africa," *Sierra Leone Weekly News,* 20 Apr. 1918. On the increasing importance of these disciplines within progressive and liberal Protestant mission circles, see Olav G. Myklebust, *The Study of Missions in Theological Education: An Historical Inquiry into the Place of World Evangelization in Western Protestant Ministerial Training with Particular Reference to Alexander Duff's Chair of Evangelistic Theology,* vols. 1 and 2 (Oslo: Egede Institute, 1955).
55. Langley, "Chief Sam's African Movement," pp. 164–176. Langley, *Pan-Africanism and Nationalism,* pp. 107–285. An anticolonial tone was continued in his later writings. In 1918 he predicted, "Race consciousness is gradually growing and with it will come race pride and independence in the right way." He also pointed out that "the government of a people has a meaning but such a thing as a government of one people by another does not and cannot exist. Either a people govern itself or that people has not a real government, but only a system of provincial administrations." Faduma, "Lessons and Needs of the Hour," *Sierra Leone Weekly News,* 12 Oct. 1918. Quoted in Rina Okonkwo, "The Emergence of Nationalism in British West Africa, 1912–1940," Ph.D. diss. (City University of New York, 1979), p. 118.
56. Langley, *Pan-Africanism and Nationalism,* pp. 107–194; Martin Kilson, "The National Congress of British West Africa, 1918–1935;" and Robert I. Rotberg and Ali A. Mazrui, eds., *Protest and Power in Black Africa* (New York: Oxford University Press, 1970), pp. 571–588.

57. Langley, *Pan-Africanism and Nationalism,* pp. 37–38, 110–111.
58. Lynch, *Blyden,* p. 250, and especially pp. 170–247.
59. Langley, *Pan-Africanism and Nationalism,* pp. 38–39, 119–120, 207–212. See the summation of Hayford's mature ideas and similarities with Faduma's in J. E. Casely Hayford, *Ethiopia Unbound: Studies in Race Emancipation* (London: Phillips, 1911). See also Hayford's call for West African unity in J. E. Casely Hayford, *United West Africa* (London: Phillips, 1919).
60. *Sierra Leone Weekly News,* 27 Apr. 1918.
61. Ibid. Langley notes that Faduma's sentiments seemed to have "unwittingly created the impression that he held that politics would be beyond the scope of the conference. This, however, he corrected." Langley, *Pan-Africanism and Nationalism,* p. 156.
62. "Work and Scope of the Conference of British West Africa," *Sierra Leone Weekly News,* 11 May 1918; Langley, *Pan-Africanism and Nationalism,* p. 156.
63. Langley, *Pan-Africanism and Nationalism,* p. 156.
64. Faduma also suggested that concerned whites be invited to participate in the conference: "I should be glad if invitation is extended to leading philanthropists, students of political and social science, ethnologists, businessmen and missionaries of the white race who are known to be interested in the development of West Africa." He argued that the conference "should invite criticism if offered constructively by our white friends. It should not be a conference of flatterers. We should endeavour to find the happy mean between what we think of ourselves and what others think of us." "Work and Scope of the Conference of British West Africa," *Sierra Leone Weekly News,* 11 May 1918.
65. *Gold Coast Independent,* 22 June 1918. Quoted in Langley, *Pan-Africanism and Nationalism,* p. 158.
66. "Welcome Address to the Overseas Delegates by I. J. Roberts, Esquire, President Gambia section, December 1925." Quoted in Langley, *Pan-Africanism and Nationalism,* pp. 135–136.
67. Langley, *Pan-Africanism and Nationalism,* pp. 128–132.
68. Ibid., pp. 130–131, 243–285; Geiss, *Pan-African Movement,* pp. 287–289.
69. Faduma, "Negro Development: Its Meaning and Aims," *Sierra Leone Weekly News,* 17 Sept. 1921.
70. Ibid.
71. *National Congress of British West Africa: Resolutions of the Conference of Africans of British West Africa, Held at Accra, Gold Coast, from 11th to 29th March, 1920,* pp. 2–7. Quoted in Langley, *Pan-Africanism and Nationalism,* pp. 128–129. See also Geiss, *Pan-African Movement,* pp. 286–287.

72. "The National Congress of British West Africa (Presidential Address)," *Sierra Leone Weekly News,* 3 Mar. 1923.
73. Faduma's proposals were essentially those listed by Hayford. They included a call for: (1) The holding of a conference of educationalists for further discussion and implementation of needed reforms; (2) compulsory education for all of West Africa's youths; (3) a more systemized plan for the training of teachers; (4) the establishment of agricultural and industrial schools; and (5) the funding of a West African university. "The Second Session of the National Congress of British West Africa," *Sierra Leone Weekly News,* 8 Mar. 1923.
74. *The Constitution of the National Congress of British West Africa: Passed by the Second Session of the National Congress, Held at Freetown, Sierra Leone, January–February, 1923,* in Langley, *Ideologies,* pp. 754–755.
75. "The Second Session of the National Congress of British West Africa, held in Freetown, Sierra Leone," *Sierra Leone Weekly News,* 10 Feb. 1923. It appears that this disclaimer, made at least partially with British governmental officials in mind, was provoked when the Reverend Canon Lewis made reference to the "fine movement of Marcus Garvey" during a Congress-related function held in St. George's Cathedral. Lewis's comments also provoked the following comments from the *Sierra Leone Weekly News:* "Those of our readers who have been reading our articles on the Congress Movement know that the policy of the Congress is quite different and in no way connected with Marcus Garvey." "The National Congress of British West Africa." *Sierra Leone Weekly News,* 10 Feb. 1923. No direct links have been discovered between Faduma and the Pan-African movements of Garvey or Du Bois. There are, however, a number of indirect links.

    The 1921 Session of the Du Bois–led Pan-African Congress, which met in London, Brussels, and Paris, was reported on in the *Sierra Leone Weekly News,* as was a letter to the editor from Robert Broadhurst, "Assistant Secretary for England to the Second Pan-African Congress." His letter called for cooperation between the Pan-African Congress and the National Congress of British West Africa. "The Second Pan-African Congress," *Sierra Leone Weekly News,* 22 Oct.1921; Robert Broadhurst, "The Pan-African Congress," *Sierra Leone Weekly News,* 22 Oct. 1921; Robert Broadhurst, "The Pan-African Congress," *Sierra Leone Weekly News,* 8 Oct. 1921. For a full discussion of West African attitudes toward diaspora African-led Pan-African efforts, see Langley, *Pan-Africanism and Nationalism,* pp. 17–103.
76. Langley, *Pan-Africanism and Nationalism,* pp. 133. Also Martin Kilson, "Nationalism and Social Classes in British West Africa,"

Journal of Politics 20 (May 1958): 368–87; Cohen, *Politics of Elite Culture,* pp. 15–16, and Akintola J. G. Wyse, *H. C. Bankole-Bright and Politics In Colonial Sierra Leone, 1919–1958* (Cambridge, New York: Cambridge University Press, 1990).

77. The impact of these currents is illustrated most prominently in the leadership roles of T. Hutton-Mills, J. E. Casely Hayford, Kobina Sekyi, and the active participation of a handful of less traditional ministers such as Faduma, his old schoolmate William B. Euba, and Patriarch James G. Campbell. On the radical religious and political posture of Sekyi (William Essuman Gwira Sekyi), the Gold Coast philosopher, nationalist, and lawyer, see Langley, *Pan-Africanism and Nationalism,* pp. 99–103. On Campbell, who was decisively influenced by Faduma, see Shepperson, "External Factors," p. 209.
78. "Nationalism in Church and State with Especial Reference to West Africa," *Lagos Weekly Record,* 20 Nov. 1920. Quoted in Thompson, *Africa and Unity,* pp. 323–326.
79. Ibid., pp. 325–326.
80. Ibid., p.324.
81. Langley, *Pan-Africanism and Nationalism,* p. 159. Langley also noted that "in most areas along the West Coast, the Western-educated and propertied Creoles generally assumed leadership of protest and political movements in the late nineteenth and early twentieth centuries." Langley, *Pan-Africanism and Nationalism,* 140.
82. The census returns are reported as follows:

Organization	1911	1923
Church of England	18,865	20,173
Wesleyan Methodist	11,826	11,898
United Methodist	3,689	3,243
Roman Catholic	1,472	1,980
Lady Huntingdon's Connection	1,805	1,179
United Brethren in Christ	790	800
African Methodist Episcopal	480	541
Mohammedam	11,451	16,611
Pagan	24,472	27,800

T. N. Goddard, *The Handbook of Sierra Leone* (London: Grant Richards, 1925; New York: Negro Universities Press, 1969), p. 69.

83. "The Approaching Session of the National Congress of British West Africa," *Sierra Leone Weekly News,* 13 Jan. 1923.
84. Geiss notes that During's sermon was the "keynote of these religious services" and "underlined the political flavour of the meeting." Geiss, *Pan-African Movement,* p. 290, and "Special Service in Wesley Church, National Congress of British West Africa," *Sierra Leone Weekly News,* 27 Jan. 1923.

85. Constitution of the National Congress of British West Africa, 1923. Printed in Langley, *Ideologies of Liberation,* p. 755.
86. Langley, *Pan-Africanism and Nationalism,* pp. 141–142, 170; Thompson, *Africa and Unity,* pp. 46–47.
87. "Second Session of the National Congress of British West Africa, Wilberforce Hall, Freetown," *Sierra Leone Weekly News,* 10 Feb. 1923.
88. Ibid.
89. Ibid.
90. The second session of the Congress was concluded by a Christian service which included a sermon preached on the text, "I am a citizen of no mean city." Geiss, *Pan-African Movement,* p. 90. Faduma was among the ministers who delivered farewell addresses to the delegates at the conclusion of the twenty-one day deliberation of the Congress. *Sierra Leone Weekly News,* 24 Feb. 1923.
91. Langley, *Pan-Africanism and Nationalism,* pp. 148–149.
92. Ibid., p. 152.
93. From Kobina Sekyi, *The Parting of the Ways,* (Cape Coast, 1925), pp. 45–48. Quoted in Langley, *Ideologies,* pp. 251–222.
94. The active existence of the Congress ended with the death of Hayford in 1930. Esedebe, *Pan-Africanism,* p. 176.
95. For example, the increasing religious pluralism of the African and diaspora African communities also presented a dilemma for the Garvey wing of the Pan-African movement. At the fourth international convention of the UNIA in 1924, the issue was explicitly addressed: "When this subject came up, and was thoroughly aired by both Clergy and Laity, the pious and the worldlian, it was decided that, as there are Moslems and other Non-Christians who are Garveyites, it was not wise to declare Christianity the state Religion of the Organization; but by establishing the Temple of God in each heart, and letting our every word and action be motivated from that Source, we could reach a state of inner Serenity so as to enable us to establish on earth the Fatherhood of God and the Brotherhood of Man—a belief which is the basis of recognized religions." Amy Jacques-Garvey, *Garvey and Garveyism* (Kingston: United Printers, 1963), pp. 133–134.
96. Faduma, "Sierra Leone Revisited." On the pedagogical controversy that centered on a critique of government educational policies and priorities, see "Report of the Education Department," *Sierra Leone Weekly News,* 2, 9, 30, June 1923. See also "Professor Faduma's Educational Work," *Sierra Leone Weekly News,* 24 Aug. 1918.
97. Langley, *Pan-Africanism and Nationalism,* p. 157.
98. As reflected in his writings on pedagogical reform, Faduma had transcended the traditional evangelical Pan-African and Pan-West

African ideal that premised its vision of a Pan-African political entity on the establishment of a "Christian state." He insisted that any attempts to establish "a sectarian state" was "out of place" among the democratic institutions required in the modern era—especially in Africa with its varied religious creeds. Sectarianism could have no place in the modern African state he envisioned. It would "draw no line between Jew, Christian, Muslim, Heathen, etc., but . . . give equal opportunity to all," respecting "the religious conscious" of Mohammedan, Heathen, Jew, and Hindu equally as that of a Christian." See Faduma, "African Negro Education: Some Demands of Modern Education," *Sierra Leone Weekly News,* 10 Aug. 1918; Faduma, "Lessons and Needs," *Sierra Leone Weekly News,* 12 Oct. 1918; Faduma, "African Negro Education," *Sierra Leone Weekly News,* 9 Nov. 1918.

7

"The Faith That Is in Me"

While there are consistent themes and concerns cogently presented in Faduma's numerous writings, he did not develop a systematic presentation of his mature theological convictions. Like most of his fellow African and African-American clergy, he addressed his existential situation as a preacher and pastor rather than as a professional theologian. He was, in short, a "practical theologian" who was more concerned with praxis than with sustained reflection upon praxis. Nevertheless Faduma's prolific writings illuminate his continuous efforts to apply his theological beliefs on behalf of the beleaguered African and African-American communities.[1]

The deadly influenza epidemic that ravaged Sierra Leone in 1918 provided the context for Faduma's theological reflections on the problem of evil and suffering.[2] In the midst of this tragedy, he drew on his liberal soteriology to offer some measure of solace to members of the Sierra Leone Christian community who found their traditional theological beliefs of little comfort. In response to the additional misery fostered by a conservative theodicy, he explicitly rejected traditional Protestant "superstitions" that taught that "sin is the cause of pain and suffering" and that the epidemic was therefore a divine winnowing of Sierra Leone's "saints" and "sinners." It was not true, insisted Faduma, "that those who escaped the dire effects of the epidemic in our land are the only saints, while those who do not are the sinners."[3] Rather, he suggested, "the problem of suffering" was "a mysterious problem" but one that was "a necessary part of man's evolution."[4]

Faduma characteristically emphasized that the lessons to be learned from the epidemic were not about humanity's sinfulness, nor God's wrathful judgment and complicity in their suffering, but rather about social responsibility and the "workings of physical laws" related to sanitary conditions. He warned that unless the lessons of sanitation were heeded, religious ritual would be of no avail: "[U]nless we repent and rectify these physical wrongs, we shall perish in spite of prayers and songs when the time of visitation comes. The good and the bad will perish."[5]

Faduma appears to have come closest to presenting a comprehensive and systematic summary of his liberal theological convictions in a series of at least ten articles published in the *Sierra Leone Weekly News* in 1923 under the title "The Faith That Is in Me."[6] He had made his initial public confession of faith and commitment to the New Theology in 1890.[7]

Now more than thirty years later, he voiced his mature theological convictions to a Sierra Leone community that had recently suffered the social, mental, and spiritual dislocations of World War I, and the misery occasioned by the influenza epidemic.

The series had its immediate impetus in the arrival of W. R. Brown on a lecture tour sponsored by the International Bible Students Association.[8] Originally from Jamaica, Brown was described as "a Bible expositor of power and ability, possessing a commanding grasp of the Scriptures." In a series of "Illustrated Bible Lectures" in Wilberforce Memorial Hall, he expounded on the teachings of the Association's founder, Charles Taze Russell. However, his lectures drew heated protests from the more traditional segments of Sierra Leone's Christian community who charged that "Russellism or Millennial Dawnism" was "a vast modern delusion" which "at its core militates against and undermines all the cardinal doctrines of the Bible."[9] Response and countercharges gave rise to an intense and prolonged theological controversy, which was chronicled in the pages of the *Sierra Leone Weekly News*.[10] The conflict eventually drew Faduma's efforts to mediate between advocates and critics of Russellism. Characteristically, he presented his own theological convictions ("The Faith That Is in Me") as both corrective and alternative.[11]

In this public and often poignant reflection of his theological development, Faduma presented a cogent analysis of the theological convictions and beliefs that shaped his life and work.[12] His assertions reflect characteristic traits of evangelical liberalism such as: (1) belief in the progressive revelation of God; (2) the necessity of continued intellectual, ethical and theological development; (3) the historical development of Christianity; (4) Scripture perceived as a means "not for our imitation but for correction and instruction in right living"; (5) belief in the immanence of God; (6) the inadequacy of human language concerning God; and (7) a fervent distaste for "errant denominationalism" and creedalism.[13] Illustrative of the christology of liberal evangelicals, Faduma affirmed that Jesus was "The perfect Man" and role model for humanity:

> I believe Jesus is the ideal man, just what every man should be and can be if Jesus is imitated. As Christ is the image of God, so is he the model and unique man for humanity. I believe he is the only sinless man held up for imitation and true copy. It is only by continuous striving and copying after Him that the Christian has his highest development.[14]

On the issue of evolution and the conflict between supporters of the evolutionary accounts of creation and supporters of more literalistic biblical accounts, Faduma again provided the characteristic liberal resolution. An awareness of "the inadequacy of human language concerning God" enabled him to reconcile the biblical account of creation with his understanding of the evolutionary process and thus to present evolution to the Sierra Leone community as the Divine method of creation.[15]

"The Faith That Is in Me" series also sounded a new note of realism in Faduma's theology. It suggests that by 1923 Faduma had tempered his earlier optimism and idealism about the efficacy of liberal theology. If so, he was among a number of theological liberals who, amid the carnage of World War I and theological liberalism's manifest failure to usher in the "kingdom of God," were forced to reexamine and temper their earlier idealism and optimism. Postwar liberals tended to embrace revised liberal theological schemas that reasserted the reality of both individual and collective sin—theological themes heretofore associated with the theological orthodoxy from which they had rebelled. The classic effort in this direction was made by Walter Rauschenbusch in *A Theology for the Social Gospel.*[16] Faduma's similar tempering of his earlier optimism and idealism was undoubtedly rooted in the additional trauma of firsthand experience with racism in the United States, the collapse of the Back to Africa Movement, and the postwar resurgence of British imperialism in West Africa. This new note of realism was reflected in his use and emphasis of traditional theological terms and concepts that had been given only minor and incidental attention in his earlier works. Hence a review of topic headings in this series reveals such concerns and preoccupations as "Law and Sin," "Divine Grace and Sin," "The Forgiveness of Sins," and "The Origin of Sin."[17]

This postwar preoccupation with the reality of "sin" was further illustrated by his perception of the war as a powerful and persuasive example of humanity's sinfulness. Yet, unlike conservatives, he viewed it less as a manifestation of original sin than as "another exemplification of the Nemesis that awaits nations that neglect moral principles and high idealism."[18] In giving added credence to the reality of "sin," Faduma still cast it within the soteriological framework of evangelical liberalism.[19] The Faduma of the postwar period was still personally committed to theological liberalism, albeit a liberalism that had been tempered and chastised by a growing awareness of its inability to fathom the problems of human evil, suffering, and tragedy. This renovated liberalism remained the core of his evangelical Pan-Africanism, providing the intellectual foundation for much of his subsequent pedagogical and missiological efforts. Thus, in the concluding section of this series, Faduma could still affirm his faith in "the New Theology preached by John over a thousand years ago which we are just grasping" and the continued—albeit slow—realization of John's vision of God "coming down . . . among men on Earth, transforming the earth to a New Earth."[20]

Not surprisingly, Faduma's presentation of his mature theological convictions served to heighten rather than reduce theological controversy in

Sierra Leone. His writings immediately provoked criticism from the defenders of orthodoxy. Hence a resident of the colony who styled himself "John the Presbyter," advised Faduma to be more careful in expressing his theological convictions to the residents of Freetown because he "launches into deep water directly [when] he begins to talk to our brethren and sisters in Freetown concerning God-consciousness."[21] Suggestive of the real source of concern was his charge that Faduma was unclear as to the precise relationship between "knowledge of God" and "faith in God" and thus presented "a conception of God" that was both "perplexing and unsatisfactory."[22] "John the Presbyter" 's critique of Faduma's theological convictions also provided valuable insight into the religious, theological, and social ethos of West Africa's oldest outpost of "Christianity and civilization." In an alarmist portrayal of creeping liberalism and secularism, "John the Presbyter" charged that an increasingly pervasive rationalism manifested in the preference of "an intellectual knowledge of God" over a "knowledge of Him which is spiritual" had undermined the social, industrial, and economic welfare of the colony:

> What is the secret of all our trouble in Sierra Leone today—social, industrial, economic and what not? Why are there no intimate friendships . . . ? Why do the young lack reverence for God and man and proceed to do the most ugly things fearlessly? Why is there no strong public opinion, indeed no public opinion *at all* to vigorously and insistently condemn wrong doings of the most notorious character? Why is marriage . . . such a dismal failure, and women so exceptionally different from the women of thirty years ago? Why, in a word, has Sierra Leone tumbled into a morass from which she is not even seeking to come out, and God and His is a thing of abhorrence to Creoles to their own utter undoing as is evident in the prevalent hunger, increasing poverty, and the blocking up of all our prosperities?
>
> The answer arising out of Professor Faduma's statement is here:—We are content to have an intellectual knowledge of God which, except in the case of a few, is slender, while *we make it our business to reject that knowledge of Him which is spiritual and which is the source of strength of character, purity of life and conduct, and of all the material prosperities* . . . .[23]

Faduma's reply to the critique of "John the Presbyter" was published in the next issue of the *Weekly News* and was cast firmly in the framework of theological liberalism. In contrast to the obvious lack of tolerance shown by "John the Presbyter," Faduma noted that it "was not to be expected" that what he believed "must be what everybody believes, even if everybody is a Christian." Furthermore, he warned residents of the colony of the dangers of becoming theological sycophants in a misguided defense of orthodoxy: "Religious faith is a matter of personal experience and not what Arius, Sabellius, Athanasius or any divine thinks, important and often enlightening as their experiences may be."[24] Elsewhere Faduma suggested that the social and economic malaise described and deplored by conservative churchmen such as "John the Presbyter" was in fact caused in large part by their own misguided efforts to keep the church a conservative rather than a progressive institution.[25]

Faduma also reminded his critics that a divisive and archaic system of traditional missionary education contributed significantly to the current state of religion and irreligion in Sierra Leone:

> [T]he educational system of the past emphasized denominationalism and sectarianism. It did not encourage the spirit of freedom. A man was a Methodist or a churchman not because he willed to be so, but because he was compelled by his environments to be so. He did not think out his creed, it was ready made for him in Europe. It fitted some but unfitted many. The most absurd dogma was believed because it came from the pulpit and because all of the education of the people was in the hands of the pulpit. Such a system encouraged religious superstition and a very narrow view of religion.[26]

Faduma's continuous quest and support for religious truth led to his involvement in and with numerous religious activities and organizations in Sierra Leone. His broad and tolerant ecumenism was illuminated in his belief that "The kingdom of God is larger both in what it connotes and denotes than any one church denomination."[27] This ecumenism allowed him to be welcomed and at home in most of Sierra Leone's churches.[28] Despite his earlier critique of the religiosity and ministry of the African-American Church, one of the pulpits that he regularly occupied was that of the African Methodist Episcopal Church. Moreover, in 1916 he presented the major address at the celebration of the denomination's centennial. His address emphasized not only the history of the denomination but also its Pan-African significance. Thus he contended that the A.M.E. Church served foremost as "a reminder as to what the black man may do for himself." In commenting on his message of racial and ecclesiastical independence the *African Mail* noted:

> Principal Faduma makes it clear to us in his powerful address that the Black race is a gifted race which may fulfill a high destiny if only it is conscious of that destiny and believes that *Possunt quia posse videntur* . . . . A Negro church is a desideratum in this land. For the present we are not standing on legs of our own. Let us work towards originality and a certain sober independence.[29]

A similar emphasis was reflected in Faduma's hagiographic tribute to the Sierra Leonean butcher and lay Christian, Father T. B. Cole. Although Cole had been "a man without any pretensions to the training of schools, a plain ordinary butcher," Faduma noted that his Christianity and theology had been both "vital and practical." Moreover, Cole was an example of the ideal African Christian who had managed to root an activist and progressive faith in an indigenous African consciousness. Especially endearing to Faduma were Cole's efforts to adapt Methodist hymns and rituals to African culture and temperament. Such efforts on behalf of both Christianity and the African race earned Father Cole a place on Faduma's register of West African "saints": "Among African saints among whom may be named 'Holy Johnson,' afterwards called Bishop James Johnson of the Anglican Church, this layman may rightly be classed. He is a glory to the African Church, a pride to African Methodism which nursed him and an example to future generations."[30]

During this period, Faduma also presented a much more "sympathetic" and balanced, though still liberalism rooted, appraisal of the religion and religious development of African-Americans. The "Negro," he noted, was still in dire need of proper "religious development," especially in light of the demands of the modern world:

> His leaders in the past have come from the church—His mode of thought, his viewpoint on many matters are churchly. [But] his religion has become formal and superficial. Religion, to meet present day needs, must not only be emotional but should be rational, it must pass through the crucible of practice and [be] reduced to life in action. It must not be substituted for beautiful songs and anthems, formal prayers and religious catch- phrases. It must not spend its energy in competition for denominational ascendancy, but should reach the soul of man in his strivings to find the infinite and be in mystic union with the infinite.

The shaping influence of environment upon religious development was also noted:

> The Negro's conception of religion in the United States of America is different from that of his brother in Africa. This is due doubtless to their different experiences of life under different environments. . . .In the canebrakes of Louisiana, in the cotton fields of Georgia and the Carolinas, down by the Sewanee and Mississippi Rivers, in the stillness of the night in his desire to "steal away to Jesus," there the Old Negro in captivity worked and wept when he remembered Africa the land of his birth, the land of his ancestors. His whole religious life has been coloured by his environments.[31]

Despite the controversial nature of the theological, missiological, and pedagogical reforms that Faduma advocated, his numerous contributions to the religious, educational, and political well-being of Sierra Leone and West Africa were not unappreciated. In 1923 the *Sierra Leone Weekly News* published "an appraisement of Professor Faduma" that summarized his contributions in both West Africa and the United States:

> From his youth up to the present he has been a writer on many interesting subjects. He has not been known to be superficial in thinking and writing. . . . [T]he scholars who have passed through his hands are masters in the art of writing and speaking the English language . . . . The education of the Negro and the psychology of education he has made a speciality. He speaks and writes clearly on the kind of education West Africa needs. A knowledge of the roots of economic and edible plants is as important to him as Greek and Latin roots, the handling of tools as needful as that of the pen, and to disconnect them is an educational blunder calculated to make the West African always subservient and dependent. In his remarkable address before the last Congress of British West Africa he anticipated in many respects the findings of the American Education Commission. Had he not been a black man! That he is appreciated by members of his race in both continents cannot be denied. A man of simple tastes and quiet manners, yet of high thinking, he goes amongst his people as one of them, absorbing and giving in return all that is best. In both continents he has inspired Negro boys and girls to noble action.

In light of Faduma's contributions, the editorial called for the compilation of his writings and a biography of his life and work:

> We should suggest (a) that lovers of the race organize efforts to compile in book form some of his literary output so as to preserve for present and future generations thoughts that are inspiring and uplifting (b) that a short biography of his life written by himself be preserved. We are sure his struggles and achievements will be incentives to African youths.[32]

Ironically, this tribute coincided with Faduma's plans to return to the United States to visit his family and "observe recent educational method."[33] On September 19, 1923, following a round of farewell services "in recognition of his valuable service to the Colony in Educational, Literary and Religious undertakings," he sailed for the United States via England.[34]

By December 1924, Faduma was reassociated with the American Missionary Association and teaching Latin and English literature at Lincoln Academy in Kings Mountain, North Carolina. Founded in 1892, the Academy was operated by the American Missionary Association as a literary and industrial school for blacks.[35] Once again an American Missionary Association–sponsored school in the rural South served as Faduma's mission station as he again preached and practiced his liberal-rooted Pan-African missiology and pedagogy on the American side of the Atlantic.[36] Moreover, the pages of the Association's official journal would again be used to advance and publicize his message of liberal Christianity, racial solidarity, and Africa's redemption.

In December 1924, Faduma's selective account of his sojourn in Sierra Leone was published in the *American Missionary* under the title,

"Sierra Leone Revisited."[37] Although noting that in 1914 he "left for West Africa, mainly for the purpose of helping to organize educational work in the Gold Coast," Faduma made no mention of the Back-to-Africa Movement or his involvement with the National Congress of British West Africa. However, he did encourage "lovers of the race and humanity" to assist African students to come to the United States, where they might "qualify themselves in the physical sciences, educational psychology and industrial training" to aid in Africa's redemption.[38]

The latter did not represent a new dimension of Faduma's pedagogical Pan-Africanism. Prior to his involvement with the African Movement, he encouraged African students such as J. S. Ocorde Terry of Sierra Leone to travel to the United States for study. Tragically, Terry died suddenly while studying at Shaw University in Raleigh, North Carolina. Faduma had the painful task of traveling to Shaw and delivering Terry's memorial address, which was subsequently published in the *Sierra Leone Weekly News* under the title "Vale: Longum Vale."[39]

Encouragement of and concern for African students studying in the United States would be an important dimension of Faduma's life and work. It was by way of his direct contact with such students that he continued to make perhaps his most direct contribution to the struggle for Africa's redemption and revitalization. As the mainstream of the Pan-African movement manifested a growing secularization and increased frustration with both Christianity and the Christian mission enterprise, he continued to teach and preach the gospel of progressive evangelical Pan-Africanism to a younger generation of Africans studying in the United States.

During the postwar period the growing number of Africans studying in the United States led to the formation of a number of African student organizations. Many of these were related to the Christian student movements then popular on American campuses and though generally moderate and Christian in their orientation, these early African student organizations effectively served as incubators for an increasingly radical Pan-African leadership.[40] One of the earliest and most important of these organizations, the African Student Union of America, was founded at Tuskegee Institute by an East African instructor in history, Simbini M. Nkomo.[41] Nkomo envisioned the Union as evangelical as well as Pan-African in its orientation and goals.[42] Both concerns were merged in the first conference of the Union, held in Chicago in 1919.[43] However, by the Fourth Annual Conference, held at Tuskegee in 1924, a deeper radicalism was discernible in an agenda that included for discussion such topics as: "Misrepresentations concerning Africa; Abolishing Restrictions on the Coming to America, for study of African Students; Native Missionaries; Cooperation between Europeans and Africans; the Returning Students and the Mission Boards; How American Negro Students may cooperate with African Students; [and] Liberia and Its Problems."[44]

The following year, Faduma addressed a joint meeting of the African Student Union and the Student Bible Institute held at Hampton Institute. His speech, entitled "Africa's Claims and Needs," was vintage evangelical Pan-Africanism.[45] To this younger generation of African students, he presented a message of "hope and responsibility":

> If Africa is to be regenerated it must come largely through her sons and daughters who are being trained and fitted for service and responsibility. The leadership that is needed and will count is a trained one. In spite of difficulties and hardships to be encountered in a foreign land in the form of climate and lack of funds the opportunity to succeed is greater than the difficulties. We can if we will.[46]

There was also his traditional warning and words of caution to the unwary African student who might be "led to imitate and adopt foreign ideas and customs, and manners without adapting them to fit his environment." Such a course, he advised, would "invariably leave him a nondescript—neither African nor European, nor an American," but rather "worse than he was before—a jackdaw in peacock's feathers." Selective adaptation from the West, not mimicry, was to be the key to Africa's redemption and modernization. "Too often," he noted, "the life of the Westerner is held up in all matters as a standard and a *sine qua non* of civilization." Yet Africans, he reminded, had also developed "a civilization" which though "hoary with age" had admirably served the needs of African people. Moreover, in "respect to obedience to authority, . . . sex morality, honesty, truthfulness, and other virtues, the African . . . [had] little to learn from the more civilized Westerner."[47]

Faduma insisted that it was now time for Africa to take her place within the modern world, and that it was "the new light of modern progress and Christian Civilization in contact with Africa's stagnant, primitive civilization which would reform and render her serviceable to humanity." Characteristically, he concluded his address with a prayer that "the hearts of the students in all the schools will be so filled with the Christian missionary spirit that they will give the very best in service to Africa for the sake of Africa and for the sake of Christ."[48]

Although increasingly out of sync with the mainstream of the Pan-African movement, Faduma's continued call for Africa's redemption via a liberal and progressive missionary and pedagogical effort did not necessarily fall upon deaf ears. One of the Africans studying in the United States upon whom his message had a direct and profound impact was Ernest Kalibala. Born in Uganda, Kalibala received his early education from agents of the Church Missionary Society.[49] While serving as a high school teacher, he was exposed to the thought and writings of Marcus Garvey, which prompted him to travel to the United States to continue his education. Resistance by the Colonial Government, however, forced him to take a circuitous route that included a number of months of theological study in England.[50] With the aid of the Phelps-Stokes Agency and Thomas Jesse Jones, he finally gained admission to the United States and entered Tuskegee Institute in the spring of 1925.[51]

After only a year of study at prestigious and "safe" Tuskegee, Kalibala transferred to Lincoln Academy, thereby incurring the displeasure of Jones and the Phelps-Stokes Agency.[52] No doubt a major factor in his finding this tiny AMA school, with few of the resources or the prestige of Tuskegee Institute, the "long desired school," was Faduma's presence on the faculty.[53] After successfully completing two years of high school study at Lincoln Academy, Kalibala moved to New York and enrolled in New York University, where he studied anthropology and obtained a Bachelor of Science degree in 1933.[54] By then regarded "as the most capable African in America," he further enhanced his reputation with the earning of a master's degree in education from Teacher's College.[55]

Kalibala's master's thesis, entitled "Education for Villages in Uganda, East Africa," coincided at numerous points with the progressive and race-conscious pedagogical theory advanced by Faduma. Kenneth King notes, "Its eighty-five pages" were "a valuable and for East Africa, very early African criticism of educational theories which were then the stock-in-trade of European experts."[56] Kalibala, as did Faduma, rejected such theories and charged that they were designed to keep the African a man-child, a perpetual hewer of wood and drawer of water for the Anglo-Saxon.

Equally or perhaps more reflective of Faduma's influence were Kalibala's mission activities and writings. Upon completing his studies at Teacher's College, he returned to Uganda with his African-American bride and associated himself with the educational division of the Church Missionary Society.[57] His association with this agency was, however, of short duration; apparently his progressive religious and educational theory was incompatible with the policies and practices of the CMS.[58]

Having broken with the CMS, Kalibala established the Aggrey Memorial School wherein he attempted to practice his progressive missionary and educational theories. The school, which was emphatically nonsectarian, was "a valuable illustration of what Kalibala had adopted and what he had rejected from his own experiences in mission schools and in American Negro colleges."[59] Unable to find adequate support, Kalibala eventually affiliated the school with the Foreign Mission Board of the largest independent African-American denomination—the National Baptist Convention, Inc.[60] He also joined Faduma in using its missionary journal, the *Mission Herald,* to project his own progressive and race-conscious missiological and pedagogical theories to a primarily African-American audience.[61]

There is no way of knowing how many students Faduma similarly influenced on both sides of the Atlantic during his more than half a century of missionary and educational activity. Students, however, were not the only group exposed to his distinctive theological, pedagogical, and ideological teachings. His numerous personal appearances before various religious and educational conventions and the publication of more than seventy articles, sermons, and lectures in major newspapers and journals projected his views to a much larger audience on both sides of the Atlantic.

In the United States, as in Sierra Leone, he functioned as a "practical theologian" and mediator of new and controversial currents to the African American community. His activities in this capacity are illuminated in his response to the smoldering conflict over the relation of science and religion that eventually gave rise to the "fundamentalist-modernist controversy."[62] The evolutionary thesis became the focus of this controversy which reached its climax in the famous Scopes trial of 1925. In an effort to help rural black ministers reach some understanding and resolution of the issues involved in the controversy, Faduma, who had long since satisfactorily reconciled the theory of evolution and the scriptural account of creation, lectured during 1925 and 1926 at conventions throughout North Carolina on "The Christian Minister's Attitude toward Religion and Science."[63]

Faduma's continued commitment to evangelical liberalism was also convincingly demonstrated by his enrollment at the age of seventy in the 1927 Summer Quarter at Chicago Theological Seminary.[64] Founded by Congregationalists in the mid–nineteenth century, the Seminary had been under the increasing influence of theological liberalism since the 1880s.[65] Affiliation in 1914 with the Divinity School of the University of Chicago, which included among its faculty liberals and modernists such as Shailer Mathews, Shirley Jackson Case, Charles Witney Gilkey, Henry N. Wieman, Walter Marshall Horton, and Edward Scribner Ames, resulted in the influence of the more radical theological leaven of modernism within the Seminary.[66]

By Faduma's enrollment in 1927, Chicago had become one of the nation's leading liberal theological institutions. Its aggregation of liberal luminaries must have been a major attraction to the aged liberal. He may also have been attracted by the Seminary's claim of "unabated concern for foreign missions."[67] Whatever the attraction, Faduma's enrollment afforded him the opportunity for brief study with a new generation of liberals. It was an opportunity similar to the one he had enjoyed at Yale Divinity School in the 1890s with an earlier generation of liberal adherents and formulators.

The courses Faduma took at Chicago reflect his continued and characteristic interest in merging social, ethical, missiological, and pedagogical concerns. His enrollment in two biblical courses, the "Religion of Paul" and "The Epistle to the Corinthians," was consistent with his long-standing appreciation of the missiological significance of the Pauline materials.[68] A third course in the education department reflected his continued interest in theological liberalism's pedagogical impact. Of special significance was his enrollment in a course in social ethics taught by Dr. Arthur E. Holt.[69] Entitled "Religion and the Major Social Evils," the course was described as "A case study . . . in which there will be an attempt to discover the major evils which prey upon the life of man . . .[and] the part which religion plays in man's struggle against these evils."[70]

Faduma remained strangely silent about his study at Chicago Theological Seminary in his later writings. Perhaps this reticence reflected his disappointment with a mediocre academic performance that earned him grades of C and B in his Biblical courses, a P in Education, and what must have been a very disheartening C in Social Ethics.[71] To the aged Faduma, who still prided himself on academic excellence and continuously stressed the same to his students, this may have been a humbling and perhaps traumatic experience. Faduma's silence and his grades may have also reflected a profound discomfort with the Seminary's theological and methodological perspective. Indeed, the tenets, methodologies, and worldview of an earlier liberalism with which Faduma was so comfortable and proficient may in fact have been a liability at Chicago Theological Seminary, where the acids of modernism emanating from the "rationalistic atmosphere" of the University of Chicago and its divinity school had fostered a theological shift in the direction of "scientific modernism."[72]

If troubled by the theological and methodological shifts fostered within the academic community by the influences of "scientific modernism," Faduma may have paused briefly at the end of the decade to appreciate the potent impact evangelical liberalism was having on the mainstream of Protestant missiology. Despite war, recession, the fundamentalist reaction to liberalism, and even the rumblings of a major theological critique emanating from Europe, the liberal perspective increasingly came to dominate the mainstream of Protestant missiology during the postwar period.

The liberalism-influenced shift, which occurred most notably between the Edinburgh World Missionary Conference of 1910 and the Jerusalem Conference of 1928, has been chronicled by a number of mission historians.[73] Stephen Neill noted that

> in these years of rapid missionary expansion, a very different Gospel had been growing up and taking hold of the minds of a great many Christians, especially in America. The liberal was not by any means so sure that Jesus Christ was the *last* Word of God to man. He was repelled by the exclusive claim to salvation through Christ alone. He tended to take a much more favorable view of the other religions than his more conservative colleagues, and to look forward to some kind of synthesis of religions rather than to the disappearance of any of them. . . . There should be no hostility between

> them, the spirit of proselytism being replaced by the willingness to learn from one another . . . . Clearly a comprehensive change was taking place in the theological climate, in attitudes to other religions, and in the understanding of the missionary task.[74]

Far from being a passive observer, Faduma was an active participant in the missiological debates of the post-Edinburgh period, occasionally using the pages of major mission journals to articulate his mature Pan-African missiology and support the liberalization of mainstream Protestant missiology.[75] Indeed, many of the adaptations and modifications made in mainstream Protestant missiology were those which he had long advocated. Among them were: the call for incorporation of the findings of modern scientific scholarship from a broad range of disciplines; the call for a greater respect and appreciation of non-Christian religions and cultures; indigenization of Christian ritual and personnel; the disassociation of mission efforts from western racial, cultural, political, and religious chauvinism; renewed emphasis on the service and social dimensions of the mission enterprise; a call for ecumenical and cooperative efforts; and the ending of the paternalistic relationship between the older and "younger" churches. In a number of extensive, often serialized post-Edinburgh articles, Faduma consistently articulated such themes as vital components of his liberal theology-based, Pan-African missiology.[76]

Of the post-Edinburgh temper of the mission movement, Faduma observed:

> We are now living in an age of intense missionary activity. The Christian Church is realizing more than ever what is meant by "the kingdom of God." The Saviour's commission, "Go and disciple all nations," is studied more closely than it ever was before . . . . The missionary temperature of the Church is rising every year.[77]

That this "missionary temperature" was being increasingly shaped and influenced by the tenets and disciplines associated with theological liberalism provided Faduma with cause for optimism. Missionary work, he noted, was "no longer tentative" but had rather "become a serious study" and "a science for all":

> Throughout the largest universities of the land are to be found bands and chairs on the philosophy of religion and comparative religions, besides annual lectures on missions from returned missionaries. Men and women are not expected to rush heedlessly into the foreign field; they are given an intelligent preparation for their prospective fields of labour.[78]

Faduma was convinced that Africa in general and Sierra Leone in particular—"the oldest missionary field in Africa"—had a vital stake in this new approach to missions.[79] Thus he called for the establishment in Sierra Leone of a "Co-operative Missionary Training Institution" to train Africans in the modern religious and mission sciences.[80] Included among its departments would be "(a) A school of Religion, (b) A school for Theology, (c) A Bible school, (d) A school of Christian Sociology and Practical ethics."[81] At the core of its curriculum would be the comprehensive and "scientific" study of religion in disciplines which "should include the study of Comparative Religion, the Philosophy of Religion, Anthropology and Race Psychology, and Religious Psychology."[82] A narrow denominational focus—the bane of traditional religious education—would have no place in such a curriculum. Faduma explained:

> We are afraid the study of Religion in the past has been in the narrow forms of denominationalism. The principal religions of the world including paganism should be studied scientifically and with open mind. The germinal truths which underlie all religions should be studied side by side with their falsities. Paganism should be studied with keener interest and sympathy in order to comprehend the inner meanings of those strivings and yearnings which have been in pagan minds for centuries. The danger in studying religion from the Christian standpoint only is that one has a narrow view not only of religion but even of Christian religion . . . . And when one has a narrow idea of the Christian Religion he easily becomes a sectarian.[83]

In defense of the broader relevance of this perspective, Faduma asserted that "The man who knows only one religion is a source of danger in any community."[84]

The more enlightened attitude toward Islam, which was rapidly spreading in progressive mission circles, was also anticipated and encouraged by Faduma. Conscious of the myriad prejudices and stereotypes regarding Islam under which most missionaries labored, he welcomed the changed perspective that modern "scientific" study brought to bear on Islamic religion and culture. Thus in 1914 he noted the increased "importance" afforded Islam at the Edinburgh missionary conference:

> So important is the subject of Islam that in the World's Missionary Conference, which met in 1910 at Edinburgh, a committee of experts was formed to study the question. The mention of such names as Le Chatelier, of Paris, Becker, and Meinhof, of Hamburg, Macdonald, of Hartford, and Westerman, of Berlin, in the committee, make us feel that the subject would be studied in a scientific way, and would be free from platitudes.[85]

In 1925 Faduma entered directly into the mainstream of the missiological discussion and reappraisal of Islamic religion and culture with the publication of his "Christianity and Islam in Africa: A Native African's View of the Situation" in the foremost missiological journal of the era, the *Missionary Review of the World*.[86] His missiological credentials had been recognized by its editors almost thirty years earlier when they praised his presentations at the 1895 Congress of Africa as "the excellent views of one of the most highly educated and broadly cultured natives concerning missionary work.[87]

However, Faduma's perspective on Islam was more than academic and missiological. His concern for the religion and its adherents was rooted in his familiarity with the Islamic community in Sierra Leone. It was a familiarity which began among the Muslims of his home village of Waterloo and was extended by his study of Arabic under Imam Alfa (Alpha) Omaru.[88] Faduma was also aware of and influenced by the controversial and provocative writings of Edward Blyden on Islam in West Africa.[89]

As early as his 1895 paper entitled "Religious Beliefs of the Yoruba of West Africa," Faduma gave evidence of his awareness of the historical and cultural impact of Islam in West Africa. In this work, which was also characterized by his application of the methodological perspective of comparative religion, he pointed out that while the "ubiquitous Arab has somewhat modified" Yoruba "civil as well as religious life" he has not "stamped it out of existence." Indeed, he noted that Yoruba civilization successfully "combines both the native and Mohammedan elements."[90] His continued interest in and concern with the topic of Islam inspired works such as "Christianity and Islam in Africa," written in 1914, and in 1922 his serialized translation of "Khalil's Mohammedan Code." In the former article Faduma discussed and compared the "practical effect and mode of operation" of Christianity and Islam "on the native of Africa."[91] The latter work reflected not only his familiarity with the broad history of Islam and Islamic culture but also his considerable sensitivity to the Islamic segment of the Sierra Leone community. He introduced it with the hope that it would "be interesting and informing to British West Africans, and especially to Muslims who are not conversant with Arabic literature."[92] Thus both academic study and personal experience with Islam in West Africa had well prepared Faduma to enter into the mainstream of the missiological discussions and reappraisals of Islamic religion and culture.

"Christianity and Islam in Africa: A Native African's View of the Situation," was an abbreviated version of his 1914 study "Christianity and Islam in Africa."[93] In both works, Faduma, reminiscent of Blyden, contrasted Islam's successful propagation in Africa with the failings of the Christian missionary enterprise. Contrary to the old missiological notions that depreciated the positive influence of Islam in Africa, he insisted that in relative terms the influence of Islam had been salutary. Convinced that Christian mission theorists had much to learn from Islam's success in West Africa, he attempted to disabuse his readers of the often superficial and stereotypical notions that hampered their understanding of the factors that accounted for Islam's rapid spread in West Africa. Among the more significant factors listed by Faduma were: (1) Islam's unity, unlike the sectarian divisions of Christianity; (2) the intrinsic and uncompromised relationship between the religious and ethical teachings of Islam; (3) Islam's tendency to respect and protect the best of indigenous African culture; and (4) Christianity's susceptibility to and Islam's resistance to the virus of racism. On this last and most important factor, he noted that "Islam practices a brotherhood of believers and recognizes no superior or inferior race," while modern Christianity is "honeycombed with Pharisaism, the spirit of separation, the spirit of race exclusiveness."[94]

Yet, Faduma contended that the problems highlighted were not inherent to Christianity but were perversions of its central tenets:

> It is not Christianity that is responsible for these inconsistencies in the religion of Jesus Christ, it is Anglo-Saxon and Teutonic imperialism which is injected into Christianity. Race consciousness, instead of being conquered by the religion, dominates the religion of Christ. . . . The problem of Christianity in Africa is not one of precept, it is one of practice, it is not one of dogmatics, but of pragmatics.[95]

Faduma concluded with what can perhaps be described as the credo of his Pan-African missiology:

> Ethiopia is now stretching out her hands unto God. The Christian Church is asked to "deliver the goods" to Africa's sons with no label on but that of Christ and His Cross. The manhood and dignity of the race will accept nothing more or less. You need not deliver the goods unless they are offered in terms of Christian brotherhood. Show Africa the Christ, not yourself, and let the transformation that comes be the result of an inward spiritual working, not of superficial accretion.

"Under those terms," he contended, "Mohammed will bow to Christ" and "Islam will be no match for Christianity."[96]

In the decades that followed, an aged Faduma would witness the emergence and maturation of a number of new theological, missiological, and ideological developments. A number of these develoments would threaten to render both theological liberalism and evangelical Pan-Africanism obsolete.

Notes

1. See for example Orishatukeh Faduma, "Lessons and Needs of the Hour," *Sierra Leone Weekly News,* 21 Sept., 5 Oct. 1918, and Or-

ishatukeh Faduma, "Father T. B. Cole, The Christian Layman: An Appreciation," *Sierra Leone Weekly News,* 3 Dec. 1921.

2. On the deadly impact of this international epidemic, see "Deaths for the Week," *Sierra Leone Weekly News,* 21 Sept. 1918. This series either had roots in or was the basis of Faduma's more explicit discussion of the theodicy issue in a 1917–1918 work entitled "The Book of Job and the Problem of Suffering." Though listed among his "literary contributions," this work has not been located.
3. Faduma, "Lessons and Needs," *Sierra Leone Weekly News,* 21 Sept. 1918.
4. Faduma, "Lessons and Needs," *Sierra Leone Weekly News,* 5 Oct. 1918.
5. Faduma, "Lessons and Needs," *Sierra Leone Weekly News* 21 Sept., 5 Oct. 1918 On the liberal emphasis on social solidarity and responsibility, see Smith, *Changing Conceptions of Original Sin,* p. 167.
6. Orishatukeh Faduma, "The Faith That Is in Me," *Sierra Leone Weekly News,* 2 June 1923; 16 June 1923; 14 July 1923; 21 July 1923; 28 July 1923; 18 Aug. 1923; 1 Sept. 1923; 15 Sept. 1923; 20 Oct. 1923; 3 Nov. 1923; 8 Dec. 1923.
7. Faduma, "The New Theology," pp. 139, 142.
8. Marillia Van, "Random Jottings (International Bible Students Association)," *Sierra Leone Weekly News,* 19 May 1923. On an earlier theological controversy, regarding the tenets of theological liberalism as affirmed by British Congregationalists, see "Theological Unrest," *Sierra Leone Weekly News,* 28 Mar. 1908; 2 May 1908. Variously known as "Russellism," "Millennial Dawnism," "Zion's Watch Tower Tract Society," as well as the "International Bible Students Association" and "Jehovah's Witnesses," the movement was one of the more zealous of the millennial groups that arose in the United States during the last decades of the nineteenth century. Its strong millennial emphasis, rooted in biblical literalism, appealed to the "disinherited." Consequently, it gained an international audience and growing numbers of converts in the wake of the shock and disillusionment of World War I. Its rapid spread throughout colonial Africa after World War I fostered political and religious controversy. On the controversial history and expansion of this movement, see Herbert Stroup, *The Jehovah's Witnesses* (New York: Columbia University Press, 1945); Marley Cole, *Jehovah's Witnesses: The New World Society* (New York: Vantage Press, 1955); Frederick Mayer, *Jehovah's Witnesses* (St. Louis: Concordia Publishing House, 1952). The movement caused considerable difficulties for traditional mission forces in colonial Africa. In 1935 a Commission of Inquiry concluded that "it is a dangerously subver-

sive movement." Quoted in C. P. Grove, *Planting of Christianity in West Africa,* vol. 4 (London: Lutterworth Press, 1958), p. 230. See also G. Guick, "Some Aspects of the African Watch Tower Movement in Northern Rhodesia," *International Review of Missions* 29 (1940): 216–226. On its contemporary impact in Africa, see Adrian Hastings, *African Christianity* (New York: Seabury Press, 1976), pp. 84, 93.

9. Marillia Van, "Random Jottings."
10. Mr. I. W. Harding, "Reply to Mr. Brown's Open Invitation to Debate on His Criticism," *Sierra Leone Weekly News,* 14 July 1923; W. Talbot Hindley, "Russellism, a Vast Modern Delusion," *Sierra Leone Weekly News,* 8 Sept. 1923; "Mr. Brown on the Platform—His Reply to His Critics," *Sierra Leone Weekly News,* 24 July 1923; W. E. Campbell, "Think and Decide," *Sierra Leone Weekly News,* 11 Aug. 1923; 18 Aug. 1923.
11. Ironically, Faduma found his writings against creedalism and sectarianism quoted by supporters of Brown. See W. E. Campbell, "Think and Decide," *Sierra Leone Weekly News,* 18 Aug. 1923.
12. In a telling introduction, he affirmed the liberal assumption of an intimate link between the dynamics of faith and moral action: "What a man sincerely believes and acts upon becomes an essential part of his life." Faduma, "The Faith That Is in Me," *Sierra Leone Weekly News,* 2 June 1923.
13. Faduma, "The Faith That Is In Me." *Sierra Leone Weekly News,* 2 June 1923; 16 June 1923; 14 July 1923; 21 July 1923; 28 July 1923; 18 Aug. 1923; 1 Sept. 1923; 15 Sept. 1923; 20 Oct. 1923; 3 Nov. 1923; 8 Dec. 1923.
14. Faduma, "The Faith That Is in Me," *Sierra Leone Weekly News,* 14 July. See also Averill, *American Theology in the Liberal Tradition,* pp. 69–94.
15. O. Faduma, "The Faith That Is in Me," *Sierra Leone Weekly News,* 16 June 1923. For the treatment of the Genesis account of creation by liberals such as Lewis F. Stearns, William N. Clarke, and William Adams Brown, see Smith, *Changing Conceptions of Original Sin,* pp. 183, 190–191, 194.
16. Walter Rauschenbusch, *A Theology for the Social Gospel* (New York: Macmillan, 1917). See also Smith, *Changing Conceptions of Original Sin,* pp. 200–201. On the similar postwar shift of liberals such as Eugene William Lyman and Harry Emerson Fosdick, see Cauthen, *American Religious Liberalism,* pp. 97–99, 127–143, 61–74.
17. Faduma, "The Faith That Is in Me," *Sierra Leone Weekly News,* 18 Aug. 1923; 1 Sept. 1923; 15 Sept. 1923; 20 Oct. 1923; 3 Nov. 1923.

18. Faduma, "The Faith That Is in Me," *Sierra Leone Weekly News,* 15 Sept. 1923.
19. See Smith, *Changing Conceptions of Original Sin,* pp. 200–201.
20. Faduma would also describe Heaven as "the Kingdom of God in my heart on earth begun. It is not far off. It is within you." Faduma, "The Faith That Is in Me," *Sierra Leone Weekly News,* 8 Dec. 1923. On the importance of the concept of the "Kingdom of God on Earth" for theological liberals, see Cauthen, *American Religious Liberalism,* pp. 11, 24, 43, 54, 55; Walter Rauschenbusch, *A Theology for the Social Gospel* and H. Richard Niebuhr, *The Kingdom of God in America* (New York: Harper & Brothers, 1937).
21. John the Presbyter [pseud.], Letter to the editor, *Sierra Leone Weekly News,* 21 July 1923.
22. Faduma, he charged, "introduces faith into his statement but does not state whether faith is the origin of the knowledge of God as a personal friend of which he speaks" nor sufficiently indicates "the nature of that faith." John the Presbyter, Ibid.
23. Ibid. (emphasis in original).
24. O. Faduma, letter to the editor, *Sierra Leone Weekly News,* 28 July 1923.
25. O. Faduma, "Drawbacks and Successes of Missionary Work in Africa," *Sierra Leone Weekly News,* 9 Mar. 1918.
26. Ibid., 6 Apr. 1918.
27. Ibid.
28. In 1924 Faduma reported that "Christian churches of many denominations had my services frequently on Sundays." Faduma, "Sierra Leone Revisited," p. 352.
29. *African Mail,* 21 Apr. 1916.
30. Orishatukeh Faduma, "Father T. B. Cole, the Christian Layman: An Appreciation," *Sierra Leone Weekly News,* 3 Dec. 1921.
31. Faduma, "Negro Development: Its Phases," *Sierra Leone Weekly News,* 24 Sept. 1921. Compare with his 1908 critique entitled, *The Defects of the Negro Church.*
32. Editorial, "An Appraisement of Professor Faduma," *Sierra Leone Weekly News,* 19 May 1923. Two weeks earlier, M. J. Oyedele M'-Cauley authored a letter to the editor that expressed hopes that Faduma's writings "not be allowed to remain in scattered forms, but that steps be taken to collate them in book form, with a view to give those who are interested in the development of African literature, an idea of the progress the race is making and contributing to civilization." In response to his request for a list of literary contributions, Faduma submitted a list that included 30 articles. M. J. Oyedele M'Cauley, "The Writings of Professor Faduma," *Sierra Leone Weekly News,* 5 May

1923. Unfortunately, the requested compilation of Faduma's most important articles in book form was apparently never completed.

33. "An Appraisement of Professor Faduma," *Sierra Leone Weekly News,* 19 May 1923.
34. At one of these functions Faduma was presented a souvenir by Mrs. E. H. Cummings, "the Mayoress of Freetown." *Sierra Leone Weekly News,* 22 Sept. 1923.
35. Thomas Jesse Jones, *Negro Education: A Study of the Private and Higher Schools for Colored People in the United States* (Department of the Interior, Bureau of Education Bulletins, 1916; Washington Government Printing Office, 1917), pp. 409–410.
36. O. Faduma, "Christianity and Islam in Africa," *African Mail,* 22 May 1914. On the significant transitions that were taking place within both the American Missionary Association and Congregationalism during this era, see Stanley, *The Children Is Crying,* pp. 73–104.
37. Faduma, "Sierra Leone Revisited," pp. 352–353.
38. Ibid.
39. Orishatukeh Faduma, "Vale: Longum Vale," *Sierra Leone Weekly News,* 13 July 1912; 20 July 1912.
40. Geiss, *Pan-African Movement,* p. 293.
41. Nkomo was from Rhodesia and attended Greenville College in Illinois as well as the University of Chicago. His master's thesis at Chicago was entitled "The Customs of the Bandowo Folk Considered With a View of Adding Certain New Arguments to the Generally Accepted View of the Unity of the Bantu race." (Master's thesis, University of Chicago, 1922). He died suddenly in 1925. King, *Pan-Africanism and Education,* pp. 69–70, 215–218, 221.
42. Nkomo earlier authored an autobiographical tract entitled, *How I Found Christ in the Jungles of Africa.* At the 1915 meeting of the North American Students Conference, he promoted plans for an African Students Christian Association that would "promote unity and love among all the students from different tribes of great Africa." Ibid., p. 216.
43. At that conference delegates drafted a petition to the foremost missionary statesman of the era, John R. Mott, President of the World Student Christian Federation, requesting support. King, *Pan-Africanism and Education,* p. 216.
44. Ibid., pp. 220–221.
45. Orishatukeh Faduma, "Africa's Claims and Needs," *Southern Workman* 54 (May 1925): 221–225.
46. Ibid.
47. Ibid.
48. Ibid. Even as he issued this prayer, Faduma must have been con-

scious of the escalating controversy concerning the refusal of white mission organizations to employ and deploy African-Americans and American-trained Africans as missionaries. This controversy evoked a hearing the following year at the International Missionary Conference held in Le Zoute, Belgium. See Edwin W. Smith, *The Christian Mission in Africa: Study Based on the Work of the International Conference at Le Zoute, Belgium, September 14th to 21st, 1926* (London: International Missionary Council, 1926). Carter G. Woodson also noted the difficulties of African-American missionaries during this era. Woodson, *History of the Negro Church,* p. 286. On the history of this controversy, see Wilber C. Harr, "The Negro as an American Protestant Missionary in Africa" (Ph.D. diss. University of Chicago, 1945).

49. Editorial, "The Foreign Mission Board Takes Over a New Station in Uganda, East Africa," *Mission Herald* 43 (Jan./Feb. 1940): 12–15.
50. The increasing difficulty that Kalibala and other African students had in gaining permission to study in the United States was rooted in the fear of British Colonial officials and missionaries that the result of such study and exposure to African-American thought would be a radicalization of African students. This fear resulted in collusion between missionaries and colonial officials to deny passports to Africans wishing to study at "unsafe" institutions in the United States. On the impact of this concern and policy, see King, *Pan-Africanism and Education,* p. 72.
51. On the Phelps-Stokes Agency and the activities of Thomas Jesse Jones, see King, *Pan-Africanism and Education,* p. 72. Also see Woodson, who charged that Jones, "financed by 'philantropists' " and "certain American 'Christian' organizations," was about the "business . . . of furnishing the world with 'hand-picked' Negro leaders to damn even the natives in Africa." Woodson, *History of the Negro Church,* pp. 286–287.
52. King, *Pan-African Education,* pp. 228–230, 240. A year later Jones expressed his displeasure and concern over the fact that Kalibala and other African students refused to remain in the ("safe") schools that had been paternalistically chosen for them. Perhaps with Kalibala in mind, he complained to an official of the International Education Board "that in the case of a few African students whom we have aided, we have found it difficult to keep them in such schools as Hampton or Tuskegee. As soon as they come in touch with the Negro intelligentsia of America, they desire to attend some of the outstanding northern institutions like Columbia or Cornell, or some of the more leading institutions of collegiate grade for Negroes in the South." This letter also expressed many of Jones' deeper fears and

concerns related to the education of both Africans and African-Americans. King, *Pan-Africanism and Education,* p. 226.

53. King, *Pan-Africanism and Education,* p. 228. An additional factor in this transfer was probably the death of Nkomo in 1925. This sequence of events also suggests a close relationship between Faduma and the African Student Union. Kalibala's letter to the Phelps-Stokes Agency explaining his transfer of schools echoed the message that Faduma had delivered a year earlier in his address on "Africa's Claims and Needs" to Hampton's African Student Union, which was that industrial education for Africans must first be firmly rooted in the full development of African intellectual gifts if it were to be of any real use to the African in the modern development of Africa. Kalibala also insisted on the necessity of securing a thorough general education before proceeding to specialize in narrower vocational studies of the kind emphasized at Tuskegee. He wrote: "From what I know of the English people, I find an industrial qualification that is not founded on a good mental equipment will be a great barrier to my usefulness when I return home. I can only be used then, as a tool and a footmat." King, *Pan-Africanism and Education,* p. 229.
54. Editorial, "The Foreign Mission Board Takes Over a New Station in Uganda, East Africa," *Mission Herald* 43 (Jan./Feb. 1940): 12–15.
55. King, *Pan-Africanism and Education,* pp. 230, 240.
56. Ernest B. Kalibala, "Education for the Villages in Uganda, East Africa," (Master's thesis, Teachers College, 1934). King, *Pan-Africanism and Education,* pp. 240–243.
57. Kalibala's wife, the former Miss Alta W. Jones, was the daughter of a retired New York minister and a graduate of Boston University, where she majored in Religious Education. Editorial, "The Foreign Mission Board," pp. 12–15. King, *Pan-Africanism and Education,* pp. 242–243.
58. King suggested that this development was predictable given the progressive pedagogical concepts and critique of traditional missionary educational theory presented in Kalibala's thesis. King, *Pan-Africanism and Education,* pp. 242–243.
59. Ibid., pp. 243–244.
60. "The Foreign Mission Board," pp. 12–15; King, *Pan-Africanism and Education,* p. 245.
61. In an article published in 1940 Kalibala echoed Faduma as he expounded upon "Africa—The Unknown Quantity" and attempted to counter the rampant falsehoods and inaccuracies about Africa that were being perpetuated by both black and white missionaries. See Ernest B. Kalibala, "Africa—The Unknown Quantity," Part I, *Mis-*

sion Herald 44 (May/June, 1940):10–12 and Part II (July/Aug. 1940): 11–13. Compare with Faduma's "Drawbacks and Successes of Missionary Work in Africa," *Sierra Leone Weekly News,* 16 Mar. 1918; 30 Mar. 1918; 6 Apr. 1918. Kalibala returned to the United States in the 1940s to pursue a doctorate at Harvard University which he successfully completed in 1946. His dissertation was entitled "The Social Structure of the Baganda Tribe" (Ph.D. diss., Harvard University, 1946). Kalibala's sojourn in the United States during this period and his active involvement in the highly politicized successor of the African Students Union, the African Students Association, indirectly linked Faduma and his tenets to more radical African students and student organizations in the United States. Kalibala served as vice-president of the African Students Association, which was founded in 1940. Its list of officers also include Kwame Nkrumah, who served as its president. Geiss, *Pan-African Movement,* pp. 374–378.

62. See Willard Gatewood, *Controversy in the Twenties: Fundamentalism, Modernism, Evolution* (Nashville: Vanderbilt University Press, 1969); Robert T. Handy, "Fundamentalism and Modernism in Perspective," *Religion in Life* (Summer, 1955): 381–394. On fundamentalism, see N. F. Furniss, *The Fundamentalist Controversy, 1918–1931* (New Haven: Yale University Press, 1954); and the pioneer study by Stewart G. Cole, *The History of Fundamentalism* (New York: R. R. Smith, 1931).

63. Orishatukeh Faduma, "The Christian Minister's Attitude toward Religion and Science," referred to in Faduma, "Some of My Literary Contributions" (n.p.,n.d.). An early response of rural black preachers to the challenge of modern science to scriptural "truths" is reflected in the sermons of the mid-nineteenth-century preacher, John Jasper. William E. Hatcher, *John Jasper: The Unmatched Negro Philosopher and Preacher* (New York: Fleming H. Revell Co., 1908), p. 80. For a revival of these concerns and related controversy among Southern black ministers during the spring of 1925, see Gavins, *Perils and Prospects of Southern Black Leadership,* pp. 36–37. On the treatment of this issue by another African-American liberal, see William H. Ferris, "Viewpoint of Science and Religion," *Negro World* 13 (13 Jan. 1923): 4; 14 (3 Mar. 1923): 4. Also see "Modernism Destroys Evangelism," *Negro Journal of Religion* 1 (Nov. 1935): 10. Faduma's mature and moderate evangelical liberalism uniquely suited him to the role of mediator of the controversy between religion and science within the African and African-American community. He had consistently argued that the development of the race both in Africa and in diaspora necessitated exposure to and selective adaptation of the findings of modern science and that

such adaptation did not require compromise of the essential tenets of the Christian faith. Moreover, he argued that the obscurantist posture of fundamentalism presented a serious challenge and potential setback to the religious, educational, and political development of people of African descent. See O. Faduma, "Negro Development: Its Meaning and Aims," *Sierra Leone Weekly News,* 17, Sept. 1921; "Negro Development: Its Period of Growth and Danger in Education," *Sierra Leone Weekly News,* 22 Oct. 1921; "*Negro Development—Its Phases,*" *Sierra Leone Weekly News,* 24 Sept. 1921.

64. Faduma enrolled in June 1927. Official transcript of Orishatukeh Faduma, Chicago Theological Seminary. Copy issued 16 May 1983 by Cheryl Miller, Registrar, The Chicago Theological Seminary.
65. Arthur Cushman McGiffert, Jr., *No Ivory Tower: The Story of The Chicago Theological Seminary* (Chicago: The Chicago Theological Seminary, 1965), pp. 3–5. Between 1883 and 1890, the crucial years in the struggle between liberals and conservatives within Congregationalism, the seminary faculty annually published *Current Discussions in Theology* which reflected a growing acceptance of the tenets of liberalism. McGiffert suggests that the appointment of Professor Clarence A. Beckwith to the Illinois Chair of Christian Theology in 1905 effectively signaled the decisive triumph of theological liberalism in the seminary. McGiffert, *No Ivory Tower,* pp. 87–90, 123.
66. On the significant impact of this group and their "Chicago School of Theology," see Cauthen, *American Religious Liberalism,* pp. 147–206.
67. McGiffert, *Ivory Tower,* p. 175; *Chicago Theological Seminary Register,* Annual Catalogue, 1926–1927, 17 (May 1927): 15.
68. These courses were presumably taught by Chester Charlton McCown, Professor of New Testament Literature and Interpretation, and Harold R. Willoughby, Assistant Professor of New Testament Literature. On the importance of Paul and the Pauline corpus for Faduma's missiology, see Orishatukeh Faduma, "The Faith That Is In Me," *Sierra Leone Weekly News,* 15 Sept. 1923.
69. Holt, following in the footsteps of Graham Taylor, projected and represented the distinctive social and ethical thrust and character of postwar liberals. Under his leadership, the Department of Social Economics was converted into the Department of Social Ethics and separated from the Department of Practical Theology. It further expanded its curriculum with the inauguration of a new type of course in American theological education—"Social and Religious Research and Survey." McGiffert, *No Ivory Tower,* p. 187.
70. *Chicago Theological Seminary Register,* Annual Catalogue, 1926–1927 with Announcements for 1927–1928, 18 (May 1927), p. 52. In

addition to an interest in social ethics, Faduma and Dr. Holt shared a concern and passion for the particular problems encountered by Christianity and the Christian worker in rural communities. Holt's interest in the problems of rural Christianity and the so-called "country-life movement" resulted in the seminary's offering special training for students who planned to become or remain rural ministers. In the mid-1930s the Merom Institute was established under Holt's inspiration as a "country-life center" which "would conserve for America and the Christian religion the native values of rural life" and "place intelligence and inspiration at the disposal of people who intended to live in rural neighborhoods." McGiffert, *No Ivory Tower,* pp. 192–194. For Faduma's expression of similar concerns, see his *Defects of the Negro Church.*

71. Official transcript of Orishatukeh Faduma, Chicago Theological Seminary.
72. On this shift within the ranks of liberals and its impact, see Averill, *American Theology in the Liberal Tradition,* pp. 95, 100–106; Cauthen, *American Religious Liberalism,* p. 30; and McGiffert, *No Ivory Tower,* p.165.
73. Neill, *History of Christian Missions,* pp. 454–455; Forman, "History of Foreign Mission Theory," pp. 95–101; R. Pierce Beaver, "North American Thought on the Fundamental Principles of Missions during the Twentieth Century" (a survey article), reprint from *Church History* 21 (Dec. 1952): 3–22; Lyman Van Law Cady, "The Liberal Attitude toward Other Religions," in *Liberal Theology: an Appraisal; Essays in Honor of Eugene William Lyman,* ed. David Everett Roberts and Henry Pitney Van Dusen (New York: Charles Scribner's Sons, 1942), pp. 137–150. Of the pervasive impact of theological liberalism within mainstream mission circles, Cady notes that "the work of liberal theology, responsive to the widened intellectual world, more and more influenced the younger generation of missionaries who were equipped to understand and use the new knowledge. Even those who would flatly repudiate the label of theological liberalism could not be wholly impervious to its influence in creating a more generous and appreciative attitude toward other religions." Cady, "Liberal Attitude," pp. 138–139. See also Roger E. Hedlund, *Roots of the Great Debate in Missions* (Madras: Evangelical Literature Service, 1981), pp. 28–40.
74. Neill, *History of Christian Missions,* pp. 454–455. The dominant ethos and agenda of the 1928 Jerusalem conference were also shaped by "the volcanic eruptions of the new nationalisms, many of them actively anti-Christian" and the "massive secularism" (much of it inspired by Marxism and Communism) that had arisen in the post-war years. The reports emerging from the conference reflect this

increased sensitivity to nationalism and the claims and needs of the "younger churches." One volume entitled, *The Relations Between the Younger and Older Churches,* was explicitly devoted to these concerns. In this context, many of the missiological concerns and correctives Faduma had long advocated came to the fore. Notably, the most blatant assumptions of Western spiritual and cultural chauvinism were toned down, though not completely abandoned as "A new interest in an indigenous Christianity and an indigenous Church was manifested, involving new respect for native cultures and a new critique of essential Christianity in differentiation from Western civilization." See Cady, "Liberal Attitude," pp. 140–141; Neil, *History of Christian Missions,* pp. 514–517; and *The Relations Between the Younger and Older Churches,* Jerusalem Report, vol. 3, 1928. In the years between the conferences, liberal themes such as the need to understand and appreciate other cultures and religions had been powerfully argued and widely publicized by liberal mission enthusiasts such as Daniel Johnson Fleming, Professor of Missions at Union Theological Seminary from 1918 to 1944. Fleming not only advanced a liberal missiology in the classroom but also published a number of works that emphasized the positive aspects of Christianity's contacts with non-Christian cultures. See Daniel Johnson Fleming *Contacts with Non-Christian Cultures: A Case Book on the Christian Movement Abroad* (New York: George Doran Co., 1923); *Attitudes toward Other Faiths* (New York: Association Press 1928); *Ways of Sharing with Other Faiths* (New York: Association Press, 1929); *Each with His Own Brush: Contemporary Christian Art in Asia and Africa* (New York: Friendship Press, 1938); *What Would You Do? When Christian Ethics Conflict with Standards of Non-Christian Cultures* (New York: Friendship Press, 1949). See also Forman, "A History of Foreign Mission Theory in America," p. 100.

75. Among the mission journals that published his articles were the *Missionary Echo* (a publication of the United Methodist Church); *American Missionary* (a publication of the American Missionary Society); *Mission Herald* (a publication of the National Baptist Convention); and the *Missionary Review of the World.*

76. It is testimony to the progressive and enlightened character of his earliest missiological formulations that much of Faduma's post-Edinburgh missiological writings were actually rearticulations of themes and concepts stressed in his earlier missiological writings. Compare, for example, his "Drawbacks to Missionary Work in Africa," *Missionary Echo* 24 (Apr. 1917): 54–56; 24 (May 1917): 71–72, and "Drawbacks and Successes of Missionary Work in Africa," *Sierra Leone Weekly News,* 9 Mar-20 Apr. 1918, with his address to the 1895 Congress on Africa entitled "Success and Draw-

backs of Missionary Work in Africa by an Eye-Witness," in Bowen, *Africa,* pp. 125–136.

77. O. Faduma, "Drawbacks to Missionary Work in Africa," *Missionary Echo* 24 (Apr. 1917): 54.
78. Ibid. On the growing popularity of the "Science of Missions" in the theological curriculum in the post-Edinburgh era, see Myklebust, *The Study of Missions in Theological Education,* vol. 2, p. 102.
79. Faduma, "Drawbacks to Missionary Work in Africa," *Missionary Echo,* pp. 71–72.
80. Orishatukeh Faduma, "Drawbacks and Successes of Missionary Work in Africa," *Sierra Leone Weekly News,* 20 Apr. 1918.
81. Ibid.
82. The study of comparative religion, which contributed so significantly to the development of the liberal missionary apologetic and played such a vital role in Faduma's own religious and missiological perspective, formed the core of the projected curriculum of the proposed missionary training institute. "It should be evident to all," Faduma contended, "that the study of Comparative Religion is vital in the study of religion. It is to study religion subjectively. It is to know what religion is to one-self and what it is to the other man." Moreover, he argued, the study of comparative religion would show "that in the highest religion, the Christian, there are ideals which are found in germinal forms in the lowest religions." Faduma, "Drawbacks and Successes of Missionary Work in Africa," *Sierra Leone Weekly News,* 20 Apr. 1918.
83. Ibid.
84. In support he quoted Otto Pfleiderer, Professor of Theology at the University of Berlin and one of the giants of German liberalism to the effect that one can only know a religion comparatively: "The statement of Pfleiderer is true. 'he knows one religion [only] when he knows more than one religion.'" O. Faduma, "Lessons and Needs of the Hour," *Sierra Leone Weekly News,* 2 Nov. 1918. On Otto Pfleiderer and the liberal German missiological school to which he belonged, see Myklebust, *The Study of Missions in Theological Education,* vol. 1, pp. 251–270, and Reardon, *Liberal Protestantism,* p. 34. Note also Otto Pfleiderer, *The Development of Theology in Germany Since Kant,* translated by J. F. Smith (London: Swan Sonneschein and Co., 1890). Elsewhere Faduma hinted at an even more pervasive influence of German theology and training in West Africa as he contended, "Long before the doors of London and Durham Universities were thrown open to the public, Sierra Leone and West Africa had produced men of great intellects in general, classical, and biblical literature, products many of them of German training whose spirit of work has not died out of the colonies."

Faduma, "Drawbacks and Successes of Missionary Work in Africa," *Sierra Leone Weekly News,* 20 Apr. 1918.

85. O. Faduma, "Christianity and Islam in Africa," *African Mail,* May 1914. Duncan Black Macdonald was considered a "great Islamic scholar." He taught at Hartford Theological Seminary and the Hartford School of Missions. The latter was "America's foremost center of Islamic and missionary study." Myklebust, *The Study of Missions in Theological Education,* vol. 2, pp. 92–93. Carl Heinrich Becker (1876–1933) authored a study entitled *Christianity and Islam* (1909). Alfred Le Chatelier (1855–1929) was a French scholar who authored a number of studies on Islam such as *L'Islam dans l'Afrique Occidentale* (Paris, 1899). Carl Meinhof (1857–1944) was an African linguist and author. Diedrich Westermann (1875–1956) was also a student of African life and culture. On the heightened dialogue concerning the growing attraction of Islam within the African-American community in the postwar period, see Martin, *Race First,* pp. 67–77.
86. Orishatukeh Faduma, "Christianity and Islam in Africa: A Native African's View of the Situation," *Missionary Review of the World* 48 (Nov. 1925): 865–868.
87. "Addresses on the Congress on Africa," *Missionary Review of the world* 19 (Sept. 1896): 693; These sentiments were reaffirmed in 1907 when the editors published excerpts from his "Christian Missions Among Less Developed Races." This speech was delivered by Faduma to a meeting of Southern Congregational workers in Memphis, Tennessee. See O. Faduma, "Christian Missions Among Less Developed Races," *Missionary Review of the World* 30 (June 1907): 543–555.
88. O. Faduma, "My Nigerian African Background," Holden, *Blyden,* pp. 831, 839.
89. Edward Blyden played a major role in efforts to project a more positive assessment of Islam's influence in West Africa. See Blyden's, collection of essays compiled under the provocative title *Christianity, Islam, and the Negro Race*. In this and other works, Blyden exploded the popular and erroneous conceptions of Islam fostered by missionary propaganda. Although Faduma did not directly quote or mention Blyden in his own works on Christianity and Islam in West Africa, there is little doubt that he was knowledgeable of and influenced by Blyden's works.
90. Faduma, "Religious Beliefs of the Yoruba of West Africa," in Bowen, *Africa,* pp. 31–36.
91. Orishatukeh Faduma, "Christianity and Islam in Africa," *African Mail,* 22 May 1915.

92. Khalil was described as a "great writer of Muslim jurisprudence" who in the fourteenth century codified the "Malikite interpretation of the Quran." Faduma felt that this would be of particular interest to the Muslims of West Africa since they "belong to the Malikite School." Orishatukeh Faduma, "Khalil's Mohammedan Code from the French of N. Seignette," *Sierra Leone Weekly News,* 24 Dec. 1921; 14 Jan. 1922; 21 Jan. 1922.
93. Orishatukeh Faduma, "Christianity and Islam In Africa: A Native African's View of the Situation," *Missionary Review of the World* 48 (Nov. 1925): 865–868.
94. *Ibid.*, pp. 866, 868. In 1914 Faduma argued that this egalitarianism was a major factor in Islam's success: "Herein lies the strength of Islam in Africa. It recognizes no rich or poor, no high or low, no superior or inferior, no white or black. In the melting pot of Islam all are one. There is no front seat for the privileged few, no back seat for the despised. Asia and Africa, Turk and Arab, embrace each other as one. Because Allah is one, all are one." Orishatukeh Faduma, "Christianity and Islam," *African Mail,* 22 May 1914. Compare with Blyden, *Christianity, Islam, and the Negro Race.*
95. Orishatukeh Faduma, "Christianity and Islam in Africa," *Missionary Review of the World,* p. 868.
96. Ibid. For a more personal account of the conflict between Islam and Christianity in Sierra Leone during the first half of the twentieth century, see Aiah Abu, "Islam Versus Christianity in Sierra Leone," in Berman, *African Reactions to Missionary Education,* pp. 92–115. For a more comprehensive study, see Peter B. Clarke, *West Africa and Islam: A Study of Religious Development from the Eighth to the Twentieth Century* (London: Edward Arnold, 1982).

8

"Like a Hound": Faduma's Final Years

The sparse materials that are available concerning Faduma's final years provide little in-depth insight into his perceptions and reactions to the major theological, ideological, and missiological transitions that occurred between 1930 and 1946. A number of these developments, most notably, the call for a more rationalistic and humanistic missiology, the neo-orthodox response to liberalism, as well as the rise of a more secular Pan-Africanism, both drew upon and challenged the tenets and convictions that informed his life and work.

An analysis of Faduma's final works reveals that amidst the intense theological, missiological, and ideological controversies of the era, he continued to adhere to the central tenets of evangelical liberalism and liberal missiology as adapted to his Pan-African ideology.[1] Although he may have been in agreement with Fosdick's admonition that liberals "must go beyond modernism," he was not among those whose minds had been "changed" by either the fundamentalist or the neo-orthodox polemic on the failings of liberalism.[2] The position of the Yale liberal theologian, Robert Lowery Calhoun, who declared himself "A Liberal Bandaged but Unbowed," perhaps best approximates the dogged liberalism of Faduma as he approached his final years.[3]

Although a persistent advocate of the application of liberal tenets and perspectives within Protestant missiology, Faduma, like many moderate liberals, was undoubtedly troubled by the rationalistic and humanistic missiology urged in 1932 with the publication of the findings of the Laymen's Foreign Missionary Inquiry. Its report, entitled *Rethinking Missions,* presented a modernist perspective on the character, aim, and motivation of the missionary task.[4] Not surprisingly, its missiological agenda proved unacceptable to many evangelical liberals as well as to theological and missiological conservatives who were galvanized into response.[5]

A more profound theological and missiological reaction to liberalism and modernism had much of its impetus and nurture in the writings and proclamations of the Swiss theologian, Karl Barth. Barth denounced the folly of liberalism and heralded the emergence of "crisis" or "dialectical theology."[6] By the mid-1930s this movement had inspired a distinctive American configuration of post liberalism known as neo-orthodoxy.[7] Rooted in a profound consciousness of the failings of liberalism, neo-orthodoxy specifically rejected liberalism's idealistic view of human nature and the liberal myth of unending progress toward realization of the "kingdom of God on earth." Neo-orthodoxy emphasized instead an acute awareness of the reality and theological gravity of both individual and corporate sin.[8]

The emergence of neo-orthodoxy had a profound impact within missiological circles. The resultant missiological shift was heralded in Hendrick Kraemer's preparatory volume for the 1938 meeting of the International Missionary Conference, entitled *The Christian Message in a Non-Christian World.*[9] Though only one of a number of missionaries influenced by Barth and post liberalism, Kraemer stood at the center of the developing neo-orthodox response to liberal missiology. With their emphasis on the uniqueness and exclusivity of the Christian Revelation—the radical discontinuity between Christianity and all other religions—Kraemer and his supporters presented a critique of liberal missiology and "the whole liberal attitude toward other religions."[10]

A measure of the extent to which a significant segment of the African-American religious and academic community was aware of the major theological and missiological issues of the era, as well as engaged in exploring and exercising its own theological, missiological, and ethical options, is reflected in the founding in 1934 and 1935 of the Fraternal Council of Negro Churches in America and the *Negro Journal of Religion.* Both were established by progressive and liberal black clergy who aspired to unite the leadership of black churches in a concerted assault on the myriad social, economic, and political injustices that afflicted the race.[11]

Of special concern to both the *Journal* and the Fraternal Council was the growing religious skepticism and secularism of black youth.[12] Indeed, this development and the accompanying charge that the Black Church and clergy were irrelevant had been among the major factors that inspired the founding of the Fraternal Council. A concern to reassert and reestablish the relevance of the Black Church and clergy induced the Council's founder and president, Reverdy Ransom, to warn: "If the Negro Church is to survive it must offer the Negro youth of today, something more than a home in heaven. Faced with the attitude of American Christianity, American business, labor, industry, and the government itself, who shall give them Faith, Hope, and Courage to persevere?"[13]

A similar concern over the growing secularization and religious skepticism among the ranks of a younger generation of blacks was also expressed by Faduma's former colleague in the American Negro Academy, William H. Ferris. Ferris, who received degrees from Yale and Harvard Universities and studied theology at Harvard Divinity School, manifested an evangelical liberalism that, like Faduma's, took a Pan-African orientation. Ferris was among the liberal and progressive black clergy who supported Garvey, and as editor of the official journal of the Universal Negro Improvement Association (UNIA), *The Black World,* he projected his increasingly eclectic theological and ideological convictions before an international audience.[14]

In an article entitled "The New Negro's Attitude Towards Theology," which appeared in the first edition of the *Negro Journal of Religion,* Ferris chronicled the impact of modernity within the African-American community and the resultant evolution of a "New Type of Negro" that rejected many of the old standards of black life and religiosity.[15] This development eventually gave rise to the "New Negro Movement" that emerged with explicitly Pan-African concerns in the postwar years.[16]

Wilson J. Moses noted that the postwar manifestation of the New Negro Movement was nourished by a remarkable group of young black intellectuals who exhibited "a characteristic ambivalence or outright hostility toward the Victorian conceptions of Christianity and civilization to which classical black nationalism [and Pan-Africanism] was sympathetic." By the late 1920s the movement had helped to produce a new secular black leadership that aggressively challenged the older, predominantly clerical leadership and its program of racial uplift.[17] Of this shift, and the broad ideological and religious pluralism characteristic of this new leadership, Hubert Harrison, the militant black nationalist and Pan-Africanist, noted in 1920:

> [T]wenty years ago all Negroes known to the white publicists of America could be classed as conservative on all the great questions on which thinkers differ. In matters of industry, commerce, politics, religion, they could be trusted to take the backward view . . . . Today Negroes differ on all those great questions on which white thinkers differ, and there are Negro radicals of every imaginary stripe—agnostics, atheists, I.W.W.'s, Socialists, Single Taxers and even Bolshevists.[18]

The new perspective that the "talented young men of the New Negro Movement . . . who celebrated their rediscovery of Africa and the African cultural heritage" would bring to bear on the Pan-African movement is reflected in the 1924 essay entitled "Apropos of Africa," by Alaine Locke.[19] Although conceding that African-Americans had a special role to play in the Pan-African movement and in efforts aimed at the uplift and the revitalization of Africa, he noted that this effort must take place in a context significantly different from that of the past.[20] Especially to be rejected and regretted was African-American participation in the traditional missionary enterprise, with its condescending and uninformed efforts at "Christianizing and civilizing" Africa:

> With a more practical and enlightened vision, the question of the redemption of Africa has become with us the question of the regeneration of Africa. We now see that the missionary condescension of the past generations in their attitude toward Africa was a pious and sad mistake. In taking

> it, we have fallen into the snare of enemies and given grievous offense to our [African] brothers.

He noted that if the Pan-African movement was to succeed it was imperative that the African-American "dismiss . . . his missionary condescension, his religious parochialism, and his pride of place." Africa in fact had much to offer her westernized offspring:

> We must realize that in some respects we need what Africa has to give us as much as, or even more than, Africa needs what we in turn have to give her; and that unless we approach Africa in the spirit of the finest reciprocity, our efforts will be ineffectual or harmful. We need to be the first of all Westerners to rid ourselves of the insulting prejudice, the insufferable bias of the attitude of "civilizing Africa,"—for she is not only our mother but in the light of most recent science is beginning to appear as the mother of civilization in general.

He added:

> Above all, it must be recognized that for the present the best channels of co-operative effort lie along economic and educational lines, and that religion and politics, with their inevitable contentiousness and suspicions, are for [far] less promising ways of approach and common effort.[21]

Similar disaffection with the traditional missionary paradigm and movement was also being increasingly expressed within mainstream Pan-African movements. As noted earlier, the growing chasm between Pan-Africanism and the mission movement can be dated at least from the 1900 Pan-African Conference and its preparatory sessions. Although religious and mission leaders played prominent roles in both the conference and its preparatory sessions, prophetic of the future relationship between the Pan-African movement and the missionary enterprise were the words issued at the close of the conference.[22] Its "Address to the Nations of the World," drafted primarily by W. E. B. Du Bois, issued a warning that reverberated with increasing intensity throughout much of twentieth-century Pan-Africanism: "Let not the cloak of Christian missionary enterprise be allowed in the future, as so often in the past, to hide the ruthless economic exploitation and political downfall of less developed nations whose chief fault had been reliance on the plighted faith of the Christian Church."[23]

Despite the continued participation and attendance of major religious and missionary activists, subsequent Pan-African congresses expanded this critique of the mission enterprise's complicity in the exploitation of African peoples and resources.[24] For example, the 1921 Congress was attended by such ecclesiastical leaders as African-American bishops

C. H. Phillips of the Colored Methodist Episcopal Church, John Hurst of the African Methodist Episcopal Zion Church, Archibald J. Carey of the African Methodist Episcopal Church, and West African clergy such as Mark Hayford and E. G. Granville Sutton. It listed among its demands "Education in self-knowledge, [and] in scientific truth" as well as "freedom in . . . religion and customs with the right to be non-conformist and different." It also lamented that "Science, Religion, and Philanthropy" had "been made the slaves of world-commerce and industry."[25] The 1927 Congress continued this critique and called for a more progressive and service-oriented missionary effort: "We believe in missionary effort but in missionary effort for health, morals and education and not for military aggression and sectarian superstitions."[26]

The Garveyite wing of the Pan-African movement also expressed an increasingly critical perspective toward the traditional mission enterprise. This was reflective of Garvey's own progressive theological and missiological tendencies, which were shared by many of his key clerical supporters such as William H. Heard, James Robert Lincoln Diggs, William Henry Moses, William Yancy Bell, and George Alexander McGuire.[27] In fact Garvey's less-than-orthodox theological and religious orientation occasionally resulted in charges that both he and the UNIA were "godless." His conviction in 1923 on charges similar to those unsuccessfully made against Chief Sam and the Back-to-Africa Movement provided one of his West African detractors with the occasion to voice concern over what he perceived to be growing secularism and religious skepticism among would-be black leaders. The difficulties and "failure" of both Garvey and his liberal predecessor, Edward Blyden, were attributed to their less-than–"Absolute Loyalty to Christ" and projected as object lessons to those who would aspire to lead the race:

> But *why* has Garvey failed? This is the question that serious minds will dwell on; and there ought to be some answer to it . . . . And the reason is *right here . . . Garvey was not a Christian. . . .* [B]y no power on earth could Garvey have been rendered quite obsolete if he had been a Christian . . . . Garvey has gone down not because he had enemies about him, but because he was NOT a Christian and that is the point which I desire the Negro people of West Africa specially to think over . . . We Negroes are yearning for the rise of our Race . . . . But this advance cannot take place unless through leaders who are Christians . . . . It is vain for men, whether they combine on their backs the hoods of all three Universities at once, to go talking lightly of Christianity. It is not only vain, it is an act of folly. Such men may shine as Orators but cannot be altogether depended on as leaders of such a great cause as that of race uplift. A leader who is not a Christian in the sense of being an absolute devotee to Jesus who is called Christ, can only go half-way. The race leadership of the late Dr. Blyden left much to be desired. . . . [H]enceforth, the Man whether he be a Jamaican as Garvey is, or a West

> Indian as Dr. Blyden was, who, brandishing a sword, presents himself as Leader of his Race . . . must be searched out, and there must be convincing proof of him that with all of his gifts of leadership he is also a loyal servant of Jesus the Nazarene. We still wait: *the Negro Race still waits* for this individual, this great personality.[28]

These comments, made by a resident of Faduma's home village of Waterloo, attest to the increasing impact of various forms of secularism within Pan-African and Pan–West African movements.[29] It was among the factors accounting for the ineffectiveness and eventual collapse of the church-centered National Congress of British West Africa. Indeed, by 1930 the Congress was being overshadowed by more "dynamic" and increasingly secular-oriented organizations.[30]

The demise and declining fortunes of the National Congress of British West Africa as well as the Du Boisian and Garveyite wings of the Pan-African movement inspired the formation of a host of smaller Pan-African and Pan-West African organizations. While directly linked to and influenced by the older Pan-African tradition, they did not share to the same extent its traditional evangelical allegiance and heritage. Most of these organizations, such as the West African Youth League and the West African Student Union, were increasingly influenced by the inroads being made within the Pan-African movement by Marxist currents of thought.[31] These currents were borne by committed Marxists and post-Marxists such as the Sierra Leone–born labor activist, Issac Theophilus Akunna Wallace-Johnson and the Caribbean-born Pan-African theorist, George Padmore.[32]

Wallace-Johnson's evolution from lay preacher to Marxist activist and Pan-Africanist is illustrative of the secular dynamic within twentieth century Pan-Africanism. Born of "poor Creole parents" in Wilberforce Village in 1895, Wallace-Johnson received a traditional mission education at the CMS Grammar School and the United Methodist Collegiate School.[33] After serving with British forces in World War I, his mission school education was supplemented by travel as a merchant marine and formal study in Britain. He was at one point a popular lay preacher and between 1928 and 1931 served as secretary of the Koppeng African Universal Church Society in Lagos.[34] This affiliation with one of the growing number of "Ethiopian"- oriented West African ecclesiastical organizations suggests that Wallace-Johnson had moved some distance from traditional missionary Christianity.[35] In explanation, Langley suggests that Wallace-Johnson had begun "to equate European Christianity with colonial subjection."[36] Subsequently, both European Christianity and the mission enterprise became targets of his increasingly radical anticolonial critique.

The gulf between Wallace-Johnson's early mission orientation and his evolving Pan-African ideology was further widened in 1932 when he entered the People's University of Moscow under the sponsorship of the Communist International.[37] After a brief period of trade union organization in Nigeria aimed at building "a broad working-class movement on the principles of the revolutionary class struggle," he settled in the Gold Coast.[38] There he established the West African Youth League (WAYL), which became "a kind of prototype for a Pan-West African political party" and "in the course of the 1930s an inveterate proponent of the most radical, uncompromising variety of African nationalism."[39] It helped to shape and harness the religious and ideological orientation and energies of a new generation of West African youth who did not share the values and orientation of their elders.[40]

In the mid-1930s the evangelical roots of Pan-Africanism and Pan-West African nationalism were further undermined by the widespread loss of confidence in Western Christendom in the wake of the Italo-Ethiopian crisis.[41] The increasingly cynical and critical posture regarding Christianity and the "Christian" West that the crisis provoked was articulated in an article written in 1936 by Wallace-Johnson. Entitled "Has the African a God?" it charged Christian Europe with deceit and hypocrisy and directly implicated Christianity and the Christian mission enterprise in Africa's continued subjugation and exploitation. In tone and language that elicited a charge of sedition from the colonial government, Wallace-Johnson proclaimed:

> [T]he European has a god in whom he believes and whom he is representing in his churches all over Africa. He believes in the god whose name is spelt Deceit. He believes in the god whose law is "Ye strong, you must weaken the weak. Ye 'civilized' Europeans, you must 'civilize' the 'barbarous' Africans with machine guns. Ye Christian Europeans, you must 'Christianise' the pagan Africans with bombs, poison gases, etc.!"[42]

This article and its sentiments had a significant impact upon a younger generation of emerging Pan-African leaders such as Kwame Nkrumah. Indeed, Nkrumah described it as "the first warning puff of smoke that a fire had been lit, a fire that would prove impossible to extinguish."[43]

Kwame Nkrumah, with whom much of postwar Pan-Africanism would be identified, also illustrated the shift among the younger generation of Pan-African activists away from the older tradition of evangelical Pan-Africanism to a more secular Pan-African ideology. Born in the Gold Coast, Nkrumah was baptized into the Roman Catholic Church and received his primary education at mission schools.[44] Despite a religious heterodoxy that manifested itself during his mission school days, Nkrumah nevertheless entertained thoughts of entering the Christian ministry.[45] After coming to the United States in 1935, he obtained a Bachelor of Theology degree and preached in a number of African-American churches.[46] His early linkage of evangelical theology and Pan-African ideology is reflected in his use of the "Ethiopian Prophesy" as the text of an oration delivered upon his graduation with honors from the theological department of Lincoln University in 1942.[47] However, Nkrumah's theology and perception of religion were increasingly at odds with Christian orthodoxy. One factor in this transition was his study of the history of religion (comparative religion) at Lincoln University. This study helped foster a critical appreciation of both Christianity and African traditional religions, which was illustrated in several papers that he wrote during his theological studies at Lincoln University.[48]

Nkrumah's increasingly nontraditional theological orientation and his defense of African traditional religion and culture eventually brought him into theological controversy with Dr. George Johnson, professor of theology and philosophy at Lincoln. This controversy had its roots in Nkrumah's participation as President of the African Students Association in an African memorial service at the grave site of the famous Gold Coast educator and missionary statesman, Dr. Kwegyir Aggrey.[49] The ceremony, which included the pouring of libations and an appeal to the ancestors, provoked inquiry from Dr. Johnson regarding the propriety of Nkrumah's participation in what he perceived to be "pagan" rites.[50] Nkrumah's reply illustrated his increasingly critical perspective of traditional Christianity and his heightened appreciation of African beliefs and culture. While he affirmed his commitment to the "best in Christianity" he also warned that he would not ignore its less savory aspects: "The burden of my life is to live in such a way that I may become a living symbol of all that is best in Christianity and in the laws, customs and beliefs of my people. I am a Christian and will ever remain so but never a blind Christian."[51]

Nkrumah's studies and experiences in the United States, coupled with his growing commitment to the struggle for Africa's independence, fostered a change both in perspective and in vocation. This transition was chronicled in verse by his biographer:

> In America, God's own country,
> Theology had Nkrumah studied:
> The Bible, the Book of books
> Puzzled him as he read—
> "To him that hath shall be given;
> To him that hath not, shall be taken away
> Even that which he hath."
> Then took he one glance at Chicago—
> Blacks segregated and lynched, he saw;
> If this is Christianity, Nkrumah exclaimed,
> Then a layman not a parson I'll be.
> Philosophy, theology, economics,

Political science and experience
In plenitude and variety.
With these he prepared
For the battle of Freedom.[52]

It was this perspective that informed Nkrumah's leadership role in Pan-African activities in the years leading up to the Manchester Conference of 1945.[53]

By the late 1930s evangelical Christianity was rapidly becoming a spent force and an outmoded ideology within an increasingly radicalized and secularized Pan-Africanism.[54] The League of Coloured Peoples, established in 1931 by the Jamaican-born evangelical activist, Dr. Harold Arundel Moody, represented the major exception and resistance to this trend.

Raised in the Jamaican tradition of British Congregationalism, Moody had been active since his youth in evangelical associations such as the Christian Endeavour Movement. In 1904, at the age of 22, he traveled to London to study for a medical degree at Faduma's alma mater, the University of London. There he earned the Doctorate of Medicine in 1919. However, neither British racism nor his vocational responsibilities suppressed his evangelical disposition, and he assumed leadership roles in a host of British evangelical organizations.[55]

Although dedicated to the uplift of the black race, Moody was disturbed by the attitudes and goals of the more radical black associations then taking shape. He was especially concerned with the increasing animosity toward whites and religious skepticism fueled by the influx of modernistic and Marxist concepts. Thus with the founding of the League of Colored People, Moody sought to harness the philanthropic heritage, zeal, and cooperative brotherhood of an earlier tradition of evangelical Protestantism and Pan-Africanism.[56] Through Moody, who remained President until his death in 1947, evangelical tenets and concerns decisively informed the goals and methods of the League.[57]

However, Moody's insistence that the League be an extension of his evangelical faith occasioned serious disagreements with members who sought a more militant posture for the League. As noted by David Vaughan:

> Many of his young colleagues had been nurtured in the environment and philosophy of pragmatism and materialism. They were greatly attracted by the experiments of Russian Communism and its Marxian economic doctrines. Interested as Moody was in all that was happening in Russia and especially its freedom from racial distinctions, the foundation of all things for him was the Christian religion and the true realities were spiritual and not material. He made no apologies for his faith and believed that the goals of the League could and would be attained only by the Christian way.[58]

Eventually, Moody's quasi-clerical style and evangelical temperament, coupled with the support he enjoyed among conservative circles, resulted in charges by radicals such as Padmore that he was "collaborating with the British Colonial Office to stifle the growing nationalism of African students."[59] Although a number of factors gradually forced the League into a less conservative posture, throughout Moody's lifetime it never abandoned his basic evangelical orientation.[60]

It is difficult to assess the extent to which the aged Faduma was fully abreast of the major developments within Pan-Africanism during the final decades of his life.[61] After retiring as assistant principal of Lincoln Academy in 1934, he served for eight years as Professor and "Acting Dean" at Virginia Theological Seminary and College in Lynchburg, Virginia.[62] At this traditional center of black Baptist theological, missiological, and ideological thought, Faduma continued to serve as a mediator of evangelical liberalism and Pan-Africanism to a later generation of African and African-American students. There he also continued to advance his Pan-African pedagogy, teaching "Negro History in Africa" as well as more traditional subjects such as Latin, Greek, and French.[63]

Faduma's affiliation with this black Baptist institution, which since its inception nurtured an aggressive race consciousness and evangelical Pan-Africanism, reemphasized symbolically and practically his linkage with the older tradition of evangelical Pan-Africanism and the more contemporary emphasis of the Garvey movement.[64] Among its alumni were such figures as John Chilembwe, the African Baptist radical and leader of the Nyasaland revolt of 1915, and a number of progressive African-American clergymen who in addition to being leaders or supporters of the Garvey movement also played prominent roles in African-American mission efforts.[65]

Perhaps Faduma's most significant contribution to the Pan-African and missiological cause during this period were his efforts to project an accurate and hence more positive and balanced portrayal of African life and customs to the mission-oriented segment of the African-American community. His concern "to lift the veil which enshrouds the continent" was made explicit in a two-part article entitled "Africa the Unknown," published in 1939 in the *Mission Herald* of the National Baptist Convention.[66] In this article Faduma critiqued the misinformed "caricatures" of Africa and her inhabitants that "always leave the impression on onlookers that they are savages." Such inaccuracies, he noted, perpetuated the unacceptable situation whereby many "see Africans in a glass darkly and refuse to see them face to face."[67]

In the fall of 1940, Faduma presented the readers of the *Mission Herald* with a much more comprehensive defense of his "African Background."[68] In autobiographical format he presented the theological, missiological, and ideological tenets that had guided his life and work. He also confessed that the source and wellspring of his long spiritual, intellectual, and physical odyssey was at once both intensely personal and yet embracing of the wider racial and human dilemma: it was the quest for identity and legitimation.

Faduma, the aged evangelical liberal, drew again upon the tenets of liberalism and its corollary disciplines to defend his African cultural and religious heritage and to set forth and affirm a cosmology and soteriology that did not negate his parents. Although they had been "born pagans," Faduma insisted that this, contrary to western misconceptions, did not mean that they did not "believe in God or have no knowledge of God." "I know of no African peoples," he asserted, "who do not believe in God." He also rejected the notion that his Yoruba ancestors were "barbarians and savages" and that they had originated "from a savage country." He stated:

> From time immemorial they were good farmers, traders, cloth manufacturers, and skilled in all kinds of handicrafts. They had and still have settled governments of their own, with a democratic as well as monarchical basis. Primitive though they were, yet they developed a morality and civilization which have stood the test of many years.[69]

In keeping with the liberal contention that non-Christian religions were preparatory to Christianity (a contention that orthodox and neo-orthodox missiology vigorously challenged), Faduma asserted that it was "under such a system" that his parents were "nurtured and prepared for the Christian religion."[70] Moreover, upon conversion to Christianity they "did not cast aside those solid qualities and virtues which they had in paganism, qualities which in Christianity were and are still needed, and not condemned." Drawing on Scripture, liberal theology, and his comparative studies of religion, he warned:

> [I]t is a serious blunder to think that Christianity has nothing to do with pagan virtues. Jesus came not to destroy but to fulfill. Whatever was good in the world He magnified and purified. All good gifts, all excellent qualities in paganism came from Him and are His. All glimpses of truth, all rays of light found in paganism, sprang from Him who is Truth, Life and Light. They all point to Him and are a revelation of Him. The Ten Commandments did not begin with the Christian religion, nor with the old religion of the Hebrews. Long before Moses delivered them to his people on two tablets of stone from Mount Horeb amid thundering and lightening, Hammurabi of Babylon had them among his people, and they were known in the court of Pharaoh in Egypt, north of Africa, where Moses had his schooling. The Hebrew account of Creation did not originate with Moses but from old pagan peoples, and was delivered to the world as a purified myth.[71]

Thus he insisted, "No foreign missionary introduces God to the African. What he does is to interpret God to him."

Rather than dismissing his "pagan inheritance," the eighty-three-year-old liberal humbly reasserted his debt to it:

> I owe much in my foundation to my pagan inheritance of qualities which are needed and exalted in Christianity. For these things I thank God. Of what can I boast? There are those who trace the present glory of the Anglo-Saxon to their ancestors. They boast of their inheritance of wealth, culture, learning, dominant power in the world. I have inherited none of these except good breeding and good manners, which are some of the characteristics of culture, even among primitive Africans. Such an inheritance of African culture, mingled with good blood in my veins, I am conscious of and yet dare not boast of having.[72]

During the waning years of his life, which were spent in High Point, North Carolina, with his wife of almost fifty years, Faduma's dogged evangelical liberalism was further assaulted by the brutalities of World War II and the continued intransigence of Southern racism.[73] In a 1943 article entitled "Some of My Experiences in the Southland," Faduma recalled his experiences with racism during the course of his thirty-nine-year ministry in the South, which he found to be "a land of conundrums."[74] He recounted the emergence and impact of "Jim Crow" in transportation, politics, education, and religion:

> When I first entered North Carolina in 1895 as a Christian Missionary there were no "Jim Crow" cars in it. It was not long before they were introduced . . . . Negro education was separate from that given to whites and was of an inferior character. The education of a superior type was conducted by Northern Missionary Societies whose white teachers were ostracized by Southern whites and won the sobriquet of 'Nigger teachers and preachers.' Negro Churches and White Churches were kept apart. Self-respect caused the former to have their own Churches with poorly trained leaders, interpreting the teachings of Jesus as best they could with a revelation that was excessively emotional . . . . The White Church filled with superiority complex, held itself aloof from the Negro Church. Its Christianity was a mixture of Christ and Phariseeism, a peculiar syncretism. The conception of the gospel that ignored the social, economic, and political advancement of the Negro was dominant.

Faduma was painfully concerned about the devastating impact that these practices continued to have in the realm of professional education for Southern blacks. He noted:

> It would seem that the average Negro mentality was and still is considered higher than that of the white, from the fact that to train the Negro, less money was and is required for his physical and mental development . . . . There is a philosophy handed down to us by Jesus, the greatest teacher, in the following words: "To whom much is given, of him shall much be re-

> quired." But the Southern States have by their mental twist stated in deeds and through legislation, "To whom less is given, of him shall much be required." This strange philosophy has given to the Southern white population schools of engineering, law, medicine, and pharmacy, but none to the Negro, and is still unwilling and reluctant to admit Negroes to them.[75]

He concluded with the observation that though in recent years there appeared to be signs of improved opportunities for blacks, much of this change was coming "crabwise."[76]

It was from High Point that Faduma issued the final summaries of his life's work. Ironically these summaries were requested by his alma mater and the source of his formal nurture in theological liberalism, Yale Divinity School. When the Divinity School mailed Faduma an alumni information form in 1944, he replied in an aged script that he was a "Retired Missionary" who had spent a total of "57" years at various mission posts and institutions in the United States and Sierra Leone.[77] He also included a listing of fifty of his "literary contributions," the typescript of his autobiographical sketch entitled "My Nigerian African Background," and a copy of his 1943 article, "Some of My Experiences in the Southland."[78]

Apparently intrigued by the aged African liberal, Dean Luther Allan Weigle of the Divinity School, who, like Faduma, had been decisively influenced by evangelical liberalism, requested additional information and Faduma's life story.[79] On May 10, 1945, Faduma, delayed in his response on account of illness, replied in a letter that rehearsed his missionary labors and sacrifices: "My life as a missionary has been very much crowded. I have spent the little money I have made in helping others. This has given me much joy."[80] He also recounted his years as a student at the Divinity School, explicitly recalling his old instructors, "Dean Day, Professors Fisher, Harris, Brastow, Stevens, Curtis, [and] Porter," all of whom, Faduma asserted, "left behind them and in my life memories which are indelible."[81]

On May 22, 1945, Dean Weigle responded with a letter that expressed the Divinity School's pride in Faduma's accomplishments: "I congratulate you heartily upon the long and effective service that you have rendered in the field of Christian missions and Christian education, and I assure you that we of the faculty of your old school take pride in what you have accomplished."[82]

Less than a year later, on January 25, 1946, Faduma died.[83] He was buried at High Point, North Carolina, in the adopted soil he had come to call home on this side of the Atlantic.[84] In both life and death he symbolized the Pan-African dialectic and paradox.

It is perhaps ironic that the fifth and in many ways the most important of the Pan-African Congresses, the Manchester Congress, was held on the eve of Faduma's death.[85] The status of the explicitly Christian-rooted

Pan-African vision that Faduma inherited, nurtured, and attempted to adapt, by way of liberal theology, was reflected in its lack of significant representation among the delegates of the Congress. The vast gulf that existed between the old Pan-African tradition, rooted in the evangelical missionary perspective, and the new secular-rooted Pan-African vision and program is noted by Geiss:

> Among the "historical" elements that were almost completely absent were the Christian missions or any of the African or Afro-American churches. It may be assumed that at least all the Africans present had been through mission schools—or at least through schools that had been fashioned or originally founded by the missions. But the missionary element lay so far back that it was only feebly represented in Manchester. The single minister present came—as was historically justified—from Sierra Leone, but he was a delegate of a modern organization, the teachers union . . . . It is equally characteristic of the situation at this time that, except for this delegate, Nkrumah was the only man present who had studied theology (even if in a very rudimentary way) and had also preached.[86]

Included among the resolutions and observations made by the Congress was the charge that "organized Christianity in West Africa is identified with the political and economic exploitation of the West African peoples by alien powers."[87] It is also significant that the only form of Christianity and mission activity endorsed by the Congress was of a decidedly social orientation.[88]

No eulogies have been found of Faduma, through whom so many of the religious, intellectual, and ideological currents of the era had converged and been creatively reshaped in defense of both his African heritage and his Christian faith. Nevertheless, the final statement made by Faduma in his autobiographical sketch serves as a most appropriate epitaph. Faduma, the aged liberal, evangelical Pan-Africanist, simply confessed:

> Like a hound, I am in pursuit of truth, retired but not tired, nor yet ready to depart, but still on the war path of duty. For me to live is Christ, and to die is gain. Again I say, retired, but not tired.[89]

NOTES

1. See especially Faduma's autobiographical sketch entitled, "An African Background," and "Africa the Unknown," *Mission Herald* 43 (Nov./Dec., 1939): 20, and *Mission Herald* 44 (Jan./Feb. 1940):16–17. This is also supported by the comments of Samuel Parham made during an interview in March 1981. Parham was a res-

ident of High Point, North Carolina, and knew Faduma during his final decade.

2. Fosdick, "Beyond Modernism," *Christian Century* 52 (Dec. 1935): 1549–1552. See the series of thirty-four articles published under the title, "How My Mind Has Changed in This Decade," in *Christian Century* 56 (18 Jan. -Sept. 20, 1939), and Hutchison's assessment of this series in *The Modernist Impulse,* pp. 304–305.
3. Robert L. Calhoun, "A Liberal Bandaged but Unbowed," *Christian Century* 56 (May 3, 1939): 701–704. Calhoun "was severely buffeted in his encounter with neo-orthodoxy, but never surrendered the hard core of theological liberalism." Smith, Handy, and Loetscher, *American Christianity,* vol. 2. p. 448. See also the position of John C. Bennett, who proclaimed himself "A Changed Liberal—But Still a Liberal," *Christian Century* 56 (Feb. 1939): 179–181.
4. Laymen's Foreign Missions Inquiry, Commission of Appraisal, *Rethinking Missions: A Laymen's Enquiry After One Hundred Years* (New York: Harper, 1932); R. Pierce Beaver, "North American Thought," pp. 7–10. The report reflected the theological orientation of its author, the Harvard philosopher and modernist, Dr. William Ernest Hocking. Cauthen classifies Hocking as an adherent of "metaphysical or rationalistic modernism." Cauthen, *Impact,* p. 36.
5. Varg, *Missionaries, Chinese, and Diplomats,* pp. 169–172; Robert E. Speer, "*Rethinking Missions" Examined* (New York: Fleming H. Revell Co., 1933); Beaver, "North American Thought," p. 7; and Forman, "History of Foreign Mission Theory," pp. 101–103.
6. On the impact of Karl Barth and the postwar impact of European theology in the United States, see Ahlstrom, *Theology in America,* pp. 77–82; Hordern, *Layman's Guide,* pp. 130–149.
7. On the rise of neo-orthodoxy within the United States, see Ahlstrom, *Theology in America,* pp. 77–84. Hordern, *Layman's Guide,* pp. 111–129; Hutchison, *Modernist Impulse,* pp. 288–310.
8. Smith, *Changing Conceptions of Original Sin,* pp. 201–229; Reinhold Niebuhr, *Moral Man and Immoral Society* (New York: Charles Scribner's Sons, 1932). On the neo-orthodox critique of liberalism's "captivity to the world" see H. Richard Niebuhr, Wilhelm Pauck, and Francis P. Miller, *The Church Against the World* (Chicago: Willett, Clarke and Co., 1935). For a broader perspective on neo-orthodoxy and the issues and concerns that contoured it, see Donald B. Meyer, *The Protestant Search for Political Realism, 1919–1941* (Berkeley and Los Angeles: University of California Press, 1960).
9. Hendrick Kraemer, *The Christian Message in a Non-Christian World* (London: International Missionary Council, 1938). Gerald H. Anderson suggests that this work was "largely a Barthian-based

reaction to the position represented in *Re-Thinking Missions*." Gerald H. Anderson, "Kraemer and After: A Survey Review Article," Studies in Mission Theology, n.p., n.d., p. 355. Kraemer was Professor of History of Religion at the University of Leiden. Hedlund, *Roots of the Great Debate,* pp. 60–67.

10. Cady, "Liberal Attitude toward Other Religions," pp. 147–148. See Reinhold Niebuhr's explicit rejection of the missiological tenets of E. Stanley Jones, in Reinhold Niebuhr, *An Interpretation of Christian Ethics* (New York: Charles Scribner's Sons, 1935), pp. 180–181. The impact of Kraemer's theology and missiology is illustrated by the Balinese Church. Of this church, founded by Kraemer, Stephen Neill observed "in all its inner and outward life the Balinese Church is more like the Dutch Reformed Church than the Dutch Reformed Church is like itself. It manifests hardly a trace of the wonderful art and culture of that most beautiful island." Neill, *History of Christian Missions,* p. 535.
11. No evidence has been found linking Faduma to these predominantly Northern-based innovations. However, they provide the broader context for Faduma's activities and writings during this era. The founding of the Fraternal Council was additional testimony to the distinctive way in which black liberals and progressives appropriated the tenets of liberalism and the social gospel in their efforts to improve the condition and status of the race. The liberal and social gospel inclinations and proclivities of the Fraternal Council were evident in its expressed concern to provide the Black Church "with united voice on any question that concerns the moral, social, economic, or political, industrial or spiritual welfare of the race as a whole." The Council also stressed racial unity and ecumenical cooperation rather than a divisive denominationalism. On the Fraternal Council, see Ransom, *Pilgrimage*, pp. 96–300; David Wills, "Reverdy Ransom: The Making of an A.M.E. Bishop;" Burkett and Newman, eds., *Black Apostles,* pp. 181–212; Reverdy C. Ransom, "Why a Federation of Negro Denominations in the United States?," *Negro Journal of Religion* (Feb. 1935): 5; and "Thus we Go," *Negro Journal of Religion* 1 (Feb. 1935): 15. The *Negro Journal of Religion,* which billed itself as "An Interdenominational Review," reflected in its format and contents the basic perspective, concerns, and goals of the Fraternal Council. Its editor, Lendell Charles Ridley, an A.M.E. minister and head of the Department of Philosophy at Wilberforce University, noted in the founding issue that the *Journal* represented an effort to meet the religious needs of the race: "It is for all the race, regardless of denomination. It comes to serve churchmen and non-churchmen. As a cross-section of religious faith it should help the most rabid sects to become more tolerant of

each other. As a general source of information on Negro religion it should be of service to the whole of Negro life. As an outlet for laymen and ministers from whose pen have come unpublished ethical and religious gems it should be a welcome door. It finally should be an encouragement to trained and gifted race scholars to write on the weightier, sociological, religious and metaphysical problems." Daniel, *Black Journals of the United States,* pp. 279–281; "Editorial," *Negro Journal of Religion* 1 (Feb. 1935): 3. A review of existing copies of the *Journal* reveals an impressive list of contributors commenting on a broad range of theological, social, racial, political and missiological issues. Many of the articles reflect a predominantly progressive (if not liberal) evangelical, theological, and missiological perspective. See, for example, Dr. R. R. Wright, Jr., "The Challenge to the Negro Church," *Negro Journal of Religion* 2 (Feb. 1936): 5; Arthur Evans, Jr., "Personalism," 2 (Feb. 1936): 6. In an editorial section entitled, "A World View of Religion," the editor attempted to keep readers informed of the issues involved in the current theological and missiological controversies via articles such as "Modernism Destroys Evangelism," *Negro Journal of Religion* 1 (Nov. 1935):10. The second issue of the *Journal* contained a sympathetic analysis of "Barthianism" and its "theology of crisis." The author, Dr. Charles L. Hill, was Dean of Turner Theological Seminary. Dr. Charles L. Hill, "The Religious Crisis of the Present," *Negro Journal of Religion 1* (Mar. 1935): 5, 6, 13. Most contributors were already members of the liberal-oriented Federal Council of Churches. On the origin and history of the Federal Council, see Elias B. Sanford, *Origin and History of the Federal Council of the Churches of Christ in America* (Hartford, 1916); John A. Hutchison, *We Are Not Divided: A Critical and Historical Study of the Federal Council of the Churches of Christ in America* (New York: Round Table Press, 1941); Smith, Handy and Loetscher, *American Christianity,* vol. 2, pp. 394–397.

12. See Arthur Evans, Jr., "College Students' Attitude toward Religion," *Negro Journal of Religion* 1 (Feb. 1935): 7, and "Address to the Country," *Negro Journal of Religion* 2 (Mar. 1936): 5.
13. "Message to the Churches and to the Public from the Fraternal Council of Negro Churches," Ransom, *Pilgrimage,* pp. 297–300.
14. Ferris, who grew up in New Haven and graduated from Yale University in 1895, may have become acquainted with Faduma during Faduma's years at Yale (1891–95). See Ferris on Faduma in *The African Abroad,* vol. 2, 570. After briefly pasturing a Congregational Church in Wilmington, North Carolina, Ferris became a member of the African Methodist Episcopal Zion Church and later the A.M.E. Church. Burkette noted that the juxtaposition of God and

Darwin was frequently made in Ferris's speeches and editorials. He became one of the chief philosopher-theologians of the UNIA during the years 1919–1923, and regularly expounded on such weighty issues as the "Viewpoint of Science and Religion," "What is Religion" or "The Black Man's Philosophy." In his major work, the two-volume treatise entitled, *The African Abroad,* Ferris confessed his faith in a God "who manifests himself in the laws of reason." Ferris, *The African Abroad,* vol., p. 416. See also Moses, *Golden Age,* pp. 212–213, for a critical evaluation of Ferris and his works.

15. William H. Ferris, "The New Negro's Attitude towards Theology," *Negro Journal of Religion* 1 (July ,1935): 6, 12.
16. On the international linkages and significance of the "New Negro Movement" see Geiss, *Pan-African Movement,* p. 315. Of special importance was its relationship with similar stirrings of "literary Pan-Africanism" in the areas and the subsequent rise of the Negritude movement.
17. Moses suggests that "Urbanization had produced a new secular leadership class no longer dependent upon the church pulpit for their livelihood, and no longer dependent upon the church-supported college." Moses, *Golden Age,* p. 249.
18. Hubert Harrison, *When Africa Awakes: The "Inside Story" of the Stirrings and Strivings of the New Negro in the Western World* (New York: Porro Press, 1920), p. 76. Quoted in Moses, *Golden Age,* p. 248. The predominantly cultural aspects of the movement were fueled by a prolific group of literary figures popularly identified with the Harlem Renaissance. They include Jean Toomer, Sterling Brown, Claude McKay, Countee Cullen, Robert Hayden, and Langston Hughes. Adelaide Cromwell Hill and Martin Kilson, eds., *Apropos of Africa: Afro-American Leaders and the Romance of Africa* (New York: Doubleday and Co., 1971), pp. 411–418.
19. Alaine Locke, "Apropos of Africa," in Hill and Kilson, *Apropos of Africa,* pp. 350–357. See also Locke's fuller articulation of the concerns and significance of the New Negro Movement in his book entitled *The New Negro* (New York, 1925). Educated at Howard and Oxford Universities and the University of Berlin, Locke was the first African-American to earn a doctorate in philosophy. Geiss, *Pan-African Movement,* p. 315. See also Jeffrey Conrad Stewart, *A Biography of Alaine Locke: Philosopher of the Harlem Renaissance, 1886–1930* (Ann Arbor: University Microfilms International, 1981).
20. Locke contended that "the American Negro must reach out toward his rightful share in the solution of African problems and the development of Africa's resources" because "as the physical composite of eighty-five percent at least of the African stocks, the American

Negro is in a real sense the true Pan-African." He also argued that "if the Negro is interested in Africa, he should be interested in the whole of Africa. If he is to link himself up with his past and his kin, he must link himself up with all of the African peoples." Locke, "Apropos," p. 412.

21. Ibid., p. 413.
22. See Owen Charles Mathurin, *Henry Sylvester Williams and the Origins of the Pan-African Movement, 1869–1911* (Westport, Conn., and London: Greenwood Press, 1976), pp. 60–82.
23. "Address to the Nations of the World," quoted in Langley, *Pan-Africanism and Nationalism,* pp. 28–29. For the full text of this address, see Walters, *My Life and Work,* pp. 257–260.
24. See "Pan-African Manifestos and Resolutions, 1900–1969;" Langley, *Ideologies of Liberation,* pp. 738–761.
25. See especially, "The London Manifesto," ibid., pp. 748–752.
26. This resolution reflected a perspective on missions not unlike that which would be dominant the following year at the World Missionary Conference in Jerusalem. The 1923 congress was addressed by H. G. Wells, an advocate of secular humanism and socialism. See "The Pan-African Congresses," *Crisis* (Oct. 1927): 263–264; Padmore, *Pan-Africanism or Communism,* pp. 117, 121.
27. On Garvey's progressive and perhaps liberal theological and missiological convictions, see Martin, *Race First,* especially pp. 67–88. See also Marcus Garvey, *Philosophy and Opinions of Marcus Garvey, or Africa for the Africans,* ed. Amy Jacques-Garvey, (1923, 1925; reprint, New York: Atheneum 1974).
28. F. H. Johnson, "Marcus Garvey and the Negro Race," *Sierra Leone Weekly News,* 25 Aug. 1923.
29. Faduma as an active member of the Waterloo Descendants Association was probably an acquaintance of Johnson. See "Waterloo Descendants Association," *Sierra Leone Weekly News,* 14 July 1923.
30. On this trend, see Bartels, *Roots of Ghana Nationalism,* pp. 160–161. On the West African Student Union founded in 1925 by West African students studying in Britain, see Esedebe, *Pan-Africanism,* pp. 95–100, 181–184.
31. Geiss noted, "For Pan-Africans Communism was from the first an uncertain ally . . . . Moreover the atheistic views propagated by the communists disturbed members of the African elite who had been educated in Christian missionary schools, especially in British West Africa. For these reasons even at the height of its influence . . . Communism was no more than a transitional phenomenon . . . [It] filled the gap in the development of Pan-Africanism between 1927 and 1934." Yet the influence of Marxist ideas and concepts became so pervasive that even the more conservative Pan-African groups such

as the League of Coloured Peoples "were unable completely to escape these influences." Geiss, *Pan-African Movement,* p. 339. Owing in part to a change of policy in 1934, Communism lost its tenuous base in Pan-Africanism. Most communists or "fellow travelers" of African descent left the movement to become active as independents within the Pan-African movement. They viewed "Pan-Africanism as an independent political expression of Negro aspirations for complete national independence from white domination—capitalist or communist." Padmore, *Pan-Africanism or Communism,* p.148.

32. Spitzer, *Creoles,* pp. 181–221; Langley, *Pan-Africanism and Nationalism,* p. 334; Thomas Wilson, *Russia and Black Africa before World War II* (New York & London: Holmes & Meier, 1974), pp. 243–244, 247. On the influential role of George Padmore, the disillusioned Marxist, see Wilson, *Russia,* pp. 133, 146, 181–188, 196–197, 280–290; Esedebe, *Pan-Africanism,* pp. 103–104, 135, 162, 167, 172, 180–182, 185, 202; Kwame Nkrumah, *Ghana: The Autobiography of Kwame Nkrumah* (New York: International Publishers, 1957), pp. 49, 52; George Padmore, *Pan-Africanism or Communism? The Coming Struggle for Africa* (New York: Roy Publishers, 1956); and J. R. Hooker, *Black Revolutionary: George Padmore's Path from Communism to Pan-Africanism* (New York: Praeger, 1967).
33. Spitzer, *Creoles,* p. 181.
34. Langley, *Pan-Africanism and Nationalism,* p. 334.
35. On the history of this development in West Africa, see Webster, *African Churches among the Yoruba.*
36. Langley, *Pan-Africanism and Nationalism,* p. 334.
37. Wilson, *Russia and Black Africa,* p. 243.
38. Ibid., p. 244.
39. Ibid., p. 247.
40. On the impact of Wallace-Johnson and the Sierra Leone branch of the WAYL on Sierra Leone's traditional Creole leadership after his return in 1938, see Spitzer, *Creoles,* pp. 182–221.
41. On the impact of the Italian invasion of Ethiopia and the refusal of Western Christian nations to aid Ethiopia, see S. K. B. Asante, *Pan-African Protest: West Africa and the Italo-Ethiopian Crisis, 1934–1941* (London: Longman Group, 1977). On the impact of the Italo-Ethiopian crisis on the African-American community, see Robert G. Weisbord, *Ebony Kinship,* pp. 89–114. See also "Mussolini vs. Christianity," *Negro Journal of Religion* 1 (Aug. 1935).
42. This article was published in the *African Morning Post* on 15 May 1936. See Nkrumah, *Ghana,* pp. 22–23. In 1936 Wallace-Johnson also authored "Lessons of Italo-Ethiopian War Clearly Tabled," in

which he again noted Christianity's complicity in the brutalization of Africans: "The white man—yea the European in this instance—has proved that Christianity and barbarism are identical. He has proved that European Christian ethics are nothing but a farce and that after all, the sum total of the Christian faith and doctrine is Blessed are the strong for they shall weaken the weak." Wallace-Johnson, "Lessons of Italo-Ethiopian War Clearly Tabled," *Gold Coast Spectator,* (16 May 1936): 838, 864. Quoted in Langley, *Pan-Africanism and Nationalism,* p. 335.

43. Nkrumah, *Ghana,* p. 23. See Bankole Timothy, *Kwame Nkrumah: His Rise to Power* (London: Allen & Unwin, 1955), pp. 43–44.
44. Nkrumah, *Ghana.,* pp. 1–13.
45. Ibid., pp. 11–47; Bankole Timothy, *Kwame Nkrumah: His Rise to Power,* pp. 20–35.
46. Nkrumah, *Ghana,* p. 32. In 1939 Nkrumah graduated from Lincoln with a Bachelor of Arts degree with a major in sociology and economics. In 1942 he received his Bachelor of Theology degree from Lincoln and in 1943 was awarded the Master of Arts degree from the University of Pennsylvania in preparation for the doctorate in philosophy. After departing New York for London in May 1945, he attended lectures at the London School of Economics and read Philosophy at University College. Nkrumah, *Ghana,* pp. 31–33, 48–51.
47. Ibid.
48. Of special significance was a paper entitled "The History of Religion in a Critique of West African Fetishism." Geiss, *Pan-Africanism,* p. 510.
49. Nkrumah credits Aggrey, who served as assistant vice-principal at Achimota, as being the source of his nationalist consciousness and the inspiration for his study in the United States. Nkrumah, *Ghana,* p. 32 On the remarkable career of Aggrey see Edwin W. Smith, *Aggrey of Africa: A Study in Black and White* (New York: Doubleday, Doran & Co., 1929). There is no evidence that Faduma attended this service. However, Mrs. Abna Aggrey Lancaster, daughter of Aggrey, reported that Faduma was a friend of her father's and visited their home in Salisbury. Telephone interview with Mrs. Abna Aggrey Lancaster, 18 Jan. 1984.
50. On this service held on November 26, 1942, see Geiss, *Pan-Africanism,* p. 371, and Timothy, *Nkrumah,* p. 32.
51. Timothy, *Nkrumah,* p. 32.
52. Ibid., pp. 43–44.
53. Nkrumah later described his religious and ideological transition: "As I grew older. . . the strict discipline of Roman Catholicism stifled me. It was not that I became any less religious but rather that I sought freedom in the worship and communion with my God, for

my God is a very personal God and can only be reached direct. . . . To-day I am a non-denominational Christian and a Marxist socialist and I have not found any contradiction between the two." Nkrumah, *Ghana,* pp. 11–12.

54. Ayandele, *Impact,* p. 237.
55. In 1921 Moody became the first black Chairman of the Colonial Missionary Society, in 1931 President of the Christian Endeavour Federation, in 1936 President of the Christian Endeavour Union of Great Britain and Ireland, and in 1943 Chairman of the Board of Directors of the London Missionary Society. See the uncritical and hagiographic biography of Moody by David A. Vaughan, *Negro Victory: The Life Story of Dr. Harold Moody* (London: Independent Press, 1950). For more critical assessments, see Geiss, *Pan-African Movement,* pp. 340–350 and Esedebe, *Pan-Africanism,* pp. 105–109.
56. Geiss noted that Moody was "still completely rooted in the earlier tradition of Christian missionary activity which . . . [had been] of such importance in the development of modern elites in the Pan-African milieu." Geiss, *Pan-African Movement,* p. 341
57. Vaughn, *Negro Victory,* pp. 62, 68
58. Ibid., pp. 65–66.
59. In 1932 *The Negro Worker,* edited by Padmore, called for students of color "to break with the sycophantic leadership of Dr. Harold Moody, a typical 'Uncle Tom.'" Esedebe, *Pan-Africanism,* p. 109.
60. Vaughn, *Negro Victory,* p. 159.
61. The post Italo-Ethiopian crisis posture of Moody and the League of Coloured Peoples appeared to have best approximated Faduma's Pan-African stance during this period. Esedebe suggests that Moody and the League's activities, especially during the war years, "plainly contradict the stereotype that Harold Moody was an Uncle Tom whose sole ambition lay in a modest improvement of the relations between the blacks and whites." Esedebe, *Pan-Africanism,* p. 136. For a correlation between the League's educational theory and Faduma's, see its 1944 memorandum on university education in West Africa. Esedebe notes, "It was a document combining most of the educational ideas of Edward Blyden, J. B. A. Horton and Casely Hayford. More important than this, it reflected the cultural ideas of the Pan-Africanists." Esedebe, *Pan-Africanism,* pp. 153–154. No evidence has been found of Faduma's involvement with Pan-African pressure groups that arose in the wake of the Abyssinian crisis.
62. Faduma, "Some of My Experiences," p. 9.
63. Faduma, "Africa the Unknown," *Mission Herald* 43 (Nov./Dec. 1939): 18.
64. Virginia Theological Seminary and College was one of a number of

Southern black church-related schools that "taught doctrines and inculcated attitudes which some call politely 'radical racialism' and others, more bluntly, 'sedition.'" Its early staff was characterized as "highly independent in spirit, believing . . . that the Negro people were perfectly capable of carrying on with their work without the white man always at their elbows." George Shepperson and Thomas Price, *Independent African* (Edinburgh: Edinburgh University Press, 1958), pp. 112–114, and Burkett, *Garveyism as a Religious Movement,* p. 114. See also Lester F. Russell, *Black Baptist Secondary Schools in Virginia, 1887–1957* (Metuchen, N.J. and London: Scarecrow Press, 1981), pp. 23–26. The existence of such institutions and attitudes were major factors in efforts by mission agencies and colonial governments to restrict African students in the Southern United States to so-called "safe" institutions such as Hampton and Tuskegee. See King, *Pan-African Education,* pp. 23–26.

65. They include James Robert Lincoln Diggs, William Henry Moses, Janius C. Austin, and W. W. Brown. In reference to this group Burkett notes, "It is striking that four of the most prominent Baptist clergymen associated with the Garvey Movement had close ties to Lynchburg Virginia Seminary." Burkett, *Black Redemption,* p. 100. Note, for example, that Diggs, President of Virginia Seminary and College, had also been one of Faduma's colleagues in the American Negro Academy. Moss, *American Negro Academy,* p. 119. Also on Virginia Theological Seminary and College, see the autobiographical work by William H. R. Powell, who was President of the Seminary during the years 1926–1929 and 1934–1936. William H. R. Powell, *Illustrations From a Supervised Life* (Philadelphia: Continental Press, 1968).
66. Faduma, "Africa The Unknown," *Mission Herald* 43 (Nov./Dec. 1939): 18–20; 49 (Jan./Feb. 1940): 16–17. Apparently this was Faduma's first publication in the *Mission Herald.* The editor introduced him with a biographical sketch taken from *Who's Who in Colored America.* These articles also reflect Faduma's continued role as a mediator of tenets of liberal theology and missiology within the African and African-American religious communities. Their publication suggests that this perspective continued to enjoy some support in these communities. The *Mission Herald* was edited during this period by Dr. Joseph H. Jackson, later to become the conservative patriarch of the National Baptist Convention.
67. O. Faduma, "Africa the Unknown," *Mission Herald* 43 (Nov./ Dec. 1939): 18–20.
68. O. Faduma, "An African Background," *Mission Herald* 44 (Sept./ Oct. 1940): 18–20.

69. Ibid.
70. Ibid.
71. Ibid., pp. 18–19.
72. Ibid., p. 19.
73. High Point was the site of a normal and industrial school for African-American students.
74. Faduma, "Some of My Experiences," p. 9.
75. Ibid., p. 10.
76. Ibid.
77. Alumni File, Yale Divinity School.
78. Ibid.
79. On Dean Weigle, see *Who's Who In America: A Biographical Dictionary of Notable Living Men and Women,* vol. 24, 1946–1947 (Chicago: A. N. Marqus Co., 1946), p. 2404.
80. Letter from Faduma to Dean Luther Allan Weigle, 10 May 1945. Alumni File, Yale Divinity School.
81. Ibid. On these figures, see Bainton, *Yale and the Ministry* and above, chapter three.
82. Letter from Dean Luther A. Weigle to Faduma, 22 May 1945. Alumni File, Yale Divinity School.
83. "Certificate of Death," North Carolina State Board of Health, Bureau of Vital Statistics, #2708. Issued 11 Feb. 1946.
84. Ibid.
85. On the Manchester Congress, see Padmore, *Pan-Africanism or Communism,* pp. 130–148; Langley, *Ideologies of Liberation,* pp. 758–761; Esedebe, *Pan-Africanism,* pp. 161–173.
86. Geiss, *Pan-Africanism,* pp. 402–404.
87. Langley, *Ideologies of Liberation,* pp. 758–759.
88. The first and second sessions of the Congress, which were devoted to a discussion of the racial problem in Britain, passed a resolution demanding that "the Negro Welfare Centre, the League of Coloured Peoples, African Churches' Mission of Liverpool and other African organizations (social and religious) which have been doing legitimate welfare work among coloured children, students, seamen and others, shall be given every encouragement and assistance by the responsible authorities to continue the vital social work in which they are engaged." Padmore, *Pan-Africanism or Communism,* pp. 140–141. This resolution was consistent with the "Christianity in Action" and "Christian Socialism" preference expressed by the Guyana-born Pan-Africanist leader, Ras Makonnen, during his earlier years of study and work in the United States. See Makonnen, *Pan-Africanism from Within,* pp. 42, 45, 47.
89. O. Faduma, "My Nigerian African Background."

Bibliography

Manuscript Collections

Booker T. Washington Papers (Library of Congress, Washington, D.C.).
Correspondence and Minutes of the Education Committee of the Colony of Sierra Leone (Sierra Leone National Archives, Fourah Bay College, Freetown, Sierra Leone).
Day Mission Collection (Yale Divinity School, New Haven, Connecticut).
Missionary Research Collection (Union Theological Seminary, New York, New York).
Schomburg Center for Research in Black Culture (New York Public Library, New York, New York).

Official Documents and Files

Certificate of Death. Orishatukeh Faduma. North Carolina Board of Health. Bureau of Vital Statistics. #2708. Issued 11 Feb. 1946.
Academic Transcript. Orishatukeh Faduma. Summer Quarter, 1927. The Chicago Theological Seminary. Issued by Registrar (Cheryl Miller) 16 May 1983.
Yale Divinity School Alumni File. Orishatukeh Faduma.
Yale University Alumni File. Orishatukeh Faduma.

Correspondence

Amos, A. M. (Central Registry, Academic Division, University of London). Letter to author, 20 Feb. 1985.
Bailey, Simon (Paleography Room, University of London Library). Letter to author, 4 Mar. 1985.
Miller, Cheryl (Director of Professional Studies/Registrar, Chicago Theological Seminary). Letter to author, 26 May 1983.
Roundtree, Louise M. (Head Librarian, Livingstone College, Salisbury, North Carolina). Letter to author, 27 Feb. 1984.
Weigle, Luther A. (Dean, Yale Divinity School). Letter to Orishatukeh Faduma, 22 May 1945.

Interviews

Faduma, Furman Du Bois. Great-grandson of Orishatukeh Faduma. Atlanta, Georgia. Telephone interviews with author, March, May 1995.

Lancaster, Abna Aggrey. Daughter of J. E. K. Aggrey. Salisbury, North Carolina. Telephone interview with author, January 1984.

Parham, Samuel. Neighbor of Orishatukeh Faduma (High Point, North Carolina). Interview with author in White Plains, New York, March 1981.

Newspapers and Periodicals

African Mail
A.M.E. Christian Recorder
A.M.E. Church Review
American Missionary
Atlanta Constitution
The Congregationalist
The Crisis
The Expected
Journal of Negro Religion
Methodist Herald
Mission Herald
Missionary Echo
Missionary Review of the World
The Outlook
Sierra Leone Outlook
Sierra Leone Weekly News
Southern Workman

Writings of Orishatukeh Faduma

Faduma, Orishatukeh, "Africa or the Dark Continent." *A.M.E. Church Review* 9 (Jan. 1893): 1–8.

———. "Africa the Unknown." *Mission Herald* 43 (Nov./Dec. 1939): 18–20; 43 (Jan./Feb., 1940): 16–17.

———. "An African Background." *Mission Herald* 44 (Sept./Oct. 1940): 19.

———. "The African Movement." *African Mail,* 7 May, 20 Nov., 27 Nov., 4 Dec. 1914; 22 Jan., 12 Mar., 19 Mar., 13 Aug., 20 Aug., 27 Aug., 10 Sept. 1915.

———. "The African Movement: Its Idea and Methods." *Sierra Leone Weekly News,* 2 Oct. 1915.
———. "The African Movement: The Perils of Pioneering—A Parallel." *Sierra Leone Weekly News,* 11 Sept. 1915.
———. "African Negro Education." *Sierra Leone Weekly News,* 3 Aug., 17 Aug., 24 Aug., 31 Aug., 9 Nov. 1918.
———. "African Negro Education: Some Demands of Modern Education." *Sierra Leone Weekly News,* 10 Aug. 1918.
———. "An African Speaks on Negro Problem." *Sierra Leone Weekly News,* 9 Aug. 1902.
———."Africa's Claims and Needs." *Southern Workman* (May 1925): 221–225.
———. "The A.M.E. Church and Kittrell Normal Institute." *Christian Recorder* 16 (Apr. 1890): 289.
———. "A Ballad on Egba Land." *A. M. E. Church Review* 5 (July 1888).
———. "Christian Missions among Less Developed Races." *American Missionary* 61 (Jan. 1907): 69–74.
———. "Christian Missions among Less Developed Races." *Missionary Review of the World* 30 (June 1907): 453–455.
———. "Christianity and Islam in Africa." *African Mail,* 22 May 1914.
———. "Christianity and Islam in Africa: A Native African's View of the Situation." *Missionary Review of the World* 48 (Nov. 1925): 865–68.
———. "Church and School at Troy, North Carolina." *American Missionary* 66 (July 1912): 225.
———. "Death of G. O. Marke." *Sierra Leone Weekly News,* 21 Dec. 1929.
———. *The Defects of the Negro Church.* American Negro Academy Occasional Papers No. 10. Washington, D.C.: American Negro Academy, 1904.
———. "Drawbacks and Successes of Missionary Work in Africa." *Sierra Leone Weekly News,* 9 Mar., 16 Mar., 6 Apr., 20 Apr. 1918.
———. "Drawbacks to Missionary Work in Africa." *Missionary Echo* 24 (Apr. 1917): 54–56.
———. "The Faith That Is in Me." *Sierra Leone Weekly News,* 2 June, 16 June, 14 July, 21 July, 28 July, 18 Aug., 1 Sept. 1923, 15 Sept., 20 Oct., 3 Nov., 8 Dec. 1923.
———. "Father T. B. Cole, the Christian Layman: An Appreciation." *Sierra Leone Weekly News,* 3 Dec. 1921.
———. "Growing Interest in West Africa." *Sierra Leone Weekly News,* 13 Feb. 1915.
———. "How to Cultivate a Love for Reading." *Sierra Leone Weekly News,* 12 Aug. 1922; 19 Aug. 1922.

———. "In Memoriam the Centenary of Sierra Leone." *A.M.E. Church Review* 5 (Oct. 1889): 239–240.

———. "Industrial Education." *Sierra Leone Weekly News,* 29 Aug. 1908.

———. "Khalil's Mohammedan Code, from the French of N. Seignette." *Sierra Leone Weekly News,* 24 Dec. 1921; 14 Jan., 21 Jan. 1922.

———. "Lessons and Needs of the Hour." *Sierra Leone Weekly News,* 21 Sept., 5 Oct., 12 Oct., 2 Nov. 1918.

———. Letter to Benjamin T. Tanner, 20 Aug. 1887. *A.M.E. Church Review* 4 (July 1888): 4.

———. Letter to Booker T. Washington, 12 Dec. 1913. Booker T. Washington Papers, Manuscript Division, Library of Congress, Washington, D.C.

———. Letter to Dean Luther A. Weigle, 10 May 1945. Yale Divinity School Alumni File.

———. "Life in the United States of America." *Sierra Leone Weekly News,* 1 Aug. 1908.

———. "The Man of Dreams." *Sierra Leone Weekly News,* 7 Apr. 1916: 3–8.

———. "Materials for the Study of the World Religions." *A.M.E. Church Review* 12 (Apr. 1896): 461–473.

———. "My Nigerian African Background." Yale Divinity School Alumni File. N.d., n.p.

———. "Negro Development: Its Meaning and Aims." *Sierra Leone Weekly News,* 17 Sept. 1921.

———. "Negro Development: Its Period of Growth and Danger in Education." *Sierra Leone Weekly News,* 22 Oct., 29 Oct 1921.

———. "Negro Development—Its Phases." *Sierra Leone Weekly News,* 24 Sept., 1 Oct. 1921.

———. "A Negro upon Self-Help and Self-Support." *American Missionary* 50 (Sept. 1896): 279.

———. "The New Education." *Sierra Leone Weekly News,* 8 Apr. 1916.

———. "Not Failure But Low Aim Is Crime." *Sierra Leone Weekly News,* 24 Mar. 1919.

———. "Obligations of the Weak to the Strong." *Sierra Leone Weekly News,* 6 Dec. 1916.

———. "An Old Boy's Tribute to Principal May." *Sierra Leone Weekly News,* 10 July 1899.

———. "The Pastoral Epistles." *A.M.E. Church Review* 11 (Oct. 1894): 215–230.

———. "The Problem of Christian Missions among Less Developed Races." *American Missionary* 61 (Mar. 1907): 69–74.

———. "The Problem of Negro Development." *Sierra Leone Weekly News,* 9 Aug. 1902.

———. "Race Destiny: The Race Problem from a Negro's Viewpoint." *Sierra Leone Weekly News,* 2 Aug. 1902.
———. "Religious Beliefs and Worship of the Yorubas in West Africa." *A.M.E. Church Review* 12 (July 1895): 150–158.
———. "Religious Beliefs of the Yoruba People of West Africa." *Africa and the American Negro: Addresses and Proceedings of the Congress on Africa,* ed. J. W. E. Bowen. 1896; reprint, Miami: Mnemosyne Publishing, 1969), pp. 31–36.
———. "Sierra Leone Revisited." *American Missionary* 78 (Dec. 1925): 352–53.
———. "Some of My Experiences in the Southland." *The Expected* (July 1943): 9–10.
———. "Some of My Literary Contributions." N.p., n.d.
———. "Some Suggestions on Native African Education." *Sierra Leone Weekly News,* 11 Dec. 1915.
———. "The Study of Science in Elementary and Secondary Schools." *Sierra Leone Weekly News,* 7 Oct. 1922.
———. "Success and Drawbacks of Missionary Work in Africa by an Eye-Witness." In *Africa and the American Negro: Addresses and Proceedings of the Congress on Africa,* ed. J.W.E. Bowen. (1896; reprint. Miami: Mnemosyne Publishing, 1969), pp. 125–136.
———. "A Tale of Egba Land." *Methodist Herald,* 25 Aug., 8 Sept. 1886.
———. "Thoughts for the Times." *A.M.E. Church Review* 5 (Oct. 1888): 121–126
———. "Thoughts for the Times, or the New Theology." *A.M.E. Church Review* 7 (Oct. 1890): 139–143.
———. "Vale! Longum Vale!" *Sierra Leone Weekly News,* 13 July, 20 July 1912.
———. "What the African Movement Stands For." *African Mail,* 25 Sept., 2 Oct. 1914.
———. "What the Study of Science Means." *Sierra Leone Weekly News,* 21 Oct. 1922.
———. "Where is Virtue?" *A.M.E. Church Review* 8 (Apr. 1891): 430–431.

Books and Pamphlets

Abbott, Lyman. *Christianity and Social Problems.* Boston: Houghton, Mifflin and Co., 1896.
———. *The Evolution of Christianity.* Boston: Houghton, Mifflin and Co., 1892.
———. *The Theology of an Evolutionist.* Boston: Houghton, Mifflin and Co., 1897.

Abell, Aaron Ignatius. *The Urban Impact on American Protestantism, 1865–1900.* Cambridge: Harvard University Press, 1943.

Ahlstrom, Sidney. *The American Protestant Encounter with World Religions.* Beloit, Wisc.: Beloit College, 1962.

———. *A Religious History of the American People.* New Haven and London: Yale University Press, 1972.

———. *Theology in America: The Major Protestant Voices from Puritanism to Neo-Orthodoxy.* Indianapolis: Bobbs-Merrill Co., 1967.

Ajayi, J. F. A. *Christian Missions in Nigeria, 1841–1891: The Making of a New Elite.* London: Longmans, 1965.

Ajayi, J. F. A., and R. S. Smith, *Yoruba Warfare in the Nineteenth Century.* Cambridge: Cambridge University Press, 1964.

Ames, Edward Scribner. *Beyond Theology: The Autobiography of Edward Scribner Ames.* Chicago: University of Chicago Press, 1959.

Anderson, Eric. *Race and Politics in North Carolina, 1872–1901.* Baton Rouge and London: Louisiana State University Press, 1981.

Anderson, Gerald H. *Kraemer and After: A Survey Review Article, Studies in Mission Theology.* N.p., n.d. (Reprint from *Encounter* 27).

Anderson, Gerald H., and Thomas F. Stransky, eds. *Mission Trends No. 3: Third World Theologies.* New York: Paulist Press, 1976.

Anderson, Robert Mapes. *Vision of the Disinherited: The Making of American Pentecostalism.* New York and Oxford: Oxford University Press, 1979.

Anderson, Rufus. *To Advance the Gospel: Selections from the Writings of Rufus Anderson.* Edited with an introduction by R. Pierce Beaver. Grand Rapids: Eerdmans, 1967.

Appia-Kubi, Kofi, and Sergio Torres, eds. *African Theology en Route.* Maryknoll, N. Y.: Orbis, 1979.

Apter, David. *The Gold Coast in Transition.* Princeton: Princeton University Press, 1955.

Asante, S. K. B. *Pan-African Protest: West Africa and the Italo-Ethiopian Crisis, 1934–1941.* London: Longman Group, 1977.

Ashby, Eric. *Universities: British, Indian, African: A Study in the Ecology of Higher Education.* London: Weidenfeld and Nicolson, 1966.

Attoh-Ahuman, S. R. B. *Memoirs of West African Celebrities, With Special Reference to the Gold Coast.* Liverpool: Phillips, 1925.

Averill, Lloyd J. *American Theology in the Liberal Tradition.* Philadelphia: Westminster Press, 1967.

Ayandele, E. A. *A Visionary of the African Church: Majola Agbebi.* Nairobi: East African Publishing House, 1971.

———. *Holy Johnson: Pioneer of African Nationalism, 1836–1917.* New York: Humanities Press, 1970.

———. *The Missionary Impact on Modern Nigeria, 1842–1914.* New York: Humanities Press, 1967.

Baeta, C. G. *Christianity in Tropical Africa*. London: Oxford University Press, 1968.

Bainton, Roland. *Yale and the Ministry: A History of Education for the Christian Ministry of Yale from the Founding in 1701*. New York: Harper & Brothers, 1957.

Barnard, Howard Cline. *A History of English Education from 1760*. Rev. ed. London: University of London Press, 1961.

Barrows, John Henry, ed. *The World's Parliament of Religions*. 2 vols. Chicago: Parliament Publishing Company, 1893.

Bartels, F. L. *The Roots of Ghana Methodism*. Cambridge: Cambridge University Press, 1965.

Beard, Augustus Field. *A Crusade of Brotherhood: A History of the American Missionary Association*. 1909. Reprint, New York: Kraus Reprint Co., 1970.

Beaver, R. Pierce, ed. *American Missions in Bicentennial Perspective*. South Pasadena, Calif.: William Carey Library, 1977.

Becker, Carl Heinrich. *Christianity and Islam*. 1909. Reprint, n.p., 1974.

Berman, Edward H. *African Reactions to Missionary Education*. New York and London: Teachers College Press, Columbia University, 1975.

Beyerhaus, P., and Henry Lefever, *The Responsible Church and the Foreign Mission*. London: World Dominion Press, 1964.

Bittle, William E., and Gilbert Geiss. *The Longest Way Home: Chief Alfred Sam's Back-to-Africa Movement*. Detroit: Wayne State University Press, 1964.

Blackwell, James E. and Janowitz, eds. *Black Sociologists: Historical and Contemporary Perspectives*. Chicago: University of Chicago Press, 1974.

Blyden, Edward W. *African Life and Customs*. London: Phillips, 1908.

———. *Christianity, Islam, and the Negro Race*. 1887. Reprint, Edinburgh: Edinburgh University Press, 1967.

Bond, George, Walton Johnson and Sheila S. Walker. *African Christianity: Patterns of Religious Continuity*. New York and London: Academic Press, 1979.

Boris, Joseph J. *Who's Who in Colored America: A Biographical Dictionary of Notable Living Persons of Negro Descent in America*. Vol. 1. New York: Who's Who in Colored America Corporation, 1927.

Boulaga, F. Eboussi. *Christianity Without Fetishes: An African Critique and Recapture of Christianity*. Maryknoll, N.Y.: Orbis, 1985.

Bowen, J. W. E., ed. *African and the American Negro: Addresses and Proceedings of the Congress on Africa*. 1896. Reprint, Miami: Mnemosyne Publishing, 1969.

Bracey, John H. Jr., August Meier, and Elliot Rudwick, eds. *The Black Sociologists: The First Half Century*. Belmont, Calif.: Wadsworth Publishing Co., 1971.

Brauer, Jerald C. *Reinterpretation in American Church History*. Chicago and London: University of Chicago Press, 1968.

Broderick, Francis L. *W. E. B. Du Bois: Negro Leader in a Time of Crisis*. Stanford: University of California Press, 1959.

Brotz, Howard, ed. *Negro Social and Political Thought, 1850–1920*. New York: Basic Books, 1966.

Brown, Jerry Wayne. *The Rise of Biblical Criticism in America, 1800–1870: The New England Scholars*. Middletown, Conn.: Wesleyan University Press, 1964.

Brown, William Adams. *The Essence of Christianity: A Study in the History of Definition*. New York: Charles Scribner's Sons, 1902.

Buckham, John W. *Progressive Religious Thought in America: A Survey of the Enlarging Pilgrim Faith*. Boston: Houghton, Mifflin and Co., 1919.

Burkett, Randall K. *Black Redemption: Churchmen Speak for the Garvey Movement*. Philadelphia: Temple University Press, 1978.

———. *Garveyism as a Religious Movement: The Institutionalization of a Black Civil Religion*. Metuchen, N. J.: Scarecrow Press, 1978.

Burkett, Randall K., and Richard Newman, eds. *Black Apostles: Afro-American Clergy Confront the Twentieth Century*. Boston: G. K. Hall and Co., 1978.

Carter, Paul A. *The Decline and Revival of the Social Gospel: Social and Political Liberalism in American Protestant Churches, 1920–1940*. Ithaca, N. Y.: Cornell University Press, 1954.

———. *The Spiritual Crisis of the Gilded Age*. De Kalb: Northern Illinois University Press, 1971.

Case, Adelaide. *Liberal Christianity and Religious Education*. New York: Macmillan, 1924.

Cauthen, Kenneth. *The Impact of American Religious Liberalism*. New York: Harper & Row, 1962.

Chadwick, Owen. *The Secularization of the European Mind in the Nineteenth Century*. Cambridge: Cambridge University Press, 1970.

———. *The Victorian Church*. 2 vols. 2nd ed. London: Adam & Charles Black, 1972.

Chaney, Charles L. *The Birth of Missions in America*. South Pasadena: William Carey Library, 1976.

Clarke, Peter B. *West Africa and Islam: A Study of Religious Development from the Eighth to the Twentieth Century*. London: Edward Arnold, 1982.

Clarke, William Newton. *A Study of Christian Missions*. New York: Charles Scribner's Sons, 1900.

Clayton, John Powell, ed. *Ernst Troeltsch and the Future of Theology*. Cambridge: Cambridge University Press, 1976.

Coe, George Albert. *A Social Theory of Religious Education*. New York: Charles Scribner's Sons, 1917.
———. *Education in Religion and Morals*. New York: Fleming H. Revell Co., 1904.
Cohen, Abner. *The Politics of Elite Culture*. Berkeley: University of California Press, 1981.
Cole, Marley. *Jehovah's Witness: The New World Society*. New York: Vantage Press, 1955.
Cole, Stewart G. *The History of Fundamentalism*. New York: R. R. Smith, 1931.
Coleman, J. S. *Nigeria: Background to Nationalism*. Berkeley: University of California Press, 1958.
Collison, Patrick. *The Elizabethan Puritan Movement*. Berkeley: University of California Press, 1967.
Cone, James. *My Soul Looks Back*. Nashville: Abingdon Press, 1982.
Conforti, Joseph A. *Samuel Hopkins and the New Divinity Movement: Calvinism, the Congregational Ministry, and Reform in New England between the Great Awakenings*. Grand Rapids: Christian University Press, 1981.
Cooke, Charles C. *Comparative Study of the Negro Problem*. Negro Academy Occasional Papers, No. 4. Washington, D.C.: American Negro Academy, 1899.
Cromwell, Adelaide M. *An African Victorian Feminist: The Life and Times of Adelaide Smith Casely Hayford, 1868–1960*. London: Frank Cass & Co., 1986.
Cronon, E. D. *Black Moses: The Story of Marcus Garvey and the Universal Negro Improvement Association*. Madison: University of Wisconsin Press, 1955.
Crowder, Michael. *West Africa under Colonial Rule*. Evanston: Northwestern University Press, 1968.
Cruden, Robert M. *Ministers of Reform: The Progressives' Achievement in American Civilization, 1889–1920*. New York: Basic Books, 1982.
Crummell, Alexander. *Africa and America: Addresses and Discourses*. 1891. Reprint, Miami: Mnemosyne Publishing, 1969.
———. *The Future of Africa*. New York: Charles Scribner, 1962.
Curtin, Philip D. *The Image of Africa: British Ideas and Action, 1780–1850*. London: Macmillan & Co., 1965.
Daniel, Walter C. *Black Journals of the United States*. Westport, Conn.: Greenwood Press, 1982.
Davidson, Basil. *Black Star: A View of the Life and Times of Kwame Nkrumah*. New York: Praeger, 1974.
———. *A History of West Africa*. Garden City, N. Y.: Doubleday, Anchor Books, 1966.

Davis, J. A., ed. *Pan-Africanism Reconsidered.* Berkeley: University of California Press, 1962.

Dean, David M. *Defender of the Race: James Theodore Holly, Black Nationalist Bishop.* Boston: Lamberth Press, 1979.

Dennis, James S. *Christian Missions and Social Progress: A Sociological Study of Foreign Missions.* New York: Fleming H. Revell Co., 1897.

Despres, Leo A. *Cultural Pluralism and Nationalist Politics in British Guiana.* Chicago: Rand McNally and Co., 1967.

Dickson, Kwesi. *Theology in Africa.* Maryknoll, N. Y.: Orbis, 1984.

Dickson, Kwesi, and Paul Ellingworth, eds. *Biblical Revelation and African Beliefs.* Maryknoll, N. Y.: Orbis, 1984.

Douglass, Harlan Paul. *Christian Reconstruction in the South.* Boston: Pilgrim Press, 1909.

Drake, St. Clair. *The Redemption of Africa and Black Religion.* Chicago: Third World Press, 1977.

Du Bois, William E. B. *Dusk of Dawn: An Essay toward an Autobiography of a Race Concept.* New York: Harcourt Brace, 1940.

———, ed. *The Negro Church: Report of a Social Study Made under the Direction of Atlanta University, Together with the Proceedings of the Eight Conference for the Study of the Negro Problem Held at Atlanta University, May 26, 1903.* Atlanta: Atlanta University Press, 1903.

———. *On the Importance of Africa in World History.* New York: Black Liberation Press, 1978.

———. *The World and Africa: An Inquiry into the Part Which Africa Has Played in World History.* New York: Viking Press, 1947.

Duffie, Cornelius R. *The Salvability of the Heathen: No Excuse for Neglect of Revealed Duty by the Christian.* New York: Daniel Dana, Jr., 1860.

Eighth General Catalogue of the Yale Divinity School. *Bulletin of Yale University,* Centennial Issue, 1822–1922. New Haven: Yale University Press, 1922.

Eliade, Mircea, and Joseph M. Kitagawa, eds. *The History of Religions.* Chicago: University of Chicago Press, 1959.

Elliott-Binns, L. E. *English Thought, 1860–1900: The Theological Aspect.* London: Longmans, Green and Co., 1956.

Elsbree, Oliver. *The Rise of the Missionary Spirit in America, 1790–1815.* Williamsport, Pa.: Williamsport Printing Co., 1928.

Esedebe, P. Olisanwuche. *Pan-Africanism: The Idea and Movement, 1776–1963.* Washington, D.C.: Howard University Press, 1982.

Fage, J. D. *A History of West Africa: An Introductory Survey.* Cambridge: Cambridge University Press, 1969.

Fairbank, John K., ed. *The Missionary Enterprise in China and America.* Cambridge: Harvard University Press, 1974.

Faunce, W. H. P. *The Social Aspects of Foreign Missions*. New York: Missionary Education Movement of the United States and Canada, 1914.

Ferris, William H. *The African Abroad, or His Evolution in Western Civilization*. 2 vols. New Haven: The Tuttle, Morehouse & Taylor Press, 1913.

Fleming, Daniel Johnson. *Attitudes toward Other Faiths*. New York: Association Press, 1928.

———. *Contact with Non-Christian Cultures: A Case Book on the Christian Movement Abroad*. New York: George Doran Co., 1923.

———. *Ways of Sharing with Other Faiths*. New York: Association Press, 1929.

Foray, Cyril P. *Historical Dictionary of Sierra Leone*. African Historical Dictionaries No. 12. Metuchen, N. J., and London: Scarecrow Press, Inc. 1977).

Fordham, Monroe. *Major Themes in Northern Black Religious Thought, 1800–1860*. Hicksville, N.Y.: Exposition Press, 1975.

Forman, Charles W. *A Faith for the Nations*. Philadelphia: Westminster Press, 1957.

Fosdick, Harry Emerson. *The Living of These Days*. New York: Harper & Brothers, 1956.

———. *The Power to See It Through*. New York: Harper & Brothers, 1935.

Foster, Charles I. *An Errand of Mercy: The Evangelical United Front, 1790–1837*. Chapel Hill: University of North Carolina Press, 1960.

Foster, Frank Hugh. *The Modern Movement in American Theology: Sketches in the History of American Protestant Thought from the Civil War to the World War*. New York: Fleming H. Revell Co., 1939.

Franklin, John Hope. *From Slavery to Freedom: A History of Negro America*, 5th ed. New York: Alfred A. Knopf, 1980.

Frazier, E. Franklin. *Black Bourgeoisie: The Rise of a New Middle Class in the United States*. London: Collier-Macmillan, 1957.

Fredrickson, George M. *The Black Image in the White Mind: The Debate on Afro-American Character and Destiny, 1817–1914*. New York: Harper & Row, 1971.

Fullinwider, S. F. *The Mind and Mood of Black America: Twentieth Century Thought*. Homewood, Ill.: Dorsey Press, 1969.

Furniss, N. F. *The Fundamentalist Controversy, 1918–1931*. New Haven: Yale University Press, 1954.

Fyfe, Christopher. *A History of Sierra Leone*. London: Oxford University Press., 1962.

———, ed. *Sierra Leone Inheritance*. London: Oxford University Press, 1964.

Garvey, Amy Jacques. *Garvey and Garveyism*. Kingston, Jamaica: United Printers, 1963.

Garvey, Marcus. *Philosophy and Opinions of Marcus Garvey,* edited by Amy Jacques-Garvey. Totowa, N. J.: Frank Cass, 1967. Reprint, New York: Atheneum, 1969, 1974.

Gasper, Louis. *The Fundamentalist Movement, 1930–1956.* The Hague: Mouton, 1963. Reprint, Baker Books House and Co., 1981.

Gatewood, Williard. *Controversy in the Twenties: Fundamentalism, Modernism, and Evolution.* Nashville: Vanderbilt University Press, 1969.

Gavins, Raymond. *The Perils and Prospects of Southern Black Leadership: Gordon Blaine Hancock, 1884–1970.* Durham, N.C.: Duke University Press, 1977.

Geiss, Immanuel. *The African Movement: A History of Pan-Africanism in America, Europe, and Africa.* New York: Africana Publishing Co., 1974.

Gladden, Washington. *Applied Christianity: Moral Aspects of Social Questions.* Boston: Houghton, Mifflin and Co., 1886.

———. *Who Wrote the Bible? A Book for the People.* Boston: Houghton Mifflin and Co., 1891.

Glasswell, M., and W. E. Fashole-Luke, eds. *New Testament Christianity for Africa and the World.* London: SPCK, 1974.

Goddard, T. N. *The Handbook of Sierra Leone.* 1925. Reprint, New York: Negro University Press, 1969.

Gordon, George A. *The Christ of Today.* Boston: Houghton, Mifflin and Co., 1895.

———. *The Gospel for Humanity: A Sermon Before the American Board of Commissioners for Foreign Missions.* Delivered at Brooklyn, New York, October 15, 1895. Boston: ABCFM, 1895.

———. *My Education and Religion: An Autobiography. Boston:* Houghton, Mifflin and Co., 1925.

———. *The New Epoch of Faith.* Boston: Houghton, Mifflin and Co, 1895.

Gossett, Thomas F. *Race: The History of an Idea in America.* Dallas: Southern Methodist University Press, 1963.

Greene, John C. *Darwin and the Modern World View.* Baton Rouge: Louisiana State University Press, 1961.

———. *The Death of Adam: Evolution and Its Impact on Western Thought.* Ames: Iowa State University Press, 1959.

Griffith, Cyril E. *The African Dream: Martin R. Delaney and the Emergence of Pan-African Thought.* University Park: Pennsylvania State University Press, 1975.

Griggs, Sutton E. *Guide to Racial Greatness, or the Science of Collective Efficiency.* Memphis: National Public Welfare League, 1924.

———. *Imperium in Imperio: A Study of the Negro Race Problem.* Cincinnati: Editor Publishing Co., 1899.

———. *Kingdom Builder's Manual Companion Book to "Guide to Racial Greatness"*. Memphis: National Public Welfare League, 1924.

———. *New Thoughts for a New Era.* Memphis: National Public Welfare League, 1913.

———. *The Story of My Struggles.* Memphis: National Public Welfare League, 1914.

Groves, C. P. *Planting of Christianity in Africa.* 4 vols. London: Lutterworth, 1948–64.

Handy, Robert T. *A Christian America: Protestant Hopes and Historical Realities.* New York: Oxford University Press, 1966.

———. *The Social Gospel in America, 1870–1920: Gladden, Ely, Rauschenbusch.* New York: Oxford University Press, 1966.

Harlan, Louis R. *Booker T. Washington: The Making of a Black Leader, 1856–1901.* London: Oxford University Press, 1972.

Harnack, Adolf Von. *What is Christianity*? Translated by Thomas B. Saunders. New York: G. P. Putnam's sons, 1901.

Harris, George. *Moral Evolution.* Boston: Houghton, Mifflin and Co., 1896.

Harris, Sheldon. *Paul Cuffee: Black America and the African Return.* New York: Simon and Schuster, 1972.

Harrison, Hubert, *When Africa Awakes: The "Inside Story" of the Stirrings and Strivings of the New Negro in the Western World.* New York: Porro Press, 1920.

Hastings, Adrian. *African Christianity.* New York: Seabury Press, 1976.

———. *A History of African Christianity, 1950–1975.* New York: Cambridge University Press, 1979.

Hatcher, William E. *John Jasper: The Unmatched Negro Philosopher and Preacher.* New York: Fleming H. Revell Co., 1908.

Hayford, J. E. Casely. *Ethiopia Unbound: Studies in Race Emancipation.* London: Phillips Press, 1911.

———. *United West Africa.* London: Phillips Press, 1919.

Hedlund, Roger E. *Roots of the Great Debate in Mission.* Madras: Evangelical Literature Service, 1981.

Hemenway, Robert, ed. *The Black Novelist.* Columbus, Ohio: Charles E. Merrill, 1970.

Hill, Adelaide Cromwell, and Martin Kilson, eds. *Apropos of Africa: Afro-American Leaders and the Romance of Africa.* New York: Doubleday and Co., 1971.

Hill, Robert, ed. *The Marcus Garvey and Universal Negro Improvement Association Papers.* Vols. 1–3. Berkeley and London: University of California Press, 1983.

Hofstadter, Richard. *The Age of Reform.* New York: Knopf, 1955.

———. *Social Darwinism in American Thought.* 1944. Reprint, Boston: Beacon Press, 1955.

Holden, E. *Blyden of Liberia: An Account of the Life and Labours of Edward Wilmot Blyden, As Recorded in Letter and in Print.* New York: Vantage Press, 1966.

Holmes, Brian, ed. *Educational Policy and the Mission Schools: Case Studies from the British Empire.* London: Routledge & Kegan Paul, 1967.

Hooker, J. R. *Black Revolutionary: George Padmore's Path from Communism to Pan-Africanism.* New York: Praeger, 1967.

Hordern, William E. *A Layman's Guide to Protestant Theology.* Rev. ed. New York: Macmillan, 1968.

Horton, James Africanus. *West African Countries and Peoples.* Edinburgh: Edinburgh University Press, 1969.

Hudson, Winthrop S. *Religion in America.* 2nd ed. New York: Charles Scribner's Sons, 1973.

Hutchison, John A. *We Are Not Divided: A Critical and Historical Study of the Federal Council of the Churches of Christ in America.* New York: Round Table Press, 1941.

Hutchison, William R. *American Protestant Thought: The Liberal Era.* New York: Harper & Row, 1968.

———. *The Modernist Impulse in American Protestantism.* Cambridge and London: Harvard University Press, 1976.

Idowu, E. B. *Towards an Indigenous Church.* London: Oxford University Press, 1964.

Ilogu, Edmund. *Christianity and Igbo Culture.* New York: NOK Publishers, L.F.D., 1974.

Jacobs, Sylvia M. *The African Nexus: Black American Perspectives on the European Partitioning of Africa, 1880–1920.* Westport, Conn., and London: Greenwood Press, 1981.

———, ed. *Black Americans and the Missionary Movement in Africa.* Westport, Conn.: Greenwood Press, 1982.

James, C. L. R. *World Revolution, 1917–1936: The Rise and Fall of the Communist International.* London: Secker & Warburg, 1937.

Johnson, Clifton H. *Our American Missionary Association Heritage.* New York: Division of Higher Education and American Missionary Association of the United Church Board for Homeland Ministers, 1967.

Johnson, James. *The Relation of Mission Work to Native Customs.* London, 1968.

———. *Yoruba Heathenism.* Exeter: J. Townsend, 1899.

Jones, Thomas Jesse. *Negro Education: A Study of the Private and Higher Schools for Colored People in the United States, Department of the Interior Bureau of Education Bulletins, 1916.* Washington, D.C.: Washington Printing Office, 1917.

July, Robert W. *The Origins of Modern African Thought*. London: Faber & Faber, 1968.

Kalu, O. U., ed. *The History of Christianity in West Africa*. London and New York: Longman, 1980.

Kendall, Elliott. *The End of an Era: Africa and the Missionary*. London: SPCK, 1978.

Kilson, Martin N. *Political Change in a West African State: A Study of the Modernization Process in Sierra Leone*. Cambridge: Harvard University Press, 1966.

Kimble, D. *A Political History of Ghana: The Rise of Gold Coast Nationalism, 1850–1928*. London: Oxford University Press, 1963.

King, Henry Churchill. *Reconstruction in Theology*. New York: The Macmillan Co., 1901.

King, Kenneth James. *Pan-Africanism and Education: A Study of Race Philanthropy and Education in the Southern States of America and East Africa*. Oxford: Clarendon Press, 1971.

Koputoff, J. H. *A Preface to Modern Nigeria: The "Sierra Leonians" in Yoruba, 1830–1890*. Madison: University of Wisconsin Press, 1965.

Kraemer, Hendrick. *The Christian Message in a Non-Christian World*. London: International Missionary Council, 1938.

———. *Religion and the Christian Faith*. London: Lutterworth Press, 1956.

Krentz, E. *The Historical-Critical Method*. Philadelphia: Fortress Press, 1975.

Langley, J. Ayodele. *Ideologies of Liberation in Black Africa, 1856–1970*. London: Rex Collings, 1979.

———. *Pan-Africanism and Nationalism in West Africa, 1900–1945: A Study in Ideology and Social Classes*. Oxford: Clarendon Press, 1973.

Latourette, Kenneth Scott. *A History of the Expansion of Christianity*. Vol. 4, *The Great Century: Europe and the United States, 1800 A.D. to 1914 A.D*. New York: Harper & Brothers, 1941.

———. *A History of the Expansion of Christianity*. Vol. 5, *The Great Century in the Americas, Australia, Asia, and Africa, 1800 A.D. to 1914 A.D*. New York: Harper & Brothers, 1943.

Laymen's Foreign Mission Inquiry, Commission of Appraisal. *Rethinking Missions: A Laymen's Inquiry after a Hundred Years*. New York: Harper, 1932.

Le Chatelier, Alfred. *L'Islam dans l'Afrique Occidentale*. Paris: G. Steinheil, 1899.

Legum, Colin. *Pan-Africanism: A Short Political Guide*. Rev. ed. New York: Praeger Press, 1965.

Litwick, Leon E. *North of Slavery: The Negro in the Free States, 1790–1860*. Chicago: University of Chicago Press, 1961.

Locke, Alaine, ed. *The New Negro.* 1925. Reprint, New York: Atheneum, 1969.

Loetscher, Lefferts A. *The Broadening Church: A Study of Theological Issues in the Presbyterian Church since 1869.* Philadelphia: University, 1958.

Logan, Rayford W. *The Betrayal of the Negro from Rutherford B. Hayes to Woodrow Wilson.* New York: Collier Books, 1965.

Luker, Ralph. *The Social Gospel in Black and White: American Racial Reform, 1885–1912.* Chapel Hill and London: University of North Carolina Press, 1991.

Lynch, Hollis. *Black Spokesman: Selected Published Writings of Edward Wilmot Blyden.* London: Frank Cass & Co., 1971.

———. *Edward Wilmot Blyden: Pan-Negro Patriot, 1832–1912.* London: Oxford University Press, 1967.

———. *Selected Letters of Edward Wilmot Blyden.* Millwood, N. Y.: KTO Press, 1978.

Makonnen, Ras. *Pan-Africanism from Within.* Edited by Kenneth King. London: Oxford University Press, 1973.

Marable, Manning. *Blackwater: Historical Studies in Race, Class Consciousness, and Revolution.* Dayton, Ohio: Black Praxis Press, 1981.

Marsden, George M. *Fundamentalism and American Culture: The Shaping of Twentieth Century Evangelicalism, 1870–1925.* New York: Oxford University Press, 1980.

Martin, Tony. *Race First: The Ideological and Organizational Struggles of Marcus Garvey and the Universal Negro Improvement Association.* Westport, Conn. and London: Greenwood Press, 1971.

Marty, Martin E. *Modern American Religion.* Vol. 1, *The Irony of It All, 1893–1919.* Chicago and London: University of Chicago Press, 1986.

———. *Protestantism.* New York: Holt, Rinehart and Winston, 1973.

———. *Protestantism in the United States: Righteous Empire.* New York: Charles Scribner's Son, 1986.

———. *Righteous Empire: The Protestant Experience in America.* New York: Dial Press, 1970.

Mather, Frank Lincoln, ed. *Who's Who of the Colored Race: A General Biographical Dictionary of Men and Women of African Descent.* Chicago: Momento Edition Half-Century Anniversary of Negro Freedom in the United States, 1915.

Mathisen, Robert R., ed. *The Role of Religion in American Life; an Interpretive Historical Anthology.* Lanham, Md.: University Press of America, 1982.

Mathurin, Owen Charles. *Henry Sylvester Williams and the Origins of the Pan-African Movement, 1869–1911.* Westport, Conn.: Greenwood Press, 1976.

May, Harry F. *The Protestant Churches and Industrial America.* New York: Harper & Row, 1949.

May, J. Claudius. *A Brief Sketch of the Life of the Reverend Joseph May, Wesleyan Minister to the Colony of Sierra Leone.* Freetown, Sierra Leone, 1890.

Mayer, Frederick E. *Jehovah's Witnesses.* St. Louis: Concordia Publishing House, 1952.

Mays, Benjamin E. *Born to Rebel: An Autobiography by Benjamin E. Mays.* New York: Charles Scribner's Sons, 1971.

M'bayinga, Elenga. *Pan-Africanism or Neo-Colonialism: The Bankruptcy of the O.A.U.* London: Zed Press, 1982.

Mbiti, John S. *African Religions and Philosophy.* New York: Doubleday, 1970.

———. *Concepts of God in Africa.* London: SPCK, 1979.

McCosh, James. *Christianity and Positivism.* New York: R. Carter, 1971.

———. *The Religious Aspects of Evolution.* 1889. Reprint, New York: Charles Scribner's Sons, 1890.

McGiffert, Arthur Cushman, Jr. *No Ivory Tower: The Story of the Chicago Theological Seminary.* Chicago: Chicago Theological Seminary, 1965.

McPherson, James. *The Abolitionist Legacy: From Reconstruction to the NAACP.* Princeton: Princeton University Press, 1975.

Meeks, Wayne A., ed. *The Writings of St. Paul.* New York: W. W. Norton and Co., 1972.

Meier, August. *Negro Thought in America, 1800–1915: Racial Ideologies in the Age of Booker T. Washington.* Ann Arbor: University of Michigan Press, 1966.

Meyer, Donald B. *The Protestant Search for Political Realism, 1919–1941.* Berkeley and Los Angeles: University of California Press, 1960.

Miller, Floyd J. *The Search for a Black Nationality: Black Colonization and Emigration, 1787–1863.* Urbana: University of Illinois Press, 1975.

Mills, J. S. *African and Mission Work in Sierra Leone, West Africa.* Dayton, Ohio: United Brethren Publishing House, 1898.

Mobley, Harris W. *The Ghanaian's Image of the Missionary: An Analysis of the Published Critiques of Christian Missionaries, 1897–1965.* Leiden: E. J. Brill, 1970.

Moore, James R. *The Post-Darwinian Controversies: A Study of the Protestant Struggle to Come to Terms with Darwin in Great Britain and America, 1870–1900.* Cambridge: Cambridge University Press, 1979.

Moorland, Jesse E. *The Demand and the Supply of Increased Efficiency in the Negro Ministry.* American Negro Academy Occasional Papers No. 13, Washington, D.C.: American Negro Academy, 1909.

Morel, Edmund D. *The Black Man's Burden: The White Man in Africa from the Fifteenth Century to World War I.* London and Manchester: National Labour Press, 1920.

Morris, Calvin S. *Reverdy C. Ransom: Black Advocate of the Social Gospel.* Lanham, Md., New York, London: University Press of America, 1990.

Moses, Wilson J. *The Golden Age of Black Nationalism, 1850–1925.* Hamden, Conn.: Archon Press, 1978.

Moss, Alfred A., Jr. *The American Negro Academy: Voices of the Talented Tenth.* Baton Rouge: Louisiana State University, 1981.

Mott, John R. *History of the Student Volunteer Movement for Foreign Missions.* Chicago: Student Volunteer Movement for Foreign Missions, 1892.

Munger, Theodore T. *The Freedom of Faith.* Boston: Houghton, Mifflin and Co., 1883.

Muzorewa, Gwinyai H. *The Origins and Developments of African Theology.* Maryknoll, N. Y.: Orbis, 1985.

Myklebust, Olav G. *The Study of Missions in Theological Education: An Historical Enquiry into the Place of World Evangelization in Western Protestant Ministerial Training, with Particular Reference to Alexander Duff's Chair of Evangelistic Theology.* 2 vols. Oslo: Egede Institute, 1955–1957.

Nash, Arnold S., ed. *Protestant Thought in the Twentieth Century: Whence and Whither*? New York: Macmillan, 1951.

Neill, Stephen. *A History of Christian Missions.* Baltimore: Penguin Books, 1963, 1973.

———. *Colonialism and Christian Missions.* New York: McGraw-Hill, 1966.

Niebuhr, Reinhold. *Moral Man and Immoral Society.* New York: Charles Scribner's Sons, 1932.

Niebuhr, H. Richard. *An Interpretation of Christian Ethics.* New York: Charles Scribner's sons, 1935.

———. *The Kingdom of God in America.* 1937. Reprint, New York: Harper & Row, 1959.

———. *Radical Monotheism and Western Culture, with Supplementary Essays.* New York: Harper & Row, 1960.

Niebuhr, H. Richard, Wilhelm Pauck, and Francis P. Miller. *The Church Against the World.* Chicago: Willett, Clarke and Co., 1935.

Nkrumah, Kwame. *Africa Must Unite.* London: Heinemann, 1963.

———. *Consciencism: Philosophy and Ideology for Decolonization.* New York: Monthly Review Press, 1970.

———. *Ghana: The Autobiography of Kwame Nkrumah.* New York: International Publishers, 1957.

———. *Towards Colonial Freedom.* London: Heinemann, 1963.

Noble, Frederick P. *Africa at the Columbian Exposition.* Chicago: Newberry Library, 1893.

———. *The Bible as Literature.* Spokane, Washington: The Research Club, 1914.

———. *The Chicago Congress of Africa, 1894.* A report in the Schomburg Collection, New York City.

Padmore, George, ed. *History of the Pan-African Congress.* 2nd ed. London: Susan Tulley, 1963.

———. *Pan-Africanism or Communism.* New York: Doubleday and Company, Inc., 1971.

Parsons, Stow, ed. *Evolutionary Thought in America.* New Haven: Yale University Press, 1950.

Payne, Daniel A. *History of the African Methodist Episcopal Church.* 1891. Reprint, New York: Johnson Reprint Corp., 1968.

Pease, Jane and William Pease. *They Who Would be Free: Blacks Search for Freedom, 1830–1861.* New York: Atheneum, 1974.

Peterson, John. *Province of Freedom: A History of Sierra Leone, 1787–1870.* Evanston: Northwestern University Press, 1969.

Pfleiderer, Otto. *The Development of Theology in Germany since Kant and Its Progress in Great Britain Since 1825.* Translated by J. F. Smith. London: Swan Sonnenschein and Co., 1890.

Phillips, Clifton J. *Protestant America and the Pagan World: The First Half-Century of the American Board of Commissioners for Foreign Missions, 1810–1860.* Cambridge: Harvard University Press, 1969.

Porter, Arthur T. *Creoledom: A Study of the Development of Freetown Society.* London: Oxford University Press, 1963.

Powell, Adam Clayton, Sr. *Against the Tide: An Autobiography.* New York: R. R. Smith, 1938.

Powell, William H. R. *Illustrations from a Supervised Life.* Philadelphia: Continental Press, 1968.

Proctor, Hugh Henry. *Between Black and White: Autobiographical Sketches.* Boston: Pilgrim Press, 1925.

Ransom, Reverdy C. *The Negro: The Hope or the Despair of Christianity.* Boston: Ruth Hill, 1935.

———. *The Pilgrimage of Harriet Ransom's Son.* Nashville: The A.M.E. Sunday School Union, 1948.

———. *School Days at Wilberforce.* Springfield, Ohio: New Era, 1890.

Rauschenbusch, Walter. *Christianity and the Social Crisis.* 1907. Reprint, New York: Harper & Row, 1964.

———. *A Theology for the Social Gospel.* New York: Macmillan, 1917.

Reardon, Bernard M. G. *Liberal Protestantism.* Stanford: Stanford University Press, 1968.

Redkey, Edwin S. *Black Exodus: Black Nationalist and Back-to-Africa Movements, 1890–1910*. New Haven and London: Yale University Press, 1969.

———, ed. *Respect Black: The Writings and Speeches of Henry McNeal Turner*. New York: Arno Press, 1971.

Reimers, David. *White Protestants and the Negro*. New York: Oxford University Press, 1965.

Reist, Benjamin. *Toward a Theology of Involvement: The Thought of Ernst Troeltsch*. Philadelphia: Westminster Press, 1966.

Richardson, Joe M. *Christian Reconstruction: The American Missionary Association and Southern Blacks, 1861–1890*. Athens and London: University of Georgia Press, 1986.

Rotberg, Robert I., and Ali A. Mazrui, eds. *Protest and Power in Black Africa*. New York: Oxford University Press., 1981.

Russell, Lester E. *Black Baptist Secondary Schools in Virginia, 1887–1957*. Metuchen, N. J., and London: Scarecrow Press, 1981.

Sanford, Elias B. *Origin and History of the Federal Council of the Churches of Christ in America*. Hartford, Conn.: S. S. Scranton Co., 1916.

Sanneh, Lamin. *West African Christianity: The Religious Impact*. Maryknoll, N. Y.: Orbis, 1983.

Sarbah, John Mensah. *Fanti Customary Laws*. London: William Clowes and Sons, 1897.

———. *Fanti National Constitution*. London: William Clowes and Sons, 1906.

Sawyerr, Harry. *Creative Evangelism: Towards a New Christian Encounter in Africa*. London: Lutterworth, 1968.

Scruggs, Otey M. *We the Children of Africa in this Land: Alexander Crummell*. Washington, D.C.: Howard University, 1972.

Sekyi, Kobina. *The Parting of the Ways*. Cape Coast, 1925.

Seymour, A. J. *Cultural Policy in Guyana*. Paris: United Nations Educational, Scientific, and Cultural Organization (UNESCO), 1977.

Schenk, Wilbert. *Henry Venn—Missionary Statesman*. Maryknoll, N. Y.: Orbis, 1983.

Schmidt, Stephen. *A History of the Religious Education Society*. Birmingham, Ala.: Religious Education Press, 1983.

Shepperson, George and Thomas Price. *Independent African*. Edinburgh: Edinburgh University Press, 1958.

Shorter, Aylward. *African Christian Spirituality*. Maryknoll, N. Y.: Orbis, 1980.

Simmons, William J. *Men of Mark: Eminent, Progressive and Rising*. Cleveland: George M. Revell & Co., 1887. Reprint, New York: Arno Press and New York Times, 1968.

Simpson, George Eaton. *Black Religions in the New World*. New York: Columbia University Press, 1978.
Smith, Charles Spencer. *A History of the African Methodist Episcopal Church*. Vol. 2. Philadelphia: Book Concern of the A.M.E. Church, 1922. Reprint, New York: Johnson Reprint Corporation, 1968.
Smith, Edwin W. *Aggrey of Africa: A Study in Black and White*. New York: Doubleday, Doran & Co., 1929.
———. *The Christian Mission in Africa: Study Based on the Work of the International Conference at Le Zoute, Belgium, September 14th to 21st, 1926*. London: International Missionary Council, 1926.
Smith, H. Shelton. *Changing Conceptions of Original Sin: A Study in American Theology since 1750*. New York: Charles Scribner's Sons, 1955.
Smith, H. Shelton, Robert T. Handy, and Lefferts A. Loetscher. *American Christianity: An Historical Interpretation with Representative Documents*. Vol. 2. New York: Charles Scribner's Sons, 1963.
Smith, James Ward and Leland A. Jamison, eds. *The Shaping of American Religion*. Princeton: Princeton University Press, 1961.
Smith, Raymond T. *British Guiana*. London: Oxford University Press, 1962.
Smyth, Egbert C., and others. *Progressive Orthodoxy: A Contribution to the Christian Interpretation of Christian Doctrines*. Boston: Houghton, Mifflin and Co., 1885.
Smyth, Newman. *Old Faith in New Light*. New York: Charles Scribner's Sons, 1879.
Speer, Robert E. *"Rethinking Missions" Examined*. New York: Fleming H. Revell Co., 1933.
Spitzer, Leo. *The Creoles of Sierra Leone: Responses to Colonialism 1870–1945*. Madison: University of Wisconsin Press, 1974.
Sprague, William B. *Lecture Illustrating the Contact between True Christianity and Various Other Systems*. New York: Daniel Appleton, 1837.
Stanley, A. Knighton. *The Children Is Crying: Congregationalism among Black People*. New York, Philadelphia: Pilgrim Press, 1979.
Staudenraus, Phillip J. *The African Colonization Movement, 1816–1865*. New York: Columbia University Press, 1961.
Stearns, Lewis French. *The Evidence of Christian Experience*. New York: Charles Scribner's Sons, 1891.
Steward, Theophilus Gould. *The End of the World, or Clearing the Way for the Fullness of the Gentiles*. Philadelphia: A.M.E. Book Room, 1888.
———. *From 1864 to 1914: Fifty Years in the Gospel Ministry*. Philadelphia: A.M.E. Book Concern, 1921.

———. *Genesis Re-Read, or the Latest Conclusions of Physical Science, Viewed in Their Relation to the Mosaic Record.* Philadelphia: A.M.E. Book Room, 1885.

Stewart, Jeffrey Conrad. *A Biography of Alaine Locke: Philosopher of the Harlem Renaissance, 1886–1930.* Ann Arbor: University Microfilms International, 1981.

Stock, Eugene. *The History of the Church Missionary Society.* Vols. 1–3. London: Church Missionary Society, 1899–1916.

Strong, Josiah. *Expansion under New World Conditions.* New York: Baker and Taylor, 1900.

———. *Our Country: Its Possible Future and Its Present Crisis.* New York: Baker and Taylor, 1885.

———. *Our World.* 2 Vols. Garden City, N. J.: Doubleday, 1913, 1915.

Stroup, Herbert. *The Jehovah's Witnesses.* New York: Columbia University Press, 1945.

Sundkler, B. *Bantu Prophets in South Africa.* London: Oxford University Press, 1964.

Swan, Michael. *British Guiana: The Land of Six Peoples.* London: H.M.S.O., 1957.

Sweet, Leonard I. *Black Images of America, 1784–1870.* New York: W. W. Norton & Co., 1976.

Szasz, Ferenc Morton. *The Divided Mind of Protestant America, 1880–1930.* University, Ala.: University of Alabama Press, 1982.

Tanner, Benjamin T. *The Descent of the Negro.* Philadelphia: A.M.E. Publishing House, 1898.

———. *The Negro's Origin, and Is The Negro Cursed*? Philadelphia: A.M.E. Book Depository, 1869.

Taylor, John V. *The Primal Vision: Christian Presence amid African Religion.* London: SCM Press, 1963.

Thomas, Owen C. *Attitudes Toward Other Religions: Some Christian Interpretations.* London: SCM Press, 1969.

Thompson, Vincent Bakpetu. *Africa and Unity: The Evolution of Pan-Africanism.* London: Longman Group, 1969.

Thurman, Howard. *With Head and Heart: The Autobiography of Howard Thurman.* New York: Harcourt Brace Jovanovich, 1975.

Timothy, Bankole. *Kwame Nkrumah: His Rise to Power.* London: Allen & Unwin, 1955.

Trimingham, J. Spencer. *Islam in West Africa.* Oxford: Oxford University Press, 1959.

Troeltsch, Ernest. *The Absoluteness of Christianity and the History of Religions.* Translated by David Reid. 1901, Reprint, Richmond, Va.: Knox Press, 1971.

Ulich, Robert. *A History of Religious Education.* New York: New York Universities Press, 1968.

Van Dusen, Henry P. *The Vindication of Liberal Theology: A Tract for the Times*. New York: Charles Scribner's Sons, 1963.

Varg, Paul. *Missionaries, Chinese, and Diplomats: The American Protestant Missionary Movement in China*. Princeton: Princeton University Press, 1958.

Vaughan, David. *Negro Victory: The Life Story of Dr. Harold Moody*. London: Independent Press, 1950.

Verkuyl, J. *Contemporary Missiology: An Introduction*. Translated and edited by Dale Cooper. Grand Rapids: William B. Eerdmans, 1978.

Von Hugel, Baron, ed. *Christian Thought: Its History and Application*. London: University of London Press, 1923.

Walker, James W. *The Black Loyalist: The Search for a Promised Land in Nova Scotia and Sierra Leone, 1783–1870*. New York: African Publishing Co., 1976.

Wallerstein, Immanuel. *Africa: The Politics of Independence*. New York: Random House, 1969.

———. *Africa: The Politics of Unity*. London: Pall Mall Press, 1968.

Walters, Alexander. *My Life and Work*. New York: Fleming H. Revell Co., 1917.

Warneck, Gustav. *Modern Missions and Cultures: Their Mutual Relations*. Translated by T. Smith. Edinburgh: Gemmell, 1883.

Warren, Max. *The Missionary Movement from Britain in Modern History*. London: S.C.M., 1965.

———. *To Apply the Gospel: Selections from the Writings of Henry Venn*. Grand Rapids: Eerdmans, 1971.

Washington, Booker T. *The Story of My Life and Work*. Chicago: J. L. Nichols and Co., 1901.

Washington, James M. *Frustrated Fellowship: The Black Baptist Quest for Social Power*. Macon, Ga.: Mercer Press, 1986.

Webb, Clement C. J. *A Study of Religious Thought in England from 1850*. Oxford: Clarendon Press, 1933.

Webster, James Bertin. *The African Churches among the Yoruba, 1888–1922*. Oxford: Clarendon Press, 1933.

Weisbord, Robert G. *Ebony Kinship: Africa, Africans, and the Afro-American*. Westport, Conn., and London: Greenwood Press, 1973.

Weisenburger, Francis P. *Ordeal of Faith: The Crisis of Church-Going America, 1865–1900*. New York: Philosophical Library, 1959.

Welch, Claude. *Dream of Unity: Pan-Africanism and Political Unification in West Africa*. New York: Cornell University Press, 1966.

West, Cornel. *Prophesy Deliverance! An Afro-American Revolutionary Christianity*. Philadelphia: Westminster Press, 1982.

White, Ellen Gibson. *The Royal Blacks*. New York: G. P. Putnam's Sons, 1976.

White, Hugh Vernon. *A Theology for Christian Missions.* New York: Willett, Clark, 1937.

———. *A Working Faith for the World.* New York: Harper & Brothers, 1938.

White, Ronald C., and C. Howard Hopkins. *The Social Gospel: Religion and Reform in Changing America.* Philadelphia: Temple University Press, 1976.

Williams, Daniel Day. *The Andover Liberals: A Study in American Theology.* 1941. Reprint, New York: Octagon Books, 1970.

———. *God's Grace and Man's Hope.* New York: Harper & Brothers, 1961.

Williams, Walter L. *Black Americans and the Evangelization of Africa, 1877–1900.* Madison: University of Wisconsin Press, 1982.

Wills, David W., and Richard B. Newman, eds. *Black Apostles at Home and Abroad: Afro-Americans and the Christian Mission.* Boston: G. K. Hall & Co., 1982.

Wilmore, Gayraud. *Black Religion and Black Radicalism.* New York: Doubleday & Co. 1972. 2nd edition, Maryknoll N.Y.: Orbis, 1983.

Wilson, Edward Thomas. *Russia and Black Africa before World War II.* New York & London: Holmes & Meier Publishers, 1974.

Wilson, Henry S. *Origins of West African Nationalism.* London: Macmillan, 1969.

Woodson, Carter G. *History of the Negro Church.* 1920. Reprint, Washington, D.C., Associated Publishers, 1972.

———. *The Mis-Education of the Negro.* Washington D.C.: Associated Publishers, 1933.

Woodward, C. Vann. *Origins of the New South.* Baton Rouge: Louisiana State University Press, 1951.

———. *The Strange Career of Jim Crow.* New York: Oxford University Press, 1966.

Wright, Richard Robert. *The Bishops of the African Methodist Episcopal Church.* Nashville: Printed by the A.M.E. Sunday School Unions, 1963.

Wyse, Akintola J. G. *H. C. Bankole-Bright and Politics in Colonial Sierra Leone, 1919–1958.* Cambridge: Cambridge University Press, 1990.

Wyatt-Brown, Bertram. *Eighty-Seven Years behind the Black Curtain: An Autobiography.* Philadelphia: Rare Book Co., 1965.

Yates, T. E. *Venn and Victorian Bishops Abroad: The Missionary Policies of Henry Venn and their Repercussions Upon the Anglican Episcopals of the Colonial Period, 1841–1872.* Uppsala: Swedish Institute of Missionary Research, 1978.

Yenser, Thomas, ed. *Who's Who in Colored America.* New York: The Author, 1933.

Articles and Unpublished Papers

"Addresses on the Congress of Africa." *Missionary Review of the World,* (Sept. 1896), p. 693.

"A Helpful Sermon." *Sierra Leone Outlook* 7 (April 1916): 9.

Ajayi, J. F. A. "Henry Venn and the Policy of Development." In *The History of Christianity in West Africa,* edited by O. U. Kalu. New York: Longman, 1980.

Allen, A. R. "Thomas Dixon, Jr. and Political Religion: From Social Reformer to Racist." *Foundations: A Baptist Journal of History and Theology* 14 (Apr./June 1971):136–152.

Asiegbu, J. U. J. "British Slave Emancipation and 'Free' Labour Recruitment From West Africa, 1840–1861." *Sierra Leone Studies* 26 (Jan. 1970): 37–47.

Batten, J. Minton. "Henry M. Turner, Negro Bishop Extraordinary." *Church History,* 7 (Sept. 1938): 231–246.

Beaver, R. Pierce. "The American Protestant Theological Seminary and Mission." *Missiology: An International Review* 6 (Jan. 1976): 75–76.

———. "Missionary Motivation through Three Centuries." In *Reinterpretation in American Church History,* edited by Jerald C. Brauer, pp. 113–151. Chicago: University of Chicago Press, 1968.

———. "North American Thought on the Fundamental Principles of Missions during the Twentieth Century." Reprinted in *Church History* 21 (Dec. 1952): 522.

Bennett, John C. "After Liberalism—What?" *Christian Century* 50 (1933): 1403–1406.

Bittle, William E. and Gilbert Geis, "Racial Self-Fulfillment and the Rise of an All-Negro Community in Oklahoma" *Phylon* (First Quarter, 1957): 247–60.

———. "A Changed Liberal—But Still a Liberal." *Christian Century* 56 (Feb. 1939): 179–181.

Bowden, Henry Warner. "An Overview of Cultural Factors in the American Protestant Missionary Enterprise." In *American Missions in Bicentennial Perspective,* edited by R. Pierce Beaver, pp. 40–62. South Pasadena, Calif.: William Carey Library, 1977.

Brown, Ira V. "The Higher Criticism Comes to America, 1880–1900." *Journal of the Presbyterian Historical Society* 38 (1960): 193–212.

Bucher, Glenn R. "Social Gospel Christianity and Racism." *Union Seminary Quarterly Review* 28 (Winter 1973): 146–157.

Cady, Lyman Van Law. "The Liberal Attitude toward Other Religions." In *Liberal Theology: An appraisal; Essays in Honor of Eugene William Lyman,* edited by David Everett Roberts and Henry Pitney Van Dusen, pp. 137–150. New York: Scribner's, 1942.

Calhoun, Robert L. "A Liberal Bandaged But Unbowed." *Christian Century* 56 (May 1939): 701–774.

Chicago Theological Seminary Register Annual Catalogue, 1926–1927 17 (May 1927).

Chicago Theological Seminary Register 18 (Jan. 1928).

Coffin, Henry Sloane. "Can Liberalism Survive?" *Religion in Life* 4 (1935): 194–203.

Cook, George William. "Comparative Religion." *A.M.E. Church Review* 3 (Jan. 1887): 277–282.

Delegates of the Fraternal Council of Negro Churches in America. "Address to the Country." *Negro Journal of Religion* 2 (Mar. 1936): 5.

Drake, St. Clair. "Pan-Africanism: What Is It?" *Africa Today* (Jan./Feb. 1969): 6–10.

Duignan, Peter. "Pan-Africanism: A Bibliographic Essay." *African Forum* 1 (Summer 1965): 90–104.

Evans, Arthur, Jr. "College Students' Attitude toward Religion." *Negro Journal of Religion* 1 (Feb. 1935): 7.

———. "Personalism." *Negro Journal of Religion* 2 (Feb. 1935): 6.

Ferris, William H. "The New Negro's Attitude towards Theology." *Negro Journal of Religion* 1 (July 1935): 6, 12.

———. "Viewpoint of Science and Religion." *Negro World* 13 (Jan. 1923): 4; 14 (Mar. 1923): 4.

Forman, Charles. "A History of Foreign Mission Theory in America." In *American Missions in Bicentennial Perspective,* edited by R. P. Beaver, pp. 69–140. South Pasadena, Calif.: William Carey Library, 1977.

Fosdick, Harry Emerson. "Beyond Modernism." *Christian Century* 52 (Dec. 1935): 1549–1552.

Fyfe, C. H. "The Sierra Leone Press in the Nineteenth Century" *Sierra Leone Studies* New Series, No. 8 (June 1957): 226–236.

Gloster, Hugh M. "Sutton E. Griggs, Novelist of the New Negro." *Phylon* 4 (1943): 335–345.

Goin, Edward F. "One Hundred Years of Negro Congregationalism in New Haven, Connecticut." *Crisis* 19 (Feb. 1920): 177–181.

Gordon, George A. "The Missionary Motive and the American Board." *Christian Union* 35 (Jan. 1887): 17–19.

Guick, G. "Some Aspects of the African Watch Tower Movement in Northern Rhodesia." *International Review of Missions* 29 (1940): 216–226.

Handy, Robert T. "Fundamentalism and Modernism in Perspective." *Religion in Life: A Christian Quarterly of Opinion and Discussion* (Summer 1956): 381–394.

Harlan, Louis R. "Booker T. Washington and the White Man's Burden," *American Historical Review* 71 (Jan. 1966): 441–467.

Hill, Charles L. "The Religious Crisis of the Present." *Negro Journal of Religion* 1 (Mar. 1935): 5–6, 13.

Hotchkiss, Wesley A. "Congregationalists and Negro Education," *Journal of Negro Education* 29 (Summer 1960): 289–290.

Hutchison, William R. "Cultural Strain and Protestant Liberalism." *American Historical Review* 76 (Apr. 1971): 386–411.

———. "Modernism and Missions: The Liberal Search for an Exportable Christianity, 1875–1935." In *The Missionary Enterprise in China and America,* edited by John K. Fairbank, pp. 110–131. Cambridge: Harvard University Press, 1974.

Kalibala, Ernest B. "Africa—The Unknown Quantity." Part I. *Mission Herald* 44 (May/June 1940): 10–12.

———. "Africa—The Unknown Quantity." Part II. *Mission Herald,* 44 (July/Aug. 1940): 11–13.

Kalu, O. U. "Peter Pan Syndrome: Church Aid and Selfhood in Africa." *Missiology* 3 (1975): 15–29.

Kilson, Martin. "Nationalism and Social Classes in British West Africa." *Journal of Politics* 20 (May 1958): 368–387.

Knapp, Stephen C. "Mission and Modernization." In *American Missions in Bicentennial Perspective,* edited by R. Pierce Beaver, pp. 146–209. South Pasadena, Calif. : William Carey Library, 1977.

Langley, J. Ayodele. "Chief Sam's African Movement and Race Consciousness in West Africa." *Phylon* 32(Summer 1972): 164–178.

Locke, Alaine. "Apropos of Africa." *Opportunity* (Feb. 1924): 37–58.

Loewenberg, Bert James. "Darwinism Comes to America, 1859–1900." *Mississippi Valley Historical Review* 28 (Dec. 1941): 339–368.

Luker, Ralph E. "The Social Gospel and the Failure of Racial Reform, 1877–1898." *Church History* 46 (Mar. 1977): 80–93.

Lynch, Hollis R. "Edward W. Blyden: Pioneer West African Nationalist." *Journal of African History* 6 (1965): 373–388.

———. "The Native Pastorate Controversy and Cultural Ethnocentrism in Sierra Leone, 1871–1874." In *History of Christianity in Africa,* edited by O. U. Kalu, pp. 270–292. New York: Longman, 1980.

McGiffert, Arthur, C. Jr. "The Future of Liberal Christianity in America." *Journal of Religion* 15 (1935): 146–60.

Martin, Tony. "Some Reflections on Evangelical Pan-Africanism, or Black Missionaries, White Missionaries, and the Struggle for African Souls 1890–1930." *Ufahamu* 1 (Winter 1971): 77–92.

Miller, Kelly. "Religion and Race." *Negro Journal of Religion* 1 (Nov. 1935): 5–6.

"Missionary Activities in West Africa." (editorial) *Negro Journal of Religion* 2 (Feb. 1936).

"Modernism Destroys Evangelism," (editorial) *Negro Journal of Religion* 1 (Nov. 1935): 10.

Moore, Moses N. "Ernst Troeltsch and the Problem of Christian Missions." Research Paper, Union Theological Seminary, 1979.

Morris, Calvin. "Reverdy Ransom, the Social Gospel, and Race." *Journal of Religious Thought* 41 (Spring/Summer 1984): 7–21.

Moses, Wilson J. "Civilizing Missionary: A Study of Alexander Crummell." *Journal of Negro History* 60 (Apr. 1975): 229–251.

Muller, Dorothea R. "Josiah Strong and American Nationalism: A Reevaluation." *Journal of American History* 53 (June 1966): 487–503.

"Mussolini vs. Christianity." *Negro Journal of Religion* 1 (Aug. 1935): 4, 13.

"Negro Christians Face a Grave Decision." (editorial) *Negro Journal of Religion* 1 (Oct. 1935): 8–9.

Nicholson, Joseph W. "Your Child and the Church." *Negro Journal of Religion* 2 (Feb. 1936): 6.

Noble, Frederick Perry. "The Chicago Congress on Africa." *Our Day* (Oct. 1893): 279–318.

Okonkwo, Rina. "Adelaide Casely Hayford: Cultural Nationalist and Feminist." *Phylon* 42 (1981): 41–51.

———. "Orishatukeh Faduma: A Man of Two Worlds." *Journal of Negro History* 68 (Winter 1963): 24–36.

"The Pan-African Congress." (editorial) *Crisis* (Oct. 1927): 263–264.

Park, Robert E. "The International Conference on the Negro." *Southern Workman* 41 (June 1912): 347–352.

Pearsall, A. W. H., "Sierra Leone and the Suppression of the Slave Trade." *Sierra Leone Studies* New Series, No. 12 (Dec. 1959): 211–229.

Persons, Stow. "Religion and Modernity, 1865–1914." In *The Shaping of American Religion,* edited by James Ward Smith and A. Leland Jamison. Princeton: Princeton University Press, 1961.

Peterson, Walter F. "American Protestantism and the Higher Criticism, 1870–1910." *Transactions of the Wisconsin Academy of Sciences, Arts, and Letters* 50 (1962): 321–329.

Phillips, Henry L. "Alfred Russell Wallace, LL.D., F. L. S., etc., on Darwinism." *A.M.E. Church Review* 6 (Oct. 1889): 161–165.

———. "Probation." *A.M.E. Church Review* 3 (Apr. 1887): 35–56.

Raboteau, Albert J. "Ethiopia Shall Soon Stretch Forth Her Hands: Black Destiny in Nineteenth-Century America." University Lecture in Religion at Arizona State University, January 27, 1983, Department of Religious Studies, Arizona State University, Tempe, Arizona.

Ransom, Reverdy. "Why a Federation of Negro Denominations in the United States?" *Negro Journal of Religion* 1 (Feb. 1935): 15.

Redkey, Edwin. "The Meaning of Africa to Afro-Americans, 1890–1914." *Black Academy Review* 3 (Spring/Summer, 1972): 5–37.

Richardson, Joe M. "The Failure of the American Missionary Association to Expand Congregationalism among Southern Blacks." *Southern Studies* 18 (Spring 1979): 55–73.

"Rev. Orishatukeh Faduma." *American Missionary* 58 (Jan. 1904): 15.

Russell, Charles L. "Extracts from the Hebrew Talmud." *Negro Journal of Religion* 2 (Feb. 1936): 10.

Schlesinger, Arthur M., Sr. "A Critical Period in American Religion, 1875–1900." In *Religion in American History: Interpretive Essays,* edited by John M. Mulder and John F. Wilson, pp. 302–317. Englewood Cliffs, N. J.: Prentice-Hall, 1978.

Shepperson, George. "External Factors in the Development of African Nationalism, with Particular Reference to British Central Africa." *Phylon* 22 (Fall 1961): 207–225.

———. "Pan-Africanism: Some Historical Notes." *Phylon* 23 (Winter 1962): 346–358.

Smith, Earl. "Pan-Africanism: A Political, Economic and Social Philosophy." *Freedomways* , 20 (First Quarter 1980): 27–35.

Smith, H. Shelton. "Christian Education." In *Protestant Thought in the Twentieth Century: Whence and Whither*? edited by Arnold S. Nash, pp. 225–246. New York: Macmillan, 1951.

———. "George Albert Coe: Revaluer of Values." *Religion in Life* 22 (Winter 1952/53): 46–57.

Smyth, Egbert. "Christianity and Missions." In *Progressive Orthodoxy: A Contribution to the Christian Interpretation of Christian Doctrines.* edited by Egbert Smyth, et al. Boston: Houghton, Mifflin, 1885.

Stearns, Lewis French. "Reconstruction in Theology." *The New Englander* New Series, No. 5 (Jan. 1882): 82–102.

Swift, David E. "Conservative Versus Progressive Orthodoxy in Latter Nineteenth Century Congregationalism." *Church History* 16 (Mar. 1947): 22–31.

Tanner, Benjamin. "Contributors." *A.M.E. Church Review* 5 (July 1888).

———. "The Origin of Man." *A.M.E. Church Review* 4 (Oct. 1887): 208–213.

———. "The Review in Foreign Lands," *A.M.E. Church Review* 5 (July 1888).

Thomas, George F. "The Philosophy of Religion." In *Protestant Thought in the Twentieth Century: Whence and Whither,* edited by Arnold Nash. pp. 73–101. New York: MacMillan, 1951.

Thompson, Elizah. "The Natural History of Religion." *Negro Journal of Religion* 2 (Nov. 1935): 9–10.

"Thus We Go," (editorial) *Negro Journal of Religion* 1 (Feb. 1935): 15.

Troeltsch, Ernst. "The Place of Christianity among the World-Religions." In *Christian Thought: Its History and Application,* edited by Baron F. Von Hugel. London: University of London Press, 1923.

Upshaw, A. W. "Biblical Criticism." *A.M.E. Church Review* 8 (Oct. 1891): 198–201.

———. "Reason and Revelation." *A.M.E. Church Review* 5 (Apr. 1889): 327–328.

Washington, Booker T. "Boley, A Negro Town in the West." *The Outlook* 98 (Jan./Apr. 1908): 28–31.

———. "The Colored Ministry: Its Defects and Needs." *Christian Union* (Aug. 1890).

Washington, James M. "Pan-African Religionists at Yale University." N.p. n.d.

White, Jr., Ronald C. "From Racial Accommodation to Reform: The Odyssey of Washington Gladden." *Reprinted Papers for the Group on American Religion.* Comp., Edwin S. Gaustad. The American Academy of Religion, 1974.

William, Walter L. "Nineteenth Century Pan-Africanist: John Henry Smyth, United States Minister to Liberia, 1878–1885." *Journal of Negro History* 63 (Jan. 1978): 18–25.

Wilson, H. S. "The Changing Image of the Sierra Leone Colony in the Work of E. W. Blyden" *Sierra Leone Studies* New Series, No. 11 (Dec. 1958): 136–148.

Wimbush, Vincent L. "Rescue the Perishing: The Importance of Biblical Scholarship in Black Christianity." *Reflection* (Jan. 1983): 9–11.

Wright, Jr., R. R. "The Challenge to the Negro Church." *Negro Journal of Religion* 2 (Feb. 1936): 5.

Wyse, Akintola J. G. "The Sierra Leone Branch of the National Congress of British West Africa, 1918–1946." *Journal of African Historical Studies* 4 (1985): 676–698.

Unpublished Dissertations and Theses

Drake, Richard Bryant. "The American Missionary Association and the Southern Negro, 1861–1888." Ph.D. diss., Emory University, 1957.

Fierce, Milfred C. "African-American Interest in Africa and Interaction with West Africa: The Origins of the Pan-African Idea in the United States, 1900–1919." Ph.D. diss., Columbia University, 1976.

Harr, Wilbur C. "The Negro as American Protestant Missionary in Africa." Ph.D. diss., University of Chicago Divinity School, 1945.

Johnson, Clifton H. "The American Missionary Association, 1846–1861: A Study of Christian Abolitionism." Ph.D. diss., University of North Carolina, 1959.

Johnson, Lillie M. "Black American Missionaries in Colonial Africa, 1900–1940: A Study of Missionary-Government Relations." Ph.D. diss., University of Chicago, 1981.

Kalibala, Ernest B. "Education for the Villages in Uganda, East Africa." Master's thesis, Teachers College, New York, 1934.

———. "The Social Structure of the Baganda Tribe." Ph.D. diss., Harvard University, 1946.

Lawrence, K. O. "Immigration into Trinidad and British Guiana, 1833–1870." Ph.D. diss., Cambridge, 1958.

Markakis, John. "Pan-Africanism: The Idea and the Movement." Ph.D. diss., Columbia University, 1965.

Martin, Sandy Dwayne. "The Growth of Christian Missionary Interest in West Africa among Southeastern Black Baptists, 1880–1915." Ph.D. diss., Columbia University-Union Theological Seminary, 1981.

Miller, George Mason. "'A This Worldly Mission': The Life and Career of Alexander Walters (1858–1917)." Ph.D. diss., State University of New York at Stony Brook, 1984.

Okonkwo, Rina. "The Emergence of Nationalism in British West Africa, 1912–1940." Ph.D. diss., City University of New York, 1979.

Roth, Donald F. "Grace Not Race: Southern Negro Church Leaders, Black Identity, and Missions to West Africa, 1865–1919." Ph.D. diss., University of Texas, Austin, 1975.

Thomas, Herman Edward. "An Analysis of the Life and Work of James W. C. Pennington, A Black Churchman and Abolitionist." Ph.D. diss., Hartford Seminary Foundation, 1979.

Wills, David W. "Aspects of Social Thought in the African Methodist Episcopal Church, 1884–1910." Ph.D. diss., Harvard University, 1975.

Index